Named in remembrance of

the onetime *Antioch Review* editor

and longtime Bay Area resident,

the Lawrence Grauman, Jr. Fund

supports books that address

a wide range of human rights,

free speech, and social justice issues.

An Independent Man

The publisher and the University of California Press Foundation gratefully acknowledge the generous support of the Lawrence Grauman, Jr. Fund.

The publisher and the University of California Press Foundation also gratefully acknowledge the generous support of the Peter Booth Wiley Endowment Fund in History.

In addition, the publisher gratefully acknowledges the generous support of the Literati Circle of the University of California Press Foundation, whose members are:

The Dido Fund at the East Bay Community Foundation
Harriett Gold
Lorrie and Richard Greene
Gary Kraut
Melony and Adam Lewis Advised Fund at Aspen Community Foundation

An Independent Man

ED ROBERTS AND THE FIGHT FOR DISABILITY RIGHTS

Scot Danforth

UNIVERSITY OF CALIFORNIA PRESS

University of California Press
Oakland, California

Library of Congress Cataloging-in-Publication Data

Names: Danforth, Scot, author.
Title: An independent man : Ed Roberts and the fight for disability
    rights / Scot Danforth.
Description: Oakland, California : University of California Press,
    [2025] | Includes bibliographical references and index.
Identifiers: LCCN 2025019114 (print) | LCCN 2025019115 (ebook) |
    ISBN 9780520412644 (cloth) | ISBN 9780520412651 (ebook)
Subjects: LCSH: Roberts, Edward V., 1939-1995. | People with
    disabilities—United States—Biography. | LCGFT: Biographies.
Classification: LCC HV3013.R63 A3 2025 (print) | LCC HV3013.R63
    (ebook) | DDC 362.4092 [B]—dc23/eng/20250527
LC record available at https://lccn.loc.gov/2025019114
LC ebook record available at https://lccn.loc.gov/2025019115

Manufactured in the United States of America

GPSR Authorized Representative: Easy Access System
Europe, Mustamäe tee 50, 10621 Tallinn, Estonia,
gpsr.requests@easproject.com

34   33   32   31   30   29   28   27   26   25
10   9   8   7   6   5   4   3   2   1

Contents

Photographs follow p. 208

Acknowledgments

I am grateful for the support of Mark Roberts, Zona Roberts, and Joan Leon. From the start, these three key people who knew and loved Ed encouraged me. I would never have taken this long, fascinating journey of discovery without their backing.

I appreciate Chapman University for supplying financial resources for travel and research costs. I am thankful to my colleagues in the Attallah College of Educational Studies for supporting my scholarly activities.

I benefited from the work of many talented librarians, who helped me find my way through their resources. I am grateful for the assistance of the dedicated staff members at the Bancroft Library, University of California, Berkeley, and the California State Archives in Sacramento. I am particularly thankful for the help provided by Adam M. Silvia of the Library of Congress.

Dozens of knowledgeable people freely offered their time and memories to this project. My heartfelt thanks go to the many formal and informal interview participants, including Tom Bates, Lonnie Hancock, Bruce Curtis, Colleen Wieck, Corbett O'Toole, Diane Driedger, Fred Collignon, Congressman George Miller, Gerben De-Jong, Lou Haas, Eric Dibner, Ralf Hotchkiss, Janice Haugan, Jeff Moyer, John Atkinson, Lex Frieden, Mark Roberts, Maggie Linden,

Marissa Shaw, Mark Dubois, Mike Boyd, Patricia Shifferle, Zona Roberts, Ramon Jiminez, Robert Gnaizda, Roger Payne, Joan Leon, Jonathan Gold, Stephen O'Connell, Bill Bronston, Congressman Tony Coelho, and Judy Heumann. To top it off, the wonderful disability studies scholar Steven Brown generously gave me a box of cassettes of his interviews with Zona and Ed Roberts. A special thanks goes out to firebrand Zona, who passed away in January 2025 at age 105. She was Ed's main mentor, the one who started it all.

I dedicate this book to my wife, MaryEllen, and son, Miles. I am lucky to enjoy a state of loving interdependence with these two caring people, who make me better and stronger every day.

1 *Fight*

"We're organized and we're taking over," Ed Roberts shouted at Dr. Henry Bruyn. A dozen long-haired University of California, Berkeley students in electric wheelchairs stuffed into one hospital room nodded in angry agreement. Two members of their group had been kicked out of campus housing for questionable reasons. Ed and his friends were pissed off, and they were ready to fight.

Roberts was the elder statesman of the zealous bunch. Entering the university in 1962 as an undergraduate, he was the first disabled student living on campus, housed in Cowell Hospital, the campus infirmary. By October 1969, he was a doctoral student in political science serving as the knowledgeable leader of this would-be band of radicals. In seven years, he had developed numerous influential contacts on campus and in the community. He knew where the strings were located and was pretty good at pulling them.

Bruyn was the medical director who oversaw the growth of the third floor of Cowell into a small dormitory for students with physical disabilities. Nothing in Bruyn's medical training or extensive experience working with polio patients prepared him for mutiny. No one really expected the patients to rise up and take over the hospital.

Deep inside, Bruyn must have smiled. He was the caring physician who took a chance on Ed when university administrators were not convinced that a neck-to-toe paralyzed man could attend college. A year later, he arranged for the formidable John Hessler, the sharp collaborator who became Ed's buddy, to join him in Cowell.

Although Bruyn disagreed with the California Department of Rehabilitation's decision to expel the two students, the physician withheld his formal approval of the students' protest. While he likely felt proud of his rabble-rousing charges, he was worried that an insurrection might jeopardize the Cowell program he had carefully built.

Bruyn and Ed Roberts both knew that the real target of the students' ire was State Rehab, the public agency that funded and oversaw the Cowell program. A year earlier, buoyed by a sudden influx of federal grant dollars, State Rehab had more than doubled the number of disabled students in the campus residence. In Fall quarter 1969, the psychedelic echoes of Jefferson Airplane and the pungent scent of marijuana filled the tile hallways of the medical ward. The disabled students and their youthful personal attendants easily smuggled alcohol past the frustrated nurse-minders. The third floor of Cowell Hospital was a party scene rivaling the most raucous fraternity.

Worried State Rehab bureaucrats assigned Lucile Withington, a hard-nosed, no-nonsense counselor, to clean up what appeared to be a rowdy mess. She instituted new academic requirements above the university's standards. She scrutinized the students' grades and class attendance. She increased the number of courses they had to take per academic quarter.

The Cowell residents saw Withington as a harsh and demeaning taskmaster. In their eyes, she was the embodiment of medical social control, tying them down at a time when they were busting loose, creating lives of independence and self-mastery. Many had wasted their adolescent years in hospitals. This was their lucky break, their big chance to be free, to be Berkeley students at the height of the hippy revolution.

Then Withington dropped the hammer. On Tuesday, September 16, 1969, she kicked undergraduates Don Lorence and Larry Biscamp out of Cowell. She claimed they were not making sufficient academic progress.

On a campus where edgy nonconformity was the norm, Ed and his friends believed Withington was making an example of the two most loudly divergent students. "She picked these two most active spokesmen for our group," Ed told the *San Francisco Chronicle*. He depicted the two as average young people in Berkeley, persecuted for their bohemian lifestyle. "We refused to cut our hair for her or use underarm deodorants. Sometimes our rooms were a little messy. We were very normal Cal students and that upset her greatly."[1]

Lorence was a gay man whose sexuality and mind-blowing wardrobe were viewed as disruptive by hospital and rehabilitation staff members. His free-flowing approach to academic study was more Zen than strategic careerism. Biscamp was a constant, critical thorn in Withington's side. He loudly agitated among the disabled students, calling them to act in defiant solidarity against the pushy counselor.[2]

Both ejected students were beloved members of the crew. But Lorence's expulsion struck a particularly sour note among the personal attendants who provided personal care to the physically disabled students. Numerous personal attendants were gay. The largely concealed, alternative lifestyle enclave of third floor Cowell was a tolerant space for gays and lesbians. The students and their attendants tended to view homosexuality and disability as analogous, two groups widely misunderstood and scorned.[3]

Ed quickly rallied the disabled students to fight back. Dinnertime rap sessions became late night political strategy meetings. Tipping their hats to the rebellious image of the Rolling Stones, the group named themselves the Rolling Quads. Ed was their leader. They were proud, united, and mad.[4]

Eleanor Smith, the ward nurse who assisted the students with hygiene and medical needs, found herself caught in the crossfire. A nondisabled man named Mike Fuss worked as her assistant. The two argued bitterly.

Fuss was a white man who had been active in the African American civil rights movement. When the Van de Camp restaurants of the San Fernando Valley refused to hire Black workers, Fuss organized demonstrations. He was one of many Berkeley New Left activists who trained originally in the ideology and nonviolent protest tactics of the civil rights movement.

With his keen political eye, Fuss viewed the Rolling Quads as a rising class of political advocates seeking the right to control their own lives. Smith wanted them to be compliant patients and good students. Upset by the students' radicalization, the nurse abruptly resigned.[5]

Ed plotted strategy. Returning Lorence and Biscamp to Cowell was the immediate goal. But he also had a longer game in mind. If they could win the fight to save their two friends, the victory could jump-start a larger movement. They would replace the common idea of a disabled person as incapable and requiring supervision with the emancipatory notion that disabled people were valued, competent citizens who could direct their own affairs.

In common thinking, disability had nothing to do with politics. Even in 1969 Berkeley, which was at the heart of the radical New Left and the youth counterculture, few observers of the conflict between the disabled students and State Rehab imagined that disability could be seen as a civil rights issue. The student residents of third floor Cowell were young people whose bodies had simply failed them. Many were paralyzed by the polio virus outbreaks of the 1940s. Others had severe spinal injuries from car crashes and diving accidents. What they needed was good medical care and effective rehabilitation, not some half-baked protest movement. What they needed to do, in traditional terms, was politely take their medicine and follow doctors' orders.

In Ed's outrageous imagination, this time the so-called cripples didn't accept their fate with a sweet smile that comforted the dominant, nondisabled community. The days of being grateful for charity-crumb attitudes were over. He envisioned people with a variety of disabilities coming together to demand access to the American dream.

While Ed's head was undoubtedly in the clouds, his actions were grounded in the realities of his own life. He had learned the practical lessons of gritty street-fighting from his mother, Zona. Whenever an authority figure calmly pushed her son aside, the small but formidable woman fought back. She was an unlikely combatant, a mild almost conciliatory person who felt deeply uncomfortable with conflict and confrontation. But she couldn't stand seeing otherwise respectable officials mistreat her son. She took on the school district leaders who refused to allow her son to graduate from high school. She battled the state rehabilitation system that declared Ed a person without useful potential. She clashed forcefully with university administrators who simply didn't care.

Zona taught Ed that living well with a disability required fighting the people that held you down. Teamed up with his Rolling Quads pals, for the first time, Ed wasn't dueling for his own life and future. He was part of an alliance of disabled people united for a shared cause. The real enemy wasn't their sick or weak bodies but the stigmatizing attitudes and societal barriers that kept them out of the game. The political science student had figured out that nothing was more political than disability.

The Rolling Quads met with Rod Carter, Lucile Withington's supervisor. They issued two simple demands. Reinstate Biscamp and Lorence immediately. Replace Withington with a more amenable counselor who would give the disabled students greater control over their campus housing.

The State Rehab strategy was to divide the disabled students. They declared that disability wasn't a unifying characteristic like race or gender. It was an individual affliction to be treated with professional interventions targeted to a patient's specific condition. Carter and Withington said they only had a problem with the two rule-breakers. Their disciplinary actions didn't involve the rest of the students. Just let the professionals do their work and go about your business.

The students remained united. They flooded Carter with letters that clearly communicated that they stood in solidarity with their friends Lorence and Biscamp. Negotiations with Rod Carter hit a dead end. He backed Withington, and she was not going to budge.[6]

The Rolling Quads did what outraged Cal students in 1969 did. They scheduled a public protest action. This is where Ed's skills shined. He believed that if they took their case to the press and the politicians, they would win in the court of public opinion.

Ed phoned reporters at newspapers in Berkeley and San Francisco, inviting them to the demonstration. He called state senators and assembly members, including mental health advocate Nick Petris. He lobbied them to put pressure on the Department of Rehabilitation.

He arranged for journalists to interview him inside his iron lung, the enormous steel contraption that pumped air into his lungs. Nothing moved the pity-filled uninitiated like sitting down next to the wheezing machine with Ed's grinning face poking out one end. What others viewed as a scary steel tomb was Ed's secret weapon.

The American disability rights movement, a multidecade, national campaign advocating for the civil rights of people with disabilities, began with a small campus protest in Sproul Plaza. Ed and John Hessler strategically set their demonstration in the sacred temple of Berkeley activism, where the free speech movement began. From Vietnam War protests to the Third World Liberation Front, and the ugly battle over People's Park, the Sproul Hall steps was the place.[7]

Sproul Plaza was a counterculture circus, a daily celebration of individuality and freedom of expression. Disabled student Bob Metz once described the "Sproul Symphony" as two guitarists and a fiddler playing the Grateful Dead's "Ripple" combined with a pair of violin-playing women in bathing suits and straw hats performing classical music, all surrounded by a chanting orange troupe of Hare Krishnas burning incense and ringing bells. It was a phantasmagoric public theater of youthful creativity.

The disabled students had a special fondness for Sproul Hall. It was the first accessible campus building. Five years earlier, Ed and Dean of Students Arleigh Williams convinced the administration to install a wheelchair ramp at the side of the building. It was an important beginning.[8]

By Berkeley standards, the Rolling Quads held a very humble demonstration. Eleven students in electric wheelchairs and an equal number of nondisabled supporters traveled from Cowell Hospital to the base of the steps at Sproul Hall. Many wore green fatigue Army jackets, the unofficial uniform of Vietnam Era protest. Carrying signs and chanting slogans, they circled Ludwig's Fountain at the Plaza's center.[9]

Many students glanced over but just passed by. A curious few wandered in, drawn by the eye-catching gathering of wheelchairs, summoned by the sound of Ed and John Hessler speaking into a megaphone. The angry rhetoric of young people berating callous and unjust authorities was familiar stuff. The stories and issues were new.

The two Rolling Quads' leaders narrated the daily lives of physically disabled students. With great patience, they detailed the kinds of accommodations they needed to attend lectures, to study, and to keep up with assignments. As essential as these arrangements were, they certainly didn't define these Cal students. The speakers touted the group's oft-overlooked talents, intellectual ability, and strong desire to earn a degree. They were not charity cases. They were college students like any other.

But the Department of Rehabilitation was letting them down. They had promised to supply the necessary support and funding so that the students could succeed. But then they pulled a cruel trick. The cold state bureaucracy yanked the rug out and walked away.

Hessler explained, "The accommodations will make the opportunity a reality. Without the accommodations, there is no reality or opportunity that can be fulfilled."[10]

Ed smartly persuaded the reporters to back the Rolling Quads. The *San Francisco Chronicle* and the *Berkeley Daily Gazette* portrayed the disabled students as victims of an unreasonable counselor and an unresponsive state agency. The decision to cut off funding to Lorence and Biscamp amounted to inhumane treatment of disadvantaged people doing their best to make it in a challenging world. A State Rehab spokesperson hung Withington out to dry, stating inaccurately that she "exceeded her authority in telling them they had to leave Cowell Hospital."[11]

Ed, the savvy graduate student who spent much of his teen years watching black and white television via a mirror hung above his supine head, knew the power of the media. His strategy foreshadowed, for example, the tactics of sophisticated gay rights groups decades later. In the mid-80s, angered by the lack of television and newspaper coverage of the AIDS epidemic, gay rights activists systematically sought relationships with television and print journalists. Depictions of gay persons shifted from illness and depravity to normality and humanity. Interpersonal connections with reporters would change media depictions of otherwise devalued persons.[12]

While Ed enjoyed a rousing public protest, it was primarily his work winning over local newspapers that turned the tide. Supervisor Rod Carter quickly reinstated the two students and reassigned Withington to other duties. Ed later observed, "We knew that when you shine the light of publicity on a state agency, they can't take it."

Carter replaced Withington with Gerald Belchick, an experienced counselor who bent over backwards to give the students control of the program. He later said, "Essentially, they [the students] got carte blanche. . . . There wasn't anything they asked for they didn't get."[13]

Ed and his Rolling Quads not only won the first fight of the disability rights movement. In the tempestuous political climate of Berkeley, California, they invented a new kind of American politics. Disability was no longer just a matter of physicians and hospitals treating sick persons. It wasn't simply a matter of rehabilitation and hopeful recovery. It was a civil rights issue, a struggle by rejected and pitied people to gain access to the opportunities of mainstream society, to gain value in the hearts of fellow citizens. The very people who many viewed as weak, incompetent, and dependent would lead the way.

Working with people with many kinds of bodily impairments, from Berkeley, across the United States, and around the world, Ed Roberts crafted his life within and through this new movement. On the long activist road from Cowell Hospital in September 1969 to the signing of the Americans with Disabilities Act by President George H. W. Bush in July 1990, the man in the iron lung became an unlikely hero. An extravagant self-promoter, an exorbitant risk-taker, an unyielding fighter who made his mother proud, he didn't just lead the national and international disability rights movement. He very consciously and forcefully created an affirmative new way of being a disabled person. As Ed Roberts elevated himself and his people, he became the most recognized and celebrated disabled person on the planet.

2   The Crippler

In February 1953, two weeks after Ed Roberts's fourteenth birthday, *Time* magazine touted the promising polio vaccine research of Dr. Jonas Salk. Preliminary tests on two groups of disabled persons near Pittsburgh, residents of the Watson Home for Crippled Children and the Polk School for the Retarded and Feebleminded, yielded positive results.

Salk's "dead virus" vaccine proved to be safe and effective, producing significant increases in bloodstream antibodies. *Time* prematurely announced that large-scale clinical trials were imminent, and Americans could anticipate a vaccine before the 1954 polio season.[1]

Although many polio researchers warned Salk to work slowly, to ignore the desperate push of the media and the National Foundation for Infantile Paralysis, he was truthfully racing the clock. Nationally, the number of polio cases in the United States had risen steadily throughout the 1940s. The worst year ever was 1952, with fifty-eight thousand cases. Three thousand died and twenty-one thousand suffered permanent paralysis.

Each summer brought a new plague season. Like grim baseball box scores, newspapers across the United States published foreboding tallies of local cases. The virus seemed to flourish in the warmer weather during outdoor activities. Adding to the scare, the illness that historically affected infants and toddlers was beginning to spread to older youth and adults.[2]

Six days after the dramatic *Time* article raised American hopes of a polio cure, Ed and his buddy Roger Huf attended a March of Dimes charity baseball game. For two sports nuts, it was an enjoyable way to spend a warm Sunday afternoon. Afterwards, Ed's pal invited him to a party hosted by his church youth group. Ed wanted to go. But his mother kept him home to rest. Zona could tell from the look on her son's face that he felt off. He admitted reluctantly that he was tired.

The next morning Ed awoke with a strange stiffness running down his back and out all four limbs. Zona called Bill Martin, the family doctor. Ed stayed in bed all day, his joints heavy and tight, his head throbbing. Zona assumed her son had a minor bug.

Like any American mother, she also thought the unthinkable.

Polio tormented the fretful minds of parents. A 1952 national survey asked Americans what they feared most. Polio was second only to nuclear war. Many other diseases—pneumonia, influenza, diphtheria, pertussis, measles—killed more American children. Yet polio filled the nightmares of American parents.[3]

This heightened state of anxiety was partly by design. The fundraising efforts of the National Foundation for Infantile Paralysis (NFIP) spread polio panic to reap donor dollars for research and treatment. Founded by President Franklin Delano Roosevelt in 1938, the foundation employed aggressive marketing techniques to rally American families and their pocketbooks in a national war against polio.

Eddie Cantor, star of silent movies and radio, launched the NFIP March of Dimes campaign on his radio show, urging listeners to send their dimes to President Roosevelt. Americans overwhelmed the White House post office with $268,000 in dimes. Cantor's radio appeal raised an immediate $1.8 million.

Beloved movie stars Jimmy Stewart, Humphrey Bogart, and Jimmy Cagney appeared in promotional shorts. On the big silver screen, Judy Garland and Mickey Rooney shared ice cream cones and told moviegoers, "Do what every good American should do . . . help those who can't help themselves." The house lights came on, and ushers walked the aisles collecting donations in theaters across the nation.[4]

Throughout the 40s and early 50s, the campaign by the March of Dimes ratcheted up parents' apprehensions and boosted donations. A public relations staff of over forty experienced, skillful specialists churned out radio and television programming and placed articles in *Reader's Digest* and other leading national magazines. Each spring they warned of the upcoming plague season, distributing tens of millions of pamphlets teaching family doctors how to identify the polio symptoms and mothers how to keep children safe. Stay away from swimming pools and theaters. Avoid overexertion. Wash hands frequently.

The darkest March of Dimes messenger was the Crippler, the haunting incarnation of the polio virus as a goblin stalking American children. A radio drama opened with an angelic lad named Peter walking to school, singing an innocent but ominous verse, "Don't step on the line." The common schoolyard adage cautioned that stepping on a sidewalk crack released the evil beneath.[5]

The Crippler, voiced in doomful tones by Academy Award nominee Raymond Massey, quickly captured the child.

"Now sing, now whistle, now walk," the Crippler taunted. "Go ahead."

"I can't," paralyzed Peter meekly protested.

"I know you can't," boasted the evil menace, "I've crippled you."

But plucky Peter and the March of Dimes weren't defeated! After much rehabilitation, with the encouragement of a caring nurse, he struggled mightily to walk for the first time.

"I did it!" the lad shouted. With the medical care provided by the March of Dimes, he was successfully rehabilitated. All those dimes defeated polio.

Sort of. Before the Salk vaccine, lacking anything that could be called a cure, the campaign actively promoted the upbeat fiction that a patient who walked a few stumbling steps with heavy leg braces and crutches had overcome polio.

The influential, misleading story of the "cured cripple" was based on the famous example of President Franklin Delano Roosevelt, who was infected by poliomyelitis in 1921 at his family's summer house. Roosevelt spent seven years trying every cure possible, including the hydrotherapy exercises he developed for the swimming pools at his beloved Warm Springs, Georgia, rehabilitation resort.[6]

After countless failed treatments, Roosevelt invented a useful personal image. His political career required him to be physically robust and vital. He strategically cast himself as the strong lead character in what historian Hugh Gallagher called the "splendid deception."

FDR leaped back onto the national political scene with two dramatic speeches, nominating presidential candidate Al Smith at the Democratic conventions of 1924 and 1928. In 1924, wearing a corset to straighten his weak torso and heavy leg braces locked at the knee, his son James holding one arm and a crutch under the other, Roosevelt shuffled effortfully to the podium. His wheelchair, his daily source of mobility, was hidden from sight.[7]

Roosevelt upgraded the act four years later by dropping the crutch, a universal symbol of physical disability. Leaning heavily on his son's arm and using only a cane, he slowly made his way to the rostrum. The convention audience embraced his heroic courage, as would voters in his own 1932 presidential election. He became the great crippled man who overcame his disability.

Americans confronting the hardships of the Great Depression looked to President Roosevelt as the leader who knew firsthand how to triumph over painful adversity. Combining iron will power and P. T. Barnumesque showmanship, with the helpful conspiracy of the

White House press corps, Roosevelt projected an image of victory over polio.

On the wall of Little Peter's bedroom, a photo of the iconic President Roosevelt watched over him. The boy emulated FDR as a young ballplayer might lovingly imitate the smooth swing of Hall of Famer Stan Musial.

As Peter took his first steps, the defeated Crippler groaned, "Where did he get the courage to do that?"

With the cloying optimism of Tiny Tim, Peter told his nurse, "You know why I could do it for the first time? I kept looking at his [President Roosevelt's] picture on the wall. I said, if he could do it, then I could."

The March of Dimes strategy was grimly brilliant. Many illnesses and accidents could result in a child's death. As tragic as such losses were, they offered the silver lining of finality. A deceased child could be mourned and remembered. In predominantly Christian America, a child passed away had only relocated to God's heavenly side.

The campaign reminded parents that paralytic polio often resulted in a fate worse than death. As historian Jane Smith observes, "To many people, there were far worse things than dying of paralytic poliomyelitis. You could get the disease and live." The fearful minds of Americans agonized over the broken child polio left behind.[8]

. . .

When Zona Lee Harvey first discovered she was pregnant, the eighteen-year-old high school senior sought an illegal abortion. She wasn't ready to be a mother. Her boyfriend Verne Roberts drove her to the rear entrance of an unmarked San Francisco office building.

Zona knew this was risky. In the late 1930s, abortion was illegal in California with the vaguely defined exception of "therapeutic abortions," procedures performed to save the life of the mother. The few hospitals offering medical abortions required difficult-to-obtain approvals from physician committees. About 65 percent of abortions were performed illegally, in most cases by persons with no medical training and under unsanitary conditions. Tens of thousands of American women each year were hospitalized due to post-procedure infections. Hundreds died.[9]

Zona didn't know if this back-alley surgeon was a moonlighting pharmacist or a greedy traveling salesman. He locked the door and directed the nervous teen to change into a medical gown behind a thin curtain. She fumbled nervously to undress with the strange man just across the room. She emerged hesitantly in the skimpy frock. He pointed to the table, and she sat down.

The man gripped Zona's bare thigh with his right hand. The touch of his cold fingers on her skin sent her into an anxious clutch. She snapped her knees up tight to her chest.

Tears raced hot down her cheeks. Her head swam, dizzy and buzzing. Jagged-edged scenes from her childhood flooded her mind. Cruel men—two of her mother's husbands—had harmed her before.

She was being dangled upside down hundreds of feet above the Snake River's rushing waters. Leo, her mother's second husband, squeezed her ankles. His forearms shaking, he shouted to the blue sky above and whitewater below, "I'll do it! I'll do it!" Zona's mother, Nada, fell to her knees and pleaded for her child's life.

Zona's thoughts flashed to a second childhood memory. Her fingers froze on the violin strings. Halfway through her recital, she stared blankly at the audience. Next to her mother was Bob, husband number three, the music professor. His lips moved, urging her to continue. But all Zona could hear was his midnight whisper under her bedcovers, "We don't talk about this. This is our secret." He masturbated at her side as she turned her head away.

Looking up at the abortionist, Zona gathered herself as best she could. Crying and trembling, she backed away. She grabbed her clothes and ran out of the office. Verne held her on the bench as she sobbed. They were going to have a child. He would be called Eddie, the first of four Roberts boys.[10]

A week before her high school graduation in 1938, Zona and Verne Roberts married. Verne's parents Catherine and Walter put money down on a four-room wooden house right across from the high school in Burlingame, California, a cozy town just south of San Francisco. The athletic field would become the daily playground for Zona and Verne's sons in the years to come. Off the back of the house was a small deck surrounded by a sprawling apricot tree. Verne expanded the little living room onto the front porch and enclosed it with glass windows.

Verne had long since quit high school to support his family. His father, Walter, was ill with a severe case of tuberculosis. His mother, Catherine, took on sewing jobs while her son loaded sugar trucks.

Before she met Verne, Zona was alone, working as a live-in maid for an affluent family. She had run away from her mother's turbid ride through four marriages, escaping a string of abusive stepfathers.

Soft-spoken twenty-two-year-old Verne came from the kind of loving, stable family that Zona had only dreamed of. Gentle and reliable, he was an attractive source of security and comfort to a young woman who knew little of either.

As Zona's pregnancy came to term, Verne lost his job. A friend who worked for the Penn Furniture Company convinced him to apply for a job driving a delivery truck. But no luck. It was the deep Depression, and jobs were scarce.

The wooden plank shelf in the bedroom closet was the family's bank. Zona neatly piled Verne's wages so that a quick glimpse gave an account balance. The shelf held a stack of three quarters. Desperate and humiliated, the newlyweds applied for welfare. A county social worker scheduled a visit to complete the application the following Saturday morning.

On Friday night, Verne spent two quarters at the bait store. He went fishing in the San Francisco Bay, trying his last ounce of luck to bring home a fish for dinner. He returned empty-handed. Zona dumped a can of sardines and the last of the milk into a saucepan to make the worst creamed sardines ever eaten.

Early the next morning, Zona awoke to a loud knock on the front door.

"Get up!" she pushed Verne's sleeping body, "The welfare lady is here." They scrambled to appear presentable. Verne hitched up his pants and Zona hurried to the door. She wondered what the social worker would think about a young couple too lazy to get up in time for her visit.

Zona swung open the door and sputtered out a frantic apology to the woman. But it wasn't her.

"Hey Verne, let's go," the big man bellowed, "Full day's deliveries." Verne smiled wide and leaped out the door for his first day working for the furniture store.

When the welfare worker arrived two hours later, Zona told her with great pride, "No, thank you. My husband has a job." Verne was making $25 per week.

When Verne's father died, his son took his place at Southern Pacific Railroad. Verne was known throughout the San Francisco railyards as Walter's boy. He proudly worked for the railroad for the rest of his life, fixing diesel locomotives and driving the sky-reaching cranes that hoisted enormous engines high above the yard.[11]

The railroad union was a powerful moral force in the home of Verne and Zona. The brotherhood was an influential fraternal organization that preached a clear vision of manhood. Good railroad men lived the priorities of hard work, loyalty to railroad brothers, sobriety, and fidelity to wife and family. Their union wives avoided employment and education. The women were the faithful keepers of the home in service to their husbands and children.

Proper gender roles weren't the brotherhood's only political concern. The San Francisco roundhouse fraternity that embraced Walter and his son Verne in a solid web of support only welcomed white men. They circled the wagons against the intrusion of African American and immigrant workers, excluding them from higher-wage positions.[12]

On January 23, 1939, Verne celebrated the birth of his son Edward Verne Roberts by joyfully tracing EDWARD on the foggy kitchen window. The dark-haired newborn was named after Verne's union buddy. They called him Eddie.

In the years to come, the Roberts home filled with boys. Ron was born in April 1942. Mark came along in late 1949 and Randy in the summer of 1952.

Although Zona felt ill-prepared to meet the World War II era's expectations of a wife and mother, she willingly accepted the circumscribed role. If her childhood was a silent struggle against the cruelty and neglect of parental figures, then her adult years would be devoted to providing a consistent, loving home for her children. She was dedicated to giving Ed, Ron, Mark, and Randy the steady family that she had never had.

Deep down, she always knew that it wouldn't be enough. She wanted more from life than baking pies and scrubbing diapers in a steel tub on the back steps. She was one of thousands of mid-century American housewives who yearned for greater personal growth than the pleasant covers of *Good Housekeeping* magazine could deliver.[13]

Verne was an unapologetic traditionalist. He took comfort from the standard social script of working-class manhood. Weekdays were spent with rolled-up shirtsleeves, sweating side by side with union brothers. Evenings and weekends were devoted to family life. Fathers and sons played softball while wives chatted in the bleachers. Verne and Zona hosted neighborhood couples for barbeques and semi-serious games of canasta. With a buddy down the street, Verne sawed planks and pounded nails for a new sunporch. He and his boys threw the aluminum dinghy onto the roof of the station wagon for a day of fishing in the Bay.

Verne moved through the war years and the conformity-oriented 50s with a soft grin and a deep ease. Unfortunately, what comforted and enabled Verne constricted and limited Zona. She loved her family with all her might. But she struggled with what feminist pioneer Betty Friedan called "the problem that has no name." Beyond the traditional family structure and the four walls of the home she tended, there had to be something more interesting and exciting. Quietly and gradually, Zona sought her own independence.[14]

She brought toddlers Ed and Ron to the cooperative nursery school at nearby College of San Mateo. The volunteer mothers gave Zona advice on how to raise her boys according to her own values. Sitting in the nursery, conversing with the other moms, Zona felt herself rising in new ways. This was the beginning of her lifelong journey of personal development through friendships with liberal women. Many were members of the local Unitarian Church. They were intelligent, well-informed about current events, and strikingly opinionated. They shared intimate discussions of gender politics that foreshadowed the empowering feminist rap sessions of the 1960s.

Zona gained confidence and felt validated in her desire to seek a life beyond the limitations of wife and mother. Her friends encouraged her to pursue her own interests, to develop herself as a strong and capable woman. She enrolled in courses at the college, but quickly withdrew when Verne objected.

She moved thirstily to the next opportunity, getting involved in the local schools. She became the leader of the Parent-Teacher Association (PTA). She created an art education program called "Your Child Is Creative" that she and other mothers delivered to local elementary schools.

With her friend Helen Foley, Zona developed controversial sex education programs for the public schools. Despite widespread concern, they arranged for University of Oregon psychologist Lester F. Beck to screen his groundbreaking sex instruction film *Human Growth* for the junior high school students. The educational film promoted an uncommonly frank and unembarrassed discussion about reproduction among a mixed-gender group of students.[15]

Zona leaped into Democratic Party politics. She served as ward captain for the 1950 Helen Gahagan Douglas campaign for Senate. Douglas was a glamorous movie star and a three-term congresswoman defeated by Richard Nixon through notorious red-smear tactics. The anticommunist hysteria that gripped the country was easily redirected toward an enterprising woman seeking national office. The media aided Nixon by frequently questioning whether a woman had the intelligence and strength to do the job. Eleven-year-old Ed's first involvement in politics was going door to door with his mother delivering Douglas campaign leaflets.

Nixon's true colors flew high nine years later when, as vice president, he tussled with Soviet premier Nikita Khrushchev while the two blustery cold warriors toured an exhibit of a modern American kitchen. Promoting the postwar American lifestyle, Nixon boasted of prosperous working men buying homes with the latest appliances. At the heart of the domestic sanctum, he bragged, was a "universal" ideal housewife who served her husband and children while enjoying the consumer benefits of "new inventions and new techniques."

Responding angrily, the gruff Khrushchev criticized his counterpart's "capitalistic attitude toward women," the vice president's condescending vision of womanhood trapped under the ties of her own apron. What made America great, in Nixon's vision, were the sweet women surrounded by the latest ovens and toasters.[16]

By 1960, television specials and newspaper columns explored the dilemma of the "trapped housewife," smothered by burdensome family obligations and yearning to break free. Journalists wondered, did she need more leisure time or psychotherapy? Congresswoman Douglas and her avid campaign worker Zona Roberts were disruptions of the dominant social order, assertive feminists busting out of Nixon's kitchen. They were part of a generation of forward women wriggling free of the Betty Crocker straitjacket to find new opportunities for self-development and expression.[17]

The psychological foundation for Ed's belief in himself began with his mother gaining confidence and strength in the postwar patriarchal society. He took mental notes as his mother asserted greater control over her life. In her struggle to become herself in male-dominated America, she became Ed's role model for a person pursuing personal independence against profound cultural obstacles. Later, to her own surprise, she would teach him how to be a disruptive iconoclast.

. • ·

Young Ed lived for athletic competition. The neighborhood boys played pickup games of football and baseball on the high school field across the street. The Roberts home was a chaotic track meet with hollering boys running in every direction. As a toddler, Ed fell down so often that he sported a near-constant split lip.

From an early age, Ed was the leader of the sandlot society, the youthful manager who organized teams, officiated games, and resolved heated conflicts. He had a unique empathy for the feelings and needs of others, especially the smaller and weaker boys who could not dominate the playing field. When a little lad fell down and cried, Ed walked the tearful child to a nearby shop to buy him a piece of candy.

School was an unfortunate necessity. Ed's teachers all said that he was very intelligent. He was talkative and knowledgeable on many topics. But he wasn't interested in something as impractical as academics.

One teacher told Zona, "I have never seen such a kid on the playground for getting the kids together, and for playing the games. But you bring him into the classroom, and it's like he goes away." Bored and unstimulated by the textbooks and math problems, Ed's mind drifted off.

Despite his obvious intelligence, Ed couldn't read. By the end of fourth grade, he had only memorized the alphabet and a dozen sight words. He seemed to be dyslexic. But without warning, in fifth grade, the words on the page came to life for him. Within a short few months Ed read with fluency and comprehension like any other classmate. His teachers and parents were delighted.

By middle school, surrounded by a loving family in a comfortable suburban town, Ed was developing as a well-rounded young man. He was talented and competitive on the athletic field, a leader among his playground pals, and sound in academics.

Ensconced comfortably in a steady middle-class household with a loving family, Zona and Verne had good reason to feel confident that Ed's future was secure.

· • ·

Dr. Bill Martin arrived at the Roberts' house in the late afternoon. He had the bedside manner of a grumpy accountant, blunt and unfiltered, brutally honest without apparent regard for the emotions of others. He completed a brief examination and walked solemnly into the bathroom. He reemerged drying his hands with a towel.

"Take him to county hospital," he ordered without elaboration. "I'll meet you there."

Ed was admitted to the polio unit at San Mateo County Hospital, a small facility six miles from the Roberts' home. The initial symptoms undoubtedly pointed to poliomyelitis infection, but Dr. Martin wanted to confirm with a spinal tap. An examination of cerebrospinal fluid was the medical gold standard for a proper diagnosis.

The lumbar puncture is a painful procedure. Dr. Martin rolled Ed over on his side, hospital gown open at the back, and knees drawn up to his chest. The boy bit down and gasped as the sharp needle pierced the lower vertebrae, sinking deep into the spinal canal to collect a small fluid sample.

Surrounded by medical personnel, deluged by bright overhead light, Ed was alone. Little did he realize that this was the start of many months of grueling loneliness in hospital wards away from his family and friends. This was the beginning of a long isolation that would be formative. Scarred by the punishing heartache of his secluded teen years, he would intentionally spend the rest of his life surrounded by people.

Verne and Zona waited at the end of the empty hallway behind a large window. At last the white-coated Dr. Martin walked toward them carrying a small glass tube of the collected specimen. He swished the contents back and forth in front of Zona's eyes.

"Well, it looks clear. Might not be polio." As he methodically discussed possible diagnoses, Zona's head swam, and her knees dipped. The sound of the word *polio* spoken aloud for the first time coupled with the raw image of her son's spinal fluid wrenched her stomach. Verne held her shaking body as she bent over and vomited on the floor.

When the sun rose on that Monday morning, only hours after the March of Dimes ballgame, Ed was able to walk to the bathroom. By the time the sun fell from the sky, Verne had to carry him.[18]

3   *Vegetable*

Ten thousand particles of poliomyelitis virus lined up end to end equal about the length of one grain of salt. Although the virus is often described as living, it is more accurately a bundle of genetic material encased in a thin protein shell that multiplies only when engaged with a supportive host.[1]

For many years, polio researchers thought that the virus entered the human body through the nose. In 1941 Johns Hopkins researchers David Bodian and Howard Howe discovered that the virus came in through the mouth, grew in the gastrointestinal tract, and then spread through the bloodstream.

Most polio infections pass like a soft breeze. The virus finds a home briefly in the digestive system and then slides quietly through and out the body via the emitted stool. About three-fourths of all polio infections are asymptomatic. Infected persons don't even know they had the disease.

Almost one-fourth of cases produce mild symptoms like headache, sore throat, and slight fatigue. Ed's mother and three brothers experienced negligible flu-like symptoms during the week he entered the hospital.

In less than one percent of the cases, the virus lodges in the brainstem, attacks the nervous system, and the patient experiences some degree of paralysis. Even when paralysis occurs, most patients gradually recover partial or complete control of their arms and legs. Future rock star Neil Young contracted polio in 1951 at age five. Returning home after a brief hospitalization, he learned to walk again by balancing against the furniture.[2]

On Wednesday, the third day of his infection, paralysis occupied Ed's body below the neck. His limp limbs tingled. Then his central nervous system stalled. Basic bladder and bowel functions shut down. A nurse snaked a catheter through the tip of his penis, flowing his urine into a bag. Heavy doses of harsh liquid laxatives—milk of magnesia and castor oil—softened the stool to avoid impaction.

That evening, Ed's chest grew heavy, as if the thin bedsheet had suddenly turned into a lead corset. His breathing was labored. Within minutes he gasped for slippery wisps of air.

The virus had invaded the medulla, a bulb-shaped brain section at the top of the spinal cord that controls respiration. Breathing is an autonomic activity, maintained like a ticking clock by a special cluster of motor neurons. The infection engulfed the medulla, disarmed the neurons, and shut off the diaphragm muscles that squeeze the lungs.

Heels clacking furiously on the hard tile floors, the nurses rushed him down the hallway on a rolling gurney. Panting and terrified, Ed watched them open an enormous steel tube. They lifted him quickly and slid his body feet first into the long tunnel. The machine's leather collar closed warmly around his neck. The electric engine thumped and whooshed into motion.

Ed gradually relaxed and his chest lightened. He could breathe easily.

The next morning he awoke to the consistent rhythm of the gigantic machine still puffing away. The brief vacation of sleep hadn't changed the reality of what had happened the night before. He now lived in an iron lung.

The negative pressure respirator was a lifesaver. Invented in 1928 by Harvard medical technologist Philip Drinker, the enormous steel pod pumped an endless mechanized tempo of alternating pressure, forcing the diaphragm to contract and expand. Thousands of polio patients whose torso muscles were temporarily or permanently debilitated survived because of an iron lung. Most required only a short period of respiration dependency before recovering the ability to breathe on their own. A rare few remained in the iron lung for months. Even fewer, for years.[3]

Although effective, the iron lung was greatly feared and reviled. Physical therapy pioneer Sister Kenny called it "an instrument of torture."

To the children on the polio unit, it was a wheezing tomb. Just as a child with braces and crutches walking out of the polio unit to go home was a heroic image of victory, the youngster trapped in the iron lung was the symbol of utter defeat. To be in an iron lung was to be sentenced to die repeatedly with each morning's rising sun.[4]

Ed found the pulsing constancy of the big barrel to be surprisingly comforting. For the rest of his life, he was swaddled every night by the gentle cadence that pressed sweet air into his body. The steel monster would become a cherished friend.

. . .

Ed wasn't out of danger. The virus was still active inside his brain.

That Friday evening, Verne visited his son after work for the usual bathing routine. Without warning, Ed's heart started racing. His face turned red. Sweat dripped down his neck. His temperature spiked to dangerous levels. Sharp pain crackled through his spine like a raging thunderstorm.

Verne and Zona waited anxiously outside the glass window for news from the nursing staff. They knew what was happening. If Ed was going to die, this would be the night. For hours the only news the Roberts heard was Ed's voice echoing down the hallway. He shouted angrily, "What are my parents still doing here?"[5]

The boy's physical distress was matched by the deep guilt he felt for causing his parents heartache and worry. He could read the poorly concealed sadness on his parents' silent faces. Like many children infected with polio, he feared that he had done something wrong to ruin his beloved family.

At first light, Dr. Martin informed Zona that Ed's high fever broke. The threat had passed. Ed was sleeping restfully. Zona sighed with relief and expressed joy that her boy had escaped death.

"This is nothing to celebrate!" Dr. Martin snapped at her. "He'll be a vegetable!"

Zona's heart caught in her throat, and she was silent.

The doctor scolded her, "How would you like it if you had to spend the rest of your life in an iron lung?"

Zona couldn't help but feel genuinely thankful that her son was alive. She wasn't thinking of what Ed's future life would be like. All she cared was that he had survived the vicious onslaught of the disease.[6]

The physician's harsh words revealed a truth that Ed would confront repeatedly in the years to come. Quadriplegics, especially those dependent on iron lungs, wasted away in hospitals or nursing homes. They were viewed as vegetables, helpless cripples unable to participate in the usual activities of American life. No one really expected them to do or become anything.

But Dr. Martin's bleak prediction was also inaccurate. The return of injured World War II soldiers brought rapid advances in the medical care and rehabilitation for paralysis, making possible longer and more physically active lives. Innovative techniques of avoiding and treating frequent urinary tract infections plus more vigorous rehabilitation regimens created new possibilities for paralyzed persons to live better than ever before.

Dr. Martin's rude comment became a favorite tale Ed would joyfully tell hundreds of times as he toured the world stumping for the rights of disabled people. In Ed's frequent retelling of the story, he toyed humorously with the physician's dire warning that the life of a vegetable is not worth living, "I'm here today as an artichoke . . . a little prickly on the outside with a big heart."[7]

Revolutionary ideas about a new kind of disabled person replacing the old-fashioned image of the cripple needing cure with themes of competence and value were many light years away. For the teenage boy just hours on the safe side of a deadly battle with polio, sleeping in a gigantic breathing machine, ambition didn't reach beyond the daily hospital routine.

At that moment, brusque Dr. Martin was starkly correct. Young Ed was no Marx-inspired artichoke, no Martin Luther King, Jr., of the disabled people, no troubadour of a new movement for disability rights. The rainbows he would spend his life chasing were still monochrome black-and-white lines that went nowhere. He was just a vegetable stuck in a metal box.

. . .

Once the lab test confirmed the polio diagnosis, Ed's treatment program shifted to physical therapy. The acrid aroma of hospital cleaning solvents was replaced by the musty hot tang of wet wool blankets. Ed joined the ranks of the crying children who suffered through daily hot packs and muscle-stretching exercises.

When Sister Kenny first brought her controversial physiotherapy techniques to the United States in the early 1940s, she was appalled at what she saw. The standard medical practice for polio patients was passive immobility, splinting and casting limbs to avoid the development of deformities. The boisterous Australian nurse preached the opposite, a vigorous program of movement and exercise along with the regular application of hot packs to relax the tight muscles.

Kenny was a powerhouse self-promoter who jolted the field of polio rehabilitation into action. Her inaccurate theory was that polio paralysis was a muscular disease, not an impairment of neurological functioning. Her approach focused on quieting spasming muscles with heat and then training them to recapture muscle memory through repeated passive motion. Although the American medical community greatly rejected her ideas as unscientific, hospitals across the country embraced her energetic, optimistic physiotherapy practices.

The Kenny treatment promised patients that if they endured the daily miseries of the physiotherapy regimen, they would see results in the gradual reclamation of arm, hand, and leg movement. The body would come back to life.

For patients with latent nerve endings and muscles ready to regain strength, it was an encouraging tonic. Many patients responded positively to Kenny's no-nonsense, optimistic style. Her exercises put many lifeless limbs back into motion.[8]

Every day, nurses dipped strips of wool in near-boiling water and administered the steaming compresses to the major muscles of Ed's body. Then they put him through an intense workout of limb motions and tendon stretches.

The tile hallways of the polio unit echoed with moans and cries. Unlike persons whose bodily paralysis was due to spinal cord injury, polio patients retained full somatosensory capability. They could still feel heat, cold, and pain.

The treatment was like grueling two-a-day preseason football workouts in the August heat, undergoing agonizing pain with the faith that suffering would later yield victories. Except Ed and his polio wardmates were merely passive objects of the therapy, subject to the whims and inclinations of the nurses. The kindest caregivers had a keen sensibility for their patient's feelings. Callous others pushed through without mercy, thinking that more crying meant more progress.

Ed watched many children and adults on his ward leave iron lungs, begin to breathe independently, gain bodily control, and even walk back to their lives with their families. He said goodbye to his friend Bob Penn, who walked off the hospital ward using leg braces and forearm crutches. Bob returned to his job at the power plant. The frequent sight of a polio comrade moving upright and going home gave many patients extra motivation and hope as they completed their daily workouts.

But not Ed. After weeks of physiotherapists religiously hot-packing and tugging his limbs, their encouraging words tapered off. His body made no progress. He could talk, chew, swallow, and turn his head. On the left side, he could tilt his wrist ever slightly, flex one finger and two toes. His right side remained dormant. The daily rehabilitation routine became an empty ritual.

•   •   •

When Ed was initially placed in the iron lung, Dr. Martin positioned a portable television behind his head so that he could watch shows in the mirror. Television sales boomed across the United States in the early 1950s. Suddenly millions of viewers tuned in to see Lucille Ball, Arthur Godfrey, and Milton Berle. Early TV journalists John Cameron Swayze and Dave Garroway kept Americans informed of national and world events. Edmund Hilary and his Sherpa guide Tenzing Norgay were the first explorers to climb to the summit of Mount Everest. Military leaders from the United States, United Nations, North Korea, South Korea, and China signed an armistice ending the Korean War. Through the new medium, Ed maintained contact with the outside world. In the seclusion of his teen years, television was a way to live beyond the confining smallness of his situation.

The medical staff began transitioning Ed from the iron lung to a respiration device called a rocking bed. Developed in the 1940s, the motorized rocking bed pivoted on a fulcrum behind the patient's lower back, swinging back and forth, first tilting up the head and then the feet. The oscillation made the diaphragm muscles work, creating a rhythm of inhalation and exhalation.

The rocking bed didn't facilitate any real mobility. The patient still needed to spend all day and night in bed. But medical professionals viewed it as an important step toward discharge. Ed's life sentence in a heaving steel barrel might be commuted to probation on a perpetual seesaw.

But the rocking bed straps were not designed to hold a scrawny six-foot-tall teenager. Ed's once-firm muscles had deteriorated from disuse. His body became a gaunt stick figure. When the top of the bed spun upward, he slid down beneath the straps and sheets. They soon abandoned the rocking bed, returned him to the iron lung. Discharge plans were put on hold.

Ed sank into a deep depression. The first six months of hospitalization had been filled with hopes—realistic or not—of regaining bodily control and functioning. Ed had watched other patients advance from the Kenny therapies of steaming wool and passive exercise to leg braces and walking. Limping on weak limbs, wearing metal leg braces and arm crutches, they were undoubtedly impaired for life. But they stood up, heads held high, and they went home.

Ed was still trapped in the iron lung, waiting long days and often sleepless nights without knowing what he was waiting for. The lung's baffle chambers whooshed a twenty-four-hour rhythm, precisely counting time when time didn't seem to matter. From where he lay, his head peeping out of the end of the colossal steel hull, the future was as empty as the present.[9]

4   *Reborn*

Making matters worse, Ed's belly hurt. Polio had weakened the lower esophageal sphincter muscle that blocked stomach acid from splashing upward. The combination of Ed's depression and his digestive troubles left him with little appetite. His parents worried as his thin frame became thinner still.

They hired a private duty nurse to cajole and coerce Ed into eating enough food to sustain his frail body. She whipped up frothy coconut milk vitamin shakes and pressed him to drink.

The teen fought back for reasons he could neither articulate nor understand. He didn't like the flavor of coconut milk. He was angry at the nurse for being too pushy. He certainly had nothing more interesting to do with his time than battle a demanding nurse. And this was a fight he could win. He clamped his teeth shut in utter defiance, and his body withered down to fifty-five pounds.

Later in his life, Ed would describe this episode as a suicide attempt. Killing yourself takes great creativity when you are paralyzed from neck to toes. The polio virus had stolen a vibrant body from a young athlete, leaving him in command of his head, one finger, and two toes. The only thing he could fully control was what entered his mouth. His feeding battle with a determined nurse was his way of rejecting the scant existence polio had apparently left him.[1]

The boy's hunger strike was much more than the oft-stereotyped wish of a disabled person to die. Captured in the concentration camp of a crippled identity, his energetic youth had been traded overnight for a personage seemingly defined by tragedy and pity. He faced the forlorn landscape of a 1950s America that offered zero possibility of a fulfilling life for a significantly disabled person. Other than FDR's frothy fables of overcoming paralysis, there were no real disabled public role models living a full and vigorous life that a boy could point to.

Lacking any positive paths or real options, Ed was pissed off and ready to fight. Refusing to eat was his personal stand against what little the world had to offer to him. He rebelled against the apparently inevitable totality of misery. He refused to inhabit an empty biography, a life story without fun, possibility, adventure, and love.

He was also taking control. With each meal turned away, Ed issued a despairing, vaguely conscious demand that his life take shape and gain significance through his own decisions and actions. Whatever body and life remained in the aftermath of polio must devolve fully to his ownership. The life ahead might not be much, but it had to be completely his. This he demanded with closed lips.

Zona called Anita Gordon, an old friend she had met through the cooperative preschool. Her husband, Dr. Gene Gordon, was a psychiatrist. He agreed to visit Ed in the hospital, conduct a brief assessment of Ed's mental condition, and make a recommendation of what to do.

After talking to Ed, Dr. Gordon advised Zona and Verne to discontinue the private duty nurse. Allow Ed to make his own decision about whether to eat or not. There was a risk that, due to his depression, he might continue to refuse food as an act of self-harm. He might end his life like an anorexic locked in a deadly mission.

One thing was undoubtedly true. The daily struggle with the nurse was not an effective way to get nourishment into his body. The only way forward was to put the angry adolescent in charge of his own feeding.

The Roberts took Dr. Gordon's advice. They released the private nurse so that Ed was under no pressure. A unit nurse was directed to feed their son only at his request. It was a risk. But Zona and Verne felt that they needed to trust their son.

The first day without a nurse urging him to eat, Ed felt incredible anxiety. With the private nurse giving him a wall to push against, his rage had a singular focus. He was like a wartime nation absolutely unified against the enemy. But with her removal, his energies had no clear direction. Tension swirled through his body and buzzed in his forehead.

Then suddenly, he felt elevated, as if a draft of air had lifted him up from his bed. Up his body rose. He floated by the ceiling, bumping against the overhead lights, looking down at his body and the iron lung below.

Ed felt a wonderful sense of ease. Finally, after many uncomfortable months, he was relaxed. The anxiety and depression were gone. He drifted gently for a moment more and then slowly returned to his body below.

Resting in his bed, still quite calm, Ed wondered what had just happened to him. Did he really fly above the bed? Was it just a hallucination? Whatever it was, he knew that his feelings had changed. His body felt strangely comfortable.

Ed knew it was time to eat. He ate simply because he felt hungry. He had no idea that this decision was a turning point. It would take him many more years to figure out how to do what seemingly no one knew how to do, to live well as a disabled man. But at that first chosen bite, the teen intentionally took moral title of his unmoving body and undefined life. He was alive, and he had some degree of control over who he would be.[2]

Fellow polio survivor and author Leonard Kriegel has written insightfully about his own adolescent identity struggle. "What seems to me to have happened when I was sixteen and seventeen was an almost instinctive recognition that I had to will myself into being, that

I had to kind of will a self, to create a self." Kriegel experienced polio as a thief that had robbed him of his identity as a human and a man. The burglar left behind an empty space where his teenaged identity would have formed. Like Ed, Kriegel's response was anger. Unlike Ed, his foe was the disease itself. "I had the polio to fight against."[3]

Ed's adversary wasn't the disease. It was the pitiful stock character the society around him told him he would have to be. There was no blank slate where he could author a new version of his self. That space was already filled with the oppressive cultural story of the helpless cripple, the tragic vegetable figure doing nothing and going nowhere.

That first voluntary swallow of food initiated a decade of intensive personal growth. Ed worked furiously to cast aside the cripple persona and replace it with a more valuable, livable self. The struggle took place both within his own psyche and in society, for the image of a disabled person as broken existed simultaneously in his mind and in the thoughts and actions of virtually everyone around him.

Ed undertook this very personal mission simply to survive. In doing so, he also made history. He spent years creating a positive new character to replace both the pitiful vegetable and the fictional FDR hero who only became fully human by defeating disability. Over years, Ed gradually and carefully authored a new kind of disabled person, one whose bodily functioning didn't limit the fullness and richness of their life story. It was a novel invention that ultimately became a role model for other disabled people to celebrate and follow.[4]

. . .

After nine months in the county hospital, despite all evidence, Zona and Verne still chased FDR's recovery dream. It was not uncommon for the parents of children who had polio to nurture a lingering, Xanadu wish that their paralyzed child would, if only blessed by the right treatment program, begin to move their arms and limbs again. At any moment, the phone could ring. A physician might say, "Your son's legs are coming back to life. He's getting better." Every parent knew that it could happen.

The Children's Hospital of San Francisco had the best infantile paralysis rehabilitation program in California. Ed traveled twenty-five uncomfortable miles lying down in the back of a station wagon without a respirator. His fellow polio patients had taught him how to temporarily breathe outside of the iron lung by swallowing gulps of air.

Glossopharyngeal breathing, or frog-breathing, was first documented among patients at Rancho Los Amigos Medical Center in Los Angeles by Dr. Clarence Dail in 1955. Although Ed would become a highly skilled practitioner of frog-breathing later in his life, allowing him to survive cross-country airline flights without a respirator, at this youthful point he was nervous to make this short journey.[5]

Ed also felt desperately scared of moving to a different hospital. The county hospital polio unit had become his entire social world. He was an outgoing, talkative kid who created a rich network of relationships with patients and nursing staff from his fixed location. He relied on these relationships to sustain him as his boyhood friendships in school and the neighborhood evaporated.

Leaving the small hospital just a few miles from his home for a big facility in San Francisco felt like an astronaut stepping from the lunar module into open space without an oxygenated suit. Frightened, Ed refused to talk for the next three days.

The Children's Hospital polio program was large and ambitious. The long, open rooms were filled with children who experienced the polio virus in many ways. Some children had paralysis from the waist down, affecting primarily their ability to walk. Others were impacted on one side, resulting in hemiplegia, or paralysis of the arm and leg on half of the body. A few had "upside down" polio, paralysis of the upper torso and arms without loss of use of the legs. And some were like Ed, respiratory quadriplegics, their bodies contained in iron lungs with their faces poking out.[6]

Throughout his life, Ed's adept social skills and powerful ability to listen to and talk to strangers guided him through new situations. He soon made friends on the ward and his anxieties faded. And the food wasn't half bad. He ate well and regained the weight he had lost.

Many polio hospitals in the 1950s allowed very limited family visitation, leaving children and teens isolated from their loved ones for months. Children's Hospital only permitted the Roberts family to see Ed twice each week. His brothers could not visit at all. Ed was even more isolated from his family.

The doctors immediately transitioned Ed out of the iron lung. They fitted him with a chest cuirass ventilator, a plastic chest shell encasing the entire torso. It looked like a medieval armor chest plate built by Tupperware with a vacuum cleaner hose running out the front. Rubber flanges sealed the device at the upper breast and lower abdomen. Every few seconds, an electric pump connected to the hose sucked air out of the cuirass to squeeze the diaphragm and inflate the lungs.

The doctors soon allowed Ed to go home for a weekend. He enjoyed spending time with his three younger brothers, whom he missed dearly. He had a special bond with five-year-old Mark, who looked up to him through the rose-colored glasses of a little brother's adoration. It wasn't that Mark didn't notice his older brother's physical limitations. He did. He couldn't imagine that anything about his beloved big brother wasn't wonderful. In his adult life, Mark would enact his love for his brother by becoming a passionate disability rights advocate in Eugene, Oregon.

Ed quickly found that the home life he knew before his illness was gone. A phone call to one of his best old friends didn't go well. Ed spoke in half sentences, his phrases awkwardly broken by the rhythm of the cuirass breathing machine. The friend didn't recognize Ed's strange, new speech pattern. He hung up thinking it was a prank call.

As Ed feared, his friends had moved on without him. As they continued through high school with the classes, friendships, and sports Ed had once anticipated for himself, he was bunkered in a hidden hospital world. Polio had traded his suburban boyhood of football games, pretty girls, and adolescent hijinks for a hospital gown, ecru tile walls, and nurses who praised him for having regular bowel movements.

Despite the quality of the Children's Hospital rehabilitation program, Ed made no progress. The hospital staff conscientiously carried out a daily regimen of Kenny hot packs and passive exercise, stretching his arms and legs, keeping the muscles limber and loose. But it was clear to Ed and the nurses that walking was not in the cards.

The staff tried to teach Ed to feed himself. His arm rested in a complex sling hooked to a wire pulley system that slowly raised a spoon to his lips. With intensive concentration, Ed's best performance with the Rube Goldberg device was a three-hour lunch. If he used the system for three daily meals, the waking hours of his day would be filled, and he would be exhausted by nightfall. Despite the unmistakable impracticality, the medical staff spent weeks training Ed on the self-feeding system that he never used.[7]

. . .

One day Zona was watching television at home when a local news report spotlighted the impressive work with infantile paralysis carried out at Children's Hospital. The reporter spoke from inside a polio unit. The camera panned gradually down the row of patients. Zooming dramatically to the body and face of each child, the somber announcer described the physical limitations of each. One boy lost use of his arms. Another could no longer stand on his legs. It was a televised freak show, dramatically staging the physical oddities that made the audience uncomfortable.

The narrator's tone suddenly turned even more dire, "But what if the child can't move at all?" The camera closed in on the face of a dark-haired boy emerging from the end of an iron lung. It was Ed.

Zona broke into tears. It was the first time she had cried since Ed fell ill over a year earlier. She had kept her chin up for her son and her family, vigilantly painting an optimistic face on the troubling situation.

Just then, Verne walked into the room to see his wife crying. She sobbed uncontrollably, feeling all the worse that he knew how bad she felt. At that moment, she could not avoid finally admitting that her son's polio paralysis was a mother's worst nightmare.

Zona was no starry-eyed dreamer. She was a realist hardened down to the bare sinew and bones by the harshness of life. But still, even Zona had hoped that rehabilitation might put Ed back on his feet. Only a few years earlier, in November 1950, all of California rallied behind Governor Earl Warren's lovely teen daughter Honey Bear when she was stricken with polio. Thousands of cards and letters flooded her room at Sutter Hospital. By Christmas, television interviews showed her recovering and smiling. The same miraculous recovery for Ed could . . . it might, if only it could happen.[8]

The television news reporter's grim statement as the camera fixed on Ed was a cold slap in the face. The anxious, positive façade, the many months of moving forward as if all was normal, dropped away. Ed's mother cried until she had no more tears left.[9]

. . .

It was time for Ed to go home. The Children's Hospital physicians scheduled his discharge. Using a cuirass respirator, he could at least live outside the iron lung.

During one of the final family visitation days, out of the blue a young woman social worker approached Zona.

"I'll bet you're excited about Ed coming home," she piped cheerfully.

"No," Zona responded bluntly, "I'm scared to death."

The social worker was concerned. "Hasn't anyone talked to you?"

"No." The physicians had given no information and Zona was terrified. She didn't feel at all ready to take care of a paralyzed teenage boy with an electric respirator. For days, Zona had been asking Verne, "How will we do it? How will we be like a whole hospital?"

The nursing staff routinely handled the million and one details of Ed's care with an expertise that Zona could not imagine. To avoid the decubitis ulcers that easily develop from the constant pressure of skin against the bed, they employed a regimen of ointments and bodily positioning, regularly propping his back and turning his limbs to the required angles. They knew when and how to clear excess fluid in the airway that potentially blocked breathing. They had multiple nurses who fed, shaved, bathed, and toileted Ed twenty-four hours per day. They knew how to operate, adjust, and troubleshoot the electric chest cuirass.

To top it off, Zona feared that round-the-clock caring for Ed would become her mothering duty for the rest of her life. Even with Verne helping, the primary care responsibilities would fall to her. Verne's insistence that she remain at home, not going to college or working a job, had always felt confining. Now the trap that kept her homebound would be doubly tight.

The social worker patiently listened to Zona's worries. Then she explained that a woman from the March of Dimes would contact her to set up in-home services. The March of Dimes had paid for all of Ed's medical bills after Verne's railroad insurance policy ran out. The same foundation that raised millions by scaring the bejeebers out of parents came through when the Roberts needed help. They would provide a care worker for four hours per day, Monday through Friday. Zona breathed a sigh of relief and thought, I might even get out of the house sometimes.[10]

5 King of the Cripples

With rows of attractive houses nestled between the green peninsula hills and the blue San Francisco Bay, soaked in year-round sunshine and cool ocean breezes, Burlingame in the mid-50s was a pleasant place to raise a family. Historian Kevin Starr described the post–World War II San Francisco suburbs as "a white place . . . just as mainstream California wanted it to be." It could also be described in the hyperbolic words of one social critic as the "standardized, vulgarized, mass-produced cheerfulness" of postwar suburbia. Social conformity, cast along lines of race, gender, sexuality, and disability, was the monochrome glue that seemingly held middle class society together.[1]

Buoyed by the World War II victory, widespread economic stability, and scientific developments promising even greater comforts, America was on top. High levels of government defense spending spurred the economy forward to full employment. With General Eisenhower in the White House, satisfied moderation was the order of the day. As historian William Leuchtenburg drily understated, "It was not a period hospitable to agitation for fundamental change."[2]

Eisenhower navigated difficult cold war tensions with communist adversaries China and the Soviet Union. The same atom bombs that obliterated Nagasaki and Hiroshima, pleasing Americans with a victory over Japan, now threatened instant annihilation as the world's superpowers built up horrifying nuclear stockpiles.

The existential nuclear standoff between the United States and the Soviet Union escalated during the 1950s. The superpowers had atomic warheads but needed an effective delivery system. The United States developed the Atlas rocket, an intercontinental ballistic missile (ICBM) designed to carry a nuclear warhead to the Soviet Union. But a June 1957 test flight failed. The Soviets countered in August with a successful test of their own ICBM. Just two months later they launched the Sputnik 1, the first satellite to orbit the earth. Alarmed by the communist rival's technological advances—the so-called "missile gap"—the US military and the new National Aeronautics and Space Administration worked desperately to catch up.

On the home front, Black activists struck the first impactful blows against long-standing racial segregation. The 1954 *Brown* Supreme Court decision required the desegregation of public schools. In December 1955, Rosa Parks crossed the color line to launch the Montgomery bus boycott. Twelve months of disciplined, nonviolent resistance resulted in victory and elevated a young African American pastor named Martin Luther King, Jr., as the leader of the new civil rights movement. A year later, a reluctant President Eisenhower (he opposed desegregation) dispatched federal troops to enforce the integration of Central High School in Little Rock, Arkansas.[3]

The white middle-class response to pervasive racial injustice was largely silence. Preferring a pleasant ignorance, most quietly quashed thoughts of the systemic oppression of African Americans. In the words of noted sociologist Gunnar Myrdal, they told themselves, "Everything is quiet on the racial front." This attitude of denial was exemplified in the popular work of illustrator Norman Rockwell, who painted over three hundred poignant *Saturday Evening Post* covers. His humorous and heartwarming tributes to everyday American life

featured amiable policemen, earnest blue-collar workers, valiant soldiers, and loyal families. At the direction of the *Post* editors, his sen-
timental scenes rarely portrayed Black Americans, and then only in
servant roles. Throughout the 50s his paintbrush dared not raise controversial social issues. As he explained, "There is no place for mud
and ugliness in my paintings. I paint life as I would like it to be."[4]

The common nostrum for the anxieties of nuclear bombs and
news accounts of bombed Black churches was shopping. Consumerism became the American pastime. Rushing to new shopping malls
to buy pogo sticks, refrigerators, and transistor radios, Americans
concentrated on "nest-building, nurturing the psyche, (and) enjoying the fruits of prosperity."[5]

Nowhere was this more true than in the homeowning families of
white, middle class California suburbia. Newspaper reports of Soviet
missile-rattling or racial violence in far-off Southern states did not
interrupt the backyard barbeques and plates of freshly baked cook-
ies. Ed's hometown of Burlingame was one of thousands of neat suburban locales that felt lucky enough to host the American Dream.

But that dream could be stolen away by polio. Parents of a child
with polio often experienced what one scholar called "the betrayal of
the American dream." Another social scientist described polio's vicious disruption of the lives of families as "un-American." America
itself, that uplifting celebrant of healthy families, respectable social
status, and financial security, had turned her back on them.[6]

The Roberts were like many polio parents: they adopted an attitude of normalization. To the greatest extent possible, they behaved
as if their son's paralysis mattered little. They tried to make Ed's return from the hospital uneventful. He would simply pick up right
where he left off.

That was more coping scheme than reality. Most kids with polio
did not settle neatly back into neighborhood life. They frequently

suffered social rejection and isolation. Friends from before the illness drifted away. The public schools were usually not welcoming.

Even greater than the loss of bodily functioning was the forfeiture of social status. Polio victims entered the hospital as normal, acceptable, whole persons. Months or years later, they returned home as social outcasts with no real place in decent society. Ed and other polio survivors were invisible ghosts, remnants of lost humanity lingering on the fringes of society.

Ed came home from Children's Hospital in October 1954. In eager preparation for his discharge, the Roberts moved from their small home on Oak Grove Avenue to a slightly larger house around the corner. They sought a new normal with the slightest modifications. A sprawling apricot tree and a long clothesline graced the backyard, just like at the old house. The dining room connected to the living room, providing an expanded area for Ed's hospital bed and cuirass respiration machine. Ed's brother Ron could still walk to nearby Burlingame High School.

Architectural accessibility decades before curb cuts did not involve a wheelchair ramp. Ed passed through the front door cradled in the careful arms of two people, often Verne and a neighbor, one of whom placed one arm under his neck propping his head and one arm under his back holding his arms, with the another person's arm under his butt and the other arm beneath his knees.

But Ed rarely moved. Planted in the large front room, he became the nucleus of the Roberts family's home life. He was the community square sundial that marked the time of the family's daily routine.

When Verne arrived home from work, he buttered a plate of soda crackers and brewed a cup of coffee. He sipped and nibbled at Ed's bedside as they talked through the details of the day.

At dinnertime, the whole family huddled around Ed. His bed was the dining room table. Randy was two, Mark five, and Ron thirteen.

They propped their dinner plates on the bedsheet. The family cat curled up against Ed's head, snatching meat off the fork as Zona fed her teenage son. After dinner, the Roberts watched the little black and white television behind Ed's head.

Later Verne gently carried his six-foot-tall, fifteen-year-old son to the bathtub. Every appendage of his sprawling frame, if not properly contained, flopped loose. An unintentional twist or pinch could bruise and cause pain. Zona systematically arranged a series of bath towels to cushion his body against the hard porcelain tub—one beneath the head and neck, two more under the lower back and the butt, and a pair along the sides for his arms. Verne set Ed in the warm water. Zona scooched his feet up toward his rear end and tucked a final folded towel under the bend of knees.

Ed's parents and brothers tenderly adjusted, toileted, and scratched his body. At the vulnerable adolescent moment when growing boys and girls worry about bodily appearance, Ed had no privacy.

Surprisingly, he didn't seem to mind. He had grown uncommonly accustomed to nurses manipulating his body. They unceremoniously stuffed a cold bed pan under his rear end and aimed his penis down to void. With a methodical lift and swipe, they cleaned his anus and dabbed his penis dry. It all happened with the disinterested casualness of running a feather duster across the top of a dresser.

Many young patients experienced this as a shocking assault that left lasting emotional scars. But not Ed. By the time he went home, he had become so inured to his own public nudity that he felt no hesitation asking for a bed pan to relieve himself in front of family, neighbors, and friends.

Ed had achieved a personal freedom from anxiety over physical appearance that would serve him well for years to come. His unusual body, the very object that bothered so many other people, didn't really bug him. As a teenager, he was already accepting the radical idea that his body—understood widely as hideous and unsightly—was wholly natural.

. . .

The electric chest cuirass really didn't work very well. The rubber edges of the plastic shell were supposed to seal tightly against Ed's torso. His narrow body swam loose inside the pulsing hull. Verne packed towels into the gaps. The pumping motion shook the towels free, and the plastic edges rubbed painful burns and rashes.

The respirator didn't supply enough air. His skin broke out in large red blotches across his arms and chest, a sign that he needed more oxygen.

By 1957, Dr. Leon Lewis at Fairmont Hospital in San Leandro, across the Bay from Burlingame, had a solid reputation for working with polio survivors. He admitted Ed to the hospital for a series of tests of heart and lung functioning.

Ed met Johnnie Lacy and Bill Tainter, two young polio patients who would later achieve their own success as disability rights leaders. Lacy would become the director of an independent living center in nearby Hayward, and Tainter would become the second disabled man to lead the California Department of Rehabilitation. At Fairmount, Lacy and Tainter organized a teen protest of the nursing staff's heavy-handed control. They led all the mobile patients to the hospital roof where they enjoyed an impish afternoon escape.[7]

Ed learned that his heart was not healthy. A cardiac catheterization discovered significant damage to the left-side heart chambers, caused either by the original polio virus or by the subsequent lack of oxygen. The weakened ventricles operated at a decreased capacity, reducing the blood supply to his entire body. This condition was permanent. Maintaining healthy oxygen levels would be a problem for Ed throughout his life.

An unexpected complication plummeted Ed's blood pressure and heart rate. Sharp pain stabbed his abdomen and groin. He fell into neurogenic shock, a dangerous disruption of the autonomic nervous system. Kidney stones had lodged in a ureter, one of the tubes between the kidney and the bladder, likely due to extended periods of catheterization. The Fairmont Hospital surgeons performed emergency surgery to remove several kidney stones.

When Ed regained his strength, Dr. Lewis set up a discharge planning conference. He wanted to make sure that Ed's respiration support at home would deliver a healthy flow of oxygen. Ed and his parents participated in the meeting with the medical team. This was a sharp break with standard hospital protocol. In prior hospitalizations, the officious doctors rarely spoke to Ed or his parents.

As the meeting started, Zona found herself crying. Dr. Lewis reached across and held her hand. She was overwhelmed by the rare opportunity to sit face-to-face with doctors and talk openly about her son's treatment. The consensus decision was to return Ed to the iron lung, at least at night, to improve oxygen flow. With his damaged heart, the lung was the safest plan.

The March of Dimes bought a shiny Emerson tank respirator for the Roberts' living room. It had a large squeezebox bellows at one end and two rubber hand ports on the side. Little Randy was deathly frightened of the huffing metal monster. Mark felt much the opposite, crawling around on the iron lung like an indoor jungle gym.

Ed slept in the iron lung every night. He gave up on the awkward and uncomfortable chest cuirass, opting instead to frog-breathe during the day.

. . .

Educationally, Ed was way behind. After two years of spotty academic instruction, he returned full-time to school. A local women's club and the Sears Roebuck store set up a two-way telephone connection to the classrooms of Burlingame High School. Ed listened on a small speaker located by his head. To speak, he tapped a switch with his left foot.

Ed wrote a sports column for the school newspaper. Verne drove him to the high school football games. At first, Ed refused to enter the stadium. He felt too embarrassed to have people see him in his wheelchair. He was afraid that everyone would stare at him. Verne and Ed watched the action from the family station wagon outside the chain link fence.

With his father's encouragement, Ed finally allowed Verne to wheel him into the stadium. At first, he was bombarded with a strange combination of half-concealed revulsion and exaggerated concern. Luckily, over the long football season, most fans lost interest in him and his chair.

· • ·

Seven-year-old Mark didn't notice the stigma. He felt privileged to push Ed's tall wheelchair up the sidewalk of Burlingame Avenue to the small shops of the downtown business district. With the high seatback and Ed's head looming above, little Mark peered around the edges of the chair to see where they were going.

At each street corner, the tall sidewalk dropped sharply to the street below. Mark carefully lowered his brother. The small front wheels dipped gently. Then the large rear tires crashed hard to the pavement. After crossing the road, Mark struggled mightily to pop the chair backwards, lifting the front tires up the curb.

A passerby approached the brothers and barked accusingly, "What's the matter with you?"

Ed stared silently at the far-off blue sky. He didn't know what to say.

Later, back in the safety of his home, he planned how to respond next time. He decided that he needed an answer that would satisfy the questioner and make him go away. He also needed an authentic answer that told the person who he truly was. It would take him years to learn how to do this.

Mark and Ed rolled into the five-and-dime store. A middle-aged woman approached Ed without a greeting. She set her hands on his head. Eyes gazing upward, she began to pray. "Please, I ask of you, Oh Lord Jesus, cure this unfortunate soul and let him walk again."

Ed glanced down at his younger brother. Catching Mark's eyes, he screwed up his mouth, as if to say, "Oh well!" Mark grinned back as they waited patiently. When she finished, they bought batteries for Ed's transistor radio so he could listen to Stanford football games.

. . .

By September 1958, the start of Ed's senior year, Zona was worn out. She had spent four years tending to Ed's needs in the family living room. His social isolation was hers. She dreamed of going to college, working a job, and maybe even traveling across Europe. Unless something changed dramatically, she and Ed would be forever stuck at home. She would never escape Richard Nixon's kitchen.

Zona decided that Ed must attend high school in person. He was able to frog-breathe out of the iron lung. His youngest brother Ron could push his wheelchair to class or arrange for other students to help. It was an unusual decision for parents to make. Kids using wheelchairs typically didn't go to school.

Ed didn't want to go. He feared that the other students would stare at his thin, limp body propped up in a wheelchair. When the dozens of teenagers locked their intrusive and mournful eyes on him, they would testify in the harshest court possible, the judgmental forum of adolescence, that Ed was repulsive.

On Ed's first day at Burlingame High School, his brother Ron guided his wheelchair into the outdoor commons area filled with hundreds of students. The horrific scene was just as Ed had imagined. Mouths hung open. Saddened eyes fixed on him. When he looked back at them, attempting to burst their gloom with a smile, they turned quickly away.

The intensity of the staring eyes decreased over time as classmates became more comfortable. Even more, Ed noticed a change in himself. He felt a separation between his own feelings and the discomfort experienced by others. If they felt pity or disgust or fear about his body, somehow those feelings didn't harm him.

Ed learned to split the social stigma of his disability into two halves. One side was the feelings and actions of the starers who unthinkingly carried out the culture's cruelty. The other side was the typically deflating experience of the person receiving stigma's wound. Ed found to his surprise that the gawkers could uphold their half of the equation while he shut down his side. Even if they sent him their pity, he learned to refuse delivery.

Beginning in the hallways of Burlingame High School, Ed began to practice a personal art of self-valuing, of granting himself esteem regardless of the opinions of others. It would take him years of arduous work, laboring like a martial artist accumulating the intricate skills of self-defense, to fully develop this complex new practice.

In later years, in his speeches, Ed told audiences that he had simply decided to be a star. Like flipping a light switch, he chose to believe that the pitying stares of his high school classmates were due not to his disfigurement or incapacity but to his fame and celebrity. The kid in the iron lung was a superstar, and all the students at Burlingame High knew it. Through a deft and powerful trick of the mind, he viewed himself not as a helpless cripple but as a combination of Rock Hudson and Marlon Brando.

In truth, it was neither that uncomplicated nor that easy. Neil Marcus, a writer and performing artist who lived with a neurological impairment called dystonia, insightfully wrote, "Disability is an art—an ingenious way to live."[8] As a high school senior Ed began an intensive practice of creative ingenuity that would become central to his life and identity.

But unlike Buddhist meditation or Tae Kwon Do, there was no tried-and-true tradition to follow. He had no wise mentor to teach him, and no well-paved road to success. What he was doing was unprecedented, and it was his own invention.

Supported by the love of his family, the uncertain, frightened teen traced the initial outlines of a life-changing innovation he and other disabled people would later call "independent living." It didn't mean standing on his own two feet or doing everything for himself. It meant living fully in the community as a valued person, not hidden away in an institution or nursing home or hospital. It all started with a glimmer of awareness that maybe, just maybe, Ed could see himself as a person of worth and talent.[9]

. . .

Ed wrote a story entitled "Is there?" for his high school literary magazine. He opened the first-person narrative lying alone in the dark staring up at the hospital ceiling, wondering, "Is there a life after this one . . . and if there is, what will it be like?"

After all the treatment and rehabilitation was done, a polio patient finally went back to the outside world. What life would there be for him?

The story shifted quickly to a dream sequence, a Hollywood movie. Ed fantasized himself as a "beautiful gray-black stallion" at "the starting gate at a famous racetrack." He defeated a field of "nine thoroughbreds." It was his "twenty-third win in as many starts," and he felt understandably "proud" in the "winner's circle."

Not only was Ed a perennial winner. He was "the first and only talking horse in the universe." He was doing the impossible.

His many victories were not the result of athletic prowess. He did not run faster than the other horses. He talked his way across the finish line. Chatting up his opponents, Ed had "completely unnerved" them, resulting in his long win streak.

It was unclear if Ed trash-talked the horses into submission, psychologically undermining their will to win, or if he jovially won them over, a triumph by consensual acclamation. Somehow persuasive words—the only tool available to a paralyzed teen—became the way to win.

The racetrack reporters were suspicious. They thought that Ed must have cheated to win twenty-three races. When questioned, Ed lashed back with fierce pride:

> What do you mean, "Is this race fixed?" It is due to my ingenuity and brains that I have won all these races. How many other horses do you think could talk their way into the winner's circle twenty-three times in a row. Answer me, if you dare!

Competitive, creative, and combative, Ed already envisioned himself succeeding in a world that had no place for him. He planned on using his powerful mind and verbal eloquence to talk his way to the top.[10]

Ed often joked with his adoring younger brother Mark that he would become "the king of the cripples." The third grader hung by the edge of his big brother's bed, cherishing every word Ed uttered. Mark didn't get the joke. A kingdom of disabled people? There was no such thing. Mark thought that Ed was already royalty.[11]

Ed humorously half-wondered about the possibility of unifying disabled people in some meaningful way. His father belonged to a supportive union of railroad men who took care of one another. Maybe he could lead a similar union of disabled people.

He had spent eighteen months in the hidden community of polio patients. Isolated from family and friends, they suffered through daily hot packs and stretching. They endured multiple painful surgeries to straighten spines and realign joints. Like soldiers at war, they shared a gallows humor comradery, a togetherness forged of unfortunate circumstances.

But the hospital ward devoted to reconstructing broken bodies was no home for the human spirit and no crucible of community. Muscles, nerves, bones, and ligaments were medically managed and shaped toward an ideal of physical normality. Neglected were the minds and hearts of the polio survivors.

As Ed labored within his own emotions and thoughts to revive his identity, to cobble together a scheme that might allow him to live with fullness and love, he pondered how he could be successful. In his silliest musings, the polio ward castaways would gather around him in a new union of disabled people. He would be their leader. It was a blue-sky fantasy too bizarre for Hollywood.

6   *Learning to Fight*

In April 1959, eighteen-year-old Ron Roberts and his twenty-year-old brother Ed were ready to graduate from high school. Zona set up an appointment with a school guidance counselor to double-check Ed's academic credits.

Zona waited as the counselor reviewed the records in his academic file. Then the woman looked up with a concerned expression.

"I'm afraid Ed is missing two graduation requirements. He hasn't taken driver's education and physical education."

"Driver's ed and PE?" Zona questioned aloud, assuming there was some mistake.

"Yes," the counselor answered earnestly. "Those two classes are district-mandated for high school graduation. He'll need to stay another year."

Zona sat dumbfounded. Did the counselor honestly expect Ed to drive a car, do jumping jacks, and climb the rope to the gymnasium ceiling? Did she even know who Ed was?

"We're talking about my son Edward Verne Roberts, born January 23, 1939 . . ." Zona kept her eyes down as she spoke. She didn't want to—or she really didn't know how to—challenge an authority figure. Nervously she rattled off a list of his completed classes. "He took Spanish and math and . . . " Finally, she just blurted, "He has very good grades."

"Yes, he has done well in the classes he has completed," the counselor answered matter-of-factly. There was nothing in her tone or demeanor that demonstrated any awareness of what she was asking Ed to do. "The problem is that he has not met all the requirements set by the district to qualify for high school graduation. He'll need to attend for one more year."

Zona mumbled a quick "thank you" and raced directly down the hallway to see the principal. Certainly, the high school's principal would realize that Ed could not take those classes.

She quickly explained the situation to the head administrator. Sitting behind his large desk, Principal Wilson listened politely as Zona pled her case. Then he said, "We have an outstanding group of guidance counselors here. If Miss Simpson says that Ed is short two graduation requirements, then I'm sure she is correct."

"You want Ed to . . ." Zona was exasperated. She didn't know where to begin to argue with him.

"He can come back in the Fall to complete these requirements," Mr. Wilson repeated as he stood up and guided her gently out the door.

Zona felt as if she was stuck in a carnival funhouse where a hundred mirrors twisted every reality into befuddling distortion. She ran the morning's discussions over and over in her mind. How could the school administrators expect Ed to drive a car or do athletic activities? Maybe they lacked knowledge about quadriplegia and respiratory paralysis. Maybe they were confused about what Ed's body could actually do.

In her naïve optimism, Zona didn't consider the possibility that both the counselor and the principal did not expect a paralyzed young man to complete a physical education course or driver's education training. What would he need a high school diploma for anyway? He was not fit for a job. Even with good grades there was no college he could attend. They saw Zona as an overinvolved mother who was sadly unwilling to accept the dreadful cards life had dealt her son.

The educators were correct about one thing. Zona was not about to accept their miserable outlook for Ed's future. During her years on the elementary school PTA, Zona built a good rapport with the district superintendent Tom Reynolds. She called his office to request a meeting. Reynolds opted to send the assistant superintendent, Mr. Evans, to visit Zona and Ed at their home.

Zona felt hopeful about this meeting. There was no way Mr. Evans could stand next to Ed's iron lung, look at his head peeking out of the giant steel drum, listen to the bellows pumping, and conclude that he would somehow drive a car or run around the high school track. The mere sight of the gigantic respirator would surely snap the man back to reality.

But it didn't.

Mr. Evans rested his left hand on the top of the enormous machine and spoke directly to Zona. "I don't see why Ed shouldn't return for one more year to complete PE and driver's education."

Then the assistant superintendent leaned down to where Ed's face rested on a pillow and looked him sincerely in the eye. Delivering a jolt of authoritative motivation to what he thought was a malingering youth, he asked, "You wouldn't want a cheap diploma, now would you?"

Zona snapped. She was livid. She couldn't believe what this man was saying.

"So we'll prop him up behind the wheel of a car? Maybe put a brick on the gas pedal? Will that satisfy your graduation requirements?"

Face filled with candor, Mr. Evans blinked, wide-eyed, fully unknowing. He had no idea why Zona was upset. In his experience, some laggard teens just needed an extra push. He tried to console Zona, reassuring her that one more year was not that big a deal.

"Get out!" Zona shouted, surprising herself and Ed with her raised voice. "I demand that you get out of my house right now."

Ed watched in silent awe. He had never seen his mother fight like that. The mild-mannered, kindly woman put her hands on the assistant superintendent's back and shoved him out the front door.

Even more, she had done it for him. It was the first time the notion crossed Ed's mind that creating a livable life for himself might involve, maybe even require, fighting.

Zona took the battle to the next level. She called up Mimi Haas, a longtime dear friend and a member of the local school board. Mimi's son Louie was Ron's best pal. Zona knew that Mimi was a person she could trust.

Together Zona and Mimi compared Ed's high school transcripts to the district graduate requirements. It was true that Ed was short the two courses. But Mimi agreed with Zona, "It sounds strange to me that they would even talk about Ed taking those classes." She arranged for Zona to meet with the superintendent.

Zona told Tom Reynolds the entire story, and he quickly agreed with her. "You know, some people can't see past the end of their nose. I think that this really shouldn't be a problem. But it will have to be decided officially by the school board at the next meeting." He alone didn't have the authority to set aside the high school graduation requirements. He asked Zona to attend the meeting to formally request school board approval.[1]

. . .

Another young man similarly sickened by polio almost a year earlier than Ed, in Spring 1952, was Hugh Gallagher. He became a top legislative aide to United States senator Bob Bartlett. In 1964, Gallagher led a campaign to convince the architects and builders of the new Kennedy Center for the Performing Arts in Washington, DC, to make the impressive cultural center fully accessible for people using wheelchairs. It was an outrageous new idea.

Multiple letters from Senator Bartlett, all authored by Gallagher, were ignored by the architect and the project director. When the two contractors appeared before a Senate subcommittee chaired by Bartlett, they deftly dodged the question of disability access, as if it didn't really matter.

Finally, at Gallagher's urging, Senator Bartlett told the two builders that the subcommittee would withhold all project construction funds until they guaranteed that the new building would be wheelchair accessible. As a result, the Kennedy Center became an early, shining example of accessible public architecture. After winning the fight, Gallagher concluded that he and the Senator had "blackmailed" the construction managers "for their own good."[2]

Ed and Zona were learning Hugh Gallagher's lesson, early. Many otherwise decent people would not take the inclusion of disabled people seriously without painful arm-twisting or a sharp slap in the face. People of stellar reputations and good intentions were the most dangerous, for they appeared to casual onlookers to be reasonable and good.

As the evening of the school board meeting approached, Zona grew increasingly anxious. The steely tactics of hardball Washington politicians were not part of her repertoire of social skills. She was not comfortable taking on respectable school officials in a public conflict. Verne, while supportive, was too congenial to question authority figures. This was Zona's fight.

Zona tried to picture herself standing at the microphone in front of a room filled with people, making her argument clearly and convincingly. All she could imagine was her knees wobbling and her voice creaking, incomprehensible squeaks and half-syllables falling from her quivering lips.

When Zona worked on Helen Gahagan Douglas's 1950 senate campaign, she learned an important lesson about politics. You had to rally your supporters if you wanted to win. She called up each of Ed's high school teachers. They all knew that he was an excellent student. She asked them to come to the meeting as a show of support. If the school board didn't listen to a student's mother, they might listen to their own teachers.

By the evening of the meeting, Zona was wired. Adrenaline raced through her body as she silently rehearsed her speech. Walking into the crowded school district conference room, she saw Assistant Superintendent Evans at the doorway. To Zona's surprise, he smiled wide and greeted her like an old friend, "Mrs. Roberts, I'm so glad to see you. We're all so very proud of your wonderful son."

Something wasn't right. The upbeat tone of his voice either meant that the school board intended to approve Ed's graduation or that creepy Mr. Evans was twisting the knife to produce extra pain. His prior performance in the Roberts' living room suggested the latter.

The businesslike panel of school board members sat behind a broad, formal dais at the front of the large conference room. Mimi smiled briefly at Zona, but her demeanor was flat and official. Parents, teachers, and community members occupied the rows of chairs facing the school board. Thankfully, Zona noticed many of Ed's high school teachers in the room.

A single microphone stood at the front of the assembly. With each discussion item, audience members went up to the microphone to comment or ask questions of the board.

The long, dry agenda crept slowly. Zona replayed her planned speech in her head, doubting her words more with each repetition, sinking deeper and deeper into her seat. She felt like rushing out the back door to the parking lot where she might get a full breath of air.

The school board chairman finally announced, "Next for the matter of Edward Verne Roberts."

Notes in her shaking hand, Zona bounded to her feet. She tried to scramble down the aisle to the waiting microphone, but her feet froze in place. She couldn't move.

Then the man's voice called to her, "Mrs. Roberts?"

Zona clenched. The room was quiet. She looked up from her notes. The entire room stared at her.

The chairman continued, "Your son Ed has accumulated an outstanding academic record at Burlingame High School. We congratulate you and Mr. Roberts on your son's excellent achievements. The board is pleased to issue a high school diploma for Edward Verne Roberts."

Zona looked around the room and then down at her hands. They were gripped in tight fists ready to punch. Her hands opened and fell to her side. Her notes scattered to the ground.

She tried to speak. She came fully prepared to tell the school board about her incredible son Ed and how they were damned wrong to stop him from graduating. She came ready to swing her fists.

All she could muster was a quick "thank you." She collapsed into the chair in a burst of tears.

When his mother told him the news, Ed's heart filled with pride. She went toe to toe with school district leaders. In the years to come, Zona became a more confident and capable fighter for justice. Ed followed in her instructive wake, learning how to bust open the many doors that were closed to a disabled person. If he was going to find a life of fulfillment and, just perhaps, dignity, he would have to punch and kick. His mother would show him how.[3]

The opposition would not be an army of overtly cruel jerks organized into a rabid antidisability hate squad. There was no equivalent of the Ku Klux Klan that burned wooden wheelchairs on the lawns of disabled people. The opposition would be otherwise kindly, well-meaning neighbors, community members, leaders, and professionals who simply didn't understand how their unquestioned attitudes squashed the hopes and dreams of people like Ed.

. . .

In September 1959, Ed's younger brother Ron went to Berkeley to attend the University of California. Ed also had excellent grades, but he started classes at nearby College of San Mateo so that he could continue living at home. Zona drove Ed to campus and pushed his wheelchair to the lecture halls. Classmates hoisted Ed and his bulky wheelchair over curbs and up staircases.

Ed distributed sheets of carbon paper so he could get copies of notes from other students. For written assignments, Ed dictated to Zona, and she wrote out his examinations and papers longhand.

At the community college, Ed met his first mentor, a brilliant and warm English instructor named Jean Wirth. The two shared a bond built on parallel adolescent experiences of being the strangest kid in school. Wirth had sprouted suddenly at age twelve to a height of six foot five inches. School classmates viewed her as a freak show exhibit. Ed found someone who understood what it felt like to be an object of curiosity and mockery. More importantly, she believed he had a successful future ahead of him.

Wirth was an educational innovator who understood how the community college system failed the many talented students of color. The most capable African American and Hispanic students found the standard curriculum personally meaningless, lacking real connections to their lives and cultures. Instructors often wrote them off as lazy or unintelligent. She devoted herself to keeping them in school despite their discouragement.

She emboldened Ed to question social conventions and battle against injustice. When the College of San Mateo required all faculty members to sign a loyalty oath declaring themselves to be patriotic anticommunists, a common practice in the 1950s when Senator Joseph McCarthy accused State Department officials of being Soviet spies, she brought the oath text to class. She and the students studied the document and discussed the political ramifications of such a requirement in a democratic society.

When Ed took his first course in American government, he was hooked. He was fascinated with the intricate workings of power, how decisions were made through legislative processes and executive actions. His mentor encouraged him to study political science.

After completing an associate degree in three years, Wirth called Ed and Zona to a meeting. She encouraged him, "Where are you going next?"

"I'm thinking about going to UCLA." Ed responded.

Wirth asked, "Why UCLA?"

"Because they have a program for disabled veterans there. Parts of the campus are accessible for people using wheelchairs." In the years following World War II, the Veteran's Administration developed programs supporting veterans with physical disabilities at the University of Illinois and UCLA.

Zona was surprised. She had occasionally slipped Ed brochures about colleges that provided some minimal assistance for disabled students. But he had been dismissive, muttering bitterly, "I've seen enough crippled people in the hospitals." He didn't want to be surrounded by disabled people in some special program.

Wirth pressed Ed to go to UC Berkeley. "You're a fine political science major, and Berkeley is the place you need to be. They have the best political science department. Plus, UCLA is more of a commuter school. In Berkeley, there is a village next to campus where you can move around in your wheelchair."

Ed had visited his brother Ron a few times, and he liked the campus and the town. The university was large and sedentary, like a venerable dinosaur sleeping on a leafy hillside in the afternoon shade. The commercial district around the school was quaint and inviting, lined with pleasant avenues of restaurants and shops. For a nice kid from Burlingame, it would be a comfortable place. And Wirth was right about the quality of the political science department.

Ed decided to go to Berkeley, beginning in Fall quarter 1962. He expected to study the art and science of politics in the detached, safe environs of textbooks and faculty lectures. He had no idea that he would also learn the street-level politics of civil disobedience. He had no idea he was rolling into a roaring firestorm of political upheaval. He didn't imagine that the incendiary world of oppositional protests would suit him perfectly.[4]

7 Dr. Bruyn's Program

The twenty-eight-mile drive from suburban Burlingame on the San Francisco peninsula across the Bay Bridge to Berkeley was a passage from a gray flannel world of rarely questioned social norms to a bohemian village ready to burst into paisley flames. The 1950s orderly veneer of wholesomeness and security concealed powerful undercurrents of dismay and anxiety. Not all was as right as the surface joviality might suggest. When the 1960s firestorm of youthful discontent erupted, Berkeley was ground zero.

As the nuclear rivalry with the Soviet Union grew, California was the nation's cold war staging ground, the hub of the dramatic growth of new aerospace and defense industries. By 1959, Golden State corporations and universities filled 40 percent of all American defense contracts. Caltech and the University of California, Berkeley emerged as scientific centers of the rising military-industrial complex.[1]

While the defense industries funded expansion of California's suburbs, wars abroad were confusing and inconclusive. The American military battled faraway communism in Korea and Vietnam. From June 1950 until July 1953 United Nations forces overwhelmingly supplied by the United States and South Korea fought a North Korean military backed by China and the Soviet Union. Approximately three million civilians died. American troops dead and missing topped forty thousand. Unlike the clear-cut, patriot victory of World War II experienced just a few years earlier, this puzzling conflict ended in a stalemate.

For Americans at home struggling to understand newspaper headlines filled with battles fought in unpronounceable Asian locales, the Vietnam War seemed like more of the same. Again the United States supported the South against a communist North backed by China and the Soviet Union. Hoping to keep American troops home, the United States initially supported France and South Vietnam to the tune of $3 billion. By the November 1963 assassination of President John Kennedy, sixteen thousand US troops had been sent to Vietnam. Hundreds of thousands more soon followed, and Vietnam became America's own tumultuous, unpopular war.

Matching the war in intensity was the civil rights movement exploding across the American South. In early 1961, college students of the Congress of Racial Equality (CORE) challenged local segregation practices. Black and white activists, including future congressman John Lewis, organized the Freedom Rides, taking Trailways and Greyhound buses across hostile Alabama and Mississippi. At many bus stops, the local police sat back while raging white mobs brutally beat the riders and set the vehicles on fire. In Washington, DC, President Kennedy and Attorney General Robert F. Kennedy pleaded unsuccessfully with state authorities to stop the violence.

Beginning in Greensboro with a group from North Carolina Agricultural and Technical University, African American students conducted sit-in protests at store lunch counters. Young activists, often trained in Ghandian practices of peaceful resistance, followed the principle of laying their bodies on the line. Sit-ins, swim-ins, and pray-ins spread quickly across the South, occurring in Winston-Salem, Raleigh, Richmond, and New Orleans.

In October, Martin Luther King, Jr., and a group of eighty students requested service at a Rich's department store lunch counter in

Atlanta, leading to mass arrests. Sentenced to four months hard labor on a chain gang, King was released from maximum security prison only due to the intervention of Attorney General Kennedy.[2]

Modeled after the insurgent African American civil rights movement, numerous other social justice movements were spawned. Among those were the gay rights movement, the women's movement, and the disability rights movement, each basing their ideas and practices primarily on the Black civil rights approach. Each adopted the minority group model as a powerful way of understanding the systemic oppression they all faced. Each employed a variety of nonviolent civil disobedience tactics, confrontational but passive, including street marches, rallies, and sit-ins.

In the 1950s and 60s, the early foundations of the gay rights movement were built by homophile groups like the Mattachine Society for gay men and the Daughters of Bilitis for lesbians. These social support organizations stayed under the radar. They were fearful of being discovered. Homosexuals were routinely viewed by the police, newspapers, and the general public as immoral perverts jeopardizing the common decency of American society. These groups offered safe and secret spaces of friendship, a culture of discrete camaraderie that maintained social respectability.

While the homophile organizations engaged in small picket protests marked by respectful attire and politeness, as well as lawsuits against federal agencies that fired gay employees, their primary approach was not dramatic confrontation. Frank Kameny, the influential leader of the Washington, DC, Mattachines, wanted to persuade the America public that gays and lesbians were not sick or immoral. He believed that the cultural acceptance of homosexuality could be "marketed just like toothpaste."[3]

Respectful salesmanship was replaced by street demonstrations after the 1969 Stonewall Inn riot in New York City. Potent new LGBT activist groups—including the Gay Liberation Front (GLF) and the

Gay Activists Alliance (GAA)—created a distinct gay minority identity seeking social equality within a familiar civil rights narrative.

The modern women's movement—often called the second wave of feminism—began when John F. Kennedy entered the White House. In 1963, he formed the President's Commission on the Status of Women. The diverse commission included leading women representatives from the NAACP, American Association of University Women, Teamsters, and numerous Christian and Jewish faith groups. Congress passed the Equal Pay Act, outlawing wage and salary discrimination against women.

Led by Eleanor Roosevelt, the Commission on the Status of Women proved to be the organizational vehicle for a national women's rights campaign. Although the commission's final report largely confirmed the traditional necessity of women being homemakers in charge of the care of husbands and children, it also collected an enormous amount of data about women's lives. Armed with new information, all fifty states created similar commissions to track the status of women.

At a June 1966, national conference of the state commissions, Betty Friedan, author of the groundbreaking book *The Feminine Mystique*, scribbled the acronym NOW on a napkin and passed the note around the dinner table. The National Organization for Women (NOW) was founded with Friedan as the first leader. In the 1970s NOW become the largest and most influential national organization pursuing equality for women.[4]

In September 1962, Zona and Verne Roberts drove the family station wagon with Ed sprawled out flat to Berkeley, the calm and studious town that housed a great political science department perfect for Ed. Historian Kevin Starr described California at the end of the 1950s as tidy and anxious, concealing the underlying frictions of multiple tectonic plates soon to burst. Berkeley would become a main fault line for the 1960s political earthquake. The Roberts had no idea they were delivering their son straight into an explosion of bitter dissent.

Ed had no idea that the Berkeley cauldron of political fury would be his best teacher.

. • .

When Ed enrolled at Cal, his focus was imminently practical. He could only attend with assistance from the California Department of Rehabilitation. He needed an accessible place to live and competent care workers. These support services would seem to perfectly fit the State Rehab's goal of helping disabled people make it in society. Ed quickly found it wasn't that simple.

The State Rehab bureaucracy had a system of code numbers marking the status of each case. The most desirable code for any rehabilitation counselor was a 26. This meant that a client was successfully rehabilitated resulting in continuous employment. Rehabilitation completed. A home run for the counselor. Filling the statistics ledger with 26s was central to the organizational purpose of State Rehab, displaying the agency's overall effectiveness.

The department evaluated individual cases on a strict cost-benefit scheme. On the cost side of the accounting ledger was the financial expenditure necessary to prepare a client for work. On the benefit side was a cold mathematical prediction of the future dollars recovered if the disabled person became a tax-paying worker.

The agency's barely hidden strategy was called "creaming." Rehabilitation counselors accepted clients with relatively minor injuries and solid employment histories who could be quickly flipped into new jobs. This meant keeping people who had more significant disabilities out of the system.

Ed's rehabilitation application was quickly denied. After running him through a battery of psychological tests, State Rehab decided that his chances of long-term employment success were too low. People with respiratory paralysis were bad investments.

Zona and Ed met with the rehabilitation counselor to appeal this decision. To their surprise, the counselor had a disability. He moved slowly about his office, dragging one leg behind.

"Our psychological instruments," the counselor explained in flat professional tones, his eyes staring past Ed and Zona, "indicate extremely high levels of hostility. In our professional opinion, a client with this clinical profile is . . . well, Mr. Roberts is infeasible."

Ed choked and spit back, "Infeasible?"

"What hostility?" Zona challenged, trying to cut through the professional jargon.

"Aggression and anger," explained the counselor. "It is not uncommon for persons with partial or full paralysis to experience psychological distress due to the loss of bodily functioning." The counselor expressed a common belief in the field of rehabilitation that persons with mobility impairments were limited less by unmoving limbs than by psychopathology. What held them back were the mental health disorders caused by a physical disability.

Ed was steamed. "If you were paralyzed from the neck down and you wanted to do something in your life, don't you think being aggressive would help you?"

"Well, yes," the counselor nodded in reluctant agreement. "But your numbers on the MMPI were way off the scale." The Minnesota Multiphasic Personality Inventory (MMPI) was a widely used psychological measure designed to reveal mental disorders.

Ed shot back, "I think being angry makes me more likely to succeed."

The counselor's decision was not unusual for the times. A physician named Paul Corcoran, later a leader in the disability rights movement in Boston, went through a specialized rehabilitation training residency at New York University. The famous Dr. Howard Rusk supervised him from 1963 to 1966. Rusk was the foremost international authority in the new field of physical rehabilitation, the medical expertise devoted to bringing broken bodies back to functioning, and NYU had perhaps the best program in the nation.

Yet Corcoran found that the advanced Rusk NYU program would not treat people with quadriplegia. "They were felt to be too disabled to benefit from rehabilitation." Ed would have been turned away by the very best.[5]

The State Rehab counselor wouldn't budge. Zona and Ed filed a second-level appeal.

They decided to let Ed's teacher Jean Wirth and Phil Morse, the College of San Mateo's vice president, meet with the rehabilitation bureaucrats. The educators argued that Ed had already proven himself to be an outstanding college student. At their urging, Ed's application for state rehabilitation assistance was finally approved.

Meanwhile, Ed had received an acceptance letter from the university. Wirth, Morse, Zona, and Ed traveled to Berkeley in August to search for campus housing.

Zona had visited the University of California many times. Ed's brother Ron had enrolled two years earlier. She knew Cal was a challenging place for a student pushed in a manual wheelchair. The large campus sprawled down a series of hills and across low culverts. The sidewalks and roads were lined with fierce concrete curbs, making wheelchair travel slow and laborious.

But this time, as Zona guided Ed's wheelchair past the rows of enormous stone buildings, her eyes focused on one thing. Steps. Rising, insurmountable, everywhere, rows and rows of steps. Staircases towered like medieval curtain walls and bastions defending the mighty castles of knowledge.

Many Cal buildings were built in a majestic Beaux Arts style with noble French and Italian Baroque features including arched windows and grand tile entranceways. The main entries were usually elevated one level, raising the first floor to second-story height. A long row of dramatic steps flowed from double doors down to the sidewalk far below.

Any student climbing the long staircases would be psychologically humbled by the time they climbed up to the front lobby. For students using crutches, canes, or wheelchairs, the humility was double. The raised royal portals seemed to sneer and shout, "Go away! We don't want your kind."

Zona bumped Ed's wheelchair up the formidable steps leading to Sproul Hall, the main administration building. The first university administrator who met with the group stared at Ed with his mouth open.

"We didn't know he was handicapped when we admitted him," he complained, claiming they had unknowingly violated their own policy. "We tried cripples before, and it didn't work."

Zona mused silently that no one in university admissions wondered why an applicant over six feet tall weighed only eighty-five pounds. The annoyed administrator sent the foursome to meet with the Dean of Students. He had the authority to politely send them away.

While Zona and Ed waited for this dean to block his enrollment at the University of California, in faraway Oxford, Mississippi, a similar but vastly different drama unfolded. James Meredith, an African American man, accompanied by Chief US Marshal James McShane and Fifth Circuit Court representative John Doar, walked past a nasty, taunting crowd of two thousand to enter the Woolfolk Building at the University of Mississippi. Constance Baker Motley, a Columbia-trained NAACP lawyer who would later play a supportive role in disability rights history, secured a federal court order allowing him to be the first African American to enroll at the historically white college. Despite legal authorization and the intervention of US Attorney General Robert F. Kennedy, Mississippi governor Ross Barnett personally blocked Meredith's enrollment.

Playing to their segregationist supporters, Barnett and his lieu-tenant governor, Paul B. Johnson, turned Meredith back four times. A New Orleans federal judge convicted the two Mississippi leaders of contempt of court and set a firm deadline for Meredith's enrollment. Armed with rebel flags and coolers of beer, thousands of white su-premacists flooded the picturesque southern college town to defend against race mixing. That Saturday the raucous stadium crowd at the Ole Miss Rebels football game versus Kentucky chanted Governor Barnett's name. Raising his fist at the fifty-yard line, he shouted over the stadium loudspeakers, "I love our customs!" The ecstatic white crowd roared.

When President Kennedy made a television address reassuring America that he was enforcing the federal court order in a peaceable, orderly way, thousands of students and ruffians rioted on campus. They crashed a bulldozer into the university administration building, heaved Coke-bottle Molotov cocktails and rocks, and fired shotgun rounds, wounding 160 police and federal marshals. Finally, an exas-perated Attorney General Kennedy sent in Army troops to put down the racist rebellion. Meredith was enrolled at Ole Miss.

The unnoticed aspect of the analogy between Ed Roberts and James Meredith was the failed attempt four years earlier of another African American man to enter the University of Mississippi. Clennon King, an affluent resident of Albany, Georgia, who later became a college professor, was not only denied admission. Local authorities declared him insane and incarcerated him in Whitfield Asylum. Officially, he was rejected and locked up for having a psychiatric disability.[6]

The almost polite, bureaucratic effort to deny Ed admission to the University of California, Berkeley was a quiet incident of private mis-ery, not a high-level political crisis accompanied by a violent upris-ing. Jim Crow racism enforced segregation with intimidating verbal threats backed by fists, shotguns, and a bulwark of the South's apart-heid laws. By comparison, disability exclusion was boring, a whispered violence operating at the dullest octave. Not the explosive stuff of front-page news, it was quieter than the whining creak of a rusty door hinge swinging shut.

If the "we tried cripples before" administrator thought that Dean of Students Arleigh Williams would quickly dispatch Ed and Zona, perhaps with an empathetic lament that the university just wasn't ready for people like Ed, he was wrong. Dean Williams was a competent, kind college leader with a different attitude. He really didn't know what to do. But he wanted to be helpful, to find some way to house Ed on campus. The main problem was finding a room that could hold an iron lung the size of a Volkswagen in a building with an elevator. The group left William's office with a map and a list of suggested housing options.

Ed and company rolled up Bancroft Avenue on the south side of campus to the first dormitory Dean Williams recommended. Phil Morse backed the chair up a set of tall steps to the lobby. They searched out a resident assistant who showed them a room on the first floor. It was obvious that an iron lung wouldn't fit.

Next they checked out the International House, a campus housing facility primarily for students from foreign countries. At the sight of the building, Ed chuckled. The three-story stone mansion with an imposing rampart of two levels of steps was a glorious monument to inaccessibility.

Jean Wirth found the house manager. The small man's nervous eyes bounced first up at her towering frame and then down at seated Ed. He backstepped and sputtered, "No, we don't have any students who—oh, no, we couldn't have him."

They found nothing that day. Dean Williams's helpfulness hadn't been helpful enough. On the drive home, the typically energetic group was silent. They felt deflated.

But Phil Morse and Zona didn't give up. They returned to campus and met again with Dean Williams. Morse spoke to Williams as one college administrator to another, pressing him to dig up more housing options.

Williams had one Hail Mary pass left. He dialed Dr. Henry Bruyn, the medical director of Cowell Hospital, a four-story, 110-bed student infirmary. Maybe Ed could live in the university hospital.

"Henry, I've got a very disabled young man who's done very well in San Mateo College. And he would like to come to Berkeley. But he's in a wheelchair and he has to sleep in a respirator. I don't know how in the world we could take care of him."[7]

The physician who ran Cowell Hospital was ideally suited for the challenge. Bruyn had extensive prior experience working with polio patients from outbreaks in the 1940s. He knew that many adult "polios" languished in nursing homes and community hospitals. They were ambitious and talented, but they were overlooked by colleges and employers. He believed strongly that polio survivors living with paralysis should be integrated into universities.

The hospital director invited Ed and Zona to meet with him. He had something in mind. The entire third floor of Cowell Hospital was empty. If he could get the medical staff to cooperate, there was no reason Ed and his iron lung couldn't move in.

Right away Dr. Bruyn liked Ed. He found him to be intelligent, outgoing, and articulate. If this plan could work, it would work for a student like Ed. Bruyn explained his vision to Zona and Ed. The orderlies and nurses would serve as his personal attendants for bathing, toileting, and feeding. Student workers could push him to and from his classes. If he needed anything, he could push a button twenty-four hours a day and an orderly would come immediately.

Ed was miffed. "I don't want to live in a hospital," he griped. He had spent eighteen lonely, painful months in hospitals. He wanted to go to college. Dr. Bruyn reassured him that the arrangement would work. Ed reluctantly moved in to start his classes.[8]

Soon Ed discovered that many nurses didn't want to care for him. Some were afraid that his iron lung would shut down during a power outage. Some felt revulsion handling his thin, unmoving body. They were unaccustomed to caring for a "patient" that didn't get better.

Ed did what he knew how to do. He charmed them. He cracked corny jokes. He captured them with his dewy dark eyes. He gave them compliments about their appearance. He asked them questions about their lives, their problems, husbands, homes, and children. His voice was warm and his demeanor inviting. He listened with tender devotion and unwavering intensity.

The nurses soon found themselves wanting to talk to the odd patient on the empty third floor. They spent their coffee breaks leaning on his shoulder, sharing worries and joys. They found themselves feeling strangely at ease conversing with the disabled young man they had feared only days earlier.

Although living in a hospital was far from ideal, it worked. Ed was a Cal student. He majored in political science, earned top grades, attended football and basketball games, and felt comfortable with his campus life.[9]

.   .   .

Even though Ed was generally healthy, he was always susceptible to serious illness. While spending the 1962 Christmas holiday break at home with his family, he came down with pneumonia. Within a couple of days, his breathing became labored and painful. Zona and Verne loaded him in the back of the station wagon and sped across the bridge to Cowell Hospital.

Dr. Bruyn diagnosed him with double pleurisy. The tissue surrounding his lungs was infected and filled with liquid. The nurses began administering intravenous antibiotics immediately.

Ed felt terrified. That first night in Cowell he tried to stay awake. He was convinced that if he fell asleep he might never wake up. As he lay staring up into the darkness, half-dreaming with anxiety and a rocket-high fever, he spied a dark figure entering his room. It stopped at the edge of his bed.

"You are killing yourself," the shadow said forcefully. "Don't cling so hard. Let go. This is your body. You have to trust it."

The apparition left the room as quickly as it had entered. Ed didn't know if it was a real person or if the combination of nerves and fever had conjured up a ghostly hallucination. Reassured by the visitor, he slept soundly. In the morning, he started to feel better.

Of all the lessons he learned at Berkeley, Ed always remembered what the mysterious visitor taught him. Polio had changed his body, stealing physical abilities that would never return. It was natural to doubt the capacity of his paralyzed body to be stable and vigorous. Whoever or whatever entered his room that night advised Ed to do the exact opposite, to wholeheartedly place all bets on his body to hold and sustain a good life. Despite his polio illness and paralysis, his was a sturdy body that could carry him forward with strength and hope.

Later the next day, Ed asked Dr. Bruyn if he was the shadowy figure who gave him wise advice the night before. Dr. Bruyn denied it. Ed never believed him.[10]

· · ·

In early 1963, Dr. Bruyn received a phone call from a doctor at Contra Costa County Hospital a few miles north of Cal. He said, "I've got somebody in the hospital that might be a candidate for your program at Berkeley."

"What program in Berkeley?" Bruyn responded with surprise.

"I hear you have a program for disabled students."

The rehabilitation community already knew that something big was brewing in Berkeley. A December article in the *Berkeley Gazette* announced, "Helpless Cripple Attends UC Classes Here in Wheelchair." Ed's attendance was described by hesitant university administrators as "experimental."[11]

Dr. Bruyn informed the inquiring physician that there was no disabled student program. He admitted, "I have a disabled student living in our infirmary and it's working fine."

The doctor invited Bruyn to visit. "Come out and talk to this guy."

When Dr. Bruyn arrived at Contra Costa County Hospital, he was escorted to a small paralysis unit housing four long-term patients who had languished for years. Three lay in bed watching television.

At the far side of the room, a fourth bed was hidden behind mounds of books. A very tall young man with dark hair wore stereo headphones amidst a clutter of radio equipment. He was too busy to notice the visitor.

"Is that John?" Bruyn asked.

"Yes," grinned the doctor. "He's listening to short wave broadcasts from Paris. He's studying French. He wants to teach languages."

"OK," Bruyn agreed immediately. "He's accepted . . . to our program." John Hessler's five-year confinement on the back ward had finally ended.

In September 1963, John Hessler joined Ed as the second disabled student resident of Cowell Hospital. The two became fast friends and allies. They fought the pushy nurses, smuggled beer into the hospital, and helped one another navigate a campus filled with obstacles.[12]

. . .

Ed and John Hessler were both big basketball fans. They often used their connection to Dean Williams to score courtside seats beneath the backboard at Cal Bears men's games in Harmon Gym. One time an enormous Cal player leaped toward the rim and careened past the baseline.

"Oh shit!" shouted Ed as the player soared toward him. He landed on top of Ed, toppling his wheelchair and crushing his foot.

After the game, Ed's injured foot ached. The two friends decided logically that beer would be the best medicine. Their student attendants pushed their wheelchairs down Telegraph Avenue, the main drag in Berkeley, to Blake's, a popular beer hall known for its sawdust floors. After a few pitchers of suds, the pain subsided.

Ed needed to urinate. His wheelchair wouldn't fit into the men's room. No one had even begun imagining accessible restrooms. In the empty alley behind the bar, his attendant helped him pee into an empty beer pitcher.

A police cruiser pulled up with lights flashing. A cop jumped out and arrested Ed for urinating in public.

"We're taking you in," the officer barked. "You'll be released in the morning." He opened the prowler's back door and motioned naively for Ed to climb in.

"I don't think you want to do that, officer," Ed advised with a smart-aleck grin.

"If you had the common sense to use the bathroom inside, you wouldn't be in this fix," the cop snapped.

"OK, sir," Ed sighed with an air of resignation. "As long as your jail is equipped with an iron lung. You do have a negative pressure Drinker respirator?"

"A what?"

"You know, an iron lung." Ed continued playfully. "I'm completely paralyzed. If I don't sleep in a respirator tank the size of a submarine, I'll be dead by morning."

"You're breathing right now, aren't you?" the officer scowled. He wasn't going to be fooled by a bunch of drunk college kids.

Ed gave the police officer a quick demonstration of frog-breathing. He watched in amazement as Ed gulped down mouthfuls of air.

"But I can only swallow air when I'm awake. That's why I sleep in an iron lung."

"An iron . . . a lung, huh? Let me check on that." The officers sat in the driver's seat of the squad car and radioed his supervisor. After a short conversation featuring lots of "I don't knows" and quizzical expressions, he returned shaking his head.

"OK, just this once—one time only—I'm gonna let you go with a warning. But if I catch you pissing in public again, I'll take you straight to jail. You got it?"

"Yessir! Yessir!" Ed and his three friends repeated in joyful submission. The police car pulled away, and the college chums laughed and celebrated all the way back to Cowell Hospital.[13]

. . .

John Hessler was an enigma. He was a working-class ruffian who read French literature aloud to savor the melodious flow of the language. He was a macho teen hell-raiser who broke his neck in a swimming accident in the delta of the San Joaquin River and enjoyed writing sensuous poetry. Raised in a family where men worked with their muscles and hands, he studied in Berkeley and Paris to earn a master's degree. A quadriplegic, his formidable physique and stern facial expression often intimidated people into acquiescence.

The two Cowell residents were an odd couple and a great team. Ed was jovial, humorous, hopelessly disorganized, and deeply connected to the people around him. His eyes lit up as he swirled big ideas in the tallest clouds. Hessler was firmly planted on the ground. He was a clear, strategic thinker, an effective manager with a commanding voice who could get things done.

The duo was assisted by Mike Fuss, a nondisabled personal attendant and civil rights activist. He teamed up with Hessler to build strategic alliances with administrators and staff members across campus. Fuss and Hessler befriended the staff members in academic departments—the unsung women who worked the typewriters and phones—to get classes moved to more accessible buildings.

Dean Williams hired Ed and John Hessler to advise committees beginning the enormous task of making the campus accessible. They worked on installing what they called "ramps"—now known as curb cuts. They gave architectural guidance on campus building projects, including a new library and performance hall.

With the support of Dr. Bruyn and Dean Williams, Ed and Hessler were both successful students who later advanced to graduate programs. Dr. Bruyn grew the population of physically disabled men on third floor Cowell to half a dozen. He truly did have a college-based rehabilitation program, a little enclave of highly focused students taking full advantage of the unique opportunity.[14]

8   *Death and Renewal*

While Ed was home for the 1963 winter holiday, his father coughed and wheezed. He stifled a painful grimace and struggled to catch his breath. He had been dogged by heavy fatigue for months, but Verne was proud that he hadn't missed a single day of work.

Zona planned on making Verne a special whiskey Alexander to toast the New Year. But he was too exhausted. He went to bed long before midnight. Verne's illness was more severe than either of them thought. A couple days later, Zona received a phone call from the local hospital informing her that her husband had been admitted. Verne's condition had deteriorated quickly. Without a word to his wife, he asked a neighbor to drive him to the hospital.

Verne had a large, malignant tumor on his lung. When he heard the word "cancer" he didn't ask the doctors or nurses any questions about his condition. No one was allowed to say the word in his presence. He bore his fate in resolute silence, a stoic man carrying his burden alone.

"I don't want you here," he barked at Zona. "Go home. Take care of the boys." He didn't want their sympathy. This was a small matter. He promised he would be home soon.

Contrary to her husband's wishes, Zona rounded up the two youngest boys to visit their father at the hospital. Eleven-year-old

Randy refused to get in the car. He had always been Verne's favorite son. He couldn't bear to see his dying father.

When Zona and Mark entered Verne's hospital room, the teen halted at the foot of the bed. He looked at his father's ashen face and the tubes running into his arm and nose. He started to cry.

"What's wrong?" Verne snapped. He turned to Zona and demanded, "Why'd you hit him?" His denial about his illness was so complete that he thought Zona must have caused the boy's tears.

For the first six years of Ed's life, as the new Roberts family took shape, Thanksgiving was always celebrated at Verne's parents' home. Ed's grandmother Catherine served a delicious turkey and stuffing dinner that raised the spirits and soothed the heart. Verne felt best in his childhood family home surrounded by the warmth and love he had always known.

One year, though, Verne decided suddenly to break the old tradition. He had his own family with a wife and two young sons, Ed and Ron. He wanted to have Thanksgiving at home with his family. Zona couldn't begin to match Catherine's culinary skills. She did her best to cook a big roast chicken dinner.

After the plates were cleared, Verne took the two boys across the street to attend the Burlingame High School football game. Entering the crowded stadium, Ed held his father's right hand, and Ron the left. Head high, grinning proudly, Verne walked through the crowd like a man who had just won the lottery. He was a father with his own family now. He beamed as he greeted neighbors and wished them a happy Thanksgiving. It was everything he ever wanted.

Verne Roberts died on February 15, 1964. The aggressive cancer had spread throughout his body. He didn't want his family at his side. To the end, he refused to speak of the disease.

Ed always remembered the best day he ever spent with his dad. Verne surprised him by showing up without notice at his elementary school. He looked out of place, a father in his rough work clothes standing awkwardly outside the classroom. He waved through the little window for Ed to play hooky with him. It was a day of wonderful adventure.

Verne drove Ed to the old Southern Pacific railroad station in Richmond. They boarded a diesel freight engine heading back across the Bay to San Francisco for maintenance. Verne sat high in the engineer's seat and boosted Ed up into his lap so that he could pretend he was driving. It was a rare moment when the proud father offered his son a glimpse of the railroad life that he cherished. His father had passed it down to him, and now he was sharing it with his oldest boy.

The Roberts railroad men sat up front at the dashboard filled with gauges and meters, enjoying the view as the train dove into the dark tunnel under the Potrero San Pablo ridge. On the other side, they burst into sunshine and raced out to the eastern shore of San Francisco Bay.

Within minutes they arrived at the old Port Richmond pier, a dilapidated wooden structure first constructed in 1899 to support rail ferry service across the Bay. Long ago the ferries that carried entire trains had been replaced by rusty barges towed by tugboats.

The freight engine slid onto a small barge and began the short journey southwest across the Bay. They passed Alcatraz Island and the towering Golden Gate Bridge to the west. At the San Francisco pier, they transferred from water back to rails and drove the mighty engine the final few miles to the Bayshore Roundhouse.

From Verne, Ed learned what it meant to be a man. This was a mixed legacy for a young, disabled guy in 1960s Berkeley. In a town creatively eclipsing traditional norms of family, gender, and community, Ed learned that living with a physical disability required an alternative lifestyle. Verne sternly opposed any alterations to the traditional structure of family and society. Yet he fully supported Ed's individual journey toward success and happiness.

Confronted by his son's paralysis, Verne remained steadfast. Many fathers felt tremendous disappointment and embarrassment having a son with a physical disability. A son's sudden paralysis often felt like a dramatic loss of cherished masculinity. The powers of manhood, the strong hands and vigorous body that made athletics and skillful labor possible, were gone. Certainly Ed would not be the third Roberts man to work the mighty rails.

But Verne responded to Ed with complete love.

When Ed was hospitalized, Verne visited him daily after work. It was bathing time in the afternoon care routine, and the nurses asked Verne to help wash his son. He hesitated as the nurse put the sponge into his calloused hand. Touching his teen son's bare body pushed him far beyond his comfort zone. It wasn't what a father did for a son.

But something told him that this incredible situation called him to step outside of the normal boundaries. Everything in their lives was out of control. Even though he didn't know what would happen, Verne wanted to somehow reassure his son that he would be alright.

Verne grasped the dripping sponge. He gently rubbed Ed's chest and shoulders. The water ran gently off the boy's back, and the bubbles lingered until he wiped them away.

The father returned every afternoon to wash his son's body. Sometimes without words, sometimes chatting about Stanford football, they held each other close with the caressing sweep of a wet sponge.[1]

Ed also learned lessons about the power of solidarity from listening to his father talk about the railroad workers' union. Verne's strong devotion to the union taught his son about how an alliance of people could come together to fight for the well-being of every member.

As Ed worked to create solidarity among disabled people, he carried forward his father's lessons about the importance of unions. A solitary worker who could easily be mistreated by an uncaring company gained new strength when united with other colleagues. Ed and his friends would extend this world-changing idea to the historically fragmented and invisible population of disabled people.

Verne also passed on the retrograde beliefs and practices of mid-century American sexism. By the time of his father's death, Ed was aware that his father's gender politics were a black and white movie in a world quickly exploding into technicolor. Betty Friedan's *Feminine Mystique* was published in early 1963. Women across America, and especially in the Bay Area, were holding rap sessions, sharing their deepest emotions and experiences, and raising their collective consciousness.[2]

During the 1960s, feminist groups became highly active in Berkeley, greatly supported by the unofficial women's movement librarian, Laura X. Originally named Laura Murra, she dropped her patriarchal surname following the Nation of Islam's naming practice. She published a newsletter called SPAZM that reported on women's liberation work around the United States and developed the Women's Herstory Library, a vast resource of movement documents and publications. She traveled the country, urging state legislatures to change old laws that allowed husbands to rape their wives.

In 1969, women Cal students held a campus protest rally, demanding that the university start a women's studies program and house it in the ROTC building. Graduate students and faculty tossed their university degrees into a burning fire, symbolizing the worthlessness of an education that ignored the experiences and wisdom of women.

Seventy-five members of a faction called Berkeley Women's Liberation took over the offices of the *San Francisco Examiner*, demanding an increase in female hiring across all departments and a freeze on advertising exploiting women. The Radio Free Women Five, a guerilla team of feminist activists, sneaked into the KPFA radio studio one summer night in 1970, confronting the on-air announcers.

Soon the station launched new programming on women's issues, news, and events.

Longtime women's movement activist Pat Cody, cofounder of Cody's Books, a mainstay of the Telegraph Avenue business strip, attended a regular women's discussion group for three decades. In the early 1970s, she led an influential effort to question the negative health effects of diethylstilbestrol (DES), a medication widely prescribed to prevent miscarriages.[3]

By 1974, the women's movement in Berkeley connected with the disability rights movement. Corbett O'Toole, a polio survivor from Massachusetts, teamed up with Kitty Cone to found the Disabled Women's Rap Group, a mutual support organization unpacking the twin oppressions of gender and disability.[4]

Through her women's friendship networks, Zona was fully engaged in these groundbreaking conversations that questioned patriarchal traditions. The antiquated gender model Ed's father embraced unraveled as new possibilities for women's freedom and achievement arose.

Regardless of his politics, Verne's sudden passing knocked Zona on her heels. She had relied on her husband for financial and emotional support for decades. He was a trusted, reliable partner. Without him, she felt uncertain and hesitant. She scraped by on the minimal pension the railroad union provided.

But Zona also felt a fresh sense of freedom and opportunity. During the years she spent at Ed's bedside, tending to his needs in the living room, the two quietly shared a bond of parallel missions. Each was trapped by limitations imposed by society. They made an unspoken agreement to help one another find freedom, escaping the confines of the home for a larger, more gratifying life in the outside world. Ed's chance came when he moved into Cowell Hospital to attend Cal. Now it was Zona's turn.

Zona leaped into action, seizing the opportunity to work and attend community college. She moved Mark, a new high school graduate, and young Randy to Berkeley so that she too could enroll at the university. A single mom in a land of opportunity, she graduated and earned a teaching credential.

Her nontraditional home near the Cal campus was aptly nicknamed the Green House. It became an informal drop-in support center for untethered youth and long-haired street people. Zona prided herself on the racial diversity of her expanded, unconventional family.

It certainly wasn't Verne's Ozzie and Harriet–style home anymore. Zona kept the front door open. She learned how to make delicious stews and soups bubbling on the stovetop for hungry wanderers. Randy banged on his drum set, and a revolving roster of musicians filled the house with rock music. Eric Dibner slept in a wooden hut built onto the bed of a pickup truck parked at the curb and came inside for meals and community. It was a place of great love and open expectations. Friends old and new could hang out and share a joint and good conversation.[5]

9   Radical Berkeley

Starting a graduate program in political science in September 1964, Ed's true education was about to begin. On October 1, university administrators shut down the small row of student political organization tables at Sather Gate on the south side of the Cal campus. Political speech without approval of the university administration was blocked.

The police arrested Jack Weinberg, a former graduate student, for distributing information for the Congress of Racial Equality, a civil rights group that fought Jim Crow racial segregation across the South. The police loaded him into the back of their cruiser, parked on Sproul Plaza. There he sat for over thirty hours. Hundreds of students spontaneously surrounded the vehicle in protest. The sock-footed Mario Savio, recently returned from Mississippi civil rights work, and others made impromptu speeches from the roof of the cop car, denouncing the university's actions. The free speech movement (FSM) began.

For the next three months, students organized in opposition to the campus restrictions on political speech. In the view of the FSM leaders, Cal was melding with the military and corporate America, the impersonal, greed-driven machines that used young people and workers as what Savio called "the raw material" of the capitalist production process.

In Savio's famous December speech on the steps of Sproul Hall, he passionately called for the students to take decisive action, "Put your bodies upon the gears and upon the wheels, upon the levers, upon all the apparatus, and you've got to make it stop!" Human freedom depended on nonviolent bodily resistance to the cruel systems that stole the humanity of citizens.

Ed got his first taste of carefully planned civil disobedience working as an FSM organizer and activist. He marched in numerous actions, positioning his large wheelchair at the front to push through police lines. As a teaching assistant for an undergraduate political science course, he was an active member of the Graduate Coordinating Council that allied closely with Savio's FSM leadership team.

After over eight hundred protesters were arrested during a sit-in at Sproul Hall, the Graduate Coordinating Council called a campus strike. Almost half of all students refused to attend class. Ed worked on strike planning, including the alternative educational activities held across campus.[1]

The free speech movement was the birth of a distinct Berkeley culture of almost constant radical protest. Sociologist Todd Gitlin neatly captured the mindset of the youth counterculture: "To be young and American is to have been betrayed . . . to be enraged."[2]

In the film *The Wild One*, Marlon Brando's grimacing, leather-jacket clad character was asked, "Hey Johnny, what are you rebelling against?" He replied succinctly, "Whaddya got?" After the students won the battle for free speech, what constantly stoked the youthful rage of Berkeley demonstrators was the Vietnam War. The campus steps and adjacent streets filled regularly with protesters denouncing America's military engagement with distant communism.

For thirty-six hours, in May 1965, antiwar activists held a teach-in attended by ten thousand students. Speakers including the famous pediatrician Dr. Benjamin Spock, author Norman Mailer, and Mario

Savio denounced President Lyndon Johnson's bombing raids and increasing troop deployments to South Vietnam.

In October 1967, the daily civil disobedience actions of "Stop the Draft Week" swung back and forth between peaceful street demonstrations and violent clashes with the police. On the first day, three thousand protesters marched from Sproul Plaza to the Oakland Army Induction Center to distribute antiwar flyers to inductees. Demonstrators physically blocked the entrance, stopping busloads of new draftees. Police hauled away 140 activists.

The Oakland police came out swinging on the second day. The *Los Angeles Times* reported, "A flying wedge of police, swinging nightsticks and squirting eye irritant"—a troop of five hundred helmeted officers—attacked the two thousand demonstrators. Clubbing activists and news reporters, spraying mace, the cops forcefully cleared the block in front of the induction center. Nine buses of draftees passed into the military processing center. Chanting "Sieg Heil" at the police, the protesters retaliated by setting up barricades of tire-flattened automobiles, wooden benches, and garbage cans. Police arrested twenty-two demonstrators. Medical aid volunteers treated twenty-seven injured persons for lacerations and broken bones.

The next morning police and activists alike returned emotionally subdued. Frightened by the previous day's brutality, activists strictly employed nonviolent strategies. In a parking lot across the street, Episcopal priests held a communion service, praying for peace. Under fire from journalists for escalating the fight that injured reporters and photographers, police officers politely asked people to clear the roadway. They carried eighty-nine limp demonstrators into paddy wagons.[3]

Cowell personal attendant Charles Grimes observed, "There wasn't a square inch of the University of California at Berkeley that was not political, that was not seething with the potential of being political." The campus and the surrounding town were constantly enflamed in demonstrations, immersing university students in a simmering cauldron of countercultural tumult.[4]

Like so many young people around them, Ed and many of the disabled students felt drawn to campus activism. For the disabled students, the experience was unique. The widespread alienation expressed by protesters mirrored their personal feelings of rejection and outrage. It seemed like everyone suddenly felt as ripped off as they did.[5]

Berkeley wasn't alone in the uproar. Nationally, campus protests against the Vietnam War peaked in the 1969–70 school year. There were 9,408 demonstrations, 731 involving arrests, 410 with property damage, and 230 resulting in physical violence. Elite campuses such as Harvard, Columbia, Wisconsin, and Cal were the most active, but protests took place across the nation, including at community colleges and high schools. At Columbia University, activists occupied five buildings and held three administrators captive. Bombs killed a custodian at UC Santa Barbara and a graduate student at Wisconsin. An overzealous National Guard attempt to put down a Kent State demonstration ended with the shooting deaths of four students.

Historian W.J. Rorabaugh observed, "The real political division in America was no longer between the Right and the Left but between the young and the old." The old directed the war, and the young, like it or not, fought and died in it.[6]

. . .

Racial unrest also rocked Berkeley. By the late 1960s, as California became increasingly diverse, young people of color wanted a college education. The state's educational policies worked against them, keeping their enrollments low and their cultural history and perspectives out of the curriculum. The state's master plan for higher education mandated standardized testing that tracked most African

American and Hispanic students to bottom-tier community colleges. The portion of Black students at San Francisco State University, the most diverse state campus, dropped from 10 percent of the student body to a meager 4 percent.

SF State's Black Student Union (BSU) worked for three years to develop and offer Black Studies courses that represented and explored their cultural experiences. But the campus administration's repeated assurances that suitable faculty would be hired to start a new degree program proved empty.

In November 1968, enflamed by a racist article in the campus newspaper, the BSU launched a student strike that sent angry ripples across California. The BSU leaders had prior experience working with Southern civil rights organizations such as the Student Nonviolent Coordinating Committee (SNCC) and they had close ties to the Oakland-based Black Panthers. They demanded increased admissions for students of color and the creation of a Black Studies department. During the ensuing five-month battle with conservative SF State president S.I. Hayakawa, a strident leader installed by Governor Ronald Reagan, demonstrators boycotted and disrupted classes, marched and rallied. Police responded fiercely, arresting hundreds. Their wild billy clubs turned campus demonstrations into blood-soaked front page news.

The cause quickly broadened in scope and location. On multiple American college campuses, Black, Asian American, and Mexican American students united to form the Third World Liberation Front (TWLF), an expansive project seeking more minoritized student admissions and Ethnic Studies courses and programs. In coordination with SF State activists, the TWLF initiated a campus strike at UC Berkeley in January 1969. Like their colleagues across the Bay, the Cal activists called for curriculum and admission policies that more closely reflected the diverse California population.

The six weeks of Berkeley protests peaked on February 22 when the maligned Governor Ronald Reagan came to campus for a university Board of Regents meeting. At noon, the Campanile bell tower greeted the esteemed visitor with a mocking rendition of the Mickey Mouse Club song. The campus climate was apprehensive. Recent protests had turned increasingly violent. Police put down demonstrators with clubs and tear gas.[7]

Three thousand protesters and six hundred riot police from twenty different law enforcement agencies turned out for the governor's visit. In the background, just in case, waited fifty National Guard troops and an Army helicopter. The day was tense, but the demonstrations remained peaceful.

Four days later, Cal chancellor Roger Hens cut off negotiations with the TWLF, blaming the students' recent violence for his decision. Governor Reagan dispatched the National Guard to lock down the campus.

On March 4, the Academic Senate voted to create a new Ethnic Studies department. Chancellor Hens promised a new degree program focusing on the history and culture of ethnic minority groups. Similarly, at SF State, President Hayakawa established a School of Ethnic Studies. There would be disagreements about how quickly and how well these universities developed these programs. But by and large, the students won the fight.[8]

On all sides Ed and his disabled friends were surrounded by irate and provocative expressions that deeply mirrored how they felt about their own lives. The BSU leaders spoke often of their desire for "self-determination," meaningful personal control over their experiences and destiny. Rally speakers at the many Berkeley protests educated audiences about how unequal America wrongly granted self-determination to a privileged few. Even though those speakers didn't mention disability or disabled people, Ed and his friends understood that these demands should be applied to themselves as well.

.   .   .

Historians argue whether the disability rights movement followed the African American, women's, and LGBT movements as a form of imitation, or if disability rights "emerged simultaneously" with the other movements. In Berkeley, it was both.

Ed and his Cowell Hospital friends often looked out the window to witness a demonstration loudly gathering on campus and wondered, what are we protesting today? The fiery maelstrom of a multitargeted protest culture engaging numerous movements concurrently was the lively space where their disability rights activity developed. The rich, heated soil of many movements informed their ideas and provoked their actions.[9]

Beginning in September 1968, while campus raged like a combat zone, Dr. Bruyn's little program became unrecognizable. Sleepy third floor Cowell broke wide open. Excitement echoed through the dull tile halls. The California Department of Rehabilitation scored a large federal grant that suddenly tripled the number of Cowell residents. More importantly, women arrived.[10]

Cathy Caulfield was the first. She was quickly followed by Judy Taylor, Sue Ward, and Carol White. Each hired two female attendants, and the instantly made new coed hospital ward filled with high-pitched tones, jokes, and laughter. The Beatles' fierce rocker "Revolution" shook the walls.

Caulfield brought a burst of playfulness and friendship to the group. An active tennis player and swimmer, she grew up on military bases in Ohio and Alaska. Two weeks after her family moved to California, a Newport Beach wave knocked her down and snapped her spine. After two years of hospitalization and rehabilitation, she attended San Francisco City College. Her grades were excellent, and she had a strong desire to attend Cal. Dr. Bruyn invited her to be the first woman to join the program.

Cathy and Ed became close friends, sharing innermost thoughts and feelings, trusting one another like siblings. Ed believed that Cathy's rebellious toughness allowed her to not only integrate into the all-male dormitory but to remain very much "her own person." She became an outspoken, influential member of the expanded group.[11]

With the addition of three women, the moribund infirmary unit of overly serious men transformed into a rowdy college party filled with booze, marijuana, and sex. Beer smuggled past the nurses was stored in the showers. College romances blossomed quickly.

Disabled young adults warehoused in dead-end hospitals for years were thrown together in an explosion of the youthful exuberance and sexual activity. Released for an unexpected educational opportunity, set loose in the frenzied carnival of Berkeley, the new Cowell residents convulsed with unexpected new joy.

It was a time of emotional bonding. Conversations at dinner often lasted for hours after the cafeteria trays had been cleared away. The disabled students connected over shared experiences of insults and obstacles, including boring hospitals, rigid service systems, poorly designed medical devices, inaccessible college classrooms, and stigmatizing attitudes.

The Cowell rap sessions were different than the late-night chats on hospital polio units. These Cowell residents weren't patients anymore. They were students and activists. The university and the town of Berkeley offered an unexpected oasis of freedom, a chance to break away from the low expectations placed on them by their families and by society.

Gabbing late into the night, opening their hearts in a new way, Ed and the other disabled students courageously crafted a common hope. It might be possible to live as physically disabled people had never lived before—independent, active, employed, even married with family. Maybe the unthinkable could come true. Together they cooked up dreams and plans not only for their lives at Cal but for the years beyond.[12]

.   .   .

Nothing cool and exciting happens in America without a fun new vehicle. Flush with grant dollars, State Rehab issued Motorettes to all the disabled students. The Motorette was a modified standard-push wheelchair with a powerful electric motor attached to the back. A person with even minimal hand control could drive it with a joystick.

Suitably nicknamed "murderettes," the first powered wheelchairs combined head-snapping speed with instability. The disabled students zipped around like teens who had stolen their father's car keys, squealing with delight, crashing into walls and racing down long hallways.

The jerky, unreliable little motors cracked open the skies above. Power wheelchairs instantly liberated the students from their constant chaperones, the ever-present wheelchair pushers. They could go anywhere they wanted, anytime they wanted, without permission or accompaniment. This was a taste of real independence.[13]

And excitement.

A transistor blew on Don Lorence's chair and he rolled down into a creek. When passersby fished him out of the water, they found him soaked and laughing. This new chair was an all-out blast.

Herb Willsmore returned late one night with a more than ample supply of beer loaded on the back of his chair. As he drove up the steep hill in front of Barrows Hall, the jittery electric motor jolted. His wheelchair flipped over backwards. Willsmore waited under starry skies until a good Samaritan came along to right his chair.[14]

Ed's thoughts immediately turned to romance. A powerchair could be a vehicle of love. He had a crush on an attractive young woman named Judy who lived next door to Zona. He had been talking her up, sharing a few laughs. Now he envisioned riding off into the sunset with her seated gloriously on his lap.[15]

Ed had silently mourned the interruption of his developing sexuality. He had not lost sexual feelings or capacities. He certainly had no difficulty achieving an erection. The problem was that, as a person with a physical disability, people often viewed him as a perpetual child. They assumed he had no sexuality.

Even when he enjoyed flirting with the pretty girls of Burlingame High, Ed sadly knew that they did not view him as a guy to make out with in a parked car. He threw them saucy glances and provocative phrases, making the girls blush and giggle. At times, a soft, feminine hand rested on his shoulder and the sumptuous fragrance of her hair fell over his body. But Ed knew that he was viewed as sexually ineligible.

Now, with the freedom offered by the new Motorettes, in the sparkling kaleidoscope land of Berkeley, Ed saw new opportunities for romance.

But his fingers couldn't manage the powerchair controls. The joystick control required a forward push. Ed's left hand, although slightly mobile, couldn't move forcefully in that direction. It would only draw inward a few inches toward his palm.

Someone ingeniously thought of turning the toggle around, enabling Ed to pull backwards on the stick to make his chair roll forward. It worked!

Ed's new life as a freewheeling man began. He immediately began dating Judy. Just as the mass proliferation of automobiles in the

1920s offered many young people a mobile venue for their first sexual experiences, Ed's powerchair was the vehicle that initiated new opportunities for intimacy.

. . .

The October 1969, victory of the Rolling Quads over the California Department of Rehabilitation gave the disabled students sudden energy and confidence. The quixotic dreams they concocted in their Cowell dorm conversations about the possibility of creating fulfilling lives in the community felt more realistic.

Ed's thinking turned to politics. He had participated in many protests on campus for important causes. Could there be a similar movement for disabled people? He looked for guidance to an imposing figure, a professor who had fought for many years for the rights of blind persons in America. His name was Jacobus tenBroek.

Sitting in tenBroek's office, the graduate student and his faculty mentor discussed disability rights. The aging scholar's graying hair was swept back tightly. His bold forehead jutted out like a mountainside stone escarpment. His eyes were steady, as unwavering as his beliefs. He spoke with a timeless eloquence, carefully measured and neatly articulated, as if he were reciting by memory the rulings of Supreme Court justice Oliver Wendell Holmes.

Blinded in an accident as a child, tenBroek came up through the California School for the Blind to attend UC Berkeley in the early 1930s. He earned multiple degrees including a Doctor of Laws. His wide-ranging scholarship included a book on the Fourteenth Amendment that influenced Thurgood Marshall during the 1954 *Brown v. Board of Education* school desegregation case.

In 1940, tenBroek was one of the founders the National Federation of the Blind (NFB), the first organization of blind people representing themselves. He was president of the NFB for over twenty years, flying around the country to deliver speeches and meet with legislators and devoting himself fervently to the cause of blind civil rights. He maintained that the only way that blind people could be empowered to live fully and independently in society was to unite in their own advocacy organization. They alone understood their needs and goals. They alone could best articulate and advocate for their rights.

Often tenBroek found himself battling the venerated blind establishment, the landscape of long-standing charities created and run by sighted people in the name of assisting and often speaking for the blind. He thought these powerful groups were well meaning but ultimately harmful.

In his groundbreaking "Within the Grace of God" speech, he blasted the unacknowledged paternalism of the blindness charities. Looking down upon blind people with pity, the nondisabled charity leaders acted to control a population they viewed as deficient.

To the professor's thinking, blind people were simply normal people who didn't see well. All their other abilities, talents, and interests were intact, ready for development and expression in a wide range of jobs and careers. In one NFB convention speech, he told his comrades that blind people were equal in every way to sighted people, ready "to find their place in the community with the same degree of success and failure to be found among the general population."[16]

What held blind people down, tenBroek reasoned, was the "age-old stereotype of blindness as witlessness and helplessness." Society perpetuated a discriminatory myth that blind persons were unable to handle the usual activities of everyday life. They couldn't go to school, work, manage their finances, own and maintain a home, marry and raise a family. They needed overarching supervision and control from service agencies and professionals who truly understood their childlike status. All this oppressive thinking was what tenBroek fought vigorously.[17]

Ed listened carefully as his teacher shared deep wisdom gathered over decades of fierce political advocacy. The fresh ideas and insights that he, John Hessler, and his friends were just beginning to put together were half-formed versions of what this masterful leader presented to him in refined completion. Professor tenBroek had already traveled this road.[18]

But tenBroek also seemed out of touch with the Berkeley counterculture. The great professor, with his neatly trimmed goatee and time-honored wool suit, was a man of a prior era. He knew well the staid, orderly society of Ed's father. But he was far less informed about the dynamic new world opening up to Ed and his friends.

Young people were questioning the conventions and structures of the culture, pushing the traditional limits of freedom and authority. Ed felt gloriously captured and invigorated. He saw opportunities for disabled people to find valued places in society.

"I think what we need to really make progress, the physically disabled," Ed spoke up, "is an organization like the federation. Do you think the NFB would be open to us?" Ed wanted tenBroek's beloved NFB to represent not just blind people but all disabled people.

The learned professor shook his head. Of course, physically disabled persons couldn't join. The very identity and purpose of the NFB was built on a membership and leadership only consisting of blind persons. Although tenBroek admired Ed's enthusiasm, he viewed him as an impetuous student asking naïve questions.

Professor tenBroek certainly knew that a humble version of the national cross-disability organization that Ed described had already existed. Founded in 1942, the small but ambitious American Federation of the Physically Handicapped (AFPH) focused primarily on improving federal government employment programs. Paul Strachan, a Georgia native who incurred a spinal cord injury when a train struck his automobile, led the little two-person AFPH office with tremendous conviction. His passionate goal was to convince both the government and businesses that people with disabilities could be hardworking, valuable employees.

Strachan's prominent achievement was a mild measure at best, President Harry Truman's annual "Employ the Handicapped Week." The President's Committee gradually sought an expanded mission beyond an annual week of underpowered slogans. But the group remained chiefly symbolic. Strachan finally shuttered the AFPH in 1958 amidst disappointment and bitterness.

Ed knew nothing of Paul Strachan and the AFPH. Even if Ed accepted Strachan as a forerunner of the modern disability rights movement, the tempered lobbying of the AFPH was Montovani's cascading strings to the screaming Fender Stratocaster of the Rolling Quads. As the folksinger Bob Dylan proclaimed to Ed's generation, times were undoubtedly changing.[19]

In 1961, as the Freedom Riders strove to integrate Greyhound and Trailways buses across violent, segregationist Alabama, Attorney General Robert F. Kennedy told Martin Luther King, Jr., that he wanted a "cooling off period." After repeated incidents of brutal violence, fearful that angry mobs would continue to attack the buses and the local authorities would not provide sufficient police protection, Kennedy asked King for patience. Dr. King responded, "I see a ray of hope, but I am different than my father. I feel the need of being free now!"[20]

Like King, Ed had little stomach for the incremental patience of Strachan or the traditional, single-disability group approach of tenBroek. What Ed wanted from his mentor was an agreement to expand the NFB to include people with other disabilities. This would create a potent national, multidisability political organization to carry forward the Rolling Quad's fervent message.

Ed was disappointed that tenBroek didn't share his vision. He and his physically disabled friends were beginning to plan an alliance uniting people with different kinds of disabilities. The D/deaf, blind, physically disabled, and developmentally disabled were traditionally divided by professions, charities, and institutions. Each had national advocacy groups (mostly run by nondisabled people), who competed for attention and funds. Ed was convinced that these divisions were a big part of the problem.[21]

"But . . ." tenBroek offered his student a hint of compromise, "an organization can create coalitions with other groups." What Ed and his friends could do, the professor advised, was develop their own organization and then build a relationship with the NFB to work on common purposes.[22]

That wasn't enough. Ed believed that people with different kinds of disabilities could form a single union that would be more impactful than the NFB or any individual disability group. Soon he would find out if he was right.

10 *A New Movement*

In the opening pages of *Out for Good*, the classic history of the gay rights struggle, authors Dudley Clendinen and Adam Nagourney describe the LGBT movement erupting spontaneously from a single conflict between protesters and unwitting authorities. The New York City police had roughed up and rousted the patrons of Stonewall Inn, a popular Greenwich Village gay bar, many times before. For gay New Yorkers, accepting police mistreatment with bitter docility was a regular, demeaning routine.

That is, until it suddenly felt like too much. For reasons unexplainable, in the early hours of June 28, 1969, Stonewall customers fought back. Within minutes a few angry words snowballed into a broken window, trashcan fires, and a screaming mob throwing pennies and nickels at police officers. Years of pent-up frustration and resentment, a long-contained simmering tinder, exploded into the LGBT rights movement.

Most striking in the Clendinen and Nagourney account is how their detailed description of the downtrodden LGBT population aptly fits the population of Americans with disabilities at the same historical moment.

> They were, in June, 1969, a secret legion of people, known of but discounted, ignored, laughed at or despised. . . . They were

invisible. . . . The census didn't count them, market surveys didn't seek them, political parties didn't court them. They had no political power, no financial leverage, no legal recognition in their favor. . . . They had, as a class, much to complain about, yet they did not exist as a class.

For gays and lesbians, the Stonewall riot was the spark that started their movement. In the aftermath of that violent moment of rebellion, five hundred protesters rallied in Washington Square Park. Standing on top of the fountain, bellowing without a microphone, activist Martha Shelley ordained the gathering the "first gay power vigil." Thousands participated in pride marches in New York, Los Angelos, Chicago, and San Francisco. The Gay Liberation Front (GLF) and the Gay Activists Alliance (GAA) sponsored public disobedience actions. Gay student associations popped up at universities across the country. The LGBT minority was no longer invisible.[1]

Just four months after the Stonewall riot, Ed's Rolling Quads relished their initial victory over State Rehab. It unified them and gave them a fresh, collective confidence. But they were still invisible. The reinstatement of two students, the replacement of an unworkable rehabilitation supervisor, and a five-hundred-word article on page two in the *San Francisco Chronicle* didn't begin to change the world. Most Cal students and Berkeley residents didn't know anything had happened.

If the gay rights movement started with a resounding riot heard 'round the world, the American disability rights movement began with a college pizza and beer victory party on third floor of Cowell. The stereo blared loud enough that hospital nurses from the second floor came up to complain. It was satisfying, validating, but much too small.

After the exhilarating skirmish with State Rehab, the Rolling Quads planned the road ahead. Ed's team had the foresight to carefully map out their lives in the community after graduation. They toyed with the notion of a "halfway house" where they could all live together. But that suggestion died quickly. Cathy Caulfield quipped, "I really love all you guys, but I'll be damned if I'll live with you forever." Creating a new form of disability segregation was not the goal.

Graduate student John Hessler taught a university class where the disabled students planned together for an integrated future. The students completed real life research projects figuring out how people with physical disabilities could live independently in Berkeley. One project developed a guide detailing all the services currently provided by local agencies and organizations. A second asked disabled community members to describe the services they most needed.

By the third class, the main problem was clear. State Rehab and other agencies that assisted disabled people were run by nondisabled people who simply didn't get it. They had university professional degrees that made them so-called experts. But they didn't really understand what disabled people needed to make it in the larger community.

The students decided to create what they called the Center for Independent Living, a self-help center operated by disabled people for disabled people. It would provide many services ranging from housing to employment to attendant care referral. The grand plan was made. How to get it off the ground was another matter.[2]

.   .   .

In the early morning hours, vigilante teams of disabled students and personal attendants carried pickaxes, shovels, and buckets of premixed concrete across the quiet campus. Rolling through the darkness, Ed, Hale Zukas, and Eric Dibner led covert urban remodeling squads that lowered curbs and built small ramps. There was undeniably something joyful about clandestine raids on the offending sidewalks that blocked their wheelchairs all day long.[3]

Progress was minimal. The Rolling Quads bided their time, watching for an opportunity to expand their curb ramping program. Their chance to become a national leader in sidewalk accessibility came from an unexpected source.

In 1968, the University of California cleared off a block of bungalows between Haste Street and Dwight Way, just east of Telegraph Ave. The empty space quickly became a weedy, mud-filled mess. The ensuing battle between the community and university over that scruffy patch of land resulted in protest, violence, and death.

In April 1969, *The Berkeley Barb*, the local radical newspaper, called on residents to turn the neglected property into a community park before the university could pave it over. Bring "shovels . . . grass . . . flowers. . . . top soil . . . colorful smiles, laughter, and lots of sweat."[4]

Residents created People's Park, an unauthorized recreation area for throwing frisbees, strumming guitars, and cooking on charcoal grills. Worried about losing the land to squatters, the university asserted control over the property, circling the weedy lot with chain link fencing plastered with "No Trespassing" signs.

On May 15 thousands of students and community residents gathered for a scheduled rally on Sproul Plaza to protest the Arab-Israel conflict. Instead, they decided to march four blocks down Telegraph Avenue to People's Park, which authorities had fenced off early that morning. Demonstrators and police played cat and mouse, sparring for hours on the streets of Berkeley. The police tried to disperse the rock-throwing crowds with blasts of tear gas and buckshot. Herrick Hospital treated nine people shot by the police on that Bloody Thursday. One man watching from a rooftop was shot and killed by a sheriff. Another man was blinded by police shotgun fire.[5]

No fan of shaggy, leftist Berkeley, Governor Reagan sent in the National Guard to clear the streets. Army helicopters dumped tear gas from the sky on the crowds below. The military took control of the city. The Rolling Quads issued a press statement in support of the People's Park dissidents.[6]

As the dust settled and radicals strategized ways to take back the park, Ed and John Hessler turned to a different chess game. The chaotic aftermath of widespread destruction offered them an unexpected opportunity.

Hoping that fresh pavement would erase the blood, carbon monosulfide, and bullet casings from the streets, the Berkeley City Council launched a downtown revitalization project. The beautification plan would repave the sidewalks, giving the people wide, pleasant walkways for an active street life.

The council members organized for the start of their regular meeting, reviewing the agenda, preparing documents and plans for discussion. As they shuffled papers and conversed in whispers, they glanced up and wondered what was about to happen. Lined up at the front of the conference room were eight long-haired young people in electric wheelchairs.

Ed and John Hessler led the group. They explained the problem to the council in a very matter-of-fact way. They wanted to live and work in Berkeley. They wanted to travel the sidewalks to restaurants and shops. They wanted to meet up with their friends to socialize. But the curbs blocked their wheelchairs when they crossed the street. They asked the city to immediately install ramps on every corner in downtown Berkeley.

Councilwoman Lonnie Hancock, a sharp politician who would later be elected Berkeley mayor, was Ed and Zona's neighbor. She grinned as Ed spoke. She could finally see her militant friend in action.

The council listened in polite silence, taking it all in, trying to comprehend the issue. They had no idea that people using wheelchairs couldn't get around the main streets of the city. They weren't aware that disabled people wanted to have greater access to the sidewalks.

None of the council members had ever seen so many people using wheelchairs in one place. The striking visible presence of the group, and their passionate unity—they clearly represented many more people in the community—hit an emotional chord with the council members.

The main obstacle for disabled people trying to gain greater access was the common impression that because disabled people were rarely seen in public, there was no problem. The lack of disabled people on sidewalks or in restaurants seemed like compelling evidence there were very few disabled people, and those few had little interest in using the sidewalks, parks, and buildings.

The council appropriated funds to incorporate curb ramps into the downtown renovation plans with a promise of more to come. The Rolling Quads left the meeting that day encouraged but also determined to keep the pressure on.[7]

Although Berkeley is often known as the first city to build widespread curb cuts, it wasn't. In 1945, the first curb cuts in the United States were built in Kalamazoo, Michigan. A disabled attorney named Frank Fisher asked the city commission to construct cement ramps on high curbs in the central business district. The City Manager, Edward Clark, had a son who used a wheelchair. Over thirty ramps were built on the main streets of Kalamazoo.[8]

In the early 1950s, the University of Illinois built a series of curb cuts and wooden ramps on campus as part of a rehabilitation program for World War II veterans with physical disabilities attending college. But the great idea carried out in Kalamazoo and the Illinois campus didn't catch on. America wasn't ready for curb cuts until Berkeley started a new trend.[9]

The first Berkeley curb cut was built in late 1969 at the corner of Shattuck Avenue, a main boulevard, and Center Street, a crossing road that connected the business district to campus. Hale Zukas and Chuck Grimes crafted a prototype ramp out of plywood and duct tape. By today's universal design standards, it was crude, steep, and narrow.

Zukas became the lead engineer and advocate for the project. He was a combination human slide rule and civil rights lawyer, figuring out the architectural angles to the third decimal point, then showing up at the city administrator's office unannounced to demand more funds and faster action.

Emboldened by their success in Berkeley, Zukas and Center for Independent Living staff members Kitty Cone and Greg Sanders set their sights on the unramped sidewalks of nearby Oakland. Cone created the Committee for Accessible Oakland, uniting old-school charitable groups such as the Easter Seals and United Cerebral Palsy to speak as one voice. She was elected to the Oakland development commission that recommended a downtown curb cuts program to the City Council. They appropriated $100,000 in the first year.[10]

In Berkeley, the disability community dubbed their beloved accessible sidewalk area "The Wheelchair Route." The accessible public trail through the central city was a visible monument of their new freedom and pride. Wheelchair users spent leisurely afternoons taking a scenic roll. Just because they could.

The ramped curbs transformed public spaces, allowing people with significant mobility impairments to travel to stores, restaurants, and on public transportation. Slight adjustments to the concrete landscape, only half-noticed by nondisabled pedestrians, represented an initial breach of the historic fortification that kept people with disabilities out of the avenues of prosperity and participation. It was just one small aperture cut through an enormous barricade, but it represented an exciting opportunity for a shut-out people.

Some municipalities took pride in leading the national trend. In 1971, Bergen County, New Jersey, initiated a community access program focused on curb ramps and barrier-free construction. "It will be done all over the country soon," reasoned Herbert H. Bennett, mayor of Ridgewood, New Jersey. Bennett and his Chamber of Commerce engaged in neighborly "arm-twisting" to create an accessible downtown business district. In addition to curb cuts, shopkeepers widened doorways and toilet stalls, added bathroom grab bars, and lowered drinking fountains. Nearby Bayonne and Hackensack likewise read the tea leaves, installing downtown crosswalk ramps.[11]

In July 1976, Chicago alderman Dick Simpson proposed an ordinance requiring designated parking spots and curb cuts. By the holiday season, activists at the Committee for an Aware Chicago celebrated the construction of new ramps in the downtown Loop.[12]

With the implementation of the 1973 Rehabilitation Act in late 1977, curb cuts spread quickly. The federal Comprehensive Employment and Training Act (CETA) program funded curb cuts in Memphis, St. Petersburg, Albion (MI), and Long Island. By 1978, Los Angeles had combined federal and local dollars to complete installation of 12,000 ramps. Nondisabled citizens suddenly found themselves sharing sidewalks with disabled people.[13]

In many cases, this created a whole new problem. Wheelchair users could travel to hair salons, pizza parlors, and taverns. They could reach the front doors of government buildings and courthouses. They could travel to bus stops and subway stations. But access typically stopped there. They often couldn't get in. The offending culprits included narrow doorways, heavy doors, the absence of elevators and ramps, undersized toilet stalls, and buses without wheelchair lifts.

The no-longer-hidden people started knocking on many doors of society, asking to enter and enjoy all the destinations now available. Sidewalks were just the beginning.[14]

11 *Humblest Beginnings*

In early 1970, a crucial door opened in Washington, DC. New amendments to the Higher Education Act created grants for colleges assisting "disadvantaged students." Indiana congressman John Brademas, an early disability rights advocate, added a requirement that 10 percent of the funds help students with "physical handicaps."

Ed's community college mentor Jean Wirth served on the US Department of Education (DOE) committee deciding how to spend the grant dollars. She arranged for the DOE to hire Ed as a consultant to help with college accessibility for physically disabled, blind, and D/deaf students.

Now Ed was both umpire and player. As he created the disability grants guidelines, he guided John Hessler and Herb Willsmore in writing a Cal proposal. With Ed pulling the strings, the Physically Disabled Student Program (PDSP) scored over $400,000.[1]

Hessler and his team also set up a campus referendum for a twenty-five-cent student activity fee. They covered the campus with tongue-in-cheek cartoon fliers emblazoned "Quarters for Cripples." The campaign won them an annual stream of thousands of university dollars.[2]

The only college disability support program run by disabled people set up shop in a shoddy apartment behind the Top Dog restaurant just two blocks from campus. When Zona graduated from Cal, Hessler offered her a job as front desk greeter and sage housemother. She helped set up students with services to support their access on campus. With her background advocating for Ed, she was an ideal liaison between the PDSP and the disabled students' parents.

The dusty PDSP office pulsed with electric conversation. The group floated above the clouds. The communal pipe dreams of the late-night Cowell rap sessions were coming true. They had created a combination social club, peer help center, and activist network.

Wheelchair repairman Charles Grimes covered one wall with an enormous sky mural, deep blue with puffy white clouds and a sweeping rainbow. The rich aroma of Zona's spaghetti, chili, and soup brought the drab apartment to life. The ramshackle office became a place of refuge and joy.[3]

Hessler articulated a vision of blind and physically disabled people working together. This cross-disability concept quickly grew to include D/deaf people. The PDSP unified disparate disability groups into a single advocacy community.

For the curious disabled student wandering in off the street, the PDSP was like nothing they had ever experienced. It was the one place on the planet where having a disability was normal. Even better, it was cool. When undergraduate Jeff Moyer first arrived on campus, Zona told him, "Come on down and meet everybody. I'll give you a key to the blind student study."

Moyer hesitated. He had always viewed himself as a member of the blind community, only. Suddenly he was surrounded by wheelchairs.

Blind students had their own study area in the basement of the university library. Moyer had an office and an assistant who recorded his textbooks on cassettes. It was a surprising step up from the miserable community college that provided no assistance or accommodations. Those instructors graded him based not on what he knew but on what he could see. With PDSP support, Moyer graduated summa cum laude.[4]

Polio survivor Bob Metts's first visit to the PDSP opened a world he had never imagined. Instantly, he found himself surrounded by a half-dozen disabled friends. He grumbled that his courses had begun, and State Rehab still hadn't bought his textbooks. His new friends urged him to advocate for himself. Right there he phoned his rehabilitation counselor and demanded that she approve his required texts. To his amazement, she did.

Energized by the unexpected victory, surrounded by people who immediately accepted his disability, Metts felt uplifted. As he left the PDSP, Zona invited him to come back for lunch. She was making soup. Tickled, he knew he would.

Metts had spent much of his childhood in the artificial quarantine world fashioned for disabled kids. Hospital wards and special education programs hid the unfortunates behind a veil of shame. Out of nowhere, two blocks from campus, he had stumbled upon the wonderfully uppity opposite, a quirky little PDSP community that self-consciously upended the traditional isolation script.

Rolling away from the PDSP on that first day, Metts was forever changed, "I felt a hundred pounds lighter. . . . I continue to think of that experience as transformative, like being born anew."[5]

Corbett O'Toole was harder to convince. At first, she recoiled from the Berkeley disability scene. When a person in a wheelchair came toward her, she crossed the street. She felt "bound and determined to stay away from those people!"[6]

Growing up in Massachusetts, O'Toole had polio as an infant. She walked with a cane. After graduating from college in 1973, she and a friend drove a Volkswagen Bug across the country. Her process of joining the new PDSP disability community was gradual. Slowly her fears softened. She found new friendships, and her identity began to shift. She became one of those people.

When she and her physically disabled chums breezed into a restaurant near the PDSP, the nondisabled customers looked up with a nervous gasp. They had never seen an unleashed gaggle of people using wheelchairs and canes.

People with bodily or mental impairments were widely considered unsightly, certainly not what the ordinary restaurant-goer wanted to see at the next table. As early as 1867, beginning in San Francisco, many American cities used a variety of what historian Susan Schweik has called "the ugly laws" to prohibit "diseased, maimed, mutilated, or in any way deformed" persons from inhabiting public spaces. Disabled bodies were to be hidden, not seen. Chicago's ordinance was passed in 1881, and Denver followed in 1889. As recently as 1974, in Omaha, Nebraska, an unhoused man was arrested for "having marks and scars on his body." Puzzled at how to handle the case, Nebraska judge Walter Cropper asked, "What's the standard for ugliness?"[7]

As Judge Cropper wondered aloud about which citizens were too unshapely or hideous to occupy public areas, the sidewalks of Berkeley were changing. O'Toole and her cheerful wheelchair-using pals rolled and caned together, creating an insurgent visual exhibition of their right to wander everyday spaces.

To her surprise, O'Toole loved it. She felt like part of the hippest rock band. She later recalled, "I thought my friends were cool, so that was a very liberating experience being in public with cripples."[8]

The PDSP became the hub of a bustling disability subculture where many disabled people felt solidarity and pride for the first time. Students hung around for hours, enjoying Zona's hot soups, savoring the sweet comfort. Many volunteered or worked part-time. Suddenly they belonged to a united community that supplied new color to the raucous rainbow carnival of Berkeley.

.   .   .

A single desk in the PDSP was set aside for a worker helping disabled people in the community beyond campus. Soon it was clear that a new services organization helping disabled people across Berkeley was needed.

The disability community's hero mythology promotes the tale of Ed Roberts founding the Center for Independent Living in Berkeley in 1972, launching a worldwide disability rights movement. Backed by a ninety-eight-piece orchestra playing the 1812 Overture complete with triumphant cannon blasts and a sky-popping fireworks display, Ed is named as the first builder of what would ultimately become over four hundred American independent living centers. His Berkeley-based CIL was the glorious model for new independent living centers around the world.

The true story began with John Hessler, Hale Zukas, Phil Draper, and other activists, who planned the CIL when Ed was out of town. For about a year, Ed pursued other interests away from the growing Berkeley disability rights community. In 1970, he rushed to the University of California, Riverside to fill in for his sick friend Joel Bryan, founder of that campus's disabled student support program.

While Ed was gone, his mentor Jean Wirth lost her teaching job. The TWLF demonstrations spread from San Francisco State and UC Berkeley to many California campuses. At the College of San Mateo, Wirth supported the protesting students. She fiercely criticized the college administrators for ignoring the needs and talents of students of color. After she spoke at the Mexican American students' campus demonstration, the top brass fired her.

The resourceful Wirth landed on her feet. She quickly raised funds from wealthy liberal donors to open a new junior college dedicated to the very students the state colleges failed. She launched Common College, a free-form, independent learning program where students created their own curriculum and learning experiences.

When Ed finished up in Riverside, he joined her. Moving with his brother Mark to the remote Portola Valley hills in early 1971, Ed taught political science. He guided students in their independent projects.

Wirth introduced Ed to her affluent benefactor network. He impressed the foundation directors with his intelligence and humor. He quickly learned the basics of fundraising while developing a host of local donor contacts.

John Hessler kept Ed abreast of the news from Berkeley. In June 1971, a formal planning team met weekly at the PDSP to discuss the start of the much-anticipated CIL. The group struggled in Ed's absence. Hessler was devoted to only running the PDSP. The CIL planning group included talented activists such as Larry Biscamp and Hale Zukas. But no one wanted to be the CIL leader.

Zukas was a man with cerebral palsy who used a wheelchair. He graduated from Cal with a degree in mathematics. His copious genius was often concealed behind his unusual modes of communication. Often his speech was intelligible only to those who knew him well. He typically wore a helmet with a long stick attached to the top. When speaking to city planners or construction contractors or transportation administrators, he tapped out his words letter by letter on a chart. The method was slow, but the message was worth the wait.

Paralyzed from the waist down as a child in a car accident, Larry Biscamp was handsome and playful. His chest and shoulder muscles bulged like a Charles Atlas magazine advertisement. He entertained his friends by diving out of his wheelchair into a handstand and walking around upside down. He was respected as one of the Rolling Quads who first defeated State Rehab.

Neither Zale nor Biscamp really wanted to run the CIL. Part of the problem was the deep skepticism the young hippies felt about being in charge of anything. They saw corporations and universities as greedy and corrupt. They envisioned the CIL as an alternate or "anti" organization, organic and freewheeling, without the usual stiff structures and stuffy systems. As Crosby, Stills, Nash, and Young sang, "Rules and regulations? Who needs 'em?"[9]

Without a leader or a coherent organizational concept, their ambitious planning talks stumbled. Just as feminist Jo Freeman observed of the 1970s women's movement, an emergent, unstructured style works well for consciousness-raising. All voices are heard and honored. People feel valued, and they gain strength. But it offers a weak organizational framework for further group action.[10]

In the planning for a CIL in Berkeley, great ideas for a range of necessary services took shape, but there was too much second-guessing about how to put it all together. The Hessler and Zukas group wondered if the PDSP might be the real prize at the end of the rainbow.

The planning team brought in Herb Leibowitz, the regional Rehabilitation Services Administration (RSA) director of research and training. He immediately saw great potential in their independent living concept. He ran back to his supervisor in San Francisco to ask for funds.

Excited, he told his boss, "I think I discovered a new kind of rehabilitation."

The regional supervisor scoffed, "That's not rehabilitation. It isn't even taught in university rehabilitation departments." It was just some long-haired disabled kids spouting off.[11]

Leibowitz couldn't help. The CIL was a dream fading more every day.

Hessler called in trusted Cal faculty member Fred Collignon. Before coming to Berkeley, he served as lead consultant to the federal Rehabilitation Services Administration. Many of the activists had explored disability accessibility in his research courses. They knew him well and valued his knowledgeable advice.

As Collignon listened to the discussion, his heart sank. They were backpedaling, making excuses, convincing themselves they shouldn't even try. The conversation focused on lack of money. There was a small pot in the state and federal coffers for disability services. The group feared that the new CIL would gobble up all the available dollars, and the PDSP would starve. They couldn't start the new organization because it would kill what they already had.

Dismayed, the professor stared at the floor. This was a sorry old chestnut he had heard too many times. Any disability group seeking more funding would just be stealing money from other worthy groups. It was one reason that disability policy never really made progress. Nobody believed that the meager government funding pot could expand.

After keeping his mouth shut for too long, Collignon finally swallowed hard. He sat up tall and spoke.

"You have to do it," he snapped cold-eyed and fierce.

The group went silent, surprised at their old professor's demanding tone.

He pushed them hard. "You have to start the independent living center. You owe it to this community."

"Why?" someone asked, "What do we owe them?"

"I just came here to go to Cal," another person countered. "I'm not going to hang around helping Berkeley for the rest of my life."

Collignon steeled his voice against their arguments, "I've had most of you in my class. I've seen what you can do. This PDSP is testimony to what you can do. You are the brightest, the most talented."

He paused. He was play-acting, putting on tough, kicking them in the butts. Underneath, the gentle college teacher's emotions twisted in a nauseous knot.

He finished his big pitch. "You have to do it. You are the privileged ones, the few disabled people with the opportunity to come to this great university, the few who broke out and became independent. You have to do this so all those other people who didn't have that opportunity can do what you've done, so they can control their lives the way you've learned to."

The committee argued for the rest of the meeting. Collignon sat back, quietly second-guessing what he had done. His words had struck a nerve. But he left that night not knowing if he had convinced anyone.

When he got home, he told his wife about the failed meeting. "I acted like a sonuvabitch," he said. He cried. He feared that the CIL was dead.[12]

Professor Collignon and Herb Leibowitz, two veteran rehabilitation professionals, knew something that Berkeley's zealous band of disabled young people didn't. Independent living for disabled people wasn't really a new idea. The field of vocational rehabilitation had rallied behind independent living services decades earlier.

In the first two decades following World War II, many people with physical disabilities were discharged from the best hospital rehabilitation programs only to end up in institutions and nursing homes. They exited the medical system with stable health and some degree of physical functioning but rarely returned to live in society.

In 1957, the National Rehabilitation Association (NRA), the group representing rehabilitation professionals in the United States, backed federal legislation to fund independent living services. NRA head E. B. Whitten proposed that state rehabilitation departments teach significantly disabled persons, even those who could not hold down a job, to take care of themselves in their own homes. The field of vocational rehabilitation would expand beyond employment to meet the everyday needs of disabled people living in the community.[13]

The NRA version of independent living services was tepid. Rehabilitation professionals would teach severely disabled persons self-care skills like bathing, feeding, and getting dressed. The professionals couldn't begin to imagine how someone like Ed Roberts who could not physically wash or feed himself could make it.

Independence only meant a person doing more for themselves. That idea, though important, was a modest step forward that unfortunately left out many people with severe disabilities.

Congress rejected the NRA-backed independent living services legislation in 1957 and 1959. Through the 1960s, the federal office of rehabilitation kept the idea alive by funding demonstration projects that taught independent living skills to adults with a variety of disabilities.[14]

These projects were unimpressive, weighed down by old, paternalistic attitudes about the incompetence of disabled persons. One program moved physically disabled adults from institutions or squalid motels to foster family placements chosen by social workers. When those placements failed, as they did 40 percent of the time, the researchers concluded that the disabled persons suffered from a "high level of psychopathology." The researchers didn't consider that adults might not want to be foster children, that they might want some say in choosing where they lived. Instead, the professionals blamed placement failures on the supposed psychiatric disorders of people with mobility impairments.[15]

Compared to the limited NRA concept, the Berkeley version of independent living was revolutionary. The flagging old independent living idea was revived with a potent new emphasis on personal empowerment. This shifted the focus from what a person could do by themselves to what they could achieve with suitable assistance. Tying one's own shoes or buttoning up one's own shirt wasn't the best use of time and energy for a disabled person who, if supported by a personal attendant, could successfully complete a college education or program computers for IBM.

This fresh approach recast independent living with political purpose, a way of coming together to fight for equality and access. An oppressively shortsighted society offered few valued social roles and opportunities to disabled people. Much of the larger society was simply off limits. Employers and schools routinely rejected disabled persons without considering how they might contribute and achieve if granted a modicum of accommodation.

Architectural access for people with physical disabilities was abysmal. Sidewalks, staircases, doorways, and restrooms kept disabled people isolated. If they couldn't use public transportation, attend a meeting or class, or find a usable public restroom, what did it matter if they could spoon corn flakes into their mouths or pull up their own socks? The self-care skills at the heart of the NRA's approach were useful but shortsighted given the broader array of obstacles to meaningful participation.

The most unfortunate element of the rehabilitation profession's rendition of independent living was the lingering belief that people with disabilities failed not because of the roadblocks society threw in their way but because of their own inadequacies. For disabled people, the depressing, widespread bigotry that they confronted in society—in schools, jobs, housing, recreation, and personal interactions—was sadly present among the rehabilitation experts who often spoke for them.

Professor Collignon understood this. He knew that if John Hessler, Hale Zukas, and the crew could pull this off, the CIL would send a lightning bolt through rehabilitation programs across the United States. It could change everything.

Collignon told his friend Ed Newman, the head of the federal Rehabilitation Services Agency, about the independent living center forming in Berkeley. He touted the CIL as a cutting-edge concept, a community services agency run by disabled people for disabled people. This was the future.

Newman immediately sent $20,000 to jump-start the project. He didn't know if he could trust this unprofessional bunch of disabled hippies. So he put Collignon down as the responsible fiscal agent. The first independent living center was born.[16]

Barely.

Larry Biscamp became the reluctant first director. Working out of a small apartment near campus, the new CIL offered a short menu of services. The team tried to raise additional funds, but their proposals failed repeatedly. Almost by design, the operation was hopelessly disorganized. For months, the fantastic dreams of the Berkeley disability activists floundered.

When Ed Roberts came back to town, he discovered that many members of the Berkeley disability community thought that he had never left. As one activist observed, Ed's shadow was so long that he "was always a presence" even when he was absent.[17]

The mythology of a new kind of folk hero was growing. Crafted of equal parts fact and rumor, inspired by a community desperate for a shining example of a militant disabled person achieving against all odds, a symbolic image began forming around Ed. Weaknesses and gaps ignored, strengths and victories enhanced, an inspiring narrative of the disability prophet gathered in the winds.

Beginning with his return to Berkeley, Ed intentionally embraced and cultivated this iconic character, allowing himself to be cast as what one adoring admirer called "the Martin Luther King, Jr." of the disability rights movement. His ego undoubtedly enjoyed the adulation. But even more, the elevated image helped him to get important things done.[18]

With his friends John Hessler running the PDSP and Larry Biscamp leading the struggling new CIL, Ed initially turned to what seemed like an even bigger idea. The key to helping disabled people live independently in the community, Ed believed, was putting them in charge of the services and assistance they received. It was all about control. His pals working in the PDSP and the CIL were implementing this necessary idea by creating new service organizations run by disabled people.

But they struggled to gain legitimacy. They were viewed with heavy skepticism by the old-line charities, hospitals, and state welfare agencies that made up the disability service establishment. Luckily the PDSP drew steady funding from the university. But the CIL, standing alone in the community, was starved for dollars.

Ed had his eye on a second path, to infiltrate the mainstream medical and social welfare system run by nondisabled professionals. Those systems were undeniably legitimate, and they enjoyed consistent funding streams. If only the disability community could take over the traditional systems and redirect them to more empowering directions.

Ed wanted to steal the keys to the establishment Cadillac.

A disturbing event provided an opportunity. In September 1972, a quadriplegic man experiencing respiratory distress was transported to the Herrick Hospital in southside Berkeley. Herrick was the main healthcare provider for many low-income disabled people. The ill man remained on a gurney untreated for eight hours. The news of his mistreatment quickly spread through the disability community.

Backed by his old friend Dr. Henry Bruyn, Ed approached Herrick physicians and administrators. In the political fallout of the emergency room mishap, they wanted new ideas for improving services for people with physical disabilities. Ed teamed up with the doctors to establish a new outpatient health clinic for disabled persons.

Ed was the Trojan horse that smuggled his disabled friends into Herrick Hospital. He ushered the entire disability community to the table of medical power. He organized a giant community meeting to launch the new clinic. Graduate student Charles Coles called it "the largest gathering of wheelchair persons ever held in Berkeley."[19]

This was Ed's ideal venue. He was the jubilant and radical master of ceremonies at an event half insurgent protest and half strategic planning. He staked out the moral high ground, helping disabled people describe their miserable experiences in the medical system. The hospital administrators sweated and wiggled uncomfortably through hours of critical testimony.

Under intense community pressure, they named Ed a board member of the new clinic. Seeking a strong say in how the clinic operated, he secured seats for other disability activists.

The trustees who ran Herrick Hospital were not pleased. The inmates were not going to run the asylum. They quickly rebuffed Ed's attempt to put disabled people in charge. The trustees seized back managerial control of the clinic.

Ed's coup was short lived. Although ultimately ineffective, he showed the Berkeley disability community that their hero was in outrageous top form, rallying them together to stick it to the coldhearted medical establishment. And have fun doing it.

As Ed poked the bear, the wallowing CIL plunged into a dark scandal. Director Larry Biscamp was accused of sexually abusing the young daughter of his girlfriend. Child welfare authorities investigated and found the allegations credible. The district attorney filed criminal charges against Biscamp.

It was an era when sexual assault accusations were often discounted. To many friends of Biscamp, the words of a young girl seemed suspect. Spinning with wild rumors, the tight disability community split into two factions, one side defending Biscamp and the other calling for his removal. The already struggling CIL collapsed in disgrace and infighting.

Ed's outsized presence created further division. Critics of Larry Biscamp rallied around Ed as the CIL's only salvation.

John Hessler and Ed met secretly. The two men were no longer the immature kids who first allied as undergraduates in Cowell Hospital a decade earlier. Now in their early thirties, they were the seasoned veterans of the movement.[20]

Ed had the long-term vision in mind. The CIL was just the first step, a necessary initial building block for a national disability rights movement. It had to be saved, stabilized, and expanded. The long-time friends came to a secret agreement. They quietly contacted individual CIL board members in advance of the next meeting. They arranged for all the necessary votes.

The takeover was ugly, and it happened quickly. At the board meeting, Hessler made a motion to replace Larry Biscamp as CIL director with Ed Roberts. The motion was unceremoniously seconded.

"It looks like everyone wants to get rid of me," Biscamp mumbled in defeat. His friends were sacrificing him to rescue everything they had built together. It was a painful moment that no one felt good about.[21]

Biscamp was a beloved brother from the Cowell Hospital days. He worked on the early CIL planning in one of Professor Fred Collignon's research courses. His rebellious hands helped mold the sand, clay, and lime into the bricks that built the first independent living center. Now suddenly he was humiliated and tossed aside.

A hasty voice vote named Ed the new CIL director. For the rest of his life, the worldwide disability rights community would celebrate Ed as the creator of the first independent living center. He always consciously described himself as "one of the founders," tipping his hat to the necessary contributions of many.

The important role that Larry Biscamp played, and the sexual abuse scandal that led to his ouster, were quickly lost from the collective memory of disability rights activists. The clean company line was that Ed gloriously started it all.

During Ed's first days trying to revive the CIL, the outgoing Biscamp gifted him an unexpected opportunity. An Alameda County council staff member bumped into the dispirited Biscamp one day in a park. Biscamp grumbled that the CIL had big plans but no money. The staffer encouraged him to apply for county funding.[22]

A local real estate man named Tom Bates had just been elected to the council. The Nixon administration in Washington, DC, redistributed tax dollars back to local governments for their own use. The president's 1974 block grants for community development overloaded the council with a growing stockpile of federal money. The new councilor was searching for worthy projects.[23]

Bates had an unusual background for a 1970s liberal. He was a member of the Cal Bears 1959 Rose Bowl team, an Army veteran, and a small businessman. But he believed that government should focus its attention and money on helping society's outcasts. He had faith that people pushed to the margins by prejudice and cruel capitalism could succeed if given a boost of government support.

CIL administrator Phil Draper and Ed Roberts met with Bates to discuss what the CIL was doing and how to expand its reach in the community. As the two men steered their power wheelchairs into Bates's small office, the councilman's breath caught in the back of his throat. He had little personal experience with people with disabilities.

As Ed boasted about the little CIL, Bates fixated on how he paused intermittently to puff on a tube suspended at his cheek. It took him five minutes to put aside his fascination with Ed's mouth working the breathing apparatus. Then he appreciated what Ed had to say. His words were articulate and savvy.

Bates took a shine to the enterprising team. Draper was a capable manager with a detailed grasp of every way the underfunded CIL was already supporting disabled people. Ed's words catapulted off Draper's, projecting the numerous new programs the brash group promised to implement with additional money.

Bates was tickled by the way the two men fully believed their grandiose plans about starting a disability revolution. They came off somehow as both neatly organized and arrogantly irreverent, as if they knew that they were miles ahead of everyone else. But their actual daily work was completely practical, focusing closely on supporting the needs of disabled people.

This was exactly the kind of project Bates was looking for. He could change the world with a few thousand dollars. The council appropriated $70,000 for the CIL in the first year and created a line item that increased funding every year.[24]

The scandal-drowned, left-for-dead CIL leaped to life with Ed at the helm, creating new programs and services. Equally important, Tom Bates became Ed's crucial political ally, backing his bombastic plan to cover California, America, and the world with independent living centers. Ed would build castles in the air, and they would be fully accessible.

12 *Joan*

A woman was about to change Ed's life.

Joan Leon climbed the narrow stairs to the dusty office above a natural foods store on University Avenue in Berkeley. A friend had recommended that she drop by the Center for Independent Living because they needed her help.

An experienced, skilled public relations officer and fundraiser, Leon had worked previously for the Philadelphia College of Art and the Tom Dooley Foundation, a nonprofit devoted to offering medical care in impoverished nations. She had a gift for putting other people's ideas and goals into words and using those words to raise large sums of money. She had no idea what the CIL was. All she knew was she was bored and ready for an adventure.

Stepping into the office, Leon was surprised to see wall-to-wall wheelchairs. She had never seen so many people with physical disabilities. Along the office walls was a row of high, thin ledges, handmade wooden desks lacquered to a serious shine. Each worker could easily slide their wheelchair under these custom workspaces.[1]

She was immediately overwhelmed by snowdrifts of loose paper flowing across the floor. Where were the file cabinets? Records and documents wandered the floorboards like fall leaves on a windy day.

There were no chairs to sit on. Leon was the only person in the room standing upright.

Shaggy-haired young people in wheelchairs chatted and joked. A couple of dogs roamed freely. In the case of both dogs and humans, it was hard to tell which were working. Many seemed to just be hanging out.

The CIL was already becoming a social club for young "crips" who were out of work and had few other places to go. The center relied on the scattered labor of many disabled volunteers, who lived off meager social security and state welfare payments. Paid staff, unpaid volunteers, friends, and clients were indistinguishable.

Herb Willsmore, a tall, slim man with a full brown beard, talked on the phone. Eight years earlier, his souped-up 1955 Chevy spun off a highway, breaking his spine and paralyzing his lower body. One of the leaders of the Rolling Quads in Cowell Hospital, he earned a master's degree in urban planning.

At the far end of the room were Phil Draper and Greg Sanders. Draper coordinated the day-to-day operations of the center. He was chair of the CIL board. His even-handed management allowed the CIL to function and grow for many years.

Sanders was a whiz at the daunting labyrinth of state and federal laws. He specialized in advocacy, helping disabled clients navigate the complex federal social security system and arrange for state in-home support services to pay for personal attendants.

Two floors up a small team of disabled hippies fixed wheelchairs. During breaks, the crew went up to the roof to pass around a joint and take in the California sunshine. They were the best in town at repairing a chair on the cheap.

"Hi, I'm Ed," a buoyant young man in a tall red wheelchair zoomed up to Leon. "Welcome to the CIL."

His giant smile seemed unaffected by the chaos that surrounded him. His eyes—once described by a journalist as "big, wide, and haunting"—embraced her in warmth. She felt his overflowing eagerness. Leon glanced shyly away and then looked back again. Ed's eyes were still there, unwavering and exalted. Leon was entranced by this strange man's audacity.[2]

Ed began talking, and he didn't stop. About himself, his friends, and the purpose of CIL. He told stories of his own life and of Cowell Hospital interspersed with grand pronouncements that sounded both far-fetched and completely reasonable. The people in this goofy office full of paper and free-range canines, Leon learned, were the sponsors of a revolution that would change the entire world. It was like listening to a Pop Warner football coach boast with all seriousness about how his snot-nosed squad of eleven-year-olds would defeat the Oakland Raiders in the Super Bowl. It was beyond ridiculous. It was self-important blather. Leon found it remarkably convincing.

Something big was going on here.

Leon had grown up with severe anxiety and suffered from anorexia as a teen. She often felt like she was an unwanted exile watching life from the cold perimeter. Ed told evocative stories of his experiences and the lives of his disabled friends. They were social castaways pushing to be let in. His narratives tapped into the feelings of rejection and mistreatment that Leon harbored silently.

But more. Ed and his CIL friends were underdogs fighting back against injustice. They were working to create a society without exclusion and cruelty. Like so many who heard Ed speak, Leon was mesmerized. Somewhere in the unyielding intensity of Ed's stories was a great idea that she could sell.

The disabled upstarts were propelled by a driving, practical question: What would it take for people with disabilities—initially physical disabilities and blindness, but later other kinds of impairments—to live and work in the community? The list written by the hippy wheelchair coalition was long and detailed.

Transportation. Buses and trains were not wheelchair accessible. Vans with wheelchair lifts were too expensive for disabled people, who often had low incomes.

Sidewalk ramps. Even with the installation of curb cuts in Berkeley and Oakland, most of the Bay Area's sidewalks were still blocked off.

Accessible apartments. They needed residences with ramps and accessible bathrooms. Very few apartments or houses in Berkeley had been modified for access.

Wheelchair repair. The motorized chairs that so many relied on every day often broke down, leaving the user stuck at home for days or weeks. Repairs were time-consuming and expensive.

Advocacy and expertise dealing with state and federal bureaucracies. Only a paperwork magician could navigate the maze of systems that provided services and financial support.

Attendant referral. Many people with physical disabilities could live in the community if they had personal attendants to assist with basic daily tasks. The state supplied a small monthly allowance for assistance. But there was no organized way to recruit, hire, and train good attendants.

Friendship and mentorship. The Rolling Quads discovered that the emotional support and guidance of disabled friends was more impactful and empowering than any service provided by nondisabled professionals. They coined the pseudo-formal term "peer counseling" to describe this crucial kind of help.

Activism. The legislature in Sacramento as well as local and federal governments made decisions every day concerning disabled people, typically without consulting anyone with a disability. The CIL members had to stay on top of political developments and push for concrete improvements.

Leon knew how to fuel the little CIL engine with donations. Ed and Joan Leon quickly became a proficient fundraising team.

Her role was clear. Whether bouncing ideas around with Ed or listening to CIL staff discuss an unmet need, her job was to gather the diffuse ideas and refine the concepts into coherent shape. She probed with detailed questions and scribbled on a notepad like an inquisitive journalist. She needed to comprehend any new idea from the perspective of the uninitiated and unfamiliar people who ran wealthy philanthropic foundations. She worked many hours with Ed to talk through ideas and frame them into digestible written form.

Then the duo hit the road, tapping the many contacts Ed made in his brief time working with Jean Wirth at Common College. Every well-intentioned Bay Area group with deep pockets—the San Francisco Foundation, Zellerbach Family Fund, van Loben Sels Foundation, Bank of America—found them knocking at the door.[3]

. • .

A kind man with a receding hairline and slight belly paunch sat behind an oversized desk. As Joan Leon and Ed entered, he rose with his hand outstretched. Seeing Ed, he awkwardly withdrew his hand and half-smiled in timid apology.

The foundation officer anticipated hearing a pitch from a disability charity or social service group. He thought he would be talking to professionals, not a paralyzed guy in a big wheelchair. He was unprepared for the visual and verbal onslaught of Ed.

Sensing the moment of discomfort, Ed saw his opportunity. He started to perform. A deep puff from the respirator hose drew the observer's eyes to his face. Watch me now. The man found himself unconsciously following Ed's lead.

First was the Wheelchair Dance. Flipping his fingers skillfully on the armrest controls, Ed raised his outstretched legs up until his feet bumped the edge of the desk. Then suddenly he lowered them down, the machinery humming in robotic motion. Next he rolled the chair back and forth repeatedly like an automobile driver struggling to parallel park, repositioning himself until the chair was angled just so.

Then came the pyrotechnics. Ed flashed the wheelchair's lights on and off. He was a salesman proudly wowing the prospective buyer with flashy acrobatics. Grinning widely, enjoying himself immensely, he watched his host's eyes leap from light to light. It was really too much fun.

There was nothing the foundation manager could do but watch Ed run the chair through its choreographed paces. Ed guided him, held him, and toyed with him. The man was bewitched by his own guilty curiosity, trapped in the silent snare of his own queasiness.

The administrator feigned upbeat patience as Ed masterfully extended the uncomfortable moment from a few seconds of initial staring into two excruciating minutes. When Ed had finally reduced the good fellow to shriveled submission—when his tense eyes cried "Uncle!"—Ed began to talk. His spiel began.

Ed unleashed a catalog of biographic stories that filled his speeches for many years. A foolish public school administrator told him he couldn't graduate from high school until he completed classes in PE and driver's ed. An uninspired rehabilitation counselor denied his application for support to attend the University of California, crudely calling him "infeasible."

The plot of each story was the same. Ed was the earnest and worthwhile disabled protagonist—representing all disabled people— held back not by the brokenness of his body or the pathology of his mind but by cruelty, injustice, and ignorance. Ed and his friends wanted what anyone else wanted, a chance to go to school and work, have a home, enjoy loved ones and family.

Each narrative smacked the foundation man's stomach like a lead cannonball, dropping him deeper into a well of conflicted feelings.

His eyes reddened and welled up with sadness. But he also found himself cheering for Ed to defeat his tormentors.

Then Ed told his favorite story.

"When I was fourteen, I got polio. When the doctor took my parents aside, my mother asked, 'Will he live?' The doctor looked at her and said, 'You should probably hope he dies, because if he lives, he will be nothing more than a vegetable for the rest of his life.' Well, I'm here today as an artichoke. You know they're a little prickly on the outside with a big heart."[4]

The corny artichoke story brought a smile to the overwhelmed foundation leader's face. Ed gifted him a moment of humorous relief, a welcome respite from the narrated chain of cruelties.

Ed had turned the tables. The disabled man who suffered years of heartbreaking hardships gently offered comfort to the nondisabled man who, until a few minutes ago, had never thought seriously about the injustices experienced by disabled people.

Ed's accomplice knew it was her turn to jump in. Leon poured on the facts, describing the CIL, its founding and purpose. There was a whole team of Eds rolling about in an office on University Avenue. She told about the many important services they provided and what a difference those services made to disabled people in Berkeley.

Then back to Ed for the finale. He pitched the big vision, how CIL was changing the community so that people with a variety of disabilities could live fulfilling lives. He told of a disability rights revolution. Of course, you want to get in on the ground floor of changing the world.

The foundation man was exhausted and fascinated. He didn't know what to do. He had no idea if Ed's CIL idea would work. If Ed was feeding him pie in the sky, it was undoubtedly a tasty pastry. Foundation after foundation made initial small investments of $5,000 and $10,000. As the managers befriended Ed and Joan Leon, the dollar totals quickly rose tenfold and more. The CIL's coffers soon burst with new donations.[5]

Meanwhile the regional rehabilitation administrator Herb Leibowitz was still looking for a way to support the CIL. He arranged to meet Ed. Of course, he had heard all about Ed Roberts. But he had never really talked to him.

The two men instantly connected. They traded ideas rapid fire, easily speaking the same language. Ed articulated a broad, expansive vision of independent living that began with services in the Berkeley community and spread quickly into a national movement.

Leibowitz saw himself as the intermediary between the disability community and professional rehabilitation, helping Ed and his team take dollars from the conservative rehabilitation system to grow their movement. Despite his supervisor's discouragement, Leibowitz set up an initial $50,000 grant.

One specific practice that Ed and his team called "peer counseling" caught Leibowitz's eye. Loosely defined, it meant one disabled person giving emotional support and guidance to another. It was the heart of what the self-help organization was all about, disabled people helping other disabled people.

With Leibowitz's coaching, Ed and Joan Leon worked with two CIL staff members, Hal Kirschbaum and Peter Leech, on a large federal grant proposal to fund peer counseling. They scored on the first try. The CIL was soon flush with hundreds of thousands of dollars.[6]

Joan Leon and Ed Roberts were a formidable team. She became his best friend and faithful collaborator. Within eighteen months, flooded with private foundation dollars and the new federal grant, the CIL bank account topped one million dollars.

From the first glint of Ed's eyes, hearing the lofty words that passed the tube bobbing at his lips, Leon was intrigued. She had an overpowering feeling that this bizarre man was the bearer of a magical secret. He had cracked the code of life. The trials of polio, paralysis, and isolation had somehow left him with a transcendent wisdom that only he knew.

In Ed she saw a wheelchair guru who knew how to live well in a harsh and disappointing world. Warmed and nourished by his secret, Joan Leon stayed at his side for the rest of his life.[7]

13 *Judy*

"Who is this?" the impatient young woman snapped. Some guy from California on the phone was yapping a mile a minute. He was full of energy.

"This is Ed Roberts. I'm director of the Center for Independent Living in Berkeley. I want you to come out and work with us. You can go to grad school at the University of California." Ed recruited hard. He had read about her impressive work in New York. She was the best disability rights activist on the East Coast.

If the CIL was to become not just a small city services provider but the dynamic hub of a growing movement, it would need the best talent. Ed knew that meant one person. Judy Heumann.

Like Ed, Heumann was a polio survivor. She grew up in a close-knit Jewish family and supportive community in Brooklyn. Most of her schooling took place in segregated special education programs. When she attended general education classes in high school, she felt alone. The academics were stronger than what she experienced in special education, but she was socially isolated.

For Heumann, the typical teen friendships and dating happened at summer camps for kids with disabilities in New Jersey and New York. Those early experiences taught her the value of a disability community that included people with a variety of disabilities. She learned how to create a unique social space where disability was normal and accepted.

At Long Island University, she was the first student using a wheelchair to live in a dormitory. She was active in the development of the campus program for disabled students that provided services to students on a largely inaccessible campus. Heumann graduated with honors in 1970.

Her activism career began when she applied for a job as a public school teacher. She passed the required written and oral exams to earn a New York state teaching license. The third prong of the assessment was a medical examination.

Heumann showed up to find a dismissive doctor, an older woman who was annoyed to even go through the motions with an applicant using a wheelchair. She already knew the result.

"How do you go to the bathroom?" the physician asked. For some unknown reason, her questions focused closely on toileting habits.

The flinty Heumann sat still, stunned by the foolish questions. She didn't know where to begin to talk to someone who doubted her ability to use a bathroom. Finally, exasperated, she spat bitterly, "If you're wondering if I can teach young children how to use the bathroom, I can."

While taking down a lengthy medical history, the evaluator realized that Heumann had once worn leg braces and walked with crutches. To her, this was an opening, a possibility that Heumann might pass. Just as Ed discovered on the polio ward, standing up was the key to social acceptance in the land of the walkies.

"I've been using a wheelchair for years," Heumann explained.

"But you can use braces with crutches, walking upright?" the doctor persisted.

"Yes," Heumann admitted reluctantly, "but if I'm in a classroom with children, I don't want to be using crutches. I need to be stable. The wheelchair is best."

The doctor ordered her to return for a second medical examination. Only this time she should bring her leg braces and crutches. If she could stand and walk well enough, then maybe Heumann could become a teacher.

Heumann came to the second physical with a supportive ally. Theodor Childs, a nondisabled African American man, was the director of the Long Island University's program for disabled students. He was ready to attest to her many collegiate accomplishments.

The medical examiner came with her own reinforcements, two additional doctors. The stern, white-coated trio barred Childs from the room. He had to wait in the hall. They didn't want to hear about what a great university student Heumann was. They wanted to know if she could stand and walk.

The lead physician leaned forward to peer behind Heumann's wheelchair. Wrinkling her nose in disapproval, she demanded, "Where are your crutches?"

"I didn't bring them. I haven't used them in many years."

Heumann watched the doctor's pen scribbling, "Applicant is insubordinate." The old myth that people with physical disabilities were held back by their own anger and psychological problems lived on.

The examiner then turned to each of her partners, whispering audibly, "She wets her pants sometimes."

"What are you talking about?" Heumann cracked angrily. Tears of frustration rolled down her face. She worked hard for four years to earn a teaching degree, and the foolish doctors were obsessing over the perplexing mysteries of how a wheelchair user urinates in the toilet.

The New York Board of Education denied Heumann a teaching license. She failed the physical exam because she traveled by wheelchair.[1]

A friend put her in touch with *New York Times* reporter Andrew Malcolm. Within two days, his sympathetic article appeared. He quoted Theodor Childs praising Heumann, "Here's a person who through great adversity has been able to finish college, which probably took a lot more drive than another regular student who has less trouble finding a job."

The board physician claimed that Heumann would be unable to help students evacuate a school building in the case of an emergency. Heumann countered this argument by saying that if elevators were not available, she could teach on the ground floor. She could effectively lead the emergency evacuation of the students. In fact, her electric wheelchair traveled much faster than the average walking person.[2]

The next day, the *Times* followed with a blunt editorial, "License Miss Heumann." The editors derided the education board's decision as "heartless and thoughtless nonsense." They encouraged the public schools to see Heumann as an ideal role model for young students. "Sitting in her wheelchair, she can show students, handicapped or normal, that the desire to teach and learn is the first educational step."[3]

A media frenzy of support for Judy Heumann's cause erupted. The *New York Post* and the *Daily News* ran similar editorials berating the narrow-minded state Board of Education.

Heumann appeared on *The Today Show,* a national morning television program hosted by Barbara Walters and Hugh Downs. The federal Department of Education sent Robert Herman, a mild-mannered senior administrator, to begrudgingly debate her on whether people with physical disabilities could work as public school teachers.[4]

The ugly case against Heumann was most fully articulated in a *New York Times* letter sent in by school administrator Charles M. Shapp. "In my own experience there have been many emergencies where classrooms had to be evacuated," he wrote, "the teacher must be able to move swiftly through the corridors and down stairways."

Shapp appealed to parents' worst fears. "What of the point of view of the parent whose child was caught in an emergency where the teacher is confined to a wheelchair? What if several children were hurt? What of the feelings of the parent whose child was injured?"[5]

The educational leader drew from the worst disability stereotypes to arouse parents' worries for their children's safety. The misfortune embodied in Heumann's disability would bring harm to the children. She was a danger to students.

Heumann was filled with anger and disgust: "I was so tired of being called a fire hazard that I could vomit."[6]

She decided to take the Board of Education to court. She contacted the American Civil Liberties Union (ACLU) to represent her. The ACLU had a long, proud history of helping persons from oppressed minority groups fight against prejudice and ignorance.

Beginning in 1963, the ACLU filed a series of employment discrimination lawsuits on behalf of a gay men against the federal Civil Service Commission (CCC). District of Columbia ACLU director David Carliner viewed gay Americans not as perverse moral violators, the government's stance, but as worthy citizens targeted by bigotry. In 1973, after losing appeals decisions in the *Scott v. Macy* and *Norton v. Macy* cases, the CCC changed its hiring policies to include LGBT applicants and workers. The ACLU defeated the federal government on behalf of gay Americans.[7]

Oddly, the New York ACLU didn't view disabled citizens as a minority group subject to discrimination. Their thinking about disability politics was out of date. They quickly reviewed the case and told Heumann she had no legal recourse. This was not a civil rights issue.

Heumann was shocked. If the ACLU didn't recognize the reality of disability discrimination, who would?

Luckily, two attorneys, Ray Lucas and Elias Schwarzbart, volunteered to take the case. Schwarzbart approached Heumann's father in his butcher shop, offering to help out. Lucas was a constitutional law expert who would soon be part of the legal team that argued for abortion rights in the *Roe v. Wade* case. They filed a lawsuit in federal court, seeking for her a teaching license and monetary damages.[8]

The federal judge assigned to the case was Contance Baker Motley. A calm but imposing figure, she was the first African American woman appointed to the federal bench. One of the most prominent women involved in the civil rights movement, on behalf of the NAACP she won court cases that opened up the University of Georgia, Clemson, and Ole Miss to Black students. She was the only woman who worked on Thurgood Marshall's *Brown* school desegregation case legal team. This was someone who could smell bias a continent away.

Judge Motley had little patience for the public schools' thin argument. She immediately ordered the Board of Education to conduct a new, fairer medical examination.

The board sent a different doctor to evaluate Heumann. The woman looked at her and immediately apologized, "This never should have happened." Heumann won her teaching license. She found a job teaching in the same Brooklyn elementary school she attended as a young girl.[9]

The groundswell of publicity was enormous. Heumann spent months doing interviews for magazines, radio shows, and television. Drivers honked horns and shouted as they passed her on the street. People stopped her in stores to give her support and encouragement.

Public speaking didn't come naturally to the nervous young woman. In moments of stress, her eyes filled with tears. As a teenager singing at her family's synagogue, she once hit a single sour note and broke down crying. Her father rescued her, carrying her off the stage.

But the recent college graduate held strong and spoke clearly in the many media engagements. She felt a passion for the cause that settled her nerves and carried her smoothly forward.

At age twenty-two, in 1971, Judy Heumann became the most prominent national spokesperson for the new cause of disability rights. She smartly used the moment of heightened publicity to organize a new disability rights group.

The country had many organizations focused on disability issues. Some were charities like Easter Seals and the Muscular Dystrophy Association, the sponsors of the annual Jerry Lewis Telethon, that raised money for medical care and research. Disability-specific groups like the National Federation of the Blind and the National Association of the Deaf lobbied for programs and funding on Capitol Hill. Professional organizations like the National Rehabilitation Association represented the status and perspectives of service providers.

But what Heumann put together was different. Disabled in Action (DIA) was a cross-disability alliance that fought against the pervasive discrimination and structural oppression that disabled people confronted every day. By comparison to other disability organizations, they were impolite, demanding, and dramatic. In a single year, DIA grew to fifteen hundred members from New York to Washington, DC.[10]

Heumann's DIA dove immediately into the political fray.

Eunice Fiorito, a blind woman who ran the New York City Mayor's Office for People with Disabilities, gave Heumann a heads-up about Section 504, a single sentence in the proposed 1973 revision of the federal Rehabilitation Act. Word circulated among disability groups that, for the first time ever, federal law might recognize and outlaw discrimination against disabled people.

If passed, Section 504 would apply to any entity receiving federal funds. Private corporations and organizations would be exempt. But federal dollars flowed to every state, county, and municipal government, including public transportation systems and schools, in the country. This was groundbreaking.

Twice President Richard Nixon vetoed the Rehabilitation Act, not because of Section 504 but due to the bill's hefty price tag. There is no evidence he even noticed 504. He wanted to save money and halt the expensive growth of federal disability support programs.

In October 1972, Heumann rallied Disabled in Action to fight Nixon's vetoes. They staged dramatic public protests, taking to the streets in the nonviolent but provocative civil disobedience style of the civil rights movement. Their in-your-face strategy relied on the visual shock of people in wheelchairs angrily shouting in the city streets. The unseen people traditionally assumed to be passive and cheerful objects of charity exploded with rage and passion. It was not what Americans driving to work or walking to the grocery store expected.

The DIA went after President Nixon at every opportunity. They planted their wheelchairs in the middle of busy Madison Avenue, in front of Nixon's reelection campaign headquarters, and halted traffic for an hour. Police threw up their hands, knowing they had no realistic way to forcibly haul away fourteen people in wheelchairs.[11]

But the New York news media didn't notice. Seeking greater coverage, the DIA next targeted Times Square, the teaming center of tourist traffic in the city. Heumann coordinated with the George McGovern presidential campaign and the Vietnam Veterans of America. Journalists would pay more attention to disabled veterans, Heumann reasoned.

Vietnam Vets leader Bobby Muller thought Heumann was crazy. But he felt her energy and went along for the glorious ride. The demonstrators blocked all Times Square traffic for twenty minutes. Muller shouted at frustrated automobile drivers through a bullhorn: "It may be a matter of you being late for dinner, but maybe it's a matter of life and death for us."[12]

The *New York Times* coverage of the DIA actions was minimal. The same newspaper that boosted African American civil rights with wall-to-wall front page coverage of the 1963 March for Jobs and Freedom in Washington, DC, seemed to view the protests as oddly cute, as if the streets were blocked by Girl Scouts holding cuddly puppies. They didn't understand disability issues as significant political matters involving millions of citizens.[13]

Annoyed at the weak newspaper coverage, the DIA demonstrated outside the *Times* offices. The newspaper managers finally agreed to meet with Heumann and DIA leaders. The DIA tried to educate the *Times* leadership that the problems disabled people faced involved prevalent attitudes and structures of widespread prejudice. After careful and thorough instruction, the otherwise brilliant people at the nation's top newspaper somehow couldn't grasp the concept.

Heumann's skillful organizing talents were fully displayed in a large protest of Nixon's veto of the Rehabilitation Act in Washington, DC, in May 1973. Two simultaneous organization meetings, the President's Committee on the Employment of the Handicapped (PCEH) and the United Cerebral Palsy Association (UCP), brought hundreds of disabled people to the Capitol. DIA collaborated with the American Council of the Blind to stage a large demonstration drawing in the many participants.

DIA directed the sharpest attack at the President's Committee on the Employment of the Handicapped, the purveyors of the pity-perpetuating "Hire the Handicapped" slogan. Over three thousand nicely dressed people gathered in an auditorium in the Washington Hilton to listen to President Nixon's daughter Julie Eisenhower. At the podium was the polite, well-intentioned member of the president's family, who had little day-to-day experience with disability issues or disabled people. She spoke in seemingly positive and inspiring words about employing disabled people while the White House she represented refused to sign a bill that would expand rehabilitation services and create a national antidiscrimination law that protected disabled people.

It was empty political theater. Pay no attention to the real actions of the leaders. Watch the nice lady at the microphone. Look at these beautiful award certificates on White House stationery. Clap politely on cue.

To the DIA members in the audience, silent compliance was too much to ask. They shouted Eisenhower down, interrupting her, telling the whole audience how President Nixon was failing. Why did the president veto the Rehabilitation Act? Why doesn't Nixon want to employ disabled people?

Many in the crowd viewed the disruptions as deeply disrespectful. They tried to shush the loud protesters. But this only emboldened DIA further. With a roar, a chorus of thirty disability activists chanted together, completely halting Eisenhower's presentation. They held up signs and shouted in unison. Then they loudly stormed out of the room.

Hundreds of activists held a candlelight vigil and sang protest songs at the Lincoln Memorial. Senator Bob Dole, a Republican and himself disabled from a World War II injury to his arm, spoke in support of the Rehabilitation Act.

Singing in front of the enormous statue of Lincoln the Great Emancipator, his gentle eyes seeming to look down with empathy, gave the activists an incredible high. In 1957, on this same spot, Martin Luther King, Jr., and thirty thousand civil rights activists gathered on the third anniversary of the Brown decision mandating the desegregation of public schools. Six years later King gave his famous "I Have a Dream" speech to a quarter million, calling for federal civil rights legislation. Students from seventy-five seminaries—Catholic, Protestant, and Jewish—had maintained a round-the-clock prayer vigil on this hallowed spot, asking God and perhaps Lincoln to break the Senate filibuster to pass the 1964 Civil Rights Act.[14]

Heumann, the DIA, and the humble group of five hundred strong stayed with Lincoln all night. The next day the groggy masses, energized by the feeling of togetherness, marched two miles to the Capitol.

There was a new feeling of cross-disability solidarity forming as protesters had fun and made new friends. The dominant group of people with physical disabilities using wheelchairs were joined by many D/deaf and blind persons. An alliance joining different disability organizations that would become important in the years to come was beginning to take shape.

East also began to connect with West. At the Lincoln Memorial, Heumann met two leaders from the Berkeley CIL, Dick Santos and Larry Biscamp. They told her about the CIL and their work. It was the first time that she heard about the California activists.

She found the independent living concept intriguing. Her·work with DIA and other East Coast activists was focused on changing government policies. But the CIL idea of putting disabled people in charge of the services they received was completely new. It mixed activism and assistance in a way that directly impacted individuals in the community. Heumann came away from the conversation wanting to know more about the CIL and independent living.

At Ed's insistent invitation, in Autumn 1973, Judy Heumann joined him in Berkeley as a staff member at the CIL. She enrolled in a Cal graduate program in public health.[15]

Ed was the goal-focused head coach who needed the best players on his team, and Heumann was the star athlete. The country's two top disability rights activists were united. Working with a talented and passionate Berkeley team, they charted a disability rights movement to change California, the United States, and the world.

14 *I'm Here, We're Here*

The CIL's secret sauce was an inside-out strategy: opening the closed doors of society through careful attention to the emotional needs of disabled people who had been harmed by prejudice. The warmth of counseling and friendship created an activist community ready to charge forward for justice. Solidarity was healing and empowering.

Peer counseling provided the psychological restorative that made the CIL flourish. Ed believed deeply that "Nothing is as important as seeing and talking with a person who has conquered the problem you have." A life pummeled by years of cruel, demeaning experiences could rise again with the loving support of another disabled person.[1]

Hal Kirschbaum was the capable manager of the peer counseling program. He was the embodiment of the smart and savvy disabled persons who gravitated to Berkeley from around the country. Raised in a leftist Jewish family, he studied at progressive Antioch College in Ohio. He and his wife, Megan, fought for African American civil rights and protested the Vietnam War.

After earning a Ph.D. in philosophy, Hal Kirschbaum took a faculty post at Coe College in Iowa. He befriended Jim Campbell, a professor who had severe kidney disease. Kirschbaum had multiple sclerosis. The two men shared their experiences living with chronic illnesses.

Soon the conversation of mutual support involved their wives. The two women discovered a unique space of support and learning as they shared thoughts and feelings about being the spouse of a person with a disability. For Hal Kirschbaum and his wife, who was a trained psychotherapist, this profound connection with another couple dealing with chronic health issues taught them the powerful potential of peer counseling.[2]

The CIL counseling clients contended with a wide range of everyday psychological issues, just as nondisabled people do. But disabled clients also carry the deep wounds of invisibility. Kirschbaum found that, above all, they longed for full recognition: "Just to get known, just to be considered as a real person, not ignored any more. Say, 'I'm here, we're here, notice us, we're a part of this.'"[3]

With the caring empathy of Carl Rogers and the exuberant exhortations of Billy Sunday, Ed served as the unofficial therapist-in-chief. The liberation of his people went beyond securing rights to participate in society. There was a deeply emotional underside that needed thoughtful, gentle attention.

Ed developed a complex understanding of how disabled people too often attacked and limited themselves. Oppression was more than a series of outdated attitudes and dehumanizing barriers maintained by a callous society. It had a sneaky, toxic way of convincing disabled people to apply the worst, most stigmatizing stereotypes to themselves.

Using his own life as an object lesson, Ed invited other disabled persons to look closely at their own experiences. As a teen in the hospital, he was subjected daily to the belittling words of doctors and nurses. "[They were] calling me cripple. . . . Constantly around me somehow feelings were reinforced, people telling me about my limits, about how I wouldn't be able to do [anything] and how I had to accept this." The medical personnel were authoritative voices teaching him the demeaning attitudes of the broader society.[4]

Initially Ed accepted an "incredibly destructive" view of himself, a dark stereotype offering nothing but misery. "I bought it. . . . All of us bought it." Given the lack of credible alternatives, it was incredibly hard not to.

In Berkeley, the love and support of disabled people who understood what he had been through helped Ed recognize the cruelest, most painful fact. In the late-night consciousness-raising conversations at Cowell Hospital, he and his friends realized that they had accepted "a bunch of shit." Acknowledging that they had unknowingly bought a noxious pile of excremental lies, often fed to them by otherwise caring professionals and family members, was the first step toward growth and healing.[5]

Peer counselors helped their clients go through a difficult, often prolonged process of confronting the limiting myths. At the end of this treacherous path was an unexpected but not guaranteed opportunity in the form of a choice. Ed repeatedly encouraged other disabled people to view their own history of mistreatment as offering them a crucial life decision about what they could choose to believe about themselves.[6]

"You can either take the experience and turn it inward and kick the hell out of yourself and destroy yourself—you've seen people do that—or you can take the energy and the anger . . . you can take that kind of anger . . . and you can say, hey, that's a tremendous force within yourself to help do something different."[7]

While Ed and the peer counselors emphasized the possibilities for positive growth, too many talented, valued friends succumbed to self-destruction. Larry Langdon was the most notable. He was the son of loggers on the green northern coast of California. Nurturing his intellectual gifts, his parents sent him away to prep school in Canada. The summer after high school graduation, he dove into the Mad River, struck the shallow bottom with his head, and snapped his spine.

An early resident of Cowell Hospital, Langdon was one of the creative masterminds behind the independent living concept. He and Jim Donald were the first Cowell residents to move into their own apartments, showing hesitant friends that independence was more than a theoretical idea. He completed two degrees at Cal despite ongoing alcohol addiction.

In April 1969, Langdon married his hometown sweetheart, Carol Billings. The newlyweds struggled as Langdon's drinking spiraled out of control. Filled with booze, he wasn't the same caring man. Billings divorced him after only one year, citing his abusive behavior.

Four years later, after a weeklong binge of drugs and alcohol, Langdon fell into a coma. When he finally regained consciousness, Billings visited him at Herrick Hospital. But he couldn't even recognize his ex-wife.

Living in a halfway house in San Jose, addled by memory loss, Langdon had a stroke in 1977. Isolated from his friends and the woman he loved, no longer a part of the movement and community he helped to build, he died alone.[8]

The volatile inner energy that made both self-destruction and personal growth possible was anger. To Ed, the bedrock foundation of individual and political progress for disabled people arose from this one emotion. It was high-octane rocket fuel ready for intentional activation.

Ed invited disabled people to gather up their anger as the useful wellspring of a better life. A finely focused bitterness made purposeful fighting possible. It was the generative spark needed to make it in a cruel society.

The result was the surprising and wonderful development of personal strength unique to disabled people. "Strength comes through first surviving physically and then beginning to cope as a devalued person and beginning to come out on top not only [as] a person that values himself but has some value to society."[9]

Ed often preached, "We know what it means to survive. We know what kind of strength can come through disability."

The radical idea that disability was a source of personal strength turned everything people thought about disabled people upside down. At a conference of behavioral psychologists—professionals fully trained in the supposed psychopathologies of disabled people—Ed opened his keynote address with a brazen declaration: "I'm here to talk about strength and not about weakness." It would take decades before psychology became interested in human strengths.[10]

Love and friendship shared with other disabled people were necessary to pull this off. What made peer counseling powerful, and what gave the solidarity of the Berkeley disability community such potency, was the way they nurtured individuals through this harrowing psychological process. For the many who were healed by the sturdy and steady love of other disabled people, they emerged with new lives of action and impact.

·   ·   ·

The CIL was an incredible hothouse of invention. During Ed's eighteen roaring months at the helm, as well as the succeeding years of continued rapid growth under the leadership of Phil Draper and Judy Heumann, many new projects spun off to become self-sustaining, highly impactful organizations. The culture of the CIL attracted talented people, many of whom graduated from Cal and others who traveled across the country to get involved in this innovative place. The CIL became a staging platform for numerous disability advocacy and service groups.

Two notable organizations born of the CIL were Through the Looking Glass and the Disability Rights and Education Fund (DREDF). The former focused on advocacy and support for families with disabled children, parents, or grandparents. While numerous groups assisted parents in raising children with disabilities, none before Looking Glass championed disabled adults as parents. The Disability Rights Education and Defense Fund (DREDF) filled a national need for legal advocacy on disability issues similar to the gay rights movement's Lambda Legal and the NAACP's Legal Defense Fund.

Beginning in 1975, Megan Kirschbaum worked closely with her husband as a therapist in the peer counseling program. Simultaneously, she pursued her doctorate in clinical psychology. Over the course of seven years, she grew disheartened with how psychotherapists and family counselors in the community undervalued disabled children. They were hopelessly stuck on what she called "pathological in focus ... negative and objectifying of the disabled babies, rather than recognizing their strengths and individuality—their humanity."[11]

In the minds of deficit-fixated therapists, the stigma of the disabled child darkened their families. Counselors believed that the young child's "pathology tended to spread to the family system too, so that they would kind of look at the parents through a pathology lens too." The entire family system was viewed without awareness of robust human capabilities, powerful love, and supportive relationships. What they saw was weakness and incompetence.[12]

Similarly, she noticed that counselors assumed that disabled adults could not take care of their children. Disability rendered a person completely unable to become a loving and effective parent. Again, stigmatizing attitudes blocked most professionals from providing useful assistance.

The gap between Megan Kirschbaum's experience of the proud and capable disability community in the CIL and the counseling profession's undernourished view of disabled people and their families was alarming. How could counselors and family therapists offer respectful, validating, and helpful services to families of disabled children if they were trapped in depressing, misleading stereotypes?

This professional negativity hit home in 1978 when the Kirschbaums' baby was born with a heart defect that required numerous surgeries. Megan, Hal, and their son, Noah, entered a strange world of early childhood specialists who had no awareness of the rich and full lives of people living with disabilities. The only goal was "fixing the deficits and fixing the disability" before age three. The professionals engaged the family in a headlong, desperate race to achieve so-called normal functioning before preschool. After that mythical threshold, the "normal" life maps were lost. Disabled children and families descended into dangerous, unknown oceans filled with sea monsters and dragons.[13]

With a $5,000 March of Dimes grant and butterfly-filled stomach, Megan Kirschbaum launched Through the Looking Glass in a backyard cottage. Quickly, she added a second prong to the new organization's services, providing counseling to parents with disabilities. The general attitude among doctors, psychologists, and social workers was that disabled adults could not be effective, loving parents. In cases of divorce, the family courts often removed young children from the homes of disabled parents.

Through the Looking Glass injected the lived lessons of the CIL into the counseling profession. People who had disabilities could live fulfilling lives with their disability. They could be terrific mothers, fathers, sons, and daughters. This disability-positive approach allowed Kirschbaum's innovative agency to effectively assist thousands of parents, families, and children over decades.

Undoubtedly, the CIL offshoot with the greatest political influence was DREDF. The legal branch of the CIL was started by Bob Funk, a man who had a leg amputated after contracting leprosy while serving in the Peace Corps in Nigeria. He returned to earn a law degree at the University of California, Davis. His move to Berkeley to start a public interest law practice coincided with Health, Education, and Welfare secretary Joseph A. Califano, Jr.'s, 1977 signing of the

Section 504 regulations. Multiple branches of the federal government needed immediate assistance to provide training to rehabilitation workers and other professionals about the new rules prohibiting discrimination against disabled persons.

Funk wrote a series of hurried grant proposals. Every one came back funded. In late 1978, the Disability Law Resource Center (DLRC), the short-term precursor to DREDF, set up operations in an unfurnished warehouse—a crude space lawyer Arlene Mayerson said "looked like a prison"—in collaboration with Legal Services of Alameda County.[14]

Funk hired skilled directors for the two main programs. Mary Lou Breslin ran the Section 504 training project. She scrambled to put together a staff of four dozen lawyers and administrators in a few weeks. Arlene Mayerson supervised the legal services unit that provided representation to disabled people and parents of children with disabilities. Often Mayerson helped clients mount discrimination lawsuits under the new 504 statute.

Contracting polio as a chubby twelve-year-old growing up in Kentucky, Mary Lou Breslin went through physical rehabilitation at FDR's famous Warm Springs, Georgia, facility. The warmth and gentle beauty of the backwoods resort didn't feel like a hospital. The caring doctors and therapists helped her move past her initial fear and learn to take control of her life.

Breslin entered the University of Illinois in 1962, the same year Ed started at Cal, and discovered that the campus rehabilitation staff promoted the idea that an independent disabled person didn't require any assistance. Contrary to the Berkeley approach, at Illinois disabled students were not allowed to use personal attendants.

At Illinois, she befriended Kitty Cone to begin her political education. Breslin joined the Student Nonviolent Coordinating Committee (SNCC) to fight for African American civil rights. The two friends staged a freezing January antiwar protest, camping overnight outside the Chanute Air Force Base, a remote training center supporting the Minuteman ICBM program.

Across the western states, Breslin's legal team delivered training sessions about the practical uses of Section 504. With no experience and no materials, starting from scratch, they created a full curriculum. They taught disability community leaders and service professionals how to leverage the new federal law to defend disabled people against discrimination. Their curriculum was then distributed to 504 education units across the country.

Like a bell echoing in the distance long after it was rung, the Section 504 training project had far-reaching impact for many years. The education of over five thousand community leaders around the country fostered a widespread shift in solving the daily problems of exclusion experienced by disabled persons. They taught their communities how to view specific situations not in terms of what a disabled person was unable to do but in relation to the obstacles in the social and built environment.

For Breslin, this change was groundbreaking: "The problem is the inaccessible city hall, not that I can't walk up the steps. That basic shift—that's what we did. . . . 504 was a tool, a way of embodying that principle and giving it to people in a way that they could make it be personal and could use it. . . . 504 shifted their own thinking." Disability activists, local community members, and government personnel learned that Section 504 meant a radical change in mindset.[15]

Her program also seeded the nation with political activists. The hundreds of 504 training groups became a useful network of knowledgeable advocates. In the following years, as DREDF defended Section 504 and later worked on the development of the ADA, they repeatedly called on this grassroots network to pressure federal leaders.[16]

Arlene Mayerson was a nondisabled woman who grew up in a conservative, loving Jewish family in Cincinnati. At Boston Univer-

sity, her tight-laced world exploded in the protests and cultural upheaval of the late 1960s. After graduation, she cofounded a small legal assistance center in a poor district of Boston. She was impressed
by the many dedicated community workers supporting disenfranchised residents of low-income neighborhoods. They advised her to
go to law school and specialize in public interest law to make a difference at a larger level.

After graduating from Boalt Law School at UC, Berkeley, she in-
terned with Judge W. Arthur Garrity to enforce the contentious racial
desegregation of Boston schools. After doing a public interest law fellowship at Georgetown University, she brought her keen civil rights
mind to the CIL.

The young attorney discovered that Bob Funk, her supervisor,
had a "management style (of) basically finding talented people that
he could then leave alone." With virtually no guidance and no desk,
charting out a new field of disability law with few case precedents,
Mayerson flourished. Pioneering the practice of disability advocacy
law without professional role models and forebears to follow, she became a national leader.

In her first case, Mayerson represented parents of children with
disabilities battling public schools over the implementation of the
1975 Education for All Handicapped Children Act. The new special
education law specifically required schools to provide students with
needed physical or occupational therapy. Many California schools
outsourced this professional work to medical agencies that didn't believe the students needed the therapies. Mayerson and the parents
negotiated directly with federal Department of Education officials,
who in turn threatened to withhold millions in California education
funds. The California Department of Education quickly arranged for
the mandated services for children.[17]

Bob Funk's office phone rang with hundreds of inquiries from
across the country. Disabled people and parents of children with

disabilities needed legal and legislative assistance. The necessity of a national legal defense group focusing on disability issues quickly became evident. There were national legal organizations supporting the rights of African Americans, women, the LGBT community, and Mexican Americans, but none related to disability. Leaving the CIL in 1979, DREDF went on to provide national leadership on the law and advocacy for disabled citizens.[18]

Key to the future success of DREDF was the addition of the cogent, forceful legal advocate named Patrisha Wright. After suffering a severe head injury as a teen, Wright remained unconscious for six weeks. When she came to, she had amnesia and an unrelenting case of double vision.

Wright was a sharp, incisive thinker with a knack for firm persuasion who became the top DREDF legal strategist. She and Mayerson made a good one-two punch. Mayerson was the behind-the-scenes legal workhorse that Wright called the "secret weapon" of the movement. As her teammate composed exhaustive legal analyses and rallied the disability community to pummel the White House with thousands of letters, Wright scoped out the battlefield and directed the multidimensional assault. Her colleagues rightly dubbed her "the General."[19]

When President Ronald Reagan took office in 1981, his central mission was to downsize the federal government, shrinking social service programs he mocked as "the schemes of do-gooders." The twin evils of Soviet communism abroad and the federal government at home were coupled in Reagan's mind as a threat to Americans' freedom. He set up a task force chaired by Vice President George H. W. Bush, dedicated to weakening government programs by reducing regulations.[20]

Insider information was leaked to the Berkeley crew, warning that Section 504 was in the White House's crosshairs. The DREDF team responded by setting up a Washington, DC, office to monitor the Bush task force. They shared space with Evan Kemp, a disability rights attorney who just so happened to enjoy playing cards with C. Boyden Gray, the vice president's legal counsel. Wright and Mayerson used this personal connection to win over Gray. He facilitated their access to top federal agency directors and White House advisors, including Bradford Reynolds, the Civil Rights Division leader widely viewed as obstructing civil rights laws enforcement.

The DREDF leaders funneled a series of disability advocates into powerful, often very personal conversations with Reagan administration executives. Ron Mace, a disabled North Carolinian who innovated a new field of accessible architecture based on universal design concepts, made very persuasive arguments. The combination of personal stories of living with a disability and expertise on the practical applications of Section 504 convinced the Reagan brain trust to back off.

Equally important, DREDF established close relationships within Vice President Bush's inner circle. The Berkeley radicals, typically more comfortable collaborating with liberal Democrats, built trusted connections to high-ranking Republicans. When George H. W. Bush won the 1988 presidential election, an unlikely Texan named Justin Dart, Jr., saw an opening to augment Section 504 with bolder, more comprehensive nondiscrimination law. Driven by the vehement legal mind of Pat Wright, DREDF would provide pivotal leadership in the creation of the Americans with Disabilities Act.[21]

. . .

During Ed's time as director, the CIL prospered greatly due to the power of solidarity. The CIL was a place where disabled people united, often for the first time.

But the racial nature of that unity was problematic. In an East Bay community with a sizable African American population, the CIL was almost exclusively white.

Ed and other movement leaders were keenly aware that the warm embrace that disabled people gave to one another through the CIL largely stopped at racial lines. This wasn't new. The PDSP and the CIL grew out of the experiences of white students attending a state university with very few students of color. They mostly employed and served white people.[22]

Despite Berkeley's reputation as a liberal city, it had a mixed record on race relations. In the early 1960s, due to the influx of African Americans from the South to the Bay Area, about 20 percent of Berkeley residents were Black. But the neighborhoods were basically segregated. White residents lived in the more affluent hills. Black families often resided in the lower income flatlands.

In 1963, Berkeley voters rejected a proposed ordinance barring racial discrimination in housing sales and rentals. When the school board voted the following year to desegregate the public schools, angry conservative parents nearly recalled the four liberal board members.

The Berkeley school district was the first in the country to institute a racial desegregation plan without a court order. But a central factor in the success of the plan was white flight out of the district. The plodding four-year planning process allowed white parents who opposed integration plenty of time to move away.[23]

During the first seven years of Dr. Bruyn's Cowell program, all the students were white. Billy Barner, paralyzed by a football injury, was the first African American resident of Cowell Hospital in 1969. When Barner arrived, it didn't take long for him to feel like a member of the group. He enjoyed cherished friendships with Cowell residents and shared in the fun. Later he recalled, "The people were so nice. It was like it was a home away from home."

Barner's integration came at a price. If he won a game of pool or took the big cash pot on poker night, the white disabled students teased him, saying his prize was a watermelon. Gracefully, Barner laughed it off. Maintaining important relationships with the other disabled students required that he downplay the racist jabs and keep an upbeat attitude.

Despite the bigoted jokes, Barner viewed himself as more accepted by the disabled students than by the community of African American students at large. One day, he noticed a cluster of six African American women talking together on campus. Assuming a racial connection, he rolled his wheelchair up to join the conversation. Visibly uncomfortable, the women made quick excuses and scurried away.[24]

Johnnie Lacy, an African American woman with a physical disability who later worked for the CIL and headed up an independent living center in Hayward, had a similar experience at San Francisco State. Other African American students often viewed her as "mindless, worthless" due to her disability, a "belief [that] cancels out the black identity they share with a disabled black person." Her disability effectively disqualified her from her Black identity.[25]

As a CIL staff member, Lacey felt a depressing level of condescension from white colleagues. Despite her college degree and strong background working in antipoverty programs, they openly called her a "token," an unqualified person hired only to meet a racial quota.[26]

In the early years of the CIL, the overwhelming emphasis on solidarity among disabled people, stretching across different types of impairments, pushed racial equity concerns to the back burner. When staff members brought these criticisms to Ed, he struggled to give them full attention. He viewed the unity of people with disabilities as the greatest priority. The new movement could fall off the rails if the Berkeley disability alliance fractured.

Ed teamed with two thoughtful African American leaders, Don Galloway and Brad Lomax, to improve race relations. Their efforts met with modest success.

Galloway grew up in a large, caring family on Chesapeake Bay, Maryland. When an arrow struck his eye at age thirteen, local physicians refused to treat a Black patient. Two prestigious university medical centers, Johns Hopkins and Duke, turned him away. A serious infection developed, and he ended up losing vision in both eyes.

He attended the Maryland School for the Blind, a rural residential campus divided into two parallel tracks based on race. He learned how to read and write in Braille. He also learned how to weave fabric and use hand tools.

Although Galloway and his classmates accidentally walked into light poles on the sidewalks of Baltimore, they weren't taught to use a cane. The school administration held the widespread belief that white canes further stigmatized blind people by serving as an obvious public symbol of impairment. Disability was to be hidden.

After junior high school, Galloway's family moved to Los Angeles. He was mainstreamed into general classes at a racially integrated high school. He received an unusual education on both racial and disability civil rights by leading local chapters of the National Association for the Advancement of Colored People (NAACP) and the National Federation of the Blind (NFB).[27]

After earning a master's degree in social work at the University of California, San Diego, Galloway moved north. He heard about an innovative cross-disability services outfit running in Berkeley. Blind persons were accustomed to receiving assistance from the Lighthouse for the Blind in San Francisco or the Orientation Center for the Blind in Albany. As Professor Jacobus tenBroek had advised Ed Roberts years earlier, the blind community didn't necessarily want to be integrated with other disability groups. Drawing from his background in both racial and disability politics, Galloway saw merit in cross-disability alliances.

Galloway recruited blind people from the community to get involved in the CIL. His approach was just right. Many blind persons felt a strong loyalty to the NFB and their own disability-specific community. The NFB company line warned them to avoid affiliation with a cross-disability group like the CIL. Galloway smartly counseled people to have it both ways, maintaining strong ties to the NFB while also participating in the CIL's exciting multidisability activism.

Galloway dramatically raised the numbers of blind persons working for and receiving services from the CIL. He effectively turned the center into a coalition of persons with visual and physical impairments.

Unifying different races was a much harder task. He organized the handful of African American CIL employees and clients into a Black caucus. His request that the CIL board formally recognize the caucus found no support. Ed and Phil Draper opposed any policies that might split the disability community. They believed that total unity was required for the organization to stand for rights of all people with disabilities.[28]

Ed recognized the legitimacy of the racial concerns Don Galloway articulated. The two men worked together to improve outreach to the Black community. They hired more African American staff members, including Ron Washington, a gay disabled man who coordinated outreach to predominantly African American neighborhoods in Oakland.

The lack of a strong relationship between the CIL and the people of nearby Oakland, the national home of the Black Panther Party, reflected the racial division that marked the region. The man who took on the challenge was Brad Lomax.

The oldest of three siblings, Lomax grew up in Philadelphia. A 1963 summer trip to visit his mother's family in Alabama profoundly impacted his thinking. He was struck by the segregated restaurants and restrooms of the Jim Crow South.

While attending Howard University, Lomax suddenly struggled to walk. He lost balance and fell down. Diagnosed with multiple sclerosis, within months he was using a wheelchair.

He then experienced a prejudice both new and oddly familiar. Like Galloway, Lomax became a rare, insightful person who understood the similarities of two forms of oppression, how ignorance and cruelty diminished both disabled persons and African Americans.

At first, his political activities focused solely on battling racism. In Washington, DC, Lomax was one of the founders of the local chapter of the Black Panthers. In 1972 he helped organize African Liberation Day, a march by tens of thousands to the National Mall in solidarity with the efforts of African nations to gain independence from colonial powers.

Lomax moved to the Bay Area and took a job with the Black Panthers health clinic in Oakland. He arrived at the time when the national party was declining but the Oakland branch flourished.

In 1973, Black Panthers leader Huey Newton appointed Elaine Brown, a dynamic woman who had served as minister of information, as his number two. When Newton was indicted for murder, he fled to Cuba. Brown became party chairwoman in August 1974 and held the position for nearly three years. She expanded the array of high-quality human services—meal programs, preschools, and healthcare—in the Oakland area. Under her watch, the Panthers' elementary school won a state award for academic excellence.

Fierce but also politically shrewd, Brown traded the standard party tactics of macho strength for what she called "the softness of the times." Her approach was pragmatic and relational, including mainstream alliances with liberal Democrats. She campaigned for Democrat Jerry Brown for governor. She ran for Oakland City Council in 1975. Securing the support of the leading workers' unions, she scored a remarkable 44 percent of the vote in a solidly Republican town.[29]

As a client at the Berkeley CIL, Lomax befriended Ed Roberts and Don Galloway. The two African American men compared notes on the work of the CIL and the needs of disabled people in the Black community. Lomax was concerned about the disabled population of Oakland, who received no independent living services. He pitched a proposal to Elaine Brown to sponsor an Oakland branch of the Berkeley CIL. The healthcare programs provided by the Black Panthers did not assist disabled people with independent living. Lomax explained this unmet need to Brown, and he offered himself as a bridge between the Panthers and the predominantly white CIL.

Galloway and Lomax organized a series of meetings between the Black power firebrand Brown and the disability rights troubadour Roberts. Ed and Elaine Brown shared a keen ability to simultaneously work at the local level while understanding how their operations fit within the broader minority politics of diverse America. Both saw Lomax's proposal as a rare opportunity for two unrelated rights groups to support one another.

The CIL branch office in Oakland opened in a small storefront. Brad Lomax and a single staff member provided services such as peer counseling, attendant referral, and housing assistance.

The Oakland independent living center project was short lived. Ron Washington viewed the collaboration between the two organizations as conflict-ridden. Each organization wanted control. He believed that the Black Panthers were ultimately more interested in the new flow of dollars from the CIL than in the disability rights cause.[30]

When Brown resigned her position as Black Panthers leader in 1977, the Lomax storefront center folded. Neither the Black Panthers nor the Berkeley disability rights community developed enough investment in the goals of the other to keep the office running. Johnnie Lacy believed that the CIL leaders had good intentions but little knowledge. Even though they tried to conduct outreach into African American communities, "they didn't know how, and the mistake they made was they never learned how."[31]

The ambitious bridges that Ed, Don Galloway, and Brad Lomax built between the CIL and the African American community weren't resilient enough to overcome the deep racial divisions of the East Bay. Although numerous people of color played vital roles in the Berkeley disability community and the growing movement, and both Ed and Judy Heumann quite consciously built connections with African American civil rights groups, it was undeniable that disability rights was a predominantly white project.[32]

. . .

The CIL, and the movement in general, also struggled with persistent gender inequities. Mary Lester, a nondisabled woman who started as CIL receptionist and later became a successful grant writer, observed, "I know a lot of women felt that there was a lot of sexism at CIL in the power structure." Beginning in the Cowell Hospital days, men like Ed Roberts, John Hessler, and Hale Zukas ran the show. While the men held the top jobs, a legion of talented, ferocious women largely comprised the working engine of the movement.

Charges of sexism in grassroots civil rights activities weren't new. In 1964, Mary King, a volunteer with the Student Nonviolent Coordinating Committee (SNCC), cautiously wrote an anonymous position paper detailing the group's tendency to allocate major decisions to the men. Arising out of the many sit-in protests involving African American college students in the South, SNCC organized the 1964 Freedom Summer. They recruited hundreds of northern college students to work with local activists registering Black voters in Mississippi. When the scorched station wagon used by three young men—two white students from New York and a local Black activist—was found in the Bogue Chitto Swamp, national news reports narrated the seven-week search that ended with the discovery of their buried bodies.[33]

Many young people found the deeply egalitarian, interracial SNCC experience exhilarating. Organic, democratic processes of dialogue involved long sessions of consensus-building that erased common hierarchies of race and gender. With deliberate intentionality, SNCC leaders equally valued the talents and contributions of white and Black staff members. But still, as Mary King carefully documented, the project leaders were disproportionately men, and the clerical and cleaning tasks typically fell to the subordinate women. SNCC leader Stokely Carmichael mocked King's feminist analysis with a crude joke, "The only position for women in SNCC is prone."[34]

Similarly, gender disparities blemished the Students for a Democratic Society (SDS), a leading organization of the predominantly white New Left. Within the group that opposed the Vietnam War and organized poor people for economic justice, intense debates over issues featured authoritative male voices. The oft-silent women organized the meetings, ran mimeograph machines, and swept the office floors.

In November 1965, SDS member Mary Hayden authored "A Kind of Memo," a parallel to Mary King's SNCC leaflet, raising concerns about the diminished role of women in the movement. Her groundbreaking insights circulated widely among activist women, suddenly bringing to consciousness feelings and concerns previously dormant and unacknowledged. When SDS men brushed aside their criticisms, many talented feminists left the SDS to devote themselves to women's rights.[35]

Ed did little to address charges of sexual discrimination in the CIL. The feminism-rich Berkeley environment and his childhood experiences with his mother informed his thinking. But he didn't take specific steps to ameliorate the CIL's gender bias.

The talented women of the CIL took their lumps, soldiered on, and often thrived. The CIL's loose organizational ethos lacked traditional lines of supervision and accountability that might constrain creativity or initiative. It was, in Judy Heumann's words, "a very grass rootsy kind of place." Corbett O'Toole described it as "a very free-flowing environment [that] allowed a lot of things to happen." In a power vacuum, an assertive person with a big idea could rally together a few hardworking friends to launch a new initiative.

Numerous women created their own leadership roles by developing groundbreaking projects. Janet McEwen Brown turned *The Independent*, the CIL's regular newsletter, into the first journalistic voice of the disability rights movement. Corbette O'Toole, Jackie Brand, and Nancy Thomas developed the Keys to Introducing Disability in the Schools (KIDS) project, fostering inclusion in public schools by teaching lessons to nondisabled children about a variety of different disabilities. When Ed left the CIL director's position in 1975, Judy Heumann became the assistant director and lead strategist.[36]

Working under patriarchal constraints, suffering regular slights, the unsung women of the Berkeley disability activist community made a collective decision to remain dedicated to the movement. They were willing to work side by side with men who often didn't "get it" to maintain this unique solidarity among disabled people. As they became aware of the growth of independent living centers in Boston, Ann Arbor, and elsewhere, they believed strongly that their CIL was the necessary heart of the movement. Progress for millions of disabled Americans, in their Berkeley-centric view, rested fully on their shoulders. For many disabled women, even if it meant doing the "women's work" of taking the meeting minutes one more time, they stayed true to the cause.

15 *Across America*

During Ed's short eighteen months as director, the CIL gained national and international attention. Letters and phone calls for information came daily. Visitors toured regularly, including many from abroad. Numerous groups came from Japan, spending weeks learning the CIL model and practices. Just as Ed hoped, the Berkeley CIL became the prominent leader of independent living.[1]

Disability activists in Boston followed the Berkeley story closely. The radical political communities of the two cities already had close ties. Antiwar and civil rights advocates often traveled between the two progressive college towns, exchanging plans and ideas.[2]

In 1973, the Tufts University rehabilitation medicine program in Boston hired Fred Fay, a disabled man and psychologist, to run a national independent-living research project. He studied budding programs around the country, exploring the many variations of services as well as the challenges they faced.

Fay first learned about the CIL from Larry Biscamp. He was convinced that the Berkeley approach was a promising model for Boston. He liked that it was run by disabled people and provided many useful services for people with multiple disability types.

In late 1974, Fay called together the first national meeting of independent living leaders. He brought a dozen program developers and disability rights activists to Boston to compare notes. The group included Ed Roberts and Judy Heumann from Berkeley, Eunice Fiorito from New York, Lex Frieden from Houston, and Max Starkloff from St. Louis.[3]

Starkloff was the Ed Roberts of the Midwest. At age twenty-one, he was severely injured in a car accident. The young man spent twelve dreary years stuck in a nursing home. When he was finally liberated in 1973, Starkloff visited Ed at the Berkeley CIL. He told Ed about his plan to create "a self-contained facility where all of us could live and work together." Ed listened patiently to Starkloff's intention to build segregated housing for disabled people in St. Louis. Then he calmly but firmly replied, "That's not the way we do things here."

Ed gave Starkloff a tour of the CIL and taught him about independent living. The St. Louis activist returned home to create Paraquad, an independent living center built on the Berkeley model. He grew it into one of the largest, most comprehensive centers in the country.[4]

The leaders gathered in Boston agreed that independent living meant creating new arrangements for people with physical disabilities and other impairments to live on their own in the community. But Ed wanted a strong commitment from everyone to replicate the Berkeley CIL. He made a passionate pitch that the CIL should be the national exemplar for others to follow.[5]

Ed wanted to clone CILs like a chain store. Build one in every American community. A disabled person in Omaha or Pensacola or Bangor could benefit from the same empowering services with a feisty dose of activism. If Ed had his way, Uncle Sam's national rehabilitation system would pay the tab.

Although the leaders marveled at what the California activists had accomplished, they didn't necessarily believe they could or should follow Ed's lead. Independent living programs developing in the 1970s took a variety of shapes, often reflecting the local land-scape of government services and existing disability organizations.

Equally important was the fact that other cities simply didn't have what Berkeley had. Few cities had a tight-knit disability community. Often the very idea of disabled people unifying to fight for greater access to society was still novel. In many localities the launch of an independent living program was the initial impetus for disabled people to meet one another and begin building relationships. It was a starting point, not a culmination of years of prior advocacy work.

Most regions simply didn't have the countercultural political edge. The 1970s political environment in the Midwest and South was milquetoast mild. The battle-hardened traditions of political activism, including community organizing and public protests, that ran deep in Berkeley were absent in much of America.

Lex Frieden came away from the Boston meeting thinking that Ed's passionate vision was inspiring but completely impractical for Texas. He wasn't interested in a disability revolution overthrowing the dominant medical establishment that greatly controlled disabled people's lives. He wasn't waging war against pervasive attitudes and practices of disability discrimination. He was helping disabled people who would otherwise live in nursing homes gain a much-needed foothold in the community.

Although Frieden was a disabled man, he was also a professional rehabilitation psychologist who worked for the Texas Institute for Rehabilitation and Research (TIRR). He held a strong professional affiliation with the medical system.

As a freshman at Oklahoma State University in 1967, Frieden experienced a spinal cord injury in a car accident. He lost functioning in his legs, and he had limited use of his arms and hands.

After medical rehabilitation, he wanted to enroll at Oral Roberts University. The straight-A student was rejected because of his disability. Fortunately, the University of Tulsa saw his potential. The dean promised Frieden that his classes would be held in the newest, most accessible building on campus. He earned a degree in psychology and went on to graduate studies at the University of Houston.

Frieden was a rising star in the disability policy world. He would become a renowned rehabilitation researcher and one of the leading architects of the 1990 Americans with Disabilities Act. As part of President George H. W. Bush's Texas inner circle, he collaborated with the indefatigable Justin Dart, Jr., to pass the most sweeping disability rights legislation in American history. If there was a figure on the national disability scene in the 70s and 80s who matched Ed in vigor, intelligence, and influence, it was Frieden.

While Ed and the Berkeley crowd often didn't trust the nondisabled people who ran traditional disability-help groups, Frieden felt differently. He thought that the rehabilitation establishment supplied natural, trustworthy partners for disabled people. For Frieden, the key to success was adapting the disabled individual to the community environment. Independent living involved outfitting individuals with a set of useful life skills and then installing them into workable segments of the existing society.[6]

In Houston, he developed multiple apartment complexes for people with physical disabilities. Participants completed a six-week, live-in, independent living skills training program focusing on personal adjustment. The program taught disabled people "subjects such as financial management, consumer affairs, living arrangements, functional skills, mobility, sexuality, homemaking skills, vocational-educational opportunities, medical needs, and social skills."[7]

The politically benign Texas model of independent living services appealed greatly to the rehabilitation professionals. Frieden did not criticize doctors or rehabilitation workers for their failures to understand and support disabled people. They were invited to partner with disabled people in a fresh collaboration.

He reassured professionals that even though independent living programs often had "a sort of grass roots, down-to-earth character," they were not "political action groups." This wasn't a rebellion. His tame definition fit comfortably into the profession's identity as knowledgeable helpers teaching disabled people useful attitudes and skills. Rehabilitation professionals were still in control.[8]

Frieden established TIRR as the national academic hub for independent living research and consultation. Over the next decade, he became the leading American voice on independent living within medical and rehabilitation circles. For the many who wanted independent living without the radical, confrontational politics of Berkeley, Frieden was their man.[9]

A month after that first Boston conference, Heumann, Frieden, and Fiorito held a follow-up meeting to create a national, cross-disability organization to represent all disabled Americans. Working with John Lancaster of the Paralyzed Veterans of America and Fred Schreiber of the National Association for the Deaf, they founded the American Coalition of Citizens with Disabilities (ACCD). Fiorito and a D/deaf American studies scholar named Frank Bowe became the leaders.[10]

Ed didn't join. Uniting people with a variety of disabilities together was his goal. But he viewed the Berkeley CIL as the mechanism for this political work. He wanted to be the leader. He also didn't feel like working with Frieden, a man he was beginning to view as a rival.[11]

Returning from Fred Fay's Boston meeting, Ed felt concerned about what he viewed as watered-down versions of independent living. Particularly troubling was Frieden's Texas model that seemed to minimize the discrimination experienced by disabled people. It gave the unwanted message that segregated housing was acceptable. It left out the crucial role of an independent living center as a political organization fighting for disabled people's rights. Political advocacy and activism, in Ed's thinking, had to be central to the movement.

Ed consulted with Regional Rehabilitation director Herb Leibowitz about how to maximize the national impact of the CIL. He wanted the Berkeley CIL to be known as the holy grail of independent living, spreading the word from Berkeley outward to develop similar centers everywhere.

Leibowitz was Ed's insightful informant and teammate inside the national rehabilitation system. He understood the rehabilitation professionals and what it would take for Ed's ideas to gain their support. The federal regional leaders, those holding positions like Leibowitz, were very intrigued. Experimentation was part of their job description.

But the more influential state directors of rehabilitation were skeptical of the Berkeley approach. They feared losing a chunk of their federal dollars to a national chain of CILs. Many thought that the consumer-led programs weren't really doing rehabilitation because they were run by disabled people and the services often had little to do with employment.

Ed and Herb Leibowitz decided to shine the spotlight on the Berkeley CIL by holding the first national conference on independent living. In October 1975, they hosted fifty leading figures at the Claremont Hotel in Berkeley for three days of presentations and discussions.

Further elevating Ed and the CIL, the big meeting occurred only a week after Ed got the word that he would be the next director of the California Department of Rehabilitation. The timing was perfect. He was about to become the highest profile disabled person in America running the country's biggest disability service outfit.

Invited conference participants included cutting-edge academics, carefully selected state rehabilitation directors, and leaders of independent living programs. Vaunting the success of the Berkeley CIL were Judy Heumann, Don Galloway, and Jeff Moyer, a speaking lineup of leaders with physical disabilities and blindness.

The most influential conferee was Miriam Stubbs, the longtime right-hand assistant of Mary Switzer, the celebrated matriarch of American rehabilitation. As the federal head of vocational rehabilitation throughout the 1950s and 60s, the iconic Switzer dramatically expanded the funding and reach of her federal agency. She was also an avid, vocal supporter of independent living services. Stubbs's presence showered Switzer's symbolic blessing on the proceedings.

Selected as the highest preacher of the CIL gospel to the audience was Hale Zukas. He was the perfect spokesperson.

It was too easy to underestimate Zukas. Atop his rambling brown hair rested a plastic ring cap with a foot-long steel rod jutting forward. He used the head wand to turn book pages and select letters on a communication board. His caustic humor and deep insights were cloaked in an unusual articulation style. Listeners who knew him well understood every snappy syllable. Others leaned in, tilted their heads, and sifted through his utterances with intense concentration.

From his electric wheelchair, Zukas presented a full lesson on the power and effectiveness of the Berkeley model. First he narrated the history of the Berkeley CIL, from the Cowell Hospital days to the development of the PDSP and the initiation of the CIL. Then he expounded the potent mixture of advocacy, support services, and vocational training under one roof.

The CIL housed fourteen service areas, four advanced education and vocational training programs including a graduate degree program, and four business ventures yielding revenue. What might seem like a down-at-the-heel, hippy crash pad to the casual observer was, in Zukas's authoritative description, a well-designed, highly effective enterprise with an incredible wingspan.

A CIL client could hire personal attendants, apply for government benefits, find a job, rent an accessible apartment, learn adaptive technologies, receive peer counseling, locate accessible recreation opportunities, catch a ride anywhere in the East Bay, earn a master's degree, and get their wheelchair repaired.

The self-help agency was also a gutsy political alliance. The community affairs department kept close tabs on all local, state, and federal policy developments and mobilized the disability community to take effective action. Road trips to Sacramento to quietly advise or loudly protest state government decisions happened regularly.

The CIL's quarterly magazine *The Independent*, capably run by Jan McEwen, had a national circulation of seven thousand copies. CIL researchers funded by a large federal grant collected data on the effectiveness of peer counseling. The computer training project, working in conjunction with IBM and other corporations, taught disabled people programming skills leading to job placements.

No observer on that day could ignore the fact that Zukas was the very person with a severe disability that rehabilitation systems habitually excluded. An average person meeting Zukas would expect very little of him. His words—eloquent and expressive, comprehensive and articulate—exposed this foolish miscalculation. No one could doubt the overwhelming intelligence of this CIL spokesperson. No one could doubt the incredible breadth and success of the CIL.

Despite the careful staging and powerful presentation, the CIL's preeminence didn't fly without serious challenge. The most impressive and troubling alternative to the Berkeley approach came from the eloquent Lex Frieden. The Texan brimmed with the confidence and analytic vigor of a mature college professor.

In his presentation, Frieden tapped themes familiar to the Berkeley activists. A person with a severe disability should live in "an environment free of physical and social barriers" and be supported by "reliable and sufficient attendant care." They must have "an opportunity to manifest his independence by choosing his own course," controlling the living environment and making the most important life decisions.

But then he wandered into forbidden terrain, expressing support for segregation. A person with a severe disability "may need to be institutionalized during some times in his life," perhaps in "group residential settings." The halfway house concept that the Rolling Quads had resoundingly rejected emerged in Frieden's presentation as useful.

The main problem that Frieden confronted in Houston was the lack of available personal attendants. In Berkeley, the PDSP and the CIL had solved this issue by recruiting and training large numbers of workers to provide personal care. California had funded in-home care services for disabled and elderly persons since the 1950s. In Texas there was no state personal assistance funding scheme and no organization helping people find qualified attendants.

By Frieden's calculations, the most efficient way to share a small pool of attendants was to group disabled people together in segregated housing units. He gave multiple examples of this independent living model in Houston. One accessible apartment housed thirty disabled residents. Another accommodated twenty-four. In a large complex, a wing was set aside for eleven disabled tenants.[12]

Ed worried about the toxic presence of segregation in independent living programs. In a speech a few months later, he concluded definitively, "Segregation in and of itself has been one of the most devastating things that disabled people could have experienced."[13]

Although Ed and Lex Frieden collaborated as leading figures in the disability rights movement for years to come, Ed was not able to change his colleague's mind. The two main models of independent living, Berkeley and Texas, clashed just as the two men and their cultures did.

Ed waved the Berkeley freak flag. His thinking about disabled people's independence took shape in the Berkeley crucible of countercultural and political revolution. His mother, Zona, taught him how to fight against the oppressors. His father taught him the necessity of having a good union behind you. Berkeley brought it all together as Ed built solidarity with his disabled friends in a one-of-a-kind activist union battling for their rights.

The Berkeley approach was angry and idealistic. Authority figures hid their corruption and dehumanizing attitudes behind tall sentences and neat suits. The ragtag people of the streets and the marginalized minority groups could see what The Man was doing behind the curtain. They knew that the downtrodden and the excluded had to unite to fight back. The only way forward was to organize and struggle to remake society. Ed demanded integration immediately. Anything less was a compromise that would continue to harm and devalue disabled people.

Lex Frieden came from a different world. He carried the mid-America banner of common decency and reasonableness. The Texas approach was calm and measured. The authority figures, political structures, and social conventions that kept society rolling along were trustworthy and valuable. Disabled people merely needed a way to enter and subsist in the community. It was just a matter of finding doable ways to add disabled people into the existing mix.

Frieden gained confidence as young man under the supportive mentorship of nondisabled rehabilitation researchers in Houston. He learned that independent living was a promising new area of rehabilitation work that extended his profession to meet the everyday needs of disabled people.

He sought gradual, incremental change without a larger political project. His rehabilitation center program trained the disabled individual in an independent living curriculum that any rehabilitation professional could support. Integration occurred through transitional housing arrangements that prepared people to make it in the larger community. In the eyes of rehabilitation leaders and many government officials, it was entirely sensible.

The split between Ed Roberts and Lex Frieden and their conflicting views of independent living represented a political division among early disability rights activists that corresponded with similar rifts in other civil rights communities. In the movements for African American civil rights, LGBT rights, as well as the women's movement, schisms developed between leftists seeking liberation and moderates espousing a milder brand of assimilation. Liberation factions viewed their project in radical terms, requiring a dramatic reconstruction of economic and political institutions undergirding society. Assimilation blocs sought basic access into mainstream society, entry to the playing field without significantly changing the game itself.

In the LGBT movement of the early 1970s, the older homophile organizations—the Mattachine Society and the Daughters of Bilitis—bickered with the more militant new organizations over goals and strategies. The old guard preached respectability and conventionality, discipline and discretion. Polite, deferential negotiations with the police and politicians were the best course of action.

Wearing blue jeans and shaggy hair, the youthful and disorganized Gay Liberation Front (GLF) and their more focused offshoot the Gay Activists Alliance (GAA) adopted the confrontational street demonstration tactics of the antiwar activists. They engaged in "zaps," carefully planned, highly theatrical performances publicly spoofing politicians like New York mayor John Lindsay and Greenwich city councilor Carol Greitzer. When Lindsay hosted a high society reception at the Metropolitan Museum, GAA protester Marty Robinson snatched the microphone from Lindsay's hands and insisted, "I want to know when you intend to speak out on homosexual rights." After three dozen shouting GAA members drowned out councilwoman Greitzer's speech at the Village Independent Democrats Club, she wearily agreed to sponsor their city antidiscrimination bill.[14]

In the women's movement of the late 1970s, Betty Friedan and NOW were the disciplined veterans disrupted by the younger, insurgent women's liberation movement. NOW meetings raged into ear-splitting shouting matches as the grassroots, alternative culture youth upset the orderly proceedings they viewed as stodgy and meek. Historian Ruth Rosen has described the schism as a conflict between pragmatic moderates who "wanted a piece of the pie" and theatrical idealists who demanded "entirely new ingredients."[15]

In the early 1970s, Ed was more of a new-ingredients kind of leader, staying true to his Berkeley leftist roots by holding a firm full-inclusion party line. He felt that the CIL's approach to independent living was superior to less overtly political alternatives. Smuggling disabled people under the unattended edges of the tent was a strategy too deferential for his rebellious sensibilities. His experiences with the Rolling Quads and the CIL, as well as his graduate studies in political science at Cal, taught him that remaking the foundational institutions of American society—social, economic, and political—were necessary for disabled people to participate fully and thrive.

In the decades to come, he wouldn't remain a political purist. Over the course of his career, he gravitated toward pragmatism, pursuing moderate and radical avenues simultaneously. His heart cherished his rancorous Berkeley roots. But he discovered that every town in California or the United States wasn't militant Berkeley. And the fiery counterculture of the 1960s pretty much fizzled out by the mid-1970s. In the years to come, much like his rival Lex Frieden, Ed would come to value every opportunity for any disabled person to taste the American pie.

·　·　·

In 1975, Ed dedicated himself wholly to selling the Berkeley model. For part two of his effort collaborating with Herb Leibowitz, they invited the directors of the federal rehabilitation regional centers to the CIL. Joe Owens, the national head of the Council of State Administrators of Vocational Rehabilitation (CSAVR), the association of the state rehabilitation leaders, joined the meeting.

Realizing these esteemed leaders would soon be his professional colleagues, Ed invited them to tour the CIL, followed by an evening reception. The ambitious goal was to convince them of what Leibowitz already believed. The CIL was the future of rehabilitation.

In a meeting with the staff, CIL administrator Phil Draper pleaded, "Be on your best behavior." The visiting men were mild-mannered, middle-aged functionaries in moderately priced Woolworth suits. They were churchgoing white bureaucrats in polyester ties who had never experienced anything like Berkeley. Draper tried to slap lipstick on the hippy pig.[16]

The CIL's true colors weren't easily concealed. During the reception, staffers Wally Whalen and Jeff Moyer slipped out back to smoke a joint. Just as many American workplaces featured caffeine as the breaktime brain booster, marijuana was the go-to mood enhancer among the CIL staff. The two men desperately needed a break from the stifling propriety. Wally slunk his wheelchair behind a van in the parking lot. Jeff ducked down next to his friend, and they passed the smoke back and forth.

Wally flipped the release valve on the bag of urine attached to his leg. A catheter tube ran down to the bag. He needed to empty it periodically.

The yellow stream flowed slowly down a paved slope, across the parking lot to the front of the building. By the time Wally and Jeff finished the spliff, the urine had pooled by the CIL entrance. The elegant red carpet for the gathering of rehabilitation dignitaries was a puddle of Wally Whalen's piss.

The rehabilitation leaders came away impressed by what they learned about the CIL. But was it replicable? A hairy bunch of disabled beatniks working out of a rundown garage spouted high-minded talk about revolution. They were undoubtedly helping disabled people in the local community. But was this really a new kind of rehabilitation that could be exported to meat and potatoes America?

16 *Revolution in Sacramento*

The acclaimed British theater, television, and film actress Lisa Harrow once described Ed as the sexiest man she had ever met. She and her husband, the whale biologist Roger Payne, enjoyed taking in Broadway shows and meandering joyfully down the busy city streets with Ed in the late 1980s. Earlier in her career, tabloids linked her to the most sought-after leading men of Hollywood. Of all these, it was Ed who made her bread rise.[1]

Ed was a consummate, unrepentant flirt. He actively sought out women—tall, short, thin, wide. Their reactions to his forwardness varied. Often his warm eyes and reassuring tone melted their hearts. Other times, his too-much Rat Pack schtick met with groans of sexism.[2]

His attitudes toward women were contradictory. Deeply influenced by feminists, including his mother, Zona, the forward-thinking progressive leader often exhibited the incognizant flirty coarseness of a 1950s dance hall skirt-chaser. The feminist wave that grew around him in Berkeley impacted his ideas about civil rights and justice. But sometimes his rakish come-ons came off like stale leftovers from his father's generation.

One woman who found his self-assured playfulness alluring was a young occupational therapist at Fairmont Hospital in San Leandro. She attempted unsuccessfully to teach Ed how to feed himself with a knife and fork. Ed foolishly thought he would give occupational therapy one more try. It was a complete bust. But he returned eagerly each week because of Catherine, the attractive therapist who made ineffective rehabilitation completely worthwhile.

Almost a decade Ed's junior, Cathy Dugan was a tall, willowy, dark-haired beauty. She was a quiet young woman of little self-confidence who carried herself with a sweet demeanor. She was swept up in Ed's charm but also his powerful confidence. He spoke with the self-importance and high ideals of an ambitious politician mapping a promising future. He was like a young Franklin Delano Roosevelt in the years before he became governor of New York, a disabled man of evident brilliance who would surely leap to great heights. Caught in Ed's rising tide, Cathy adored him.

In Ed's CIL office, Cathy spent many days sitting at his feet, reading books beneath his desk shelf as he took meetings and made phone calls. Officially, Ed hired her as an occupational therapy consultant. But it wasn't clear to the CIL staff what project she was working on.[3]

Ed didn't question why a woman was content to spend the day beneath his feet. He had hoped to find such a woman, attractive and attentive. He was too thrilled by the prospects of a romantic relationship to search for flaws.

He was also elated that Cathy felt sexually attracted to him. The wheezing mechanism of the respirator tank was no turn-off. Cathy crawled inside the iron lung, venturing where no nondisabled person had dared go. Inside the lung the two enjoyed making love. For all of Ed's satisfaction sleeping in the tank, he likely had never imagined a sexual partner keen on climbing inside.

Since the day he drove his first Motorette down the Cowell Hospital hallways, Ed dreamed of finding a loving partner. It finally came true with Cathy.[4]

· · ·

Just when all seemed impossibly wonderful, more good fortune arrived. Jeff Moyer and Ed were hanging out at the CIL when the phone rang.

"Uh-huh. Uh-huh," Ed's face widened into an enormous grin. "Yes, of course. Thank you." He shouted to his friend, "Let's get out of here. I'm the new state director of rehab!"

Taking office in January 1975, Governor Jerry Brown hired Ed as the head of the California Department of Rehabilitation. He was the first person with a severe disability to lead a state rehabilitation agency. It was the largest department in the nation.

Moyer and Ed drove to Zona's house. Settling comfortably into the big tank, Ed breathed deeply. His face tilted up to view his friend. The two buddies shared a celebratory joint and joked about the incredible things Ed could accomplish in Sacramento.

"Most important," Ed proclaimed, "is ending this creaming crap. Too many people have been neglected. No more!"

"You have to tell the rehab employees on day one what your beliefs are," insisted Moyers.

"Yes," Ed agreed. "Put it right out front from the start."

"An official pronouncement from on high," Moyer jested, speaking with regal authority. He pretended he was reading a royal parchment scroll. "To all rehabilitation counselors. Starting immediately if not sooner, no more creaming crap!" The two friends snickered.

Moyer continued, "This official action stops the practice of creaming whereby only those with mild dis—"

"Less severe," Ed chimed in.

"—less severe disabilities are helped. This resulted in high statistics—"

"—high statistics, fake statistics," Ed picked up, "about the number of rehabilitations achieved. Hey, Jeff, write this down."

Moyer grabbed a pen and paper, and the two worked together on the first public communication from Ed's office. For two half-stoned men goofing around, the tone was surprisingly direct and demanding. "Severely disabled were excluded from service because their cases were considered more difficult and costly. This has to change."

The final line spoke directly to the frontline rehabilitation workers who qualified clients for services. "It will be necessary for counselors to broaden their concept of who has a reasonable expectation of being rehabilitated." From day one, Ed would be no line-toeing Babbitt. He would completely change rehabilitation in California.[5]

Governor Jerry Brown was the right boss for Ed's big plans. He was an iconoclastic liberal with a penchant for poking the buzzing beehive with a big stick. If Governor Ronald Reagan's nostalgic idea had been to restore California to a past when time-honored institutions held strong, Brown wanted to jump-start a self-serving government that had been out of touch with the citizens.

He injected civil rights purpose into bureaucratic government departments by selecting community activists as leaders. He picked Mario Obledo, a leading Hispanic rights attorney and cofounder of the Mexican American Legal Defense and Educational Fund to run the Department of Health and Welfare. Obledo was the first Hispanic to lead a state agency. Brown handed the reins of the Health Department to Bob Gnaizda, the lawyer who teamed with Cesar Chavez and Dolores Huerta to fight for the rights of farmworkers and the poor.

Ed liked to tell a perhaps tall tale about how he gained the governor's appointment. During Jerry Brown's election campaign, a group of Ed's friends attended a series of Brown events in the Bay Area. They filled the front row with their conspicuous wheelchairs. As Brown made his stump speech, they repeatedly chanted, "Ed Roberts! Ed Roberts!" Finally, the candidate asked one of his aides to find out who this Roberts guy was and set up a meeting with him.[6]

More truthfully, Brown asked Bob Gnaizda to recommend a new person to head up the state rehabilitation agency. Gnaizda visited the

Berkeley CIL. He came away impressed with Ed's ability to advocate for disabled people.

Gnaizda wholeheartedly recommended the disability rights activist to Governor Brown. But he quietly feared that Ed would be rejected in Sacramento because of his disability. The staid halls of state government politely favored conventional white men. Diversity in many forms was often viewed as unsettling by leaders who had very little awareness of their own prejudices.

Upsetting the too-comfortable applecart was Governor Brown's strategy. Ed was a natural choice. The new governor wanted California to be the national leader in rehabilitation. He had little idea what this meant in terms of policies, but he believed that Ed was the best bet to do this.[7]

When asked by a reporter about Ed's new job, a friend quipped: "It would tax your mind to the limits, what he's going to do. He's a militant, a radical. It's like appointing Mario Savio as head of a state department." Ed was just what the new governor wanted, a Cal Berkeley rabble-rouser ready to destroy the government's furniture.[8]

. . .

Delighted to have a romantic partner at his side, Ed brought Cathy with him to Sacramento. In the backyard of their small home, they created a simple wedding chapel with hanging rugs and a colorful *papel picado*. Cathy was adorned in a soft, sky-blue dress and a crown of fresh flowers. Ed sported a favorite western shirt. The couple exchanged vows before a supportive group of close friends and family.

Soon Cathy was pregnant. Ed was elated at the thought of being a father. Like his father proudly walking his sons into the Thanksgiving football game, Ed was becoming a family man.

Being a husband and a father elevated Ed in a 1970s society that largely viewed masculinity in traditional terms. A disabled man was often viewed as lacking the strength and vigor of true manhood. Fathering a child—with an alluring, nondisabled woman no less—exceeded all expectations.

When his son, Lee Brian Roberts, was born, Ed telephoned Zona. He shouted, "Bet you didn't think I'd be the first one to give you a grandchild!"

"You're absolutely right," Zona agreed.[9]

Being a father was Ed's greatest joy. There was no better feeling on earth than when Cathy set the infant on his chest to nuzzle against his cheek. As Ed turned the state capitol upside down, his life was completed by his loving wife and son.

. . .

Even before he had moved into his new office, Ed had already promised the world. He boasted that he would engineer a one-hundred-eighty-degree turnaround for the California Department of Rehabilitation.

Ed crowed that State Rehab would be the official state sponsor of a full-scale disability revolution. "We [severely disabled] were considered vegetables a few years ago. . . . The vegetables now are rising. We want to show that severely disabled persons can take charge of their own lives." From Mt. Shasta to Calexico, he promised to turn the musty old government agency into a multimillion dollar version of the Berkeley CIL, creating unprecedented access and equality across all segments of society.[10]

Ed didn't mind hurting feelings. Before he had even met the directors of other state rehabilitation departments, his new colleagues around the country, he criticized them openly. Only Massachusetts, Ed told the press, was truly carrying out the 1973 Rehabilitation Act mandate to prioritize clients with more significant disabilities. The other forty-nine states, including California, were dragging their feet.

"Well, now California is going to do it," he pronounced. "I'm going to shift priorities, shift money, and alter the measures of success." Ed vowed to double the number of people with severe disabilities receiving services in the first year.[11]

But it was more than a numbers game. The real key was to change the power dynamic between rehabilitation counselors and their clients. "We're going to directly involve disabled people on an equal basis in deciding what their own lives are going to be like." Supporting disabled clients meant empowering them to make the important decisions about their own services and goals. Rehabilitation had to help people do what Ed had learned to do, "take charge of their own lives."[12]

If they wanted to get an education, the department should send them to school. If they wanted to work, the department should support them in choosing a personally meaningful vocation. If they wanted to live in the community, escaping nursing homes and institutions, then the state should help them secure the best housing.

Across California the disability community cheered. They finally had their man at the top of the system. They believed in Ed.

Agency employees were doubtful. A scattered legion of progressive staff members felt optimistic about serving people with more significant impairments. But most of the staffers across the state were angry and afraid. They felt that Ed disrespected their efforts and skills. They complained vaguely about the rise of the "disabled mentality," the preposterous notion that putting the patients in charge of the hospital would improve medical care.

Many viewed Ed as a modern freak-show star. His accomplishments were like the theatrics of P. T. Barnum's freak-show performers from the late nineteenth century who showed off unique skills defying the limits of their bodies. Disabled side-show performers like Tom Thumb and Zip the Pinhead were the objects of perverse fascination, leaving audiences feeling simultaneously scintillated and disgusted. The most skeptical rehabilitation workers saw Ed as a curiosity well worth the ten-cent price of admission but certainly not qualified to lead them.[13]

Of course, Ed's personal success was laudable. But it was also rare. As one counselor warned, "Not everyone who is severely disabled is a genius or Superman like Ed Roberts. Dumb, unmotivated people get paralyzed, too."[14]

Other employees worried about money. Services for people with severe disabilities were costly and possibly ineffective. The agency would go bankrupt tilting at windmills. One rehabilitation supervisor voiced the fears of many: "We're in dire straits. Budgetary problems are going to totally disrupt us in a few months. It's not that Ed Roberts has bad intentions, but good administration is more than good intentions."[15]

Ignoring naysayers and critics, Ed immediately put his promises into action, making sweeping changes in the first year.

Central to Ed's plan was removing what he saw as dead wood, the incredulous late-career professionals that blocked his innovations. Working with Governor Brown, Ed created financial incentives that enticed many longtime employees into retirement.

Wielding a sharp knife, Ed gutted the bureaucracy. He wanted to decrease the distance between his office at the top of the system and the disabled client, flattening the structure, making the department nimble and creative. He sliced one hundred upper management positions and wiped out an entire layer of the multitier management system.

He was convinced that the rehabilitation counselors' obsession with quickly closing out cases, scoring well on evaluations by creaming, fostered a culture of deception. The positive statistics were fake. He hired a team of internal investigators to probe the records, searching for fraudulent recordkeeping.

The openings created by the many retirements gave Ed an opportunity to pursue another cherished mission, adding more diversity to the personnel rolls. His department had to look more like the Californians it served. The employee roster was filled with white, nondisabled men. Ed launched an initiative to hire more people of color and women.

That also meant leading the way in hiring disabled people. A state rehabilitation department, Ed believed, must became a role model to businesses and government, publicly demonstrating that disabled people could be productive workers. Ed hired a record number of disabled people in his own agency. Then he convinced the state legislature to pass a law requiring all state departments to develop affirmative action hiring policies for disabled workers.[16]

At Ed's side were two trusted Berkeley activists. He brought in his old pal John Hessler as his assistant director. He convinced attorney Jim Donald to transfer from the state attorney general's office.

Friends and foes dubbed Roberts, Hessler, and Donald the "Three Amigos." They rolled through the halls of power, three demanding men riding a humming pack of electric wheelchairs. They developed a reputation for dominating departmental meetings, ignoring the input of the nondisabled managers who had spent years with the agency. They knew what they wanted to do. Change was going to happen whether people liked it or not.

Beyond his own department, Ed enjoyed making the rounds of the legislative offices, telling his usual personal tales and building relationships with legislators and governmental leaders. He preached his ambitious disability vision to anyone who would or wouldn't listen.

Getting around the state capitol was difficult. The buildings and sidewalks were not made for a guy in a wheelchair. Physical access to the cramped hallways and offices was limited. When legislative staff met with Ed, they often carried their chairs into the hallway. There wasn't enough space in their offices for Ed's wheelchair. There was only one tiny elevator just large enough for a single person at the rear of the building. Ed and his personal attendant stuffed themselves in like clowns into a miniature car.

Many staffers and legislators were visibly afraid of Ed. If they had come upon him on the city sidewalk, they would have crossed the road. But there was no way to avoid Ed and his sprawling wheelchair in the office hallways.

To Ed's delight, staff members and elected officials pressed uncomfortably against the wall as they awkwardly tried to pass. They threw him an apologetic half-grin, as if it was their fault they couldn't get by. His audience conveniently trapped, Ed introduced himself, cracked a joke, and sparked a conversation. Ed was an evangelist on a mission, steering every conversation to the topic of achieving independence for the disabled citizens.

Ed's political skills relied on corporeal theater. He skillfully used his impaired body to play on the emotions of government leaders. He projected an optimistic exuberance that people didn't expect. He was like a homeless street beggar earnestly wishing wealthy passersby a wonderful and fulfilling day. The dramatic incongruence of a disabled man's unfortunate circumstances and his effervescent mood shocked many government leaders.

He knew how to pull their pity strings. When his department budget was threatened with possible reductions, he staged his body for maximum impact. Unloading from his van in the statehouse parking lot, he prepared for the intense finance meetings of the day.

"I'm not letting this happen," he vowed, readying to fight. He directed his personal attendant to twist his torso to the side, slouching his body to appear doubly disfigured.

"A little more," he ordered, "Pull my hips forward." His attendant did so.

"That's it," Ed beamed with confidence. "Now watch me." The performer was ready for the footlights. He zoomed into the statehouse, all set to squeeze their tender hearts into submission.

His respirator was also a powerful dramatic prop. By manipulating his mouthpiece, Ed seized control of conversations. Biting down intermittently, he staggered the air flow, forcing long pauses. Ed's sentences stumbling out in delayed pieces. His conversations partners had no choice but to politely wait.[17]

Undoubtedly, Ed's tactics were effective. One year into his post, the keen state government observers at the *Sacramento Bee* marveled at his sweeping transformation of the California rehabilitation system. "Roberts . . . has masterminded one of the most massive departmental shake-ups in recent history."[18]

For Ed, change came much too slowly. The biggest roadblock was Richard T. Soderberg, Ed's number two, the chief deputy director. Governor Brown knew that Ed had no experience leading a large government division. He was a sloppy administrator. Brown reassigned Soderberg from the state Finance Department to make sure that Ed didn't drive the multimillion-dollar state system into a ditch.

Soderberg was a career manager who, unlike Ed, faithfully adhered to the rows of three-ring binders full of government regulations. He was competent and tidy. Whatever chimerical policies Ed created, Soderberg kept the internal financial and managerial systems humming smoothly. The disability revolution would be processed in triplicate with the proper authorizing signatures and the white, yellow, and pink copies filed appropriately.

Soderberg led a small cadre of deputy directors who consistently stalled Ed's agenda. The top department brass channeled Ed's world-changing ideas through a slow labyrinth of government procedures and committees, often grinding his diamonds back into coal.

Ed had little understanding and even less interest in the daunting maze of standard operating procedures. He was a groundbreaking artist painting an entirely new portrait of disability with the enormous brush of the largest state government in the United States. He had the aesthetic sensibilities of Henri Matisse, combining jolts of energy and vibrant colors on a sprawling canvas of fresh possibility. The right-hand man implementing his visions was a button-down manager who spent his entire career painting by number. It was a combination that simply didn't work.

Ed's wife, Cathy, understood his aggravation. But she saw a different problem. Ed was utterly disorganized. He was a fireball of passion and creativity spinning off in too many directions, often missing the target. He churned out half-sketches and preliminary outlines, bursts of genius that failed to coalesce into the desired activities and impact.

Cathy knew that Ed needed Joan Leon. When Ed first went to Sacramento, Leon remained in Berkeley with her family. After much pleading, Cathy finally convinced Leon to join Ed in state government.

Joan Leon was the right medicine. Her steady presence and managerial talent helped Ed focus, direct his energies more purposefully, and make his messages count. She gathered up the details otherwise lost, and once Ed again functioned as a capable leader.[19]

Even with his best sidekick assisting him, Ed's reforms continued to be hampered by Soderberg's logjam. Ed griped to his friend Russell O'Connell, the head of rehabilitation in Massachusetts. A nondisabled man, O'Connell was an unusual free spirit in a manager's suit. The ex-Marine often walked on the beach playing his violin and smoking a cigar.[20]

O'Connell thought that if Ed's ideas could truly take shape, other states would follow. California would push the independent living agenda forward for the entire country. He told Ed, "Bring me out to Sacramento. Let me look things over. I'll tell you what I think."

It didn't take long for O'Connell to advise Ed, "You have to get rid of him."

"But how?" Ed replied. The governor appointed Soderberg. He was spotless, keeping perfect books for an operation with a $140 million annual budget and 2,500 employees. Ed worried that if he fired Soderberg, it would disappoint Brown, possibly losing the governor's strong support for his agenda.

But O'Connell had an idea. What if they could convince Soderberg to want to leave? What if it was his own choice to step aside?

Ed hired O'Connell as a slow-motion hatchet man. Over months of nagging and nudging, O'Connell gradually persuaded Soderberg to transfer to a different state agency.

With Soderberg's exit, Ed needed a top notch second in command who could handle the technical regulations and keep the finances straight. O'Connell believed so completely in Ed that he sent his own assistant, Bill McGauley, to manage the disability revolution in California. Working with Leon and McGauley, Ed finally had the team he needed.[21]

17 *Winning*

While Ed struggled with oppositional top managers in his own de-partment, he rallied state legislators to support his mission. He had a magnetic way of building political alliances. The result was a long string of impactful legislative victories that opened California to dis-abled citizens.

One late afternoon, four determined men huddled around a single telephone at the back of the California State Senate meeting room. Senator George Moscone, the canny majority leader who would soon defeat Councilwoman Dianne Feinstein to become the San Francisco mayor, held the receiver to his ear. The social justice champion was a pivotal figure in the gay rights movement, guiding a 1975 repeal of the California sodomy law to a one-vote legislative victory. He was also an early ally of the disability rights movement. As a member of the San Francisco Board of Supervisors in the mid-60s, he advocated for mak-ing the new Bay Area Rapid Transit (BART) accessible.[1]

At Moscone's side were Ed Roberts, Hale Zukas, and a young leg-islative aide named George Miller. On the other end of the line was US congressman Phil Burton, a powerful California liberal and Mil-ler's supportive mentor. Moscone had called Burton in a hasty at-tempt to answer a thorny, technical question about federal funding for California's rehabilitation programs. It was just the kind of policy tangle that couldn't be easily unpacked by four men and a congressman on a long-distance call.

Although Moscone held the phone, the real conversation was between Burton and Zukas, the resident policy expert. Moscone covered the mouthpiece with his hand to ask Zukas a question.

Zukas shook his head and mouthed a muffled "No!" Quoting the chapter and verse of the relevant federal guidelines, he explained how to correctly calculate the monies.

Moscone and Miller couldn't understand Zukas's speech patterns. Ed had known Hale for years. He comprehended completely and chimed in with clarifying interpretations for the other two. When Moscone finally got what Zukas by way of Ed was saying, he relayed the message back to Congressman Burton.

After numerous rounds of back and forth, Ed finally sighed, "I'm sorry. I need to leave."

Miller couldn't believe it. "You can't go. We're in the middle of this."

"Don't worry. Hale and I will solve this," Ed reassured him. "I really have to get back into the iron lung."

At first, Miller was flabbergasted. How could Ed leave in the middle of this important work?

Then it dawned on him. The rehabilitation director had spent the long workday using his portable respirator, a machine that almost gave him enough air. His body was worn out, and he needed to fully breathe in his iron lung.

Miller sat back for a moment, no longer following the policy discussion. There was something about that moment that smacked him on the side of the head. He suddenly noticed the overwhelming precarity of these two brilliant men. Zukas worked at the highest intellectual level, but his articulated words came out in forms that neither Moscone nor Miller could understand. Ed's life only lasted as long as a machine pushed air into his lungs.

These guys, he thought to himself, are incredible. Standing by the phone at the back of the California senate chamber, Miller knew then that he was completely captured by these disability activists.

A few months later, George Miller was off to Washington, DC, sworn in for the first of what would be twenty consecutive congressional terms. Ed, Judy Heumann, and the entire Berkeley disability delegation counted on Congressman Miller's strong support. His office was often the welcome headquarters when the Berkeley activists lobbied legislators on federal issues. Along with Senator Tom Harkin of Iowa, Congressman Miller became Ed's closest ally on Capitol Hill.

Like Miller, many California legislators fell under the spell of Ed's warmth and humor. The governor trusted Ed to take the lead on disability issues, and he won Sacramento's powerful men to his cause.[2]

. . .

In 1976, Alameda County councilman Tom Bates was elected to the State Assembly. He joined Republican Eugene Chappie and Democrat Nick Petris as Ed's main collaborators in Sacramento.

Bates quickly grasped Ed's number one goal, building a network of independent living centers across California. Every disabled person deserved what Berkeley had. The new assemblyman set his sights on passing a funding bill. He sent his lead staff member, Maggie Shandera, to visit the Berkeley CIL to start the process.

Shandera thought she knew a thing or two about people with disabilities. She grew up listening to her mother's special education teaching stories. But she was not prepared for what she experienced at the CIL. Wheelchairs were everywhere. Wheelchairs filled with busy people chatting and laughing. The old auto dealership on Telegraph Avenue bubbled like an effervescent party, a merry gathering of good friends.

A friendly woman at the reception desk gave Shandera a tour. She rolled down the hallway, explaining that visitors from all over the world came to observe and learn. Independent living was an exciting idea that was catching on everywhere.

The receptionist dropped the Sacramento staffer at the office of Judy Heumann, the number two in charge. Heumann was a small woman behind big glasses. At first glance, she seemed much too young to run anything more than a high school yearbook committee. As she spoke, her intelligence and terse seriousness aged her before the visitor's eyes.

This was a formidable woman, Shandera thought. Like reciting an encyclopedia by memory, Heumann gave a detailed overview of the many CIL programs. Shandera wondered how the happy-go-lucky crew could get so much work done.

Heumann talked knowledgeably about a range of disability policy issues that Shandera, an experienced legislative aide, hardly recognized. She was aware that the Department of Rehabilitation helped disabled people get jobs. But the policy matters Heumann confidently covered were completely new territory.

California independent living centers needed funding, Heumann explained. Ed appropriated federal dollars officially earmarked for experimental rehabilitation programs to launch ten new centers across the state. California became the first state with a network of centers based on the Berkeley model, each run by disabled people and offering a variety of useful services. But Ed was on shaky legal ground using the experimentation funds. A more reliable stream of state money was needed. Shandera left the CIL that day with that one goal.

Legislative specialist Lenny Goldberg joined Bates and Shandera to plan a bill to permanently fund independent living centers. Collaborating with Heumann, Ed, and Jim Donald, they wrote A.B. 204. The legislation not only appropriated annual dollars to the centers. It mandated that disabled people run them. Rehabilitation profession-als couldn't take over the network.

A.B. 204 passed the State Assembly without opposition. Tom Bates and Ed were thrilled. It seemed that all winds were at their backs.

As the landmark legislation rushed toward immediate passage, the clock hands froze. All government activity in Sacramento ground to an abrupt halt. The taxpayers of California had revolted. In June 1978, Proposition 13 passed in a landslide referendum, cutting the average California homeowner's property tax by 57 percent. The spigot of state revenues that had created a sizable surplus slowed to a trickle.

Governor Brown had publicly opposed Prop 13, warning of a cata-strophic reduction of state services. Initial estimates from the Legis-lative Analysis Office predicted that Prop 13 would force the governor to fire over 25 percent of the state employees.

The governor ordered both state legislatures to immediately drop all bills containing new expenditures. He wouldn't sign them. He asked legislators to return the state surplus and cut the budget by an additional $300 million.[3]

Bates was getting ready to bring A.B. 204 to the Senate floor for what he anticipated would be an easy vote. The bill was ideologically pleasing to the whole political spectrum. Democrats loved support-ing the disability community, a group they were beginning to view as an oppressed minority. Republicans loved that the bill called for dis-abled people to pull themselves up by their own bootstraps, becom-ing taxpaying workers who no longer needed welfare funds.

A group of Senate leaders knocked on Tom Bates's door. He knew it couldn't be good news. The men huddled in his small office. Their message was blunt. It was a good bill. But just let it die. Maybe they could come back to it in the future when the state's fiscal picture im-proved.

An agreeable man by temperament, Bates felt his anger rise as his colleagues spoke. They finally advised, "Please don't bring this to the floor."

Bates blew up. "Watch me!" he shouted.

The senators warned of an embarrassing down vote. But Bates didn't listen. He was already thinking of the next steps.

When bills died in the hallowed halls of the state senate, they often petered out in unobserved silence. The senators sleepwalked through parliamentary procedures like they were reading aloud the phone book. A procedural motion, a quick vote to table, and on to next business. It was legislative sleight of hand that didn't even make the newspapers.

Bates was not going to let this bill die quietly.

He conspired with Ed Roberts and Judy Heumann. They cooked up a dramatic plan to openly confront the senators. If they were going to say no to funding for the independent living centers, kicking disabled Californians in the gut, they would do their dirty work right in front of an angry crowd of disabled people.

The Berkeley disability community was energized for the fight. Scores of women, men, and children, most in wheelchairs, boarded buses early in the morning for the drive to Sacramento.

As the legislators walked from their cars into the Senate building, they watched the buses unloading in the parking lot. Most had never witnessed the careful and time-consuming process of unloading a person in a wheelchair from a bus. Heads down, briefcases clutched, trying not to stare, they scurried past.

The enormous Senate Room 4203 rumbled with expectant chatter. The senators found the usual paths to their seats blocked by gleaming steel and overflowing humanity. The chambers were packed elbow to elbow with people sitting in wheelchairs.

Ed rolled in with a big smile, joyfully greeting senators by name. He wanted them to know he was there and ready to testify.

In the front row, facing the Senate leaders, was a little girl. Her grinning face and bright eyes beamed with anticipation and joy, as if she were waiting for the start of a birthday party. She might have been six or seven years old. It was difficult to tell because her body twisted over to one side. Her hand jabbed at the joystick and her powerchair lurched forward. Then she maneuvered back into a comfortable spot to watch the proceedings.

Throughout the session, as the senators conducted themselves with procedural indifference, moving like bus drivers mindlessly traveling the usual route, they were interrupted repeatedly by the little girl. She didn't say a word. She didn't move. She just sat there smiling in her big wheelchair, stealing the senators' concentration and tugging at their heartstrings.

A room filled with disabled people was distraction enough. But it was the one small girl who threw the state representatives off their game.

As planned, the Senate procedure was methodical and drab. A.B. 204 was brought to the floor. When the parliamentarian opened the debate, the room was silent. Senators shuffled papers and looked up at the high ceiling.

The disability rights advocates scanned the chamber, looking to see who would speak up, ready to hear arguments against the bill. They were fully aware that the Senate was meeting to vote them and their independent living centers down.

Judy Heumann and other CIL leaders silently rehearsed their prepared speeches. They were ready to testify when the moment came.

But it didn't. No one was called to testify. There was no debate. Apparently rushing to complete this nasty business, A.B. 204 went straight to a floor vote. The bill was doomed.

The first voice called out from the floor, "Yea!" A senator had voted for it! There was some courageous support in the room.

Then a second person shouted from the back, "Yea!"

And then another. And another. At regular, slow intervals, they kept coming.

With each "Yea" echoing across the expansive room, the skeptical hearts of the Berkeley visitors inched upward. They knew all about Prop 13 and the state's budget problems. They had come to Sacramento prepared to fight hard, to shout angrily, and lose. Somehow it wasn't going as planned.

They held their breath and just listened. They hesitated to get too excited. It could all fall apart with a torrent of Nay votes.

But the Yeas kept coming. Tear-filled eyes met across the room. Hands clasped against breasts.

Yea, Yea, Yea. The magical vote continued.

The stream of positive votes resounded through the parliamentary chambers like the loving whispers of angels. To the disabled persons in the room, each Yea was a glorious affirmation of their worth, a golden moment of unexpected recognition. At long last, the State of California was, in painfully sweet and brief increments, declaring people with disabilities to be complete and valued citizens.

The last Yea gave way suddenly to a consuming silence. The vote was done. The room was quiet except for the soft sound of someone softly weeping. There was a long pause while the Senate leader approached the lectern.

The man announced, "A.B. 204 has passed by unanimous vote."

Senate Room 4203 erupted. Hands flew up. Squeals of joy filled the room. The little girl in the front row hugged her mother. This was much better than any birthday party. The busloads of disabled Californians sang loudly all the way back to Berkeley.

Despite his pledge to authorize no new spending, Governor Brown signed the bill into law without hesitation. Ed's dream of creating a state-funded system of independent living centers supporting disabled people across California had come true.[4]

.   .   .

Ed was lucky when he convinced Jim Donald, an attorney and old friend from the Berkeley disability community, to serve as his chief legislative consultant. During Governor Brown's first term, knowing they had legislators and the governor in the palm of their hands, the duo worked furiously to pass disability access legislation.

The first priority was outlawing discrimination against people with physical disabilities and mental conditions in hiring and employment practices. Donald wrote a bill making it illegal for employers as well as workers' unions to reject a job applicant or fire an employee due to disability.

Ed's message throughout his career touted the disabled worker as a superior employee. "Disabled people tend to be very loyal employees . . . they tend to stay on the job longer, they tend to be employees who are absent less." Contrary to the stereotypes of disabled people as weak, unreliable, and incompetent, Ed pitched them as the ideal workers, a vast untapped resource for corporations seeking talent.[5]

Lacking any real understanding of workers with disabilities, business and local government leaders spiraled into a fearful web of exaggerated suppositions. Charles Cruttenden of the Alameda County Board of Supervisors shuddered at every imaginable contingency. Disabled workers would take too many sick days. They would have heart attacks on the job. A painter with epilepsy working on high scaffolding could have a seizure and fall to his death. The dangers and corresponding costs seemed endless.[6]

The business community worried that sick and accident-prone workers would hurt their bottom line. They predicted skyrocketing costs for health insurance, worker's compensation, and other benefits. Stanley Fontez, the president of the State Association of County Retirement Administrators, predicted the price tag for county workers "would probably run into the billions statewide."[7]

Lawmakers paid surprisingly little attention to the dollars and cents. An internal legislative analysis spitballed the potential fiscal impact on employers as "unknown but probably minimal." The State Assembly's Committee on Labor Relations likewise shrugged its shoulders, admitting that the cost implications for public and private employers were unknown.[8]

Ultimately, the bill was vetted not through rigorous statistical analysis or expert testimony. In true California style, it played out under Hollywood's bright lights.

In November 1974, an episode of the popular CBS television show *Medical Center*, starring Chad Everett as the ruggedly handsome Dr. Joe Gannon, told the real-life story of a Los Angeles woman denied a job because she was being treated for cancer. The American Cancer Society gave the hospital drama a special award for shining a light on the "real and urgent problem of employment discrimination against cancer patients."[9]

The entire range of disabilities encompassed by the legislation was narrowed down to a near-histrionic focus on the vulnerability of one subgroup. Many understandably thought that the new law would only apply to people who had cancer.

In March 1975, Assemblyman Alfred Siegler held a press conference with actor Chad Everett. While photographers snapped pictures of the television star, Siegler expounded, "Every day, people who have, through modern medical treatment, recovered from the agony, pain, and sometimes social stigma of 'having cancer' face their cruelest test of all—finding someone who will hire them."[10]

Fueled by star power and mawkish accounts of unemployed cancer patients, the legislation easily earned public support. In August 1975, surrounded not by employers pledging to hire disabled people but by television executives, Governor Brown signed the new law.[11]

Ed and his chief legislative consultant, Jim Donald, anticipated delays in enacting the new labor statute. Lawsuits could take years to unfold, discouraging plaintiffs from pursuing justice. They decided to force the issue by passing additional measures beefing up enforcement. Cities and counties were mandated to set up an appeals board of five members, including two people with disabilities, to quickly hear labor discrimination complaints.

They also empowered the state Department of Rehabilitation to initiate action against any municipality violating the code. Ed was the new sheriff in town, deputized to bring charges against workplaces failing to provide accessible restrooms, sidewalks, ramps, and elevators.[12]

The Berkeley men were on a roll. In his first term, Governor Brown signed over a dozen bills creating opportunities and rights for disabled Californians. Disabled drivers received placards allowing them to park in assigned spots or use public street meters for free. Handicapped parking tags and spots would become a fixture of the American roads. Additional new accessibility mandates covered public parks, recreation areas, and children's playgrounds.[13]

Historically, blind and D/deaf citizens had been viewed as lacking the competence to serve on court trial juries. For the first time, a California defendant's right to be judged by a jury of their peers was understood to be a mandate to include blind and D/deaf persons as jurors. Courts supplied necessary American Sign Language interpreters.[14]

Disabled Californians were granted full access to all government offices. The state architectural code was updated "to insure all buildings, structures, sidewalks, curbs, and related facilities constructed . . . by use of state, county, or municipal funds . . . shall be accessible to and usable by the physically handicapped." This sweeping law included state college campuses. Every campus would have curb cuts and accessible restrooms and classroom buildings.[15]

Perhaps the greatest victory of the 1975 California legislative session was improving voting access for people with disabilities. Most states did not allow people with intellectual disabilities or mental illnesses to vote. People with other impairments were technically allowed to cast a ballot. The cruel trick historically was that voting systems blocked people with mobility impairments and blindness. Architectural obstacles at polling places and the lack of Braille or audible ballots effectively disenfranchised these voters.[16]

Not surprisingly, candidates for office didn't worry about the concerns of the legions of barred disabled voters. Election year debates weren't filled with hot "disability issues." Ed knew that bringing disabled voters into the political process created new opportunities for them to influence their representatives, a chance to push their priorities onto the political agenda.

His legislative actions put his home state decades ahead of the national curve. Full ballot access wouldn't be guaranteed nationally until President George W. Bush signed the Help America Vote Act in 2002.[17]

Triumphant after their many early successes, the Donald and Roberts duo set their sights on the long-coveted white whales of disability inclusion—total access to commercial establishments and public transit systems. In 1959, master California politician Jesse M. Unruh authored a state civil rights law that blocked discrimination by businesses due to "race, color, religion, ancestry, or national origin." Left off that early landmark legislation was disability. Disabled people wanted to ride public buses and trains, rent apartments, stay in hotels, eat in restaurants, go to the movies, and meet a friend for a drink in a favorite watering hole.[18]

With Jim Donald, backed by supportive legislators and Governor Brown, Ed passed a series of antidiscrimination laws that opened up California's social and business landscape to people with disabilities.

The expansive laws required that public transportation, housing, and virtually all business establishments grant "full and equal access" to all disabled people.[19]

Ed's plan for California to lead the way for the entire country blossomed. Over a decade before passage of the federal Americans with Disabilities Act, California had an enviable bulwark of access laws that welcomed disabled persons into society.

FIGURE 1. Kitty Cone, Judy Heumann, Eunice Fiorito, and unidentified ASL interpreter, at Section 504 protest rally, Washington, DC, April 1977.

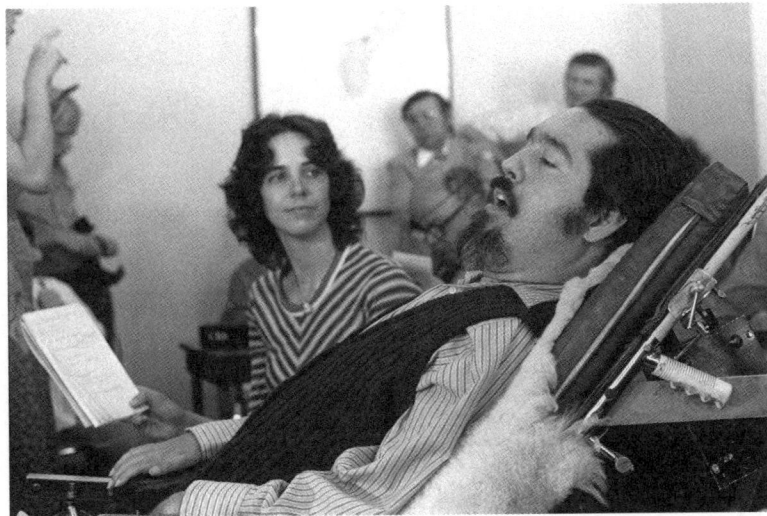

FIGURE 2. With wife, Cathy, Ed Roberts testifies at Section 504 congressional hearing at HEW offices, San Francisco, April 1977.

FIGURE 3. Ed Roberts, Roger Payne, and Jon Oda swim with dolphins in the Florida Keys, November 1993.

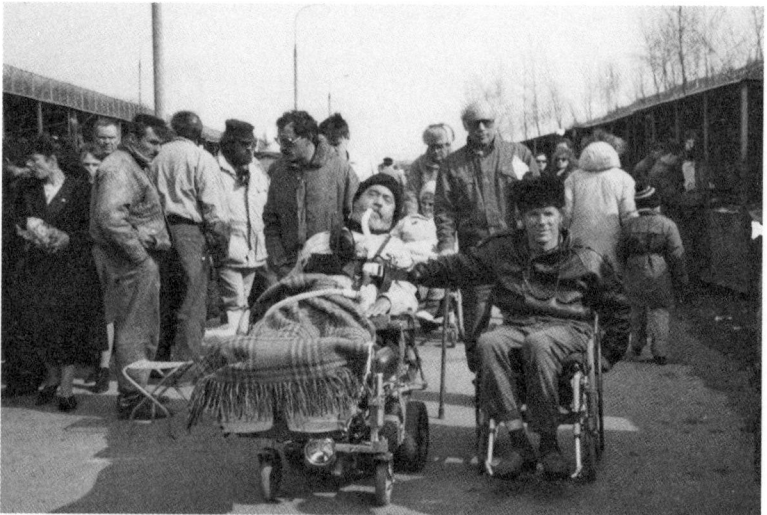

FIGURE 4. Ed Roberts and Bruce Curtis at the Izmailovski Market, Moscow, April 1993.

FIGURE 5. Ed Roberts, Joan Leon, and Judy Heumann at the World Institute on Disability in 1985.

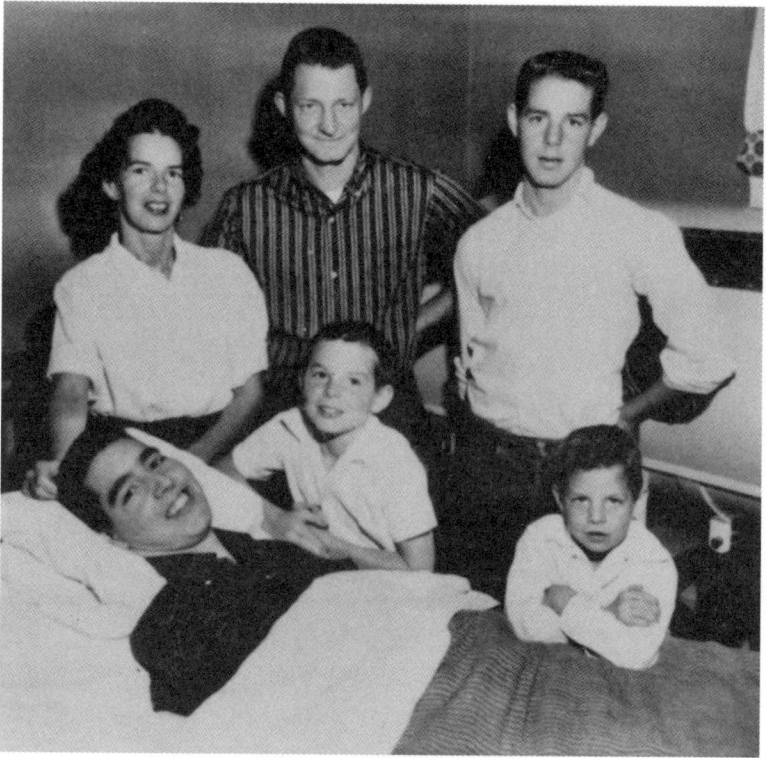

FIGURE 6. The Roberts family—Zona, Verne, Ron (standing in back) and Ed, Mark, and Randy—in Burlingame, California, in 1954.

FIGURE 7. Henry Enns (left) and Jim Dirksen (right) at the Disabled Peoples' International World Congress in Singapore, November 1981.

FIGURE 8. Lex Frieden and Justin Dart, Jr., at the Republican National Convention in Houston, Texas, November 1992.

FIGURE 9. Brad Lomax speaks with Judy Heumann and Eunice Fiorito seated at his side at a Section 504 rally in Washington, DC, April 1977.

FIGURE 10. Zona and Ed Roberts, circa 1986.

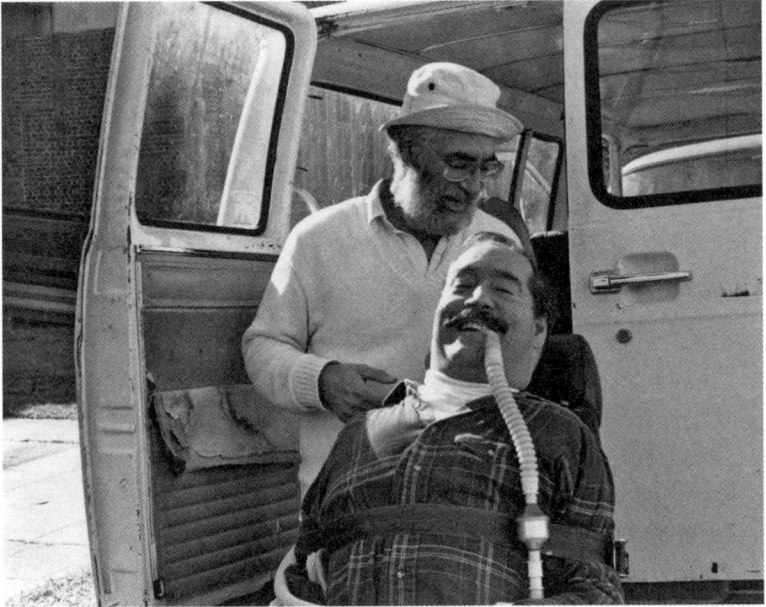

FIGURE 11. Jonathan Gold loads Ed Roberts into back of van, Berkeley, California, early 1995.

FIGURE 12. Justin Dart, Jr., speaking at Americans with Disabilities Act rally in Washington, DC, March 1990.

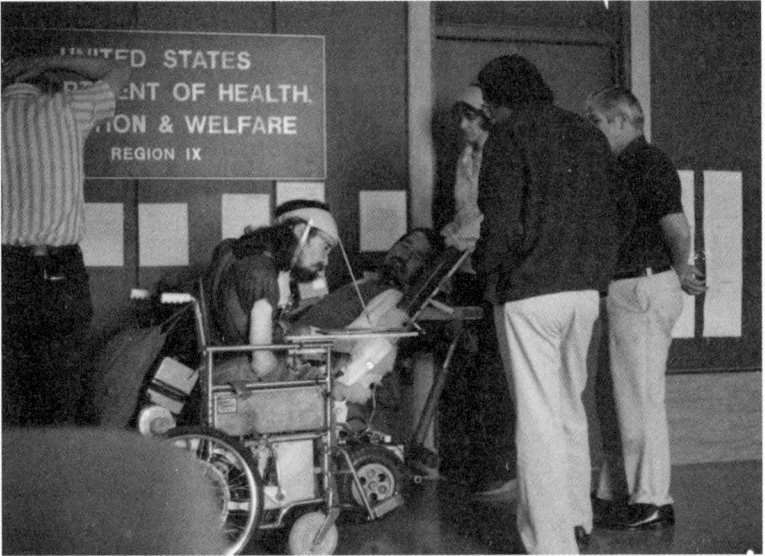

FIGURE 13. Hale Zukas (foreground), Ed Roberts, and Cathy Roberts (partially obscured at rear) at the Section 504 sit-in protest in the HEW offices, San Francisco, April 1977.

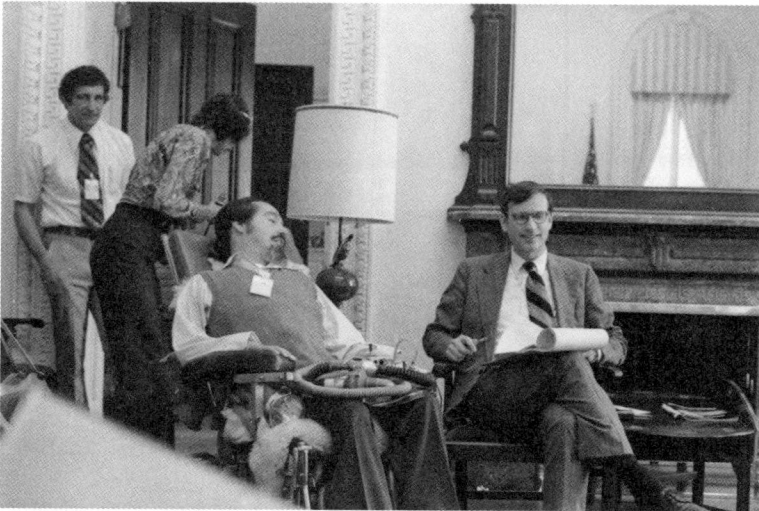

FIGURE 14. Ed Roberts and Carter administration policy advisor Stuart Eizenstat at the White House Section 504 negotiations meeting, April 1977.

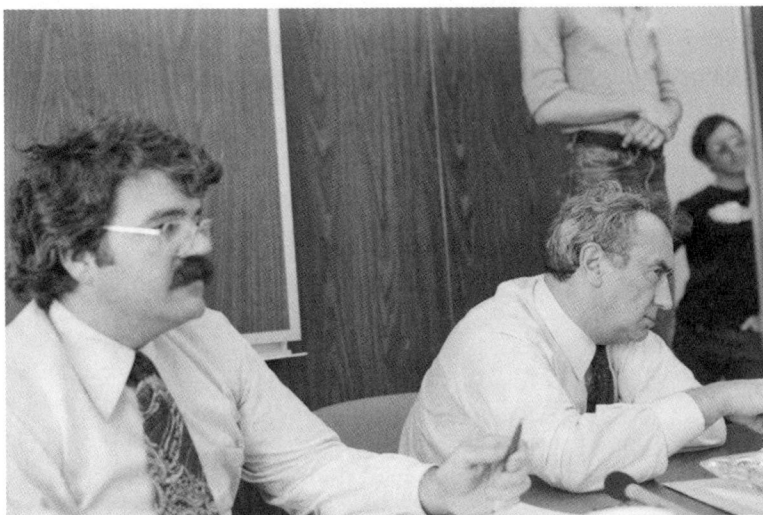

FIGURE 15. George Miller and Phil Burton at the HEW congressional hearings inside the San Francisco Section 504 sit-in protest, April 1977.

18 *Pride in 25 Days*

In April 1977, the Berkeley disability activists, led by Judy Heumann and Kitty Cone, picked a nasty fight with President Jimmy Carter. The passionate struggle resulted in the first national disability anti-discrimination law in United States history.

Tucked inside the Rehabilitation Act of 1973 was a golden egg called Section 504 that outlawed all forms of discrimination against disabled people in federal government programs. It applied to any entity receiving Uncle Sam's dollars. That meant universities, hospitals, schools, and all state or local governments. Most acts of disability prejudice and exclusion became illegal.

But there was a hitch. Section 504 could only be enacted when the Department of Health, Education, and Welfare (HEW) approved the official implementation regulations. Three presidential administrations—Nixon, Ford, and Carter—didn't sign off.

President Ford's HEW secretary F. David Mathews wrote a comprehensive set of 504 regulations that were widely accepted by the disability community. Under pressure from hospitals and universities to supply them with loopholes, Mathews refused to sign his own rules.

When President Carter took office in January 1977, the hopes of disability activists soared. After the nation's heartbreaking

Watergate experience, Carter offered America a down-to-earth decency built on his forthright Christian faith. His standard stump speech line was, "I'll never tell a lie. I'll never make a misleading statement, and I'll never avoid a controversy."[1]

The kindly Georgia Democrat, a political centrist who strongly supported human rights, had already voiced support for Section 504. With veteran disability rights activist Eunice Fiorito at his side, surrounded by people sitting in wheelchairs, he kicked off his presidential campaign on the porch of FDR's Little White House in Warm Springs, Georgia. The smiling gentleman appeared to be the kind of politician the disability community could trust.[2]

He was also a president who inherited a dysfunctional HEW, a languid bureaucracy with little taste for enforcing equity laws. When he entered office, the agency had a backlog of three to four thousand Title IX complaints. Passed originally in the summer of 1972, Title IX of the Education Amendments was a federal civil rights regulation that prohibited sex discrimination in public schools and higher education. The HEW's mishandling of Title IX foreshadowed how the agency fumbled Section 504. Tasked with writing regulations to guide enforcement of the gender equity law, HEW took two years to issue the enacting document. When women's rights lobbyists—a legion of forty groups, including NOW, the Women's Equity Action League, and the National Women's Political Caucus—objected to the vague guidelines, the HEW took an additional year to make needed corrections.

The agency was also notoriously incompetent. Lost behind cabinets or sitting unaddressed in dusty stacks, Title IX claims often languished for two or three years without action. A NOW analysis found that only 20 percent of complaints had been fully investigated. Many HEW staff members simply didn't take sex discrimination seriously.[3]

Despite the HEW's miserable record with Title IX, the disability community took the new president at his word, expecting quick approval of the 504 regulations. Their hopes were immediately dashed. The new HEW secretary, Joseph Califano, announced yet another round of 504 guidelines review.

In the Washington, DC, offices of the American Coalition of Citizens with Disabilities (ACCD), Fiorito and Frank Bowe monitored the situation closely. Government insiders warned that Califano was busy diluting 504. Behind closed doors, an HEW task force compiled a long list of what Bowe called "loopholes, waivers, and exemptions," free passes for many organizations to ignore the statute.[4]

An ugly old expression kept popping up: separate but equal. In 1896 the Supreme Court ruled that railroads could require African American passengers to travel in separate cars. It took until the 1954 *Brown v. Board of Education* decision for the court to acknowledge that segregated facilities were a cruel keystone of systemic inequality. The 1977 Califano HEW was reprising the old apartheid standard for disabled citizens.

Eunice Fiorito arranged to have a cup of tea with Secretary Califano at his office. She was a statuesque blind woman who wore crisp business suits and spoke with a Roman orator's gilded enunciation. Her every word communicated that she wasn't messing around. Califano professed in pleasant government-speak that the administration fully supported the principles of Section 504. The task force was just dotting i's and crossing t's. Fiorito asked for a definite promise that Califano would not diminish the scope of legal protections. He refused.

Fiorito held her ground, "Mr. Secretary, I won't be able to leave until you give me some kind of assurance that you're going to sign the regulations." After a tense period of hand-wringing, Califano's staff finally escorted her out of the office.

The ACCD warned President Carter: Sign the regulations unchanged by April 4, 1977, or protests will break out across the country. They went on the offensive, attacking the HEW before weakened regulations were published.[5]

The White House didn't take this seriously. Disabled people had no political power. Carter and Califano felt comforted by the stereotyped question, What could a bunch of people in wheelchairs really do?

Protests erupted on April 5 at federal buildings in ten cities. In Denver, Washington, DC, and Los Angeles, activists took over the buildings. Califano cut off food, medication, and water, quickly starving the occupiers into submission. All eyes turned to Heumann, Cone, and their coalition in San Francisco.

Heumann and Cone were not cherubic Jerry's Kids. Journalist Evan White described them as "very strong women you don't mess with." They were tough and they knew exactly what they were doing. Heumann had experience and knowledge about Washington politics, how to influence elected representatives and agency heads. Cone was a master of the politics of the street, the mass mobilization of constituencies of opposition and protest.[6]

They built a broad coalition of Bay Area organizations, including trade unions, the LGBT community, and African American civil rights leaders. They united the many disability groups, including people with developmental disabilities.[7]

On the morning of April 5, CIL worker Jeff Moyer stepped off the BART train at the San Francisco federal building. Guitar in one hand and a hastily scribbled protest song in the other, he was drenched in joyful sound, "Sign 504! Sign 504!"

In the brick square outside the six-story structure, four hundred people of different races and disabilities waved signs and shouted to the high heavens. A veteran San Francisco newsman called the scene "a visual circus. . . . None of us had ever seen anything like this before."[8]

When Ed rolled to the microphone, everyone knew him. They didn't recognize all the rally speakers. But every disabled person knew the hero who embodied everything they hoped for. Ed sharply clarified the stakes of the fight.

"504 is our civil rights act and unless its regulations are strong and positive we will continue to be deprived of the opportunities, rewards and responsibilities of our society. . . . Strong 504 regulations could permit us to attend any university or college, and to use every program or agency supported by federal funds. It would literally open doors for employment, education and recreation; without it we are second class citizens, living on the fringe of society, unable to participate and devalued."[9]

As the applause for Ed sounded across the plaza, Jeff Moyer nervously carried his guitar to the microphone. He had performed in public many times. But this was different. He was now the Pete Seeger of the disability rights movement. He sang a familiar civil rights melody. But the words were new.

Civil rights were knocking at our door,
But Carter wouldn't stand on 504.
Keep your eye on the prize. Hold on.

The crowd soared high above the plaza, bellowing anger over the Golden Gate Bridge to the north, screaming hope across the Bay's waters to the east.[10]

Then Judy Heumann seized the microphone. Every prior speaker had been enthusiastic and hopeful. Not Heumann. She was fed up. She belted out, "Let's go and tell HEW, the federal government, they cannot steal our civil rights!" She spun into the federal building followed by 150 screaming protesters.

On the fourth floor, the rumpled HEW regional director Joe Maldonado was unprepared. Fifty people pushed past his overwhelmed secretary to surround his desk. He was trapped by wall-to-wall wheelchairs.

Moldonado tried to remain calm. He wiggled in discomfort.

Heumann pummeled him with rapid-fire questions about the Section 504 regulations. Desperate, he phoned Secretary Califano in Washington. Not available. Moldonado was on his own.

Cone felt empathy for the poor man. But Heumann was unrelenting. She peppered the director with pointed questions. He finally squeaked, "What is Section 504?"

The room exploded in indignation. Heumann leaped to another level of outrage. She promised, "We're not leaving until we get assurances." They would occupy the HEW offices until the regulations were signed.[11]

Claiming he was going to bathroom, Moldonado awkwardly squeezed past the wheelchairs and beelined for the elevator. The irate mob of protesters chased at his heels, shouting in unison "504! 504!"[12]

Heumann and Cone were backed by a smart leadership team that included Mary Lou Breslin, Mary Jane Owen, Pat Wright, Ray Uzeta, Karen Parker, Joni Breves, and Jim Peachum. The group planned strategy until almost dawn. They coordinated with ACCD leaders in Washington and gathered information about the other protest sites. They called journalists, lining up interviews and answering the first round of questions. A series of working committees focused on immediate needs—personal attendants, food, bedding, water, and showers.

Food was provided by Safeway markets and the Delancey Street drug rehabilitation program. McDonald's donated breakfasts. The Black Panthers supplied many delicious, fully cooked dinners. Congregants of the Glide Memorial Church, longtime LGBT rights supporters in San Francisco, handled food deliveries.[13]

A round-the-clock sentry guarded the elevator. There was a widespread concern that federal agents would storm the building to haul them away. They planned on remaining peaceful, not fighting back, but not making it easy.

Cone curled up in a closet, Heumann in an elevator. Others sprawled out in offices and conference rooms. A few people had sleeping bags. But most slept on the hard floors. Many half-dozed, the rush of the exhilarating day passed, their bodies slumped in their wheelchairs.

Stuck in Sacramento, Ed sent his sidekick Joan Leon with a cameraman. He sensed that this would be an historic event that would define the new pride of the disability community, and he wanted it fully documented on film.

But the great American disability rights documentary over three decades before the release of *Crip Camp* wasn't to be. Legislators in the state Capitol got wind of Ed's activities and complained to the governor's office about the use of state funds to support an illegal demonstration. Governor Brown shut Ed's film project down.

On the third day, excited whispers circulated the fourth floor: "Ed's coming." He delivered the full support of Governor Brown. But even more, he told his allies that this was their time. They were each Ed Roberts. They were the heroes leading people with disabilities to a new life of freedom and dignity.

His words to the protesters defined the moment. This was a fight for 504, he instructed them, but it was more. This victory would be the defining turn in American history, the fateful juncture when disabled people claimed their own pride.

Something miraculous happened among sit-in participants. Photographer HolLynn D'Lil described it as a process of "becoming real." People who often felt "in-valid" became real humans both in their own minds and in the public square. The 504 protest experience, for those involved and for many onlookers, was a watershed opportunity of self-definition for disabled people.[14]

Following a pattern created by other movements, this was a milestone moment for disabled people. In 1969, San Francisco gay rights leader Leo Laurence observed, "The Black man found self-respect and dignity when he said, 'Black is beautiful and I am proud.' Now Homosexuals are starting to say, 'Gay is good, and I, too, am proud.'" Beginning with African American civil rights, each liberation movement in turn spun the dominant society's habitual degradation inside out, loudly proclaiming a positive opposite definition.

Disabled demonstrators in San Francisco, and, Ed hoped, disabled Americans cheering from their living rooms, could blossom into what he called a "consciousness about ourselves," creating an uplifting self-image filled with "pride (and) courage." Decades before Disability Pride Month or Disability Pride flags would become well-known cultural realities, amidst the wonderful 504 fight, Ed preached a new definition of disability as synonymous with pride.[15]

As the Carter administration expected, the tension and discomfort gradually left the protesters fatigued. Many had complex health needs requiring regular care from skilled personal attendants, including catheter changes, regimens of medication, ointments and specific care to avoid bedsores.

But the spirit and determination inside the weary bodies only increased. They understood and embraced their responsibility to represent all disabled Americans. "Everyone was committed to staying in the building until hell froze over," Ray Uzeta later recalled. Bruce Oka agreed, "Our resolve never weakened."[16]

Day and night, the rally in the plaza outside the building continued. Reverends Cecil Williams and Norman Leach of the Council of Churches led a constant vigil of support. Williams was a prominent Bay Area social justice figure who provided support and wise counsel to Black Power movement leaders. Almost fifteen years earlier, he collaborated with a small group of California progressive faith leaders to create a group called the Council on Religion and the Homosexual. When other ministers rejected gays and lesbians, Williams opened his congregation doors enthusiastically.[17]

Heumann and Cone focused on the press. If the story was spread widely and correctly, they could win over the public and the loudest voices in the Democratic Party, the two groups who could change President Carter's mind. Their strategy was to pressure Carter and Califano into submission.

Bay Area newspapers and television stations tracked the protest closely. San Francisco Channel 7 reporter Evan White showed up daily with a camera crew. He spent a day using a wheelchair to illustrate the architectural access problem to TV viewers. He discovered that he couldn't even get into the Channel 7 building.[18]

The national press was a different story. The *New York Times* thought the sit-in was foolish. Section 504 was an ill-considered regulation that would be extremely expensive to carry out.[19]

The *Washington Post* backed Califano. The same liberal newspaper that came out in support of gay equality eight years earlier seemed confused by the same goal for disabled persons. Their scathing editorial called the regulations "confusing, prolix, fuzzy, and bound to do far less for disabled citizens seeking fair play than for the lawyer seeking a guaranteed annual income." The misguided protesters were "fighting for . . . the wrong set of regulations."[20]

The reporters on the Capitol Hill beat didn't take the sit-in seriously. They were arrogantly confident, as was the Carter administration, that national political events happened inside the Beltway. So-called "cripples" holing up in HEW offices were more of an odd curiosity than a hard-nosed political concern. National news outlets treated the protests as a human-interest story.[21]

Secretary Califano cranked up the pressure on the inhabitants of the fourth floor. He shut off the hot water and killed the phone lines. Security guards sealed off the building.

The activists set up an effective communication system that Califano didn't anticipate. They used American Sign Language to relay information to outside collaborators through the lobby glass doors.

High-profile political figures offered moral support. Civil rights leader Julian Bond toured the fourth floor, giving words of encouragement. Jesse Jackson and Cesar Chavez made public statements of solidarity. Tom Bates and forty-six members of the California State Assembly publicly called upon President Carter to sign the regulations immediately. Endorsement messages flowed in from trade unions and churches across the country.[22]

Congressman George Miller, Ed's friend and political supporter, visited the demonstrators inside the San Francisco federal building. He strongly advised Heumann and Cone, "Stay in this building and don't leave until you've won."[23]

Each night, Ray Uzeta led a giant, town hall–style rap session. Every concern, wish, or opinion was heard. Then the HEW offices lit up with what Uzeta called "the best parties I ever had." The volunteer nurses who came through daily to check on health needs smuggled in booze and marijuana. Rock music rattled the office walls. Cut off from the world, trapped in a pressure cooker, the demonstrators celebrated the beauty and strength and love of being disabled persons.[24]

As the sit-in dragged into a second week, Ed feared it would end in a disappointing stalemate. The protesters inside suffered increasing discomfort while Carter and Califano played a cozy waiting game.[25]

Ed and civil rights attorney Phil Neumark hatched a preposterous idea. Ed asked his friend Phil Burton, a senior Democrat serving California's 6th District, to hold a congressional hearing about the Section 504 regulations inside the occupied building.

It was a radical scheme. Official legislative hearings were typically held in the hallowed halls of Congress or respectable public spaces like hotel conference rooms, not in the middle of an illegal occupation of government property.

The veteran congressman agreed. A hearing would attract much-needed national media coverage. But even more, Burton knew that this display of political theater would boost the pressure from the liberal wing of the Democratic Party against President Carter and Secretary Califano.[26]

Burton summoned George Miller, his protégé congressman, to meet him at the San Francisco federal building. Miller showed up not knowing what to expect.

The little conference room burst beyond capacity. The congressmen sat at microphones behind a long table across from Gene Eidenberg, the HEW representative Califano sent to speak on his behalf. For five hours, the demonstrators and representatives of various disability groups roasted Califano for failing to sign the 504 regulations. Eidenberg dutifully took it all in. To Miller, the hearings were a skillful performance of "guerilla theater," an orchestrated political attack on President Carter.[27]

Ed's testimony marked the historical character of the moment. In the most important battle of the disability rights movement, disabled people were coming together with an unprecedented sense of pride and purpose. He predicted that there was no way they would lose:

"I found, and millions of other people with disabilities are finding, that access, that my ability to move around, and my ability to regain the pride in myself as a person with a disability is one of the most important things that's coming out of what's happening here today. To see hundreds of people with disabilities—rolling, signing, using canes—the more severely retarded people for the first time joining us in this incredible struggle is one that leads me to believe that we're gonna win this."[28]

Visibly moved by Ed's words, Congressman Burton's eyes welled with tears. Gathering himself, he grilled Eidenberg. Why have the regulations been delayed? What's wrong with the regulations written by Secretary Mathews?

Eidenberg was stuck in an unenviable position. He knew nothing more about Section 504 than the list of unsatisfactory bromides he memorized on the long flight. He obediently said that the HEW wanted to install the best regulations possible. His responses were blander than government office furniture.

But then, something unexpected happened. Unwittingly, Eidenberg stumbled. While talking about the public education of children with disabilities, he used an unfortunate phrase: "Separate but equal."[29]

The room heaved a collective gasp. The activists couldn't believe what they heard. Eidenberg said that HEW was planning segregated schools for disabled children. With the social ineptitude of a man who casually drops the N-word at an NAACP meeting, the mild-mannered administrator dug the hole deeper. He divulged that the HEW task force reviewing the 504 regulations had already created a list of twenty-six different modifications. As rumored, they were watering it down!

Kitty Cone sprinted out of the room. A crowd of eight hundred strong rallied outside. She told them what the HEW man had just said. Their raucous shouts and hoots shook the windows of the fourth-floor conference room. The staid proceedings turned into a circus.[30]

If there was a single scene in disability rights history that was somehow the equivalent to Martin Luther King, Jr.'s, "I Have a Dream" speech, it was Judy Heumann's passionate response to Mr. Eidenberg.

Her short speech was not carefully written and smoothed out by the finest speechwriters. It surged from her mouth as heartfelt words longing to be said, expressing the totality of hurt and anger felt by disabled people.

Heumann began slowly, attempting a degree of restraint. She accurately detailed the legal history of the expression "separate but equal." But then emotions bubbled over. She couldn't go on like an academic in a lecture hall.

Choking on her tears, she put her head down. She paused to compose herself. Then she lifted herself back up and spoke in a taut, thumping cadence. Her eyes, now determined and gripping, fixed on the HEW representative, who stared back without expression.

"The harassment," she sighed heavily. "The lack of equity that has been provided for disabled individuals, and that even now is being discussed by this administration, is so intolerable that I can't quite put it into words."

"I can tell you that every time you raise issues of 'separate but equal,' the outrage of disabled individuals across this country is going to continue, is going to be ignited. And there will be more takeovers of buildings until finally, maybe, you'll begin to understand our position."[31]

Heumann paused for a half beat, struggling to get the words right. Then she powered forward. "We will no longer allow the government to oppress disabled individuals. We want the law enforced! We want no more segregation! We will accept no more discussions of segregation and—"

Again she broke down.

Eidenberg listened quietly, bowing his head in what seemed like empathy.

Heumann couldn't take it. "And I would appreciate it if you would stop nodding your head in agreement when I don't think you have any idea what we are talking about."

That was it. Her face fell into her hands and tears tumbled down her cheeks. There was nothing more to say. The room exploded in applause.[32]

Eidenberg ran down the hall and locked himself in an office. Burton followed in hot pursuit. He kicked and pounded on the door.

"Come out here!" the congressman shouted. Eidenberg finally emerged meek and drained.

As emotionally impactful as the hearings were, Carter and Califano seemed unmoved. The firecrackers and bottle rockets the activists shot off in San Francisco, no matter how loud and dazzling, weren't reaching Washington.

Heumann and Cone made a bold tactical decision. They would lead a small detachment to Washington to seek a direct dialogue with Secretary Califano and President Carter. The majority of the demonstrators would continue the San Francisco sit-in.

It was a risky move. They had no idea if it would work. And they had no money to pay for it.

A machinist union member named Willy Dicks, a nondisabled, African American man, gave them a personal check for $1,000. He had just attended a service at Glide Memorial Church where Reverend Cecil Williams challenged the congregation to support the protesters. Dicks persuaded his trade union to pay the lion's share. Ed's pal Werner Erhard, the famous EST personal-improvement guru, kicked in the rest.[33]

The racially mixed travel team included representatives of the San Francisco D/deaf, blind, and developmental disabilities communities. Led by Cone and Heumann, the group included Debbie Stanley, Hale Zukas, Pat Wright, Brad Lomax, Ron Washington, HolLynn D'Lil, Dennis Billups, Larry Montoya, and Mary Jane Owen.[34]

Touching down in Washington, the San Francisco activists and local ACCD leaders immediately boarded a rented box truck. The International Association of Machinists proudly affixed their banner across the side, almost covering up Hertz. It was the only way in 1977 to transport so many wheelchair users around the city. Huddled in the cargo bay darkness, the activists swayed and called out "Whoa!" at every unseen turn and stop.

They drove directly to Secretary Califano's stately home in an upscale suburb. Bleary-eyed from lack of sleep and the long flight, many wrapped in blankets against the spring chill, the protesters chanted and sang. They lit candles, the small flames flickering against the overwhelming darkness of night.[35]

As the dawn sun rose, the tall daffodil blooms in Califano's yard lifting to the first rays, Reverend Ken Longfield of Luther Place Memorial Church led a prayer service. With police monitoring closely, protestors again knocked on the front door. No response. Califano had quietly sneaked out a back door before daybreak and escaped through the woods. He was doing whatever it took to avoid them.

Each night the activists slept on wooden pews in Reverend Longfield's Dupont Circle church. Every evening they held long strategy meetings, often talking straight through until first light.[36]

President Carter and his wife, Rosalynn, frequently attended services at the First Baptist Church on 16th Street. The activists set up a loud picket line across the street on Sunday morning. As the concluded liturgy let out, worshippers walked down the tall front steps of the Greek revival basilica. Typically, President Carter and his wife strolled out together, smiling, hand in hand. But this day, uncharacteristically, the Southern gentleman sent his wife to walk down the front steps alone.

Avoiding the protesters, the president was loaded into his limousine at the rear of the church. Then the long black car drove around front to pick up the First Lady. As the stretch Lincoln pulled away, it inched slowly past the line of protesters. They peered into the vehicle. President Carter stared straight ahead, refusing to recognize them. Rosalynn, disagreeing with her husband's coldness, smiled and waved kindly to the activists.[37]

Like a recurring nightmare, the demonstrators shadowed Secretary Califano all over the city, setting up their signs and singing protest songs at every venue on his daily agenda. The HEW head went about his government business, calmly pretending they weren't there.

According to newsman Evan White, Carter and Califano viewed the activists as annoying discontents easily ignored. "They were perceived in Washington as freaks and troublemakers."[38]

President Carter and Secretary Califano didn't realize that treating the activists like misbehaving children only fed right into their narrative. The civic leaders' behavior matched exactly what the protesters were saying about the federal government's handling of Section 504, that disabled Americans were dismissed as people unworthy of serious consideration.

No one was surprised that President Carter didn't meet with the demonstrators. The real goal was to mobilize the leaders of the Democratic Party, the members of Congress and the Senate who had the president's ear. If the protesters' tactics worked correctly, Carter would receive phone calls from concerned Democrats. The president's main supporters on the Hill, the progressive friends and colleagues of Congressmen Miller and Burton, would apply the pressure.[39]

Each night, resting in the dark, empty church, the weary activists reenergized by singing together. This was a tradition going back to the gospel songs of Martin Luther King, Jr., and the early civil rights activists. Even to a group not sharing a common religion, time-honored spirituals soothed aching joints and anxious minds, restoring the bonds of solidarity worn away by the long day. One evening, while singing "Amazing Grace, " their weary voices withered to silence. They were just too tired.

Debbie Stanley, a blind woman, rose up to carry the song for everyone. Her powerful soprano voice sounded to the high rafters of the dark sanctuary, lifting the story of redemption at a moment of utter exhaustion. "I once was lost, but now am found." Tears ran down the cheeks of the beleaguered activists. They drifted off sweetly into sleep, knowing that they would get up the next morning to soldier on.[40]

A pivotal figure the activists needed to win over was the leading liberal icon, California senator Alan Cranston. He and Harrison Williams, Democratic senator from New Jersey, were the original sponsors of the Rehabilitation Act of 1973. Williams led a group of senators to add Title V provisions requiring all federal agencies to actively recruit and retain disabled workers. Judy Heumann had worked for Senator Williams as part of her graduate studies, contributing to the development of the 1975 Education for All Handicapped Children Act that created a national mandate for special education services. His support for the 504 protest was easily garnered. But Cranston would take some convincing.[41]

The Democratic whip in the Senate, Alan Cranston was a strong disability rights advocate. He had arranged appointments for Ed and Judy Heumann to the federal Architectural Barriers Board. Three years later, he collaborated with Ed on successful legislation to add independent living services to the Veterans Administration vocational rehabilitation program. A decade later, when the Americans with Disabilities Act was first proposed in the Senate, Senator Cranston would be one of the cosponsors.[42]

But he was also a cagy, detailed-oriented politician who didn't casually jump on any passing bandwagon. He needed to understand how to effectively counter the many arguments the Carter administration voiced against enacting a strong Section 504.

Ed flew to Washington to join Heumann, Cone, and Frank Bowe for the Cranston meeting. Daniel Yaholem, a Children's Defense Fund attorney, also attended. He was bringing a lawsuit against a Mississippi school district for failing to educate children with disabilities.[43]

Cranston walked the group methodically through a list of about a dozen proposed changes taken straight from the HEW regulations task force, pressing the activists to respond to each issue. Universities griped that they couldn't afford to make their campuses accessible. Did disabled students need access to every campus building? What about the expense of retrofitting older buildings? Construction costs for hospitals and local governments could be astronomical.

There was the lingering question of including drug addicts and alcoholics under the definition of disabled persons. Would employers have to hire workers who would be drunk and high on the job? Cranston took every concern seriously. The activists patiently and knowledgeably responded to every query.

After many hours, the group slumped exhausted in their chairs. The meeting was over by body-weary acclamation. But Cranston's decision still hung in the balance.

Frank Bowe, the studious academic whose 1978 book *Handicapping America* would become a foundation of the new field of disability studies, began to speak. Then he suddenly stopped. He stood up and his hands began to move. He communicated in American Sign Language, and Lynette Taylor translated.

"Senator, we're not even second-class citizens." He paused, utterly despondent. "We're third-class citizens."

Bowe's raw emotion shifted the conversation from stiff policy questions to the daily experiences of disabled Americans. Real people were suffering, and 504 would give them a chance.

Senator Cranston agreed to back the protesters. He issued a public statement advising President Carter, "Tough, effective regulations implementing Section 504 should be issued now."[44]

A George Miller–led group of twenty-nine congressional representatives likewise demanded that Carter approve the 504 regulations "without change, immediately."[45]

The Democratic leadership in Washington had turned against the president. The strategic campaign that began with a legislative hearing inside the sit-in at the San Francisco federal building had succeeded. The White House contacted Bowe and Fiorito at the ACCD. They were ready to talk.

Senior White House policy advisor Stuart Eizenstat was a thoughtful, bookish man, an Atlanta attorney with round glasses. He was a trusted, inner circle advisor to the president, a pragmatic man who skillfully steered the 1976 Democratic Party platform toward the uncontroversial ideological center.[46]

He started the meeting by defensively distancing his president from the regulations, as if the problem belonged solely to Califano. That didn't go over well with the group. But soon it became clear that Eizenstat was receptive to what Ed, Judy Heumann, Eunice Fiorito, Dan Yaholem, Bruce Curtis, and others had to say. He patiently asked the activists many questions, listened intently, and took careful notes.

The group demanded a meeting with the president. Eizenstat flatly turned them down. But his words hinted that the president believed it was time settle this matter. Even though Eizenstat promised nothing, his demeanor reassured the San Francisco activists that they had won. In Washington, nothing is guaranteed. But the activists left the White House feeling strongly that the regulations would be signed within days.

Kitty Cone and Judy Heumann felt hesitant about returning to San Francisco without an unequivocal victory. Heumann and a small group continued nightly vigils at Secretary Califano's house, unwilling to leave the Capitol until the ink of his signature dried. But the rest believed the game was over. It was time to go home.[47]

On April 29, 1977, the beleaguered demonstrators in San Francisco awoke to the incredible news. Secretary Califano had signed the 504 regulations without any changes. They had defeated the president to secure the federal law providing antidiscrimination protection to millions of disabled citizens.

Some of the protesters couldn't believe it. It simply was too good to be true. They wanted to remain in the federal building until they had concrete proof that the regulations Califano approved had not been altered.

There was also a touch of sadness among the activists. Leaving the building meant the experience of a lifetime was over. The demonstrators had bonded with one another with an intimacy and intensity they would probably never feel again. They were brothers and sisters, connected by a rare kind of love and pride.

Kitty Cone told the press they were going to remain in the building for one more day to clean up the messy HEW offices. Truthfully, it took an additional twenty-four hours for the leaders to convince everyone to leave.[48]

The ragtag bunch, weary and smiling, exited the glass lobby doors into the cheering arms of the loud crowd of supporters waiting on the plaza. They rolled out like a victorious Super Bowl team parading through the celebrating streets of their grateful city.

Kitty Cone, speaking in a raspy, brittle voice, shouted to the crowd: "Did the disabled people in the HEW building show strength beyond your wildest imagination?"

"Yes!" the raucous throng howled back.

Cone continued, "And did we show courage?"

"Yeah!"

"And did we show commitment?"

"Yeah!"

"And did we show power?"

"Yeah!"[49]

Ed told the victory rally crowd, "We, who are considered the weakest, the most helpless people in our society, are the strongest."[50]

Disabled Americans held their heads high. Kitty Cone later observed, "We brought new confidence and pride, not only to ourselves, but to the thousands and thousands of disabled people who were with us in spirit."[51]

Women activists—the CIL's Judy Heumann and Kitty Cone, working with Eunice Fiorito of the ACCD—played what was viewed as a rough and tumble men's game with vigor and mastery. They took a gut punch well and delivered back even better. In the end, they outsmarted Secretary Califano and President Carter.

19 *Nationwide Independence*

The dramatic Section 504 protest victory focused the eyes of Washington on the Berkeley CIL as federal legislators and disability advocates wrote the 1978 revision of the Rehabilitation Act. Ed and Judy Heumann saw an opportunity to pump more federal money into independent living programs across the nation. They wanted to install the Berkeley model with disabled people running the show as the national archetype of independent living. Toward this end, they asked Congressman George Miller to hold congressional committee hearings at the Berkeley CIL.

In January 1978, Miller and Congressman John Ashbrook of Ohio hosted an oversight hearing of the Committee on Education and Labor at the Berkeley CIL. It was the first hearing on the updated Rehabilitation Act, with more occurring later in Washington.

The CIL's drafty old garage space was chilly on that winter morning. Sipping hot coffee to warm himself, Miller delighted in his emcee role. The entire day was a well-orchestrated anthem of many voices praising the CIL. The message was clear. Disabled people everywhere needed their own local version of the CIL.[1]

Perhaps more important was the fact that the testimony—the first parcel of expert advice to the congressional committee on renewing the federal law—came from disabled people. The traditional roster of disability services leaders consisting of old-line charities and physicians would come later. The CIL hearings asserted, just this once, that the disabled people knew best what they needed.

Speakers included leaders of independent living centers in Santa Rosa, San Diego, Los Angeles, and San Francisco, all funded by Tom Bates's California A.B. 204. Moving testimonies came from independent living center clients with a variety of disabilities, who told how the centers helped them tackle social and bureaucratic obstacles.

Judy Heumann told the committee, "We have proven in California and in other states that ILPs [independent living programs] are, in fact, effective. Disabled people believe that these service centers are valuable and are attempting to establish programs across the country."[2]

Herb Leibowitz cheered for the home team on behalf of the federal rehabilitation system. Under Ed's leadership, "95 percent of what is going in the country" in the independent living movement was happening in California.[3]

Not surprisingly, the stars of the day were Ed Roberts and Judy Heumann. Each spoke at length and answered many questions from the two national legislators.

Wasting no time, Ed immediately addressed the challenge of duplicating the Berkeley CIL in every community. "All across the country communities, especially people with disabilities, are looking at how to import this concept to their own communities. We know it can be; we know these can be replicated." He noted that the rehabilitation agencies in Massachusetts and Michigan had already joined California in funding new independent living centers.

What stood in the way of this necessary step, Ed insisted, was prejudice against disabled people. That was the main problem. "The prevailing factor and the most difficult that people with disabilities have is the underdevelopment of our communities and our society, not only in terms of architectural barriers or in terms of services but underdevelopment in terms of attitudes."

In the face of pervasive prejudice, what independent living centers did best was raise the tragically low expectations that too many people had for what disabled people can do and can be. For Ed, it was simply a question of human faith. "I believe in people, and that comes from my gut."[4]

Judy Heumann compared her experiences moving to Berkeley and Washington, DC, illustrating the difference between living with or living without the support of an independent living center.

"I came to Berkeley, was met at the airport by a disabled friend driving a van with a hydraulic lift. I stayed in a home that was accessible and was given a loaner electric wheelchair to use, and I was assisted with personal care by a paid attendant. My life quickly began to change. I was in charge of my own activities, getting up when I wanted, going to bed when I wanted, taking a shower when I wanted, and the like. All these things may appear small to you, but for me it was the first time that my handicap did not completely control my life. I decided to stay in California."[5]

Later, when she took a graduate school internship in Washington, the lack of independent living center services in the nation's capital was disheartening. "Living in DC, after having lived in Berkeley, is an incredibly frustrating experience that can truly strip one's pride." Life without the CIL was damn hard.

Heumann pushed the congressional committee to establish independent living centers like the CIL in every community, backed by federal rehabilitation funds as well as local government dollars. Allow them to operate as nonprofit agencies run by disabled people, not by rehabilitation system professionals.

Returning to Washington, DC, the congressional committee held four additional hearings on the Rehabilitation Act in April 1978, gathering testimony from dozens of interested parties. This is where the exclusionary character of Washington disability politics was evident. By the late 1970s, for example, the women's movement was represented on Capitol Hill by forty different lobbying organizations, from the liberal NOW to the moderate Women's Equity Action League. Feminist women had effectively positioned themselves as the experts on legislation impacting women, including educational equity, financial credit, and abortion.

The same congressional committees that often sought informed counsel from leading women's groups didn't hesitate to ask nondisabled people for guidance on what disabled people needed. Often without a single disabled participant in the room, Congress tapped medical professionals and old-fashioned disability charities for advice, a long-standing tradition that ignored the voices of disabled people.[6]

It seemed certain the 1978 Rehabilitation Act revision would include additional dollars for independent living. The real question was whether those funds would create new Berkeley model centers with disabled people in charge. Or would the dollars support traditional programs of segregated housing and professional dominance? Ed worried that the series of DC-based hearings would erase the Berkeley voices and weaken the neatly crafted depiction of the CIL as the premier example of independent living. He traveled to Washington to testify again.

Ed strategically arranged to be the first speaker in the Washington hearings, allowing him to set the standard and tone for all that followed. He very intentionally shot for the stars. He called for Congress to create an entirely new rehabilitation system, "expand[ing] the continuum of services so that a person could be picked up wherever they are basically in terms of their own development, their own awareness, their own really strong belief in themselves, and that magic word 'motivation,' take them to a vocation, complete independence, or the ability to live in the community."[7]

Essential to Ed's fantastic system of "incredible comprehensiveness" was a new, national network of independent living centers. Put a Berkeley CIL in every community. The first thirty-five were already in operation. An initial commitment of $50 million would start "independent living programs up around the country."[8]

Ed's provocative opening salvo dropped the hot expression "independent living" on the tongues of the many national service and charitable organization leaders who testified. They uttered the words. But they spoke with the confusion and discomfort of electric typewriter manufacturers analyzing proposals to put new desktop computers in every American office.

"So-called independent living programs have created a Tower of Babel with a confusion of definitions and programs," grumbled James Garrett of the World Rehabilitation Fund.[9]

United Cerebral Palsy Association executive Ronald Torner admitted he was lost. "The programmatic concept of independent living is a 'popular one'. . . . But what is independent living?"[10]

Baffled and uncertain about independent living programs, the establishment leaders still took potshots at the Berkeley CIL. United Cerebral Palsy Association's Torner testified that the CIL was "an ideal model for severely physically disabled persons with normal intellectual skills" who were "aware enough and independent enough to ask for assistance." But, Torner averred, many disabled persons with "seizures, mental retardation, and substantially abnormal sensory and perceptual responses" could not be served by a Berkeley-style center.[11]

Vincent Gray of the National Association of Retarded Citizens faulted the CIL for failing to serve people with intellectual disabilities. He was unaware that the second highest disability category served by the Berkeley CIL after paralysis was intellectual disability, comprising almost 15 percent of new clients.[12]

Goodwill's Dean Phillips dramatically understated the CIL menu of programs as merely "transportation service, van, and wheelchair repair" and "peer counseling." Given the apparently severe limitations of the Berkeley model, he then advocated for "much more . . . comprehensive services to the severely handicapped." Undoubtedly, Goodwill would accept federal dollars for those expanded services that the CIL-style centers seemingly could not provide.[13]

Funding was the one point of clarity and agreement. More money was needed. Phillips doubled Ed's funding request. "Authorization for such a program should begin at not less than $100 million."

"New funding," testified James W. Wilson of the National Easter Seals Society for Crippled Children and Adults, "aimed at providing medical and rehabilitation services to foster independent living goals would be most desirable." If the new independent living idea, whatever it was, pried open the federal wallet, every organization and program queued up for a lion's share.[14]

What the inveterate disability charities didn't understand was fully grasped by top medical researchers. The hearings concluded, to Ed's delight, with the testimony of top physicians who were well informed about the independent living movement.

Dr. Henry Betts of Chicago applauded the Berkeley CIL at length. "Handicapped people have organized independent living considerations, and they have organized systems that can get care to people wherever they live. . . . The consumers themselves must be brought into the planning of this. They, you will find, have the most brilliant, innovative ideas."[15]

The congressional representatives struggled to balance new rehabilitation ideas coming from disabled people with the tried-and-true system of professionals and traditional service providers. What Ed and his activist colleagues saw as groundbreaking and even necessary struck many in Congress as disruptive and risky. At issue was the injection of radical activism into human service programs.

In the women's movement, this question divided developers of early shelters for battered women. Starting with the first American women's shelter in St. Paul, Minnesota, in 1974, feminists in numerous cities created safe houses that provided wives refuge from their violent husbands. Often operated by a combination of paid staff and volunteers, the shelters supplied accommodation for mothers and their children and twenty-four-hour crisis lines.

The first battered women's shelters did more than just offer a safe bed, hot food, and helpful counseling. The earliest shelters were sites of political activism that framed domestic violence within the broader economic and sociological subjugation of women. The dedicated feminists running the shelters—mental health professionals, social workers, and lawyers—and their injured, frightened charges were sisters bonded in the mission of women's rights.

When tax dollars became available in the late 70s to support new shelters, feminists worried that the services of safe housing and psychological support would be detached from the politics of the movement. Nonfeminist social workers secured grants and set up shelters lacking the foundation of grassroots feminist activism. These depoliticized programs obviously had value, but to the founders of the first shelters they lacked the essential purpose of empowering women in a patriarchal society.[16]

No doubt cautious legislators also recalled how the community action programs of President Lyndon Johnson's failed War on Poverty had stirred up trouble. Targeting urban ghettos of African Americans, Hispanic, and Appalachian migrants left behind by the postwar economic boom, Johnson's 1964 Economic Opportunity Act created community action programs (CAPs) designed to coordinate social services, employment, housing, and education programs. Bypassing distant federal bureaucracies, CAPs invested authority in local leaders to focus efforts in their own communities.

A controversial CAP principle called "maximum feasible participation" placed substantial program control in the hands of leaders from the low-income neighborhoods. Like the CIL, the people receiving assistance rose up to direct those services. In many cities, including Los Angeles, Philadelphia, and New York, this participation encouraged and empowered citizen activists to organize politically against city governments, conducting demonstrations and sit-ins. The blowback was the so-called "Mayor's Revolt," a revolt by city government managers critical of the Johnson administration for organizing and paying the poor to fight against local authorities.[17]

Two national rehabilitation leaders, June Rothberg, president of the American Congress of Rehabilitative Medicine, and Robert Humphreys, director of Rehabilitation Services Association, provided the middling advice the guarded Congress sought. Rothberg warned that "the independent living movement is quite new." Programs developed in Berkeley, Boston, and Houston were each worthwhile. But she advised supporting multiple approaches to independent living services. Humphreys suggested Congress begin "on a limited scale through project grants," a meager request to experiment with a small number of independent living centers.[18]

After the hearings, Lex Frieden called a meeting of disability advocates in Houston, bringing together the same group that Fred Fay had organized earlier in Boston. Ed and Judy Heumann attended. The group hashed out a compromise between the progressive Berkeley model and the politically mild Texas approach.

Then Heumann and Frieden worked closely with Joe Owen, the influential lobbyist of the Council of State Administrators of Vocational Rehabilitation (CSAVR). The text agreed upon in Houston was ultimately accepted into the independent living provision of the bill. From Ed's standpoint, the legislation was much too limited and timid. Ten new independent living centers for the entire country was far less than what was needed. California already had more than that. And there was no guarantee that disabled people would run them.[19]

The 1978 Rehabilitation Act was both a win and a defeat. Ed worried that a newly minted series of federally funded independent living centers stripped of activism and disability community leadership was a cup less than half full. The gutsy heart of the whole independent living idea was missing.

But Ed also understood how this game was played. The 1978 bill opened the door for federal funding for independent living centers as a legitimate piece of the national rehabilitation system. A small, initial flow of dollars could later become a rushing river. The Rehabilitation Act would come up for reauthorization every few years. Every time, Ed and the national community of disability activists charged to Washington. They successfully expanded allocations to create more independent living centers led by disabled people.

Within a decade, over three hundred federally funded independent living centers had been established. Today, as Ed originally envisioned in 1978, there are over four hundred independent living centers run by disabled people in the United States plus a hundred more in Europe and other countries.[20]

20 *Vegetables Unite!*

When Ed was invited in May 1980, to speak at a conference in Vancouver, British Columbia, he knew that he was bringing independent living ideas to Canada. He didn't realize that he was joining a team of activists who would soon spread the disability rights agenda to the entire world.

The conference leaders, Henry Enns and Jim Dirksen of the Coalition of Provincial Organizations of the Handicapped (COPOH), had grandiose plans straight from the Ed Roberts playbook. The savvy duo understood that the Canadian national government paid close attention to shifts in international policy, especially the pronouncements of the United Nations. If they could create international momentum for disability rights, influencing the UN in a new direction, they could also attract the support of their national government.

They invited Gerben DeJong, an innovative young rehabilitation scientist at Tufts University, to speak in Vancouver. A nondisabled man, DeJong was friends with Fred Fay and Paul Corcoran, two of the founders of Boston's independent living center. He authored a widely read 1979 article that cast the independent living movement as transforming the whole science of rehabilitation. DeJong and Ed brought the Canadians a strong double dose of American disability rights.[1]

Ed found Henry Enns, the forward-thinking leader of the Canadian disability rights movement, to be surprisingly mild and soft-spoken. Unlike Ed, Enns had the mellow demeanor of a country parson. He was an introvert, a faithful Mennonite who viewed his political work as humble earthly service to a just cause.

The son of Russian immigrants, Enns grew up on a Manitoba farm. Diagnosed with rheumatoid arthritis at age fifteen, he was using a wheelchair by the time he went off to college. He navigated the urban University of Winnipeg campus in the mid-60s before accessibility was even a conversation.

Allowing strangers to carry him up staircases to reach his classes was demeaning. But Enns had bigger aspirations in mind. If he was going to lead the way for other people with disabilities, he had to suffer indignities. It was a price he willingly paid.

For graduate school, Enns strategically picked a service profession that made everyday decisions about the lives of disabled people. He was determined to inject the missing voice of a disabled person into the field of social work.

The social work faculty at the University of Manitoba had a different take on the value of a disabled man's presence in their profession. Despite his strong undergraduate grades, they denied Enns admission due to his physical disability. Enns persuaded the reluctant professors to give him a temporary tryout. They granted him provisional admission, three months to prove himself. He earned high grades, and he was allowed to remain at the university.

As he finished his first year of study, university hospital physicians recommended he undertake a program of physical rehabilitation over the summer break. With the right training regimen and enough sweat investment, they predicted he would be walking by the time school began in autumn.

Enns obediently followed the doctors' orders. He dedicated himself to the daily schedule of strenuous exercise and stretching, pushing his sore body to the limits. When his fall classes started, his joints were inflamed. His arthritis flared up like angry fireworks crackling painfully through his knees and hips. Contrary to the expert medical forecasts, he couldn't walk. He set his aching body back into his wheelchair and returned to classes.

This agonizing ritual of hope and disappointment repeated the next summer. And the summer after that. Each June, as Enns completed the year's studies, university medical experts held out an enticing brass ring if only he would return to the rehabilitation carousel. The lure of walking—the golden prize chased for years by FDR and so many others—was too strong to ignore.

Each fall semester Enns was back in his wheelchair. He was the doomed patient whose recovery failed again and again.

One summer day he exited the hospital after another tiring workout. In the parking lot, he met an animated man using a wheelchair. He looked like a hippy in his colorful shirt and ragged hair. Jim Dirksen, a polio survivor, was entering the medical center not for rehabilitation but for a weekly meeting of disabled activists. He invited Enns to join him.

The passion and purpose of the group's discussion was a welcome tonic for the disheartened Enns. They were keen on improving their lives. But they weren't talking about walking away from their wheelchairs. They were making plans to influence the government, improve support services, and make the community more accessible.

Unexpectedly energized by that first meeting, Enns decided to quit the physical rehabilitation program and join Dirksen's rabble-rousing gang. He would stop trying to fix his body and start reforming Canadian society. He decided that the civil rights movement for disabled people was his life's true calling.[2]

After Ed and Gerben DeJong met with Enns, Dirksen, and their COPOH comrades in Vancouver, the Berkeley independent living center model spread in Canada. Enns founded the first center in

Kitchener, Ontario, in 1982. He convinced the Mennonite Central Committee (MCC), a religious body devoted to community service, to bankroll the creation of a national association to develop independent living centers across Canada.[3]

Canadians Enns and Dirksen kept a strategic eye on the international landscape as they worked in their homeland. The United Nations declared 1981 as the International Year of Disabled Persons. Rehabilitation International (RI), the worldwide professional association of rehabilitation professionals, scheduled their Summer 1980 conference to take place in Winnipeg.

In Ottawa, Liberal prime minister Pierre Trudeau elevated a lower level parliamentary committee on disability to a top policy priority. Four legislators from different parties and disability community representative Jim Dirksen held their first meeting at the RI World Congress in Winnipeg. Dirksen's committee wrote a comprehensive national policy document based on a framework of human rights and full citizenship. It provided a national plan for an accessible and inclusive society.[4]

Enns and Dirksen shared their ambitious worldwide scheme with Ed. Their first move targeted Rehabilitation International for takeover. In California, Ed had largely commandeered the state rehabilitation apparatus for the disability rights cause. Would a similar strategy work on the international stage? Rehabilitation International was a powerful organization of rehabilitation professionals and the most respected authority on disability in the world. If disabled people could take control, they could immediately influence the UN as well as countries around the world.

The initial sparks of unrest had ignited at the RI World Congress in Tel Aviv in 1976. Among the eight hundred official delegates was a small contingent of disabled healthcare professionals. To their frustration, the conference halls, lodging accommodations, and transportation lacked the most basic accessibility. Conference leaders arranged for a fleet of uncomfortable, conspicuous military vehicles to haul the wheelchair users around the city. The disabled delegates felt humiliated. They expressed their dismay to RI leaders, but the response was less than satisfying. By the end of the conference, the disabled participants sadly concluded they were being ignored.[5]

The Canadians prepared a resolution for the 1980 RI world conference in Winnipeg. They asked for increased participation of disabled people, improved accessibility, and greater equality between disabled and nondisabled delegates. A Swedish group led by blind activist Bengt Lindqvist wrote a similar motion.

A difficult procedural hurdle blocked the way. The Canadians could only submit their resolution to the RI assembly if COPOH was approved as an official member organization. The single formal representative of Canada was the Canadian Rehabilitation Council for the Disabled (CRCD). The nondisabled rehabilitation professionals of CRCD would have to allow the disabled activists of COPOH to stand with them as an equal national representative. The CRCD rejected the request.

Enns and Dirksen took a page from Judy Heumann and Kitty Cone's Section 504 protest script. They threatened to stage a demonstration at the Winnipeg conference, a public embarrassment for the Canadian government, who had planned to turn the prestigious international event into a high-profile public relations win.

The Ottawa administration as well as local authorities were pumped up to host the RI World Congress. The federal government issued a new postage stamp commemorating the conference. The new Winnipeg phone book featured photos of disabled people using Manitoba Telephone System access devices. The Winnipeg Convention Centre installed push button entrance doors, and the Winnipeg International Airport boasted four new elevators operational just in time for the arrival of disabled guests.[6]

All levels of government and commerce were using the Winnipeg conference to celebrate the positive new direction of Canadian disability policy. The national government desperately wanted to avoid the humiliation of public protests. Ottawa quietly intervened in the RI membership conflict. They persuaded the CRCD to approve the COPOH as a Canadian member organization.[7]

Feeling less than sanguine about their equality resolution's chances, Enns and Dirksen hedged their bets. They organized a team of fifty disabled activists from Winnipeg to attend the RI conference, dramatically increasing the representation of disabled people. They ran their squad through three days of intensive training, practicing techniques to effectively raise issues disabled people faced every day in a forum dominated by nondisabled professionals.[8]

Dark clouds gathered as the conference launched. The *Winnipeg Free Press*, the largest local newspaper, gave the disabled conferees from forty different nations a harsh reminder of the eugenic attitudes they were up against. A blistering headline asked, "Are Handicapped Spoiled?"

The nasty hit piece denounced government policies stipulating equal access for disabled people as "so much sloppy good feeling." Curb cuts and accessible buildings were a "preposterous idea," highly expensive measures that removed "inconveniences" for a disadvantaged few while harming the "majority of the fit who are the producers and earners." The able-bodied "do the work," keeping the economic machine pumping, while the disabled who "contribute much less" selfishly demand undeserved "privileges."[9]

Dirksen and Enns were prepared. They arranged for a Canadian Broadcasting Corporation (CBC) film crew to follow their delegation, documenting their activities for a planned television special. Any negative incidents would be broadcast in living rooms across Canada.

Dirksen set up a shadow media operation to educate the press daily. His team carefully monitored every conference session, tracking the sadly regular presence of ableism in the presentations and discussions. At the close of each day, they compiled the notes into a newsletter and stuffed copies under the hotel doors of journalists.

These tactics were effective. Even the *Free Press* changed their tune, highlighting the positive involvement of disabled people in the conference and their disability rights message.

Dirksen criticized sheltered workshops for paying disabled workers "less than a dollar a day." Liam Maguire, a disabled activist from Ireland, compared the *Free Press*'s editorial of a few days earlier to "the philosophy of Goebbels and Hitler."[10]

National health minister Monique Begin admitted, "Regarding disability, we are still in the Dark Ages." She promised dramatic improvements in health services and education for disabled Canadians. The Trudeau government would lead the way in changing the society's attitudes toward disabled people.[11]

The delegations from Canada and Sweden submitted a proposal calling for at least half of the RI member organizations to consist primarily of disabled persons. They asked the RI professionals to equally share power with disabled people.

The RI Delegate Assembly voted down the equality proposal, 61–37. The message was clear to Ed, Henry Enns, and the hundreds of disability rights leaders who had traveled thousands of kilometers to attend the conference. Rehabilitation International would never represent their interests.[12]

Enns immediately requested a large convention center room to hold a meeting of disabled delegates. They needed to plan their next move. Hoping to block the insurgent group, the RI leadership refused to give the activists a meeting space. Only the intervention of Ron Chandran-Dudley, a disabled man from Singapore who served as RI vice chair, secured a room.

An angry and exuberant crowd of 250 disabled people gathered. People from all corners of the planet speaking dozens of different languages shared an almost unnamable understanding that they were members of the same family. Divided by kilometers, oceans, wealth, and politics, all disabled people were one.

Joshua Malinga of Zimbabwe told of disabled Africans starving in dire poverty, crawling on the ground because of a lack of wheelchairs. Jacqueline Carreres said that the disabled people in her native Argentina were "third class citizens." ACCD leader Eunice Fiorito urged her international comrades to push aside the arrogant professionals who often controlled the possibilities available to disabled people. "The time has come for us to speak for ourselves."[13]

Then Ed rolled up to the microphone. The audience listened fully. Everyone knew Ed. Stories about the Berkeley hero had circumnavigated the earth. Tales had traveled to the farthest reaches of the globe of a paralyzed Californian with an air tube in his mouth who climbed to the top of the largest rehabilitation agency in the United States. They knew he could fly his wheelchair above the clouds to touch the sun.

Ed took a deep huff of air. Then he belted out the delicious phrase he had been dying to shout since the family doctor had first scolded his mother for wishing him to survive.

"Vegetables of the world unite!"

The crowd roared. Karl Marx never envisioned his words in this context. But he was the ally of the downtrodden. And there was no one more down and trodden upon than the world's disabled people.

Very intentionally, Ed chose the ugly old slur "vegetable" because it emphasized the shared lowly status of every person in the room. With his usual high-spirited flair, he rollicked in the glorious irony of the world's artichokes rising to power.

Henry Enns spoke next. If Ed was the strutting Frank Sinatra of the world stage, Enns was the well-organized production manager who typically did his best work hidden in the wings. At that moment, the self-effacing Enns had no difficulty speaking to the electric crowd. The historical moment caught him and carried him forward. He had one important thing to say.

"Do I hear you say you want a world coalition of citizens with disabilities?"

"Yes!" the crowd screamed back in raw-throated jubilation.

The convention room fell apart. Tearful friends and overwhelmed strangers embraced, hugging and shouting. Cheers rang out as if every nation had simultaneously won the football World Cup. For the many disability advocates who fought daily for basic dignity in their villages and cities, this was too much. No one had imagined that a worldwide union of people of all kinds of disabilities dedicated to human rights, access, and equality was even possible. But here it was.

On June 23, 1980, with nearly empty pockets and no government backing, Disabled Peoples' International (DPI) was born.

That was the easy part. Ed joined Henry Enns's leadership group. Representatives from Canada, Costa Rica, India, Japan, Sweden, and Zimbabwe developed organizational goals and structure. Enns was elected chairperson of the new DPI steering committee. Bengt Lindqvist was tapped as secretary. They picked Liam Maguire, with his extensive background in labor unions, to write the DPI constitution.

In the first year, the new DPI leaders met in Dublin, San Francisco, and Toronto. The sessions were filled with long, heated arguments. The activists disagreed on basic goals of the organization as well as strategies for progress. Some wanted to create a polite, diplomatic body that worked closely with governments and the United Nations. Others wanted to sponsor an international activist team and create a political firestorm, taking their energy to the streets and staging dramatic protests around the world.

Thorny issues divided the group. Should they allow representatives from South Africa's apartheid regime? Would there be members from both Israel and Palestine? China and Taiwan?

Behind the long-winded arguments that seemed to go nowhere, the biggest problem was money. They needed hundreds of thousands of dollars just to get started.

With his usual bombastic flair, Ed promised his colleagues that raising an initial ten million dollars would be, as Americans like to say, a piece of cake. He boasted of his prior success with private philanthropic foundations. He assured the entire room that he could readily round up the necessary donations.

They believed him. He was the famous Ed Roberts.

Ed didn't deliver on his extravagant promise. The Bay Area network of funders that backed the Berkeley CIL were not interested in global issues. In February 1981, Ed hosted the DPI leadership group in San Francisco. He quietly paid for the meetings out of his own wallet.[14]

The San Francisco sessions were a disaster. The uplifting unity initially felt in the Winnipeg hotel conference had faded. The discussion deteriorated into a verbal brawl filled with nasty accusations. Enns led with a gentle hand, calmly mediating the heated struggles. But his soft demeanor was overwhelmed by the loudest voices.

Ed played the role of optimistic peacekeeper, encouraging his counterparts to keep their eyes on the prize. This was an incredible opportunity and responsibility, he reminded them. They couldn't squander it. Frustrated, the group reached an impasse and gave up. They left the meeting to soak their frustrations at a local bar. Unexpectedly, calmed by alcohol and the change of venue, the talks continued. Gradually, the activists worked through the divisive issues. Tamed by happy hour, unity prevailed.[15]

The biggest early test of the new DPI was the Singapore conference planned for November 1981. Holding a World Congress a little more than a year after the underfunded and barely united group was founded was ambitious to say the least. No one knew if disabled activists would travel from every corner of the world to a meeting of the fledgling organization. Even if they did, the conference plans greatly exceeded the group's paltry bank account.

Enns quickly cobbled together small pots of money. The Canadian International Development Agency (CIDA) gave $200,000 to support the travel and accommodations of people from developing countries. The United Nations kicked in another $100,000.

It wasn't enough. The DPI's inaugural international conference, its first public statement as a real global organization, was in jeopardy. When the leadership team considered cancelling the event, Ron Chandran-Dudley, the blind activist from the host country, mortgaged his house to cover the final batch of convention bills.

Enn's assistant Diane Driedger ran up travel agency lines of credit to buy over fifty round-trip airline tickets for activists from lower income countries. If this fiscally risky strategy worked, the first DPI World Congress would include participants from Argentina, Nicaragua, Venezuela, Cameroon, Senegal, and Sierra Leone.[16]

Communicating with activists from the developing nations was like tossing handwritten notes into the wind. Telephone service alternated between spotty and nonexistent. Driedger mailed the airline tickets to the addresses she had on record and hoped somehow the intended recipients would show up in Singapore.

The DPI leaders checked into the conference hotel a couple days early, knowing that they needed another $40,000 to pay for the airline tickets. They contacted the Canadian ambassador to Singapore. Maybe he could help them squeeze the last few dollars out of the Canadian government. The ambassador immediately drove to the hotel to talk to Enns and Dirksen about their dire financial situation.

To their surprise, the ambassador arrived with a large suitcase, as if he was checking into the hotel. He carried the luggage to their hotel room. Then he unzipped the bag and dumped out its contents. The Canadian disability advocates watched wide-eyed as $40,000 in cash fell onto the bed.

Everyone in the room knew that government agencies do not make large cash payments. No one knew where the money came from, and no one bothered to ask.

The next day the miracle continued. Enns, Dirksen, and Driedger waited in anxious anticipation at the front door of the hotel, hoping to greet the delegates arriving from the airport. They didn't know if the dozens of airline tickets had ever reached activists at the farthest corners of the earth. Nervously they wondered, Would people really show up?

All day long a steady stream of accessible airport vans and taxis pulled up at the hotel entrance. Out stepped weary, smiling activists from lands far away. Every single airline ticket Driedger mailed out carried back a conference participant. She later wrote, "Disabled people came, 400 strong, from all ends of the earth to Singapore—to proclaim that they would no longer be silent."[17]

At the Singapore conference, Ed was the most well-known speaker. Many looked to him for reassurance that this fledgling DPI outfit was real, that the least powerful people on earth could truly unify for the first time in history to create a single, influential voice. The very idea of such an organization was both perfect and preposterous. Ed's job was to tell them this was no pipedream. They were real. They were together. And yes, they would change the world.

Ed emphasized the power of disabled people coming together as one. Our strength is our unity. Not only within our countries but around the world. As we fight together, as we gain strength and recognition for that strength, we are going to see one of the most massive social changes this world has ever seen.

"I expect that within the next few years we will create together the most important social revolution this world has ever seen. When we bring that severely and profoundly retarded person, or that severely physically disabled person, back into our society, remove him from institutions, help the family allow the person to take the risk to be free, we will together have created a new world. One that is based on human rights. We will do that together."[18]

Ed was right, largely because of the leadership of Henry Enns. In the decades to follow, under Enns's careful stewardship, DPI became the leading international advisory to the United Nations on disability policy. Not surprisingly, counseled by disabled people, the UN moved in new directions.

The 1982 World Programme of Action Concerning Disabled Persons expanded beyond the old goals of impairment prevention and rehabilitation to pursue a rights-based agenda of access and equal participation. Human rights, citizenship, and educational and economic opportunities for disabled people became top UN priorities. The years 1983 to 1992 were declared the Decade of Disabled Persons, a dramatic commitment of the UN to focus on the intensive work of disability rights.

A long sequence of impressive UN commissions, conferences, and reports, including the 1994 Salamanca Statement calling for the inclusive education of children with disabilities, culminated with the 2006 Convention on the Rights of Persons with Disabilities. The convention articulated clear human rights and equality principles with a global program of action.

While most American disability rights leaders spent the 1980s building the ramp that finally led to the 1990 passage of the Americans with Disabilities Act, Ed often traveled the world. He was busy in the Bahamas and Australia and Japan, working closely with Henry Enns and other DPI colleagues, spreading ideas about independent living and freedom for disabled people. The revolution was indeed worldwide.

21 *A Magical Place*

Wriggling in the discomfort of almost-business attire, a tall slender man with long hair and a rarely trimmed beard sat in the waiting room outside Governor Jerry Brown's office. Mark Dubois was more comfortable in his usual river rat uniform—shirtless, sun-faded shorts, and bare feet. An experienced whitewater rafting guide, he was leader of Friends of the River, an environmental group fighting to save California's Stanislaus River from decimation by the federal New Melones Dam project.

Dubois was also the courageous man who steered Ed down the rollicking Stanislaus to bring publicity to the cause. The tale of how Ed went whitewater rafting is really a story of the intimate ties between California environmentalists and the Berkeley disability activists.

The rushing, glistening Stanislaus wound through miles of awe-inspiring natural beauty in the Sierra Nevada foothills, sweeping past ancient limestone caves, majestic rock walls the height of three foot-ball fields, and forests filled with old redbud and alder. In the 1970s, it was the second most popular whitewater rafting destination in the United States, attracting tens of thousands of outdoor enthusiasts every year.[1]

But it was under threat. The federal government had initially authorized a new dam and hydroelectric plant to curb river flooding during World War II. Dubois and his friend Jerry Mural founded Friends of the River in 1973 in an unsuccessful attempt to stop the project.

After construction of the New Melones Dam was completed in 1978, the dispute between environmentalists and the agricultural and energy interests entered a new phase. The conflict shifted to the question of closing the dam and filling the valley lowlands with river water. Once flooded, there was no turning back. Friends of the River, backed by Governor Brown, fought to keep the dam open and the river flowing freely.[2]

Dubois made national headlines in May 1979. A bill was introduced in Congress seeking to protect the upper nine miles of the Stanislaus River under the federal Wild and Scenic Rivers Act. Dubois dropped a letter at the governor's office, notifying Jerry Brown of what he was doing. Then he chained himself to the bedrock at the base of the river canyon. If the Army Corps of Engineers closed the dam and raised the lake waters to the planned levels, the flood waters would overwhelm Dubois. He would drown.

Corps district engineer Colonel Donald M. O'Shea held the dam open as county sheriffs and federal officials searched miles of lush riverbed for the environmental activist. DuBois was too well hidden. They never found him. After seven days, the governor sent a hand-delivered letter to Dubois guaranteeing that the dam would remain open.[3]

As Dubois waited outside the governor's office, two men in power wheelchairs zipped past. One man raced full speed like a daredevil toward the secretary's desk. At the last second, he spun his vehicle a furious one hundred and eighty degrees to a sudden halt. Dubois marveled that the man's outstretched foot missed the desk by mere inches.

Working with the Bay Area group Environmental Traveling Companions (ETC), Dubois had taken many people with physical disabilities down the river, bouncing and diving through the roughest rapids. But this disabled guy, who he soon learned was Ed Roberts, struck him as unusually fearless.

Ed and Jim Donald introduced themselves to the environmental activist. They chatted briefly. Ed expressed a strong interest in conservation issues and the campaign to save California's rivers.

The Berkeley disability community had deep roots in the Stanislaus. The efforts of ETC created regular access to the remote canyon for disabled Californians. A steady roster of disabled rafters traveled the rough waters throughout the 1970s.

While wheelchair users across the country were fighting for curb cuts so they could cross the street to enter the local ice cream shop, the disabled people of the Bay Area already savored what they viewed as their greatest freedom. Under blue skies they rafted headlong down a mighty river through the heart of American wilderness.

Mary Regan, a woman with multiple sclerosis, described the river as "our greatest teacher . . . it became for us a wilderness cathedral." Disabled bodies limited by bad architecture and stigmatized in many avenues of society were free, natural, and joyful on the ancient river.[4]

Dennis Fantin and Bob Metz were the pioneers, becoming the first and foremost expert team of disabled river-runners. They developed a buddy system of navigation and paddling that neatly combined their talents. Metz, though not strong enough to row, had a sharp eye for reading the rocks, drops, and chutes in the waters ahead. Fantin, though blind, was a powerful and capable helmsman. He sat at the front of the raft, matching his friend's shouted instructions with careful and potent paddle strokes. Onlookers on the shore cheered them as they steered adeptly through the most challenging rapids.[5]

Other disabled rafters followed their lead. After supposedly proficient, nondisabled paddlers repeatedly dumped him into the river waters, a frustrated Michael Pachovas turned to his friend Mark

Sutton, a blind man. Sutton was a skillful oarsman who kept the quadriplegic Pachovas high and dry. They became a rafting team that functioned on the Fantin-Metz model of synchronized capabilities.[6]

As many Berkeley disability activists became devoted rafters, they formed their own environmental action group. The Stanislaus Wilderness Action Committee (SWAC) worked closely with Friends of the River. Disabled people were perfect emissaries for the environmental message. They were the most ordinary citizens battling the wealthy and powerful who siphoned profits from the earth's waters.[7]

Emulating Mark Dubois's courageous act of chaining himself to river rock, the disabled environmentalists also put their bodies on the line. In January 1980, the environmentally friendly President Jimmy Carter was vacating office to the far less supportive Ronald Reagan. Carter's final days in office were likely their last chance for federal intervention to save the river. Three SWAC members mailed a padlock key to the White House and chained themselves to the riverbed. They repeated DuBois's threat. Unleash the waters and you'll kill us.

Michael Pachovas, polio survivor Rick Spittler, and a fifteen-year-old nondisabled boy named Kael Fisher braved ten cold nights hidden at the bottom of the valley. To the annoyance of the Reagan administration, Carter granted last-minute federal protection to a series of wilderness areas under the Wild and Scenic Rivers Act. To the disappointment of Pachovas and SWAC, Carter ignored their stunt. The Stanislaus didn't make the list.[8]

A bill to save the river, H.R. 4223, made its way through Congress. Ed testified in the Congressional hearing as the Committee on Interior and Insular Affairs took up H.R. 4223. Despite the likely Reagan veto, the environmentalists battled on.

Ed explained to the legislators the unique value of the Stanislaus River for the disability community. "It's an experience that I have seen day to day with so many of our people with disabilities who don't recognize their own strength and power and ability. . . . This canyon has been a place for the past four years where people with disabilities have been experiencing this kind of change, this kind of growth. . . . It has become a magical place."[9]

As the pivotal committee vote on H.R. 4223 approached, the fight for the river slogged into the summer months. Ed soon had his chance to experience that river magic firsthand.

Friends of the River activist Patty Shifferle rustled up a group of high-profile politicians for a whitewater rafting trip. The purpose was to draw attention to the plight of the Stanislaus by attracting journalists to follow top Washington and Sacramento politicos into the California wilderness.

Shifferle used political skills that she had learned from Ed. As the two worked together for the Stanislaus on Capitol Hill, knocking on the doors of members of Congress, she took careful note of his approach. He always put his values up front, articulated in a way that challenged politicians to act on their own values. He knew they were pushed and pulled by other interests. His strategy was to reach them as human beings who cared.

Ed taught Shifferle lessons drawn from disability activism. Behind the scenes he was constantly strategizing, thinking through how to make new connections and use those relationships to create further connections. No never meant no. It meant take another path. Talk to another person. It was all a baseball game with unlimited extra innings. No matter what happened, he fought tirelessly, ignoring setbacks and moving ahead without hesitation.[10]

On July 17, 1980, a throng of national reporters followed a crew of noted politicians deep into the valley to watch them run the frothy Stanislaus. Congressman Don Edwards was the author and sponsor of H.R. 4223. He was joined by Bay Area Congressman Pete Stark and Huey Johnson, head of the California Natural Resources Agency. Ed's presence further demonstrated the State of California's opposition to the federal dam project.[11]

Shifferle's efforts to convince the supportive congressman Phil Burton to join the rafting outing failed. Ed's friend and frequent collaborator begged off the backwoods adventure, "I'm an armchair environmentalist."[12]

Even for river guides with the expertise of the Friends of the River members, this was an intense day that required extra attention to safety. Dubois and Shifferle were both especially concerned about Ed. They had run many people with physical disabilities down the river. This was their first time rafting the whitewater with a quadriplegic man who was frog-breathing for air in the turbulent spray.[13]

It wasn't uncommon for inexperienced rafters to fall into the water at some point on the nine-mile trip above the Parrots Ferry Bridge. *The New York Times* reported that both Stark and Edwards tumbled into the river. Dubois had scooped many rookie rafters out of the drink and set them safely back in the raft. He feared it wouldn't work that easily with Ed.[14]

The problem was that Ed was strapped to a wooden frame that propped him upright in the raft. Dubois didn't think the foam life vest would keep Ed afloat with the bulky structure fastened to his back. If he slipped over the side of the boat, the makeshift seat might weigh him down, sinking him past Dubois's grasp to the river bottom.

Dubois and expert rafter Sharon Negri packed Ed into a secure nest of duffel bags and backpacks at the center of the raft. Sharon and Ed's wife, Cathy, sat at either side, and Dubois paddled at the rear.[15]

Steering with technical precision, Dubois slid the craft down fast shallows and swept neatly between rising rocks. He knew every challenge and readied himself well in advance. Soaring over high swells, the boat repeatedly plunged through the air, slapping down on the hard water surface. Ed's ballcap-covered forehead dropped forward. He groaned in pain. Ed later told Congressman Edwards that the constant, heavy pounding left his body aching for weeks.[16]

The cost to Ed's body in soreness was more than offset by the outrageous joy of racing swiftly down the raucous Stanislaus. The unbridled freedom of running the mighty waters was the sweetest amalgam of chaos and beauty. Like a kid on his first roller coaster, he was hooked. In the years to come, he would seek out more water adventures, swimming with dolphins in the Florida Keys and chasing whales in Hawaii.

One of Ed's consistent messages to disabled people and the many professionals that assisted them was the need to embrace risk. Disabled people had historically been viewed as vulnerable and fragile. For decades institutions, nursing homes, and controlling service providers had carefully shielded disabled people from potential harms. No need to add to their misery, the logic went.

Ed believed that the stifling cloak of safety stole the vitality of life. Disabled people had to get out and live.

In a speech to an audience of young disabled leaders just two months before his journey down the Stanislaus, he counseled: "I want to urge you to take risks. One of the great values in learning to take risks is that you discover that you have many more options than you ever thought possible. I can't count the times I've been told that I'm unrealistic. I've learned that it is a fundamental mistake to let other people define what's realistic and what's not."[17]

Ed relished the bountiful danger of rafting down the Stanislaus River. After that wonderful day, Ed was like a mountain climber seeking out a more challenging peak. He felt drawn to find richer experiences, bigger risks, and as he often preached, greater opportunities to live more fully than anyone imagined.

The environmental education and the political groundwork established by Friends of the River paid off in their future efforts to save many California rivers. But H.R. 4223 failed. The House committee on Interior and Insular Affairs voted on the bill to save the Stanislaus on September 17, 1980. All the Republicans voted against the measure. The Democrats split. The Stanislaus lost, 20 to 19. Five months later, the New Melones Dam was closed tight and water filled the valley. The Stanislaus River became a lake, flooding over the Parrots Ferry Bridge.[18]

Patty Shifferle and Ed both understood how politics worked. In defeat, Ed quipped bitterly about his opponents, "That Senator and I have a lot in common. I'm paralyzed from the neck down. He's paralyzed from the neck up." There were more losses than victories. The human values driving their actions remained the same. The struggle continued.[19]

22 *Grief and Genius*

Early Sunday morning, August 9, 1981, the ringing telephone rousted Ed from sleep. Zona gave him the news. His brother Randy, the youngest of Verne Roberts's four sons, was dead at age twenty-nine.

"How?" Ed asked through his tears.

His mother told the little that she knew. Randy was hanging out with his girlfriend in his Oakland apartment. A stranger knocked on the door. This wasn't uncommon. Randy's passionate vocation was jazz music. He played in a local band. He spent much of his childhood banging away on his drum set in the attic of the Roberts home. But his real income came from selling marijuana, a job that involved clandestine meetings with sketchy people at odd hours.

Randy let the man enter the apartment. The details from this point, based on what the Oakland police officer told Zona, weren't completely clear. Was the stranger a buyer? Was he Randy's supplier? A rival dealer?

The man suddenly pointed a pistol at Randy and his companion. He demanded that they hand over their stash of marijuana. Randy refused. After a brief shouting match, the man shot him in the chest. The shooter ran off, leaving the young woman holding Randy on the floor. He bled out before an ambulance arrived. Randy's girlfriend told the police that the assailant first pointed the gun at her. Randy stepped in front, protecting her from the firearm with his body. He took the bullet, and she was unharmed.

The last person that Ed might imagine as the victim of violence was his sweet and tender brother Randy. Peaceful and artistic, he was a young man too caring and gentle for the illicit drug distribution world he navigated.

As a young schoolboy, when a playground bully threatened him, Randy just folded. He had no defense. His older brother Mark advised him to creatively fend off the thug by claiming that he was a judo expert. That's what Mark did. But Randy couldn't pull it off. He didn't have the nerve to stand up for himself. He later dropped out of Berkeley High School. The harsh social world of American teenagers was overwhelming.

Friends from all over Berkeley gathered at Zona's house to offer their condolences. Ed traveled from Sacramento to share the sorrow with his mother and friends. Randy was a favorite son of the disability community. He had worked driving a CIL van. Everyone knew him as Ed's little brother, the one who was creative, sensitive, and kind.[1]

.   •   .

Novelist Kurt Vonnegut once quipped that "everybody wants to build and nobody wants to do maintenance." For Ed, the exhilarating departmental reforms and policy breakthroughs of Governor Jerry Brown's first term deteriorated into the budget belt-tightening frustrations of his second. The fun of creating something new turned into the depressing grind of trying to keep it funded and operating.[2]

After Prop 13 passed in 1978, Brown embraced the taxpayer revolt, recasting himself as a tightfisted financial manager. With hopeful eyes on the White House, he correctly embraced the nation's growing appetite for fiscal conservativism.

Beginning in 1981, the Ronald Reagan administration moved federal dollars from public assistance to defense. Federal tax code reforms cut taxes for all income groups but disproportionately benefited the wealthy. He halted decades of welfare state expansion that created an almost livable safety net for people with disabilities. Federal vocational rehabilitation spending grew sevenfold in the 1960s and doubled again in the 1970s. But no more. In his first two years in office, Reagan boosted military spending by over $22 billion while slashing rehabilitation department budgets by 12 percent.[3]

Ed's jubilant, state-authorized disability revolution never shifted into second gear. He fought just to maintain a reasonable level of services for disabled Californians. Even the Berkeley CIL, by this time heavily dependent on federal grants, had to cut staff from two hundred to a skeleton crew of thirty-eight.[4]

In January 1981, Ed and his Berkeley friends staged a protest rally of hundreds of disability advocates at the state Capitol. All fifty state departments of rehabilitation budgets were frozen. Ed criticized Reagan, arguing that any reductions in spending should be borne by his own administration. If Reagan wanted to trim what he thought was excess fat, start with the bloated federal bureaucracy. Don't cut the services and supports that disabled people rely on.[5]

But that's exactly what happened. In January 1982, Ed testified to a congressional committee on the dire situation facing many people with disabilities. President Reagan's budget cuts to social programs hit California's most vulnerable citizens hard. An impoverished underclass that struggled in the best of times was pushed to the desperate edge:

"There is an atmosphere of fear and depression taking hold of the disabled poor in California. This population is totally dependent on IHSS, SSI, Medi-Cal and a broad range of state, county and city services in order to live in the community, free of institutionalization. Even prior to the recent cutbacks, the ability of the disabled poor to survive on their own has been tenuous; but over the last six months, it has become evident that this population is unable to cope with the service cutbacks and the closing of neighborhood offices that is now taking place."[6]

The social support web built of federally funded programs carried out by state agencies and supplemented with California tax dollars, a tattered patchwork quilt inadequate even before Reagan's cuts, was falling apart. People who counted on In-Home Support Services (IHSS) to pay for personal attendants saw reductions in hours. Social Security Insurance (SSI) offices delayed monthly checks that paid the rent, leading to many evictions. Medi-Cal health insurance stopped paying for transportation to hospitals and physician appointments, effectively blocking people from accessing their own healthcare.

Ed warned that the trickle down from federal budget reductions to state programs that appeared manageable and reasonable in bureaucratic reports hit the disability community like a punch in the jaw. "There is a fundamental difference between the information you will receive from a government agency that is adjusting to funding cutbacks and the people in the community who are feeling its effects. . . . A human services system can look as though it works on paper and then not work in the community. That's what I fear is happening."[7]

By the end of 1982, Governor Brown's final year in office, Ed was weary. Not only was he feeling emotionally drained by budget woes. He no longer found comfort at home. His strained marriage had already lasted well beyond its expiration date. Sacramento had been kind to Ed but not to Cathy. She struggled without friends in a strange town.

Loving Ed was difficult. Not only did he work long hours and spend many weeks traveling around the state. When he was home, there was almost no way for Cathy to enjoy being alone with her husband. He had a personal assistant at all times. When Cathy arranged for a bit of cherished privacy, she took on the personal care tasks. Often she felt more like Ed's employee than his wife.

In her sadness and isolation, she turned to alcohol. At first, it was just a couple glasses of wine in the evening. Over time her drinking snowballed.

Ed had a remedy. He suggested she join Erhard Seminars Training, or EST, a popular self-help program. The seminars preached radical personal responsibility. EST shined a brutal, bright light on every psychological strategy used to deny complicity in life's disappointments. Whatever had gone wrong, whatever had brought suffering and hardship, was yours. You made it. You chose it. You owned it.

Health Department leader Bob Gnaizda had introduced Ed to the charismatic EST founder Werner Erhardt. Well-connected in liberal political circles, the brash, opportunistic self-discovery shaman delighted in recruiting top political figures and activists to his human potential workshops. David B. Goodstein, the wealthy publisher of *The Advocate*, the leading newspaper focusing on LGBT politics and lifestyle, was so intrigued by EST that he developed a version marketed specifically to gay men.[8]

Ernhardt and Ed quickly bonded, each seeing something of himself in the other. Highly intelligent, deeply empathetic, doggedly ambitious, both leaders relied on their magnetism and intellect to persuade people.

Erhardt repeatedly encouraged Ed to take his EST seminar. Perhaps he imagined Ed bringing EST to the disability community. Ed chuckled but passed on the invitation. Erhard got nowhere with Ed. Finally, he realized why.

"You're the only person I've ever met who doesn't need EST," the self-improvement master admitted. "Everything you would learn in the training you already know."

Ed had been forcibly schooled by polio. Confronted with long, dark hours of loneliness in hospital beds, and the near-complete loss of physical abilities, he fully accepted his life as a disabled man. He had become an EST expert.

Erhard found a willing and ready subject in Cathy. Her ardent devotion to EST had confounding results. Almost overnight, she burst out of her timid cocoon with a sudden assertiveness. But her drinking didn't slow. The combination of EST-fueled boldness and alcohol abuse only made her more ferocious. Often the couple's prolonged quarrels ended with Cathy storming out the door and leaving town for days.

By the end of Governor Brown's second term, Ed and Cathy were emotionally detached, two isolated housemates bickering bitterly over everything and nothing. When they departed Sacramento, they went in separate directions. Ed settled into the small apartment behind Zona's house, a few miles from the Cal campus. Cathy took their son Lee to her family's home 150 miles north in Shasta County. They soon divorced.[9]

Watching his wife decline into alcoholism was painful. Losing her to divorce broke Ed's heart. But his greatest loss was Lee. It was a wound that did not heal.

Throughout Lee's childhood, Ed saw his son on weekends and during the summer vacations. He took him to ballgames. He bought him pretty much anything he asked for, spoiling the boy lavishly. When they visited a shop filled with rare baseball cards, Ed told his son to choose any one he wanted. Lee selected a rare collectible costing over a hundred dollars, and Ed bought it.

Maybe buying Lee more stuff would alleviate the aching in Ed's heart. Maybe not.

As a teenager, Lee accompanied his father on work trips to fascinating destinations around the world. But even then, Ed was often too busy. He attended long meetings during the day, and his son spent much of his time playing with Ed's personal attendants. Ed would hand his attendant a credit card and send him out with Lee for a day of fun without Dad.

Throughout his life, Ed made effusive, heartfelt statements about Lee, telling any listener available that his son was the brightest light of his life. Behind those undoubtedly true statements, hidden beneath Ed's glowing, ever-present smile, was an enduring depth of sadness. The recurring pain of waking up each morning without his son under the same roof never went away. It was the greatest hardship of his life.[10]

.   •   .

Ed spent his final Sacramento months planning next steps. He would return home to Berkeley, but he didn't want to work for the CIL. His goals for the movement were now national and global, reaching far beyond Berkeley and his home state.

Independent living centers continued to grow across the United States. In 1982, Chicago activist Marca Bristo and Ed's friend Max Starkloff started the National Council on Independent Living to foster the continued development of centers. Lex Frieden compiled a national directory of all independent living programs, most formed on the Berkeley model. In 1981, there were 111 in the United States. California led with 29.[11]

Ed worked with his old friends Judy Heumann and Joan Leon on an idea for a disability think tank. They gloriously called it the World Institute on Disability (WID). WID's purpose was to combine research and advocacy, developing effective policies that benefited disabled people while changing public attitudes through media campaigns. Ed was already consulting with new independent living centers in Australia and Japan. Of course, three jobless friends could take on the entire planet.[12]

Ed's standard assumption that dollars would flow like the un-dammed Stanislaus River was wrong. Initial fundraising was frus-tratingly slow. It took a year to scrounge up enough to rent an unramped little space in an abandoned school building. Joan Leon begged local businesses for donations of paint and used office furniture.[13]

Ed had a longshot strategy to supply a five-year stream of consis-tent funding that would get WID off the ground. His scheme was to be the first disability rights activist awarded the prestigious MacArthur Foundation genius grant. The foundation honored noted academics, artists, and leaders as well as relatively obscure innova-tors and changemakers. The award paid fellows a substantial annual salary plus health insurance for five years, freeing them up to pursue their creative, philanthropic, and scientific endeavors.

The secretive foundation was not open to applications or self-nominations. The fellowship selection process had all the magic and mystery of the Roman Catholic conclave selecting a new pope be-hind sealed Vatican doors.

Unsubstantiated rumors circulated of award winners politicking on their own behalf. Reportedly, environmentalist Patrick Noonan solicited John D. MacArthur himself at his regular Palm Beach coffee shop. Annoyed at the rude intrusion, the billionaire snapped at Noo-nan and made him pay for his coffee. Noonan received the fellowship a few years later.[14]

Ed asked his pal Bob Gnaizda to pitch his name to the MacArthur inner circle. Gnaizda agreed to approach fellowship director Kenneth Hope.[15]

Gnaizda's word carried some weight. He was a rock star in left-wing political circles, a true believer and legal activist famous for rep-resenting the poor and people of color in battles against the govern-ment policies that favored affluent corporations. He helped migrant farmworkers organize a union to seek livable working conditions. He fought discriminatory hiring practices by police and fire departments. He sued mortgage lenders that redlined African American and Hispanic borrowers out of white neighborhoods.[16]

Enthusiastically campaigning for Ed, Gnaizda told Hope, "I know of no other human being whose way of being, philosophy, aspirations, and character embodies the spirit of the Fellows program [more] than Ed Roberts."

Ed's accomplishments as an effective leader in the independent living movement and Governor Brown's administration were strong enough evidence. But more importantly, Gnaizda implored the fellowship director, was the character of the man, "proving by deed that the mind needs no superficial body shell to effectively carry out the highest callings of human beings."[17]

In October 1984, over twenty months after Ed had left gainful employment, he received a telephone call from Chicago informing him that he had been selected as a MacArthur Fellow. Ed later joked, "I thought it was one of my creditors calling." The award came at just the right time. The former leader of the largest state rehabilitation agency in the country was broke.

The sizable award enabled Ed, Joan Leon, and Judy Heumann to start WID. The trio of friends immediately sought legitimacy by creating a board of directors heavy on academic researchers. Ed's good friend Dr. Phil Lee of University of California Health Policy Institute took the helm. In the second year, Brandeis University medical sociologist Irving Zola and former Massachusetts rehabilitation commissioner Russell O'Connell joined.[18]

A polio survivor and activist, Zola became the American founder of the academic field of disability studies, shaking up university disciplines across the sciences, humanities, and arts with the powerful lived experience perspectives of disabled persons. He was one of the founders of the Society for Disability Studies and their influential journal, *Disability Studies Quarterly*.[19]

Backed by an impressive, supportive board, the WID gathered the brightest disabled researchers and experts to fill the many gaps in domestic research and policy. The federal government spent millions of annual dollars on research in the fields of special education, rehabilitation, and medicine. Mostly it was stuck in a deficit orientation, the unfortunate way that too many people viewed disability. WID brought disability rights perspectives to tackling the obstacles blocking disabled children and adults from success.[20]

Big goals didn't translate immediately into success. At first, private foundations and government funding agencies were confused by an organization that combined research with fierce political advocacy. Traditionally, science and politics remained separate. Many rehabilitation researchers questioned the scientific legitimacy of a group with a political agenda.[21]

What the doubtful researchers called bias—that subjective personal ingredient that ruins good science—Ed, Judy Heumann, and Joan Leon called realism. Nondisabled researchers with their dismal fetish for human defects and low expectations were the wrongheaded ones. WID set an ambitious goal "to stimulate a more realistic societal view toward disability." They would teach America, and indeed the world, what disability really meant and what disabled people truly needed to live well.[22]

The Ed and Joan team again hit the road, reviving their fundraising partnership that had been effective in expanding the CIL. The WID leaders knocked on every door with money behind it. Building a funding profile of private and public grants, WID expanded exponentially. In 1984, the annual budget was $60,000. Five years later, it was over $700,000. By 1993, it topped $2.3 million.[23]

· · ·

Tales of the remarkable successes of disability activists like Ed Roberts and Judy Heumann, including the growth and accomplishments of WID, hide an enduring fact of disability politics. Unlike other minoritized groups that achieved a fair degree of progress and empowerment in American politics, disabled people did not have the money or votes to attract the attention of national politicians. During Ed's lifetime, and greatly continuing today, disability politics was grassroots work on the fringes of the big-money, big-power electoral system.

A prime example was the 1980 presidential campaign of Governor Jerry Brown, offering insight into the growing connection between LGBT advocacy groups and the Democratic Party. During Ed's years working closely with Brown passing many disability access laws, the governor longed for Pennsylvania Avenue. In October 1979, Governor Brown's presidential campaign coffers dropped to $90,410. If he was going to remain in the race against Massachusetts senator Ted Kennedy and the unpopular president Jimmy Carter, he needed a quick influx of cash. Although he took left-wing positions on social issues, he had almost no experience working for gay rights. He filled the upper ranks of his Sacramento administration with activists from various social justice movements without appointing a single gay or lesbian leader to a top post.

Starting with a lavish fundraiser at attorney Sheldon Andelson's luxurious Bel Air estate, the opportunistic Brown turned to the wealthy gay community to rescue his financially strapped campaign. Before that night sipping cocktails poolside by handsome young homosexual men, he had never (knowingly) met an openly gay person.

Andelson and the leaders of Municipal Elections Committee of Los Angeles, a political club of affluent gay men, connected Brown to a national network of gay political donors. He swept across the country, appearing at similar fundraisers in Chicago, New York, and Boston.

In November, candidate Brown spoke to an enthusiastic crowd of five hundred gay activists at The Pier disco in Washington, DC. One month after meeting his first gay man, he pledged them his unwavering support. The newcomer to LGBT rights became the chosen presidential candidate of gay advocacy groups across the country.

Chasing fat checks and electoral influence, the opportunistic Jerry Brown traveled a national network of gay political organizations developed in major cities during the 1970s. In New York, Los Angeles, and Washington, DC, large cities with significant LGBT populations, shrewd local clubs of lawyers, professionals, and businesspersons raised campaign donations and organized the LGBT community into effective voting blocs. By the late 1970s, candidates for mayor and city council in these cities and others competed for the necessary support of local LGBT political organizations. Capitalizing on success in large cities, the Human Rights Campaign Fund (HRCF) was launched in Washington, DC, creating a national gay lobbying organization.[24]

Making swift inroads in the Democratic Party, the HRCF quickly turned the wallets and votes of gay and lesbian Americans into a compelling minority voice that could not be ignored. In October 1982, the HRCF held a $150 per plate fundraiser at the Waldorf-Astoria Hotel in New York. The festive evening netting $50,000 was hosted by an honorary committee that included such Democratic Party heavyweights as Senators Ted Kennedy, Daniel Patrick Moynihan, and Alan Cranston. Presidential hopeful Walter Mondale, like Governor Brown a recent convert to the cause, gave the evening keynote.

Washington Post columnist Colman McCarthy commented, "A decade ago, a national politician siding with the gay rights lobby, or what there was of one back then, would have been risking political suicide. Today it would be a political death wish *not* to be for gay rights." Democrats flocked to the HRCF for campaign donations and tens of millions of gay and lesbian votes.[25]

At no point during Ed's life or since has either of the two main political parties seriously worried about filling a portion of convention delegate seats with disabled persons. Even though the number of eligible disabled American voters topped twenty million by 1980, Democratic candidates didn't sip martinis and make speeches in hotel ballrooms filled with disability rights leaders.

With a single phone call from one Sacramento state office to another, Governor Brown could have easily tapped his friend and colleague Ed Roberts to arrange introductions to the top disability movement leaders across the country. Ed could have sent Brown on a national tour, meeting Fred Fay in Boston, Eunice Fiorito and Frank Bowe in Washington, DC, Marca Bristo in Chicago, and Lex Frieden in Houston.

As impressive and accomplished as this group was, they didn't have what the politicians wanted. They couldn't introduce a presidential hopeful to a fat Rolodex of wealthy disabled business leaders, real estate moguls, and bankers. Throughout the 70s and 80s, the cost of national political campaigns—for Congress, Senate, president—skyrocketed. More than ever, candidates and political parties sought relationships with affluent donors.[26]

Very few Americans with disabilities had wealth. Disabled citizens tended to be poor, scraping by on the skimpy support of Social Security and other welfare programs. According to a 1980 census report, for every dollar the average nondisabled person made, the average disabled American pocketed only sixty-two cents. Only one of three disabled adults was employed, often working part-time and lower income jobs. Disabled women in particular remained on the sidelines of the job market.[27]

A second political currency Ed couldn't deliver was a large, unified faction of disabled voters. His disability leadership network consisted primarily of grassroots activists who could quickly organize a protest rally. But they couldn't round up large numbers of votes.

Many persons with disabilities didn't vote at all due to ballot box obstacles. The few who did cast a ballot voted as individuals, not as disabled persons joined together by a shared group identity.

At strategic moments in the disability rights movement, skillful political tacticians like Judy Heumann, Kitty Cone, and Justin Dart, Jr., successfully gathered enough support from disabled and nondisabled citizens to win key national victories. Despite the many passionate speeches that Ed and Judy Heumann made to local disability organizations in towns and cities across the United States, a national disability coalition didn't become a power player in electoral politics.

. . .

In March 1988, the WID board of directors made a surprising decision that placed Ed in a difficult position. He could either raise his voice against their action, standing up for the ethical principles he publicly espoused. Or he could accept their judgment quietly, betraying his most basic values, and directly insulting his two best friends.

As the coffers grew, and the number of programs expanded, the board of directors struggled to establish WID on solid organizational footing. The three founders were effective activists and fundraisers with spotty records as administrators of going concerns. The board tried to build the institute according to the norms of similar nonprofit think tanks. That meant establishing the standard hierarchical leadership chart.

The board concluded that a triumvirate of equal managers was unworkable. Joan Leon, Judy Heumann, and Ed had founded WID together. But only one could be chief executive. They named Ed the boss, and demoted Leon and Heumann to his assistants. Salaries were commensurate with rank. Ed was paid more than his two pals.

When the board notified the two women, they were shocked. Leon and Heumann grumbled bitterly to each other but never discussed the decision directly with Ed. They felt disrespected by Ed's willingness to quietly go along with what they knew was a clear act of workplace sexism. To their credit, they both labored on with full energy and enthusiasm despite the board's decision.[28]

An external consultant recommended that the WID board give the three leaders equal pay but continue Ed's role as senior executive. The board increased the two women leaders' salaries, though only partially closing the pay gap.[29]

Given Ed's powerful sensitivity to prejudice and inequity in any form, his decision to passively endorse the board's decision is hard to understand. His own growth as a disability rights leader greatly relied on his mother's development as a feminist. He often cited the influence of the women's rights movement on his equity-focused thinking.

Moreover, Joan Leon and Judy Heumann were his two best friends. Over fifteen years of disability justice activity, the three had built trusted, warm relationships. Undoubtedly, he noticed their concealed chagrin at both the board's actions and his acquiescence.

Ed was caught believing his own headlines. Eight years as a celebrated state agency leader and worldwide acclaim in the founding of Disabled Peoples' International were topped off with the MacArthur genius honor. He had reached the tipping point where the sum of public accolades finally exceeded his many years of intensive internal work pumping up his own self-esteem.

Beginning in his hospital bed decades before, Ed had spun adolescent grief into an outrageous way of living that bannered the sky with his own name. Strategically he developed an exuberant persona, the proud and adventurous disabled person living beyond all expectations. He not only lived it. He bellowed it with a megaphone at earsplitting volume.

Central to Ed's role as folk hero of the movement was the assumption that his own success advanced his people's civil rights. If he won, then disabled people won. It was a fever dream that had, until this episode, worked well.

In this instance, it didn't. He reached the winner's circle by knocking aside his two best friends, devaluing two outstanding women leaders. It wasn't the act of a hero.

. • •

Full public validation of Ed's status as the international star of the growing disability rights movement came in April 1988 when well-known journalist Harry Reasoner traveled to Berkeley. He brought the *60 Minutes* television crew to film Ed and Zona in his small apartment.

60 Minutes was a weekly news magazine program, a top-ratings broadcast reaching millions of American households every Sunday evening. Journalists Reasoner and Mike Wallace had a reputation for aggressive questioning, grilling interviews that disarmed the world's most powerful figures.

Reasoner didn't pack his arsenal of sharply pointed questions. Dropping the usual *60 Minutes* astringent tone, he took a wide-eyed, delightful journey through Ed's world. With uncommon ease, Reasoner cozied up to the side of the colossal iron lung, connecting emotionally with his smiling subject. The two men chatted amiably like old Cal pals sharing a joint.

The interview topics—Ed's usual life stories about overcoming obstacles, his sexual ability to father a child, and his life's work in disability activism—undoubtedly came from Ed. He led the way, and the hardened muckraker followed like an enthusiastic fan boy.

Ed made sure that the interview fully included his mother. Her years of advocacy on his behalf, teaching him to fight, were recognized on national television.

With Zona grinning at her son's side, the camera zoomed in tight to capture the expressive face popping out of the steel respirator. There was nothing lifeless or hopeless in this figure. He taught couch and coffee table America of a civil rights movement fueled by the outrage of disabled people. Unlike the San Francisco television news report that had shocked Zona, reducing her to tears many years earlier, the complimentary camera appreciated Ed's rare spirit. With gracious praise, Harry Reasoner offered Ed to American audiences as a glorious triumph of humanity.[30]

. . .

Ed and Judy Heumann relied on personal attendants every day for personal care, mobility, and small household tasks. The entire Berkeley disability activism community would have never developed into an advocacy powerhouse without the State of California paying for their care assistants. But there was no national program supplying attendants for all disabled Americans. Most could not go to school or work because there was no one to provide reliable assistance.

Of the many important World Institute on Disability projects, the highest priority was to expand the availability of attendant care services. The first step was to simply document the national landscape of attendant care service, what states were providing and how well those programs worked. In late 1983, Ed secured funding from the Charles Stuart Mott Foundation for a multiyear national study.[31]

The research was directed by Simi Litvak, a disabled woman, and a lesbian who also worked for LGBT rights. An occupational therapist by training, she worked with a thoroughness and clarity that often elevated the practical WID research above more esoteric academic scholarship.

Litvak and her research team examined the national landscape of personal attendant services (PAS). They discovered an incomprehensible mishmash of fragmented state policies and underfunded programs. Over 3.8 million disabled persons were poorly supported by a haphazard hodgepodge of uncoordinated services. Most were simply out in the cold without support.

The country needed a comprehensive, fully funded, national PAS system that would assist disabled persons regardless of where they lived or what kind of disability they had. Litvak's team recommended a coherent, sensible federal policy that not only paid for personal attendants but allowed the disabled persons themselves to take control of their own care. The basic principle of the independent living movement—putting disabled people in charge of their own assistance—was crucial.[32]

Litvak presented the findings to numerous influential national policy groups, including the National Governors Association. The WID research ignited a new conversation, bringing fresh attention to a neglected area of disability policy and service.[33]

Most importantly, WID's efforts shifted thinking about what disabled people needed to live and thrive in the community. The traditional idea among physicians and rehabilitation workers was that people with disabilities most needed improved levels of functioning. If their bodies (or brains) worked better, they could perhaps live on their own and hold down a job. But the WID research on PAS, led skillfully by Litvak, proposed that specific kinds of help provided by personal assistants were often more important.[34]

Despite the WID research, the national needle on PAS services moved little. Activists asked for federal dollars that usually flowed to nursing homes to be freed up to support attendant services. Many states received waivers from federal rules redirecting Medicaid dollars to PAS programs, often with mixed results.[35]

Washington had little appetite to pass national PAS legislation. In 1989 Congressman Claude Pepper introduced a bill to provide comprehensive long-term in-home care insurance coverage for all persons with severe disabilities. The legislation never made it to the House floor for a vote.[36]

A 1991 national study of PAS concluded sadly, "The reality is that the vast majority of persons with severe disabilities have no contact with formal programs. Instead, they rely very heavily, if not exclusively, on family." The skimpy muddle of local and state programs, funded partially with federal money, fell far short of meeting real assistance needs.[37]

The big opportunity for PAS came with President Bill Clinton's universal healthcare proposal. After three Republican administrations, Ed thought that perhaps this folksy Arkansas Democrat could put the United States medical system on par with other affluent nations.

In September 1993, Clinton told Congress the time had come "to fix a health care system that is badly broken . . . giving every American health security—health care that is always there, health care that can never be taken away." Costs for medical care were skyrocketing, and many Americans still had insufficient or no medical insurance.[38]

Hillary Clinton directed a large White House task force that focused chiefly on questions of acute care and prescriptions. A smaller workgroup led by Robyn Stone, a researcher and member of the Pepper Commission, tackled the provision of long-term care for people with disabilities and the elderly. Simi Litvak and Susan Daniels, a federal administrator for developmental disabilities programs, supplied expertise on the needs of disabled people.

Stone's task force debated a range of complex issues. Provide in-home care only for older Americans or create a larger plan to supply personal assistance for disabled persons of any age? The latter approach, favored by Litvak and WID, was substantially more expensive. Pay for care in segregated facilities like nursing homes or institutions? Or prioritize in-home services? Supporting people in their own homes, the WID choice, was widely acknowledged to be cheaper than the residential programs.

Ultimately, the working group's plan for long-term care followed Litvak's advice on all the major provisions. People with disabilities of any age would receive in-home personal assistance from a state-run provider without fear of forced relocation to a nursing home or institution. The government would lead the way in caring for all disabled persons, regardless of impairment, age, or income. States would match federal dollars and design their own approach to service provision within budget limitations and the overall parameters of the legislation.

The Stone group's plan for long-term care drew varied reactions from stakeholder groups. Governors worried that the primary costs would be shifted onto the states. Senior citizens, to the president's dismay, had many qualms. The details of each state's individual long-term services strategy were up in the air. It was too ambiguous. Elderly people wanted to know specifics before backing the president's federal legislation. Plus, the AARP and other groups were concerned that the acute care portion of the bill included cuts to Medicare. The AARP ultimately withheld support for the overall package.

Disability advocacy groups, including the Arc (formerly, the Association for Retarded Citizens), the American Disabled for Attendant Care Programs (ADAPT), and the Consortium for Citizens with Disabilities (CCD), an organization that attempted to unify all of the disparate disability groups, largely endorsed the long-term care provisions. Although different disability groups squabbled about who would benefit least or most, they generally backed the president's efforts to bring new money and coordination to services.

Polls showed that national support for healthcare reform that provided comprehensive coverage for all Americans was at a forty-year high. Clinton had a Democratic majority in Congress. It appeared that the politic winds were at the president's back.

But ultimately his enormous plan suffocated under its own weight. It was too complicated and unclear, and the whole development process dragged on far too long. The president and his supporters never successfully explained the bill to the media or the public. Conservative opponents easily tagged the 1,342-page proposal as the worst kind of bureaucratic big-government spending fiasco. The eighteen-month deliberation process pushed Democrats dangerously into the 1994 midterm elections, scaring many to back away from the high-priced legislation.[39]

Opposed strongly by the Republicans, insurance companies, and the nursing home industry, dogged by overall budget worries, the Health Security Act failed. Long-term care, Litvak's cherished PAS, and the WID goal of widespread, easy-access personal attendant programs for every disabled person remained unfulfilled.

As one Stone working group participant noted, for younger persons with disabilities long-term care wasn't really about healthcare. It was about life, about having the home-based assistance necessary to live fully, to go to college or work a job, to participate in all aspects of society. With the failure of Clinton's universal healthcare initiative, that dream of supported access was deferred.[40]

. . .

By the early 1990s, feeling successful in his think tank, maintaining a furious schedule of speaking engagements in the United States and abroad, Ed's health became an ongoing concern. He was dead tired.

The trouble started almost a decade earlier in Sacramento. He struggled with sleep problems and exhaustion. During long state government meetings, his head dropped down on his chest and he snored softly. Joan Leon nudged him repeatedly to wake up.

Traveling only made his fatigue worse. The iron lung wouldn't fit on an airplane. His personal attendants rigged many creative night-time breathing systems: a plastic bubble tent over his hotel bed, an air hose strapped to his mouth, the old turtle shell chest cuirass ventilator Ed had used as a teenager. All of them worked, and none of them worked very well.[41]

Ed's body—especially his torso—ached all day long. He directed his personal attendant to repeatedly reposition his body, trying to get comfortable in his wheelchair. On mornings when he didn't have an important meeting, marijuana was the medicine to ease the pain. Long before cannabis was acknowledged and legalized in some states as an effective painkiller, it became part of his daily pain-relief routine.[42]

His time outside of the iron lung was often limited to only eight hours. "Polio was supposed to do its damage, stop and leave you alone," he grumbled. It had undoubtedly come back around for more.[43]

What Ed endured wasn't new, and he wasn't the only one. As early as 1875 French neurologist Jean-Francis Charcot recounted three troubling cases of men who experienced a rebound of new symptoms decades after recovering from childhood paralytic polio. They felt weak and fatigued.

Physicians paid little attention to this surprising phenomenon until a sudden rise of patient complaints in the 1970s. Thousands of survivors of the early 50s polio outbreaks reported Charcot's symptoms.

In 1979, the widely read *Rehabilitation Gazette* ran an article by polio survivor Larry Scheider describing his lethargy, pain, and weakness at age 57. "In recent years," he observed, "I find myself being able to do less and less and tire far too easily."[44]

Initially, physicians didn't know what to make of the mysterious new symptoms. There was no official diagnosis for these complaints. Most doctors weren't old enough to remember the last polio outbreak. They knew little about the eradicated disease.

In 1981, passionate and influential polio advocate Gini Laurie collaborated with Northwestern University physician Allen Goldberg and assistive technology innovator Margaret Pfrommer to sponsor a conference on post-polio health issues. Like Ed, Pfrommer contracted bulbar polio in the mid-50s, leaving her paralyzed, breathing with a respirator. She was one of earliest developers of advanced assistive technologies like sip-and-puff wheelchair control systems.

Three years later, Laurie and a group of physicians authored the first medical book on the unrecognized condition. The same year, the Warm Springs Institute, the Georgia rehabilitation center initially founded by FDR, held the first scientific conference on the puzzling illness.[45]

Under growing pressure, medical professionals responded. By the mid-80s, nineteen clinics treating what was called "post-polio syndrome" opened across the country. Doctors struggled to understand how, after many dormant years, the polio virus somehow returned to make an unexpected second assault.

As WID grew through the 1980s, the gray streaks in Ed's hair and beard gave him the appearance of a middle-aged man. But he felt much older. His teenage illness had boomeranged painfully back with new weapons, reminding him daily that he couldn't really escape that old virus.

Laboring with bodily pain and creeping tiredness, grieved by the separation from his son Lee, Ed moved ahead with his activism. The MacArthur fellows met annually, giving him access to a fascinating community of elite scholars and companions. The *60 Minutes* story launched him to higher levels of fame. Linked arm-in-arm with his friends Joan Leon and Judy Heumann, he built the first international disability policy think tank. If he could only keep his eyes open, he would see that he was on top of the world.

23 Partners

Colleen Wieck wrapped up her speech at the May 1987, United Cerebral Palsy conference at the Minneapolis Hyatt Regency. The audience of four hundred parents of disabled children, adults with cerebral palsy, and disability service professionals clapped in warm appreciation.

Stepping from the rostrum, Weick noticed a commotion stirring in the wings. The arriving keynote speaker barked orders to a team of conference staff members, who scrambled obediently at his every word.

"These chairs here. Move these out of the way," the man directed. "I don't want any chairs. Nothing between me and the audience." He snapped clipped sentences of absolute clarity. This guy knew what he wanted. The workers quickly removed the row of chairs.

"And the podium. No podium. Just a microphone. Do you have a clip-on mike? For my shirt?"

A hotel staff member scurried off to find the required microphone. An attendant folded a tartan wool blanket and draped it over the man's legs to keep him warm.

Weick marveled at the scene. This handsome man, his dark hair and full beard with matching sweeps of frosted white on his brow and chin, presided from a gigantic power wheelchair. Using only his creaking voice, puffing on a respirator tube between phrases, he organized every detail with brutal precision. He was both kind and taxing, gentle and pushy.

Not everyone appreciated Ed's exacting schtick the way Weick did. A journalism professor who interviewed Ed for a schmaltzy book about heroic people who overcame difficult circumstances was horrified by his demanding behavior. Traveling the aisles of a gourmet grocery store in Berkeley, Ed called out items for the writer to place in a shopping bag. "Apricots. Salmon. Make sure that fish is fresh!"

The store workers and customers greeted Ed as their favorite celebrity. But the journalist was embittered: "I began to feel as if, without asking, Roberts had turned me into his valet." He concluded that "He's nothing but an ego on wheels," overcompensating for sexual ugliness by bossing people around.[1]

Weick didn't see a pitiful, neurotic wretch desperately compensating for his hideousness. She saw an assertive and effective manager. Whether the action was scratching an itchy ear or arranging for a hotel room that truly fit his needs, Ed knew how to orchestrate the constant assistance that made his life work.

"Hi, Colleen, I'm Ed," he greeted her with wide grin. "I really enjoyed your presentation. Your Partners in Policymaking is a great program."

"Thanks," Weick replied. "I've been looking forward to meeting you." Weick was a nondisabled administrator with the Minnesota Council on Developmental Disabilities, a state agency leading programs for children and adults with what was then called "mental retardation."

"Me, too," Ed replied. "You really have something good going on."

Partners in Policymaking taught disabled people and parents of children with developmental disabilities how to fight the system, how to advocate for greater inclusion in the community and the public schools. Section 504 and the 1975 federal special education law gave advocates legal levers to push employers, government, and the schools. Weick hoped that the program would empower people to know their rights and understand how to use them.

A central goal was helping parents advocate for more inclusive education, a growing but controversial trend to teach disabled students integrated with their nondisabled peers. Ed believed that too many disabled kids languished in special education classes, mired down in low expectations. The Partners program showed parents how to set up useful support and accommodations in general education classes.[2]

Weick marveled as Ed launched into his performance. With a dull electric hum, he rolled forward, then backward, shifting about until he settled in the right position. He lifted his feet up, then lowered them down. Then he raised his back and head. He flashed his lights on and off.

The audience watched in concentrated silence, following his chair and body like charmed hypnosis subjects tracking a swaying pocket watch. Faces slumped, eyes softened, and they eased into his warm embrace.

Ed gently carried the audience away from the nameless hotel conference room to his little cottage behind Zona's house in Berkeley. He was resting comfortably flat in the big tank. Like an adoring Harry Reasoner, the audience pulled a chair up close by his head to share an intimate conversation.[3]

"Before I start, I'd like introduce you to the gentleman to my right, Mike Boyd." Ed looked at Boyd sitting in the wings. This acknowledgment to the person who fed and bathed him was a regular preamble. "He's my attendant. He gets me on the plane and to the hotel. It's because of Mike that I am able to be here with you today."

The audience applauded, and Boyd nodded shyly.

"What Colleen and the DD [Development Disabilities] council are doing is helping people fight for their own freedom. It's been a long fight already. Many of us have been doing this for a long time. My own liberation . . . I started when my mother and I fought the school district. They wouldn't let me graduate because I hadn't taken Driver's Education and PE."

The crowd laughed.

"I'm not kidding. It's funny now. But it wasn't funny then. The administrator came to my house. He looked me right in the eye and said, 'You don't want a cheap diploma.' My mother kicked that guy out of the house. I learned to fight from my mother. She took on the school board. And we won.

"Saul Alinsky taught us if you start with success with something you know that you can win at, you find very soon success breeds success. I think that's the kind of thing that's happened in my own life . . . and something we see happening across this country for people with disabilities.[4]

"We have to have hope for the future. The future can be very bright. We've come a long way. But we still have a long way to go.

"We have to define the future, and it has to be through some struggle. The key to the struggle seems to me is the attitudinal barriers people with disabilities face day to day in their lives. We have to change those old attitudes.

"When I was fourteen, I got polio. I had a terrible fever. When the doctor took my parents aside, my mother asked, 'Will he live?' The doctor looked at her and said, 'You should probably hope he dies, because if he lives he will be nothing more than a vegetable for the rest of his life.'

"I'm here today . . . as an artichoke. You know they're a little prickly on the outside with a big heart.

"That doctor was so afraid of disability himself and had accepted so much of the stereotype of what it was that he had no idea that a person with a severe disability could have any quality of life at all.

"Well, it turned out that almost every prediction was absolutely wrong. It turned out that I had a very strong mother and father who weren't willing to accept all those predictions.

"These predictions, these dire predictions of the future, go on today. Go to a local hospital, and I bet you can find these same attitudes. Doctors telling parents of babies with disabilities, 'He'll have no quality of life. Put him in an institution.'

"What's happening now, I think, is that those of us who are the vegetables are uniting, and we are rising up, and we are not going to stand to be second class citizens. We are going to take our place whether we have to roll over people or around them or convince them to join us.

"We are creating together the most important social revolution this world has ever seen. When we bring that severely disabled person back into our society, remove him from institutions, help the family allow the person to take the risk to be free, we will together have created a new world. One that is based on human rights. We are doing that together.

"And we have to take risks. When I went to college, I learned that I had choices, and that to get anywhere, I would have to learn to take risks.

"One of the most obvious problems with patronization and segregation is that the system shelters too many people with disabilities from learning to take the risks that lead to personal growth.

"I remember when I was called a 'helpless cripple.' What does that mean? You are helpless. You can't control your life. People think they have to take care of you.

"We have built up professionals and an entire system to take care of us. Then the system itself becomes part of the problem. And we have little expectation that we can do it for ourselves.

"I remember when I was at the University of California, when I was first liberated . . . and I fell in love . . . it became incredibly inconvenient to have to take an attendant with me. I had been told for years that I could not drive a power wheelchair because I was so severely disabled. But I decided to take the risk because I had a lot at stake. I crashed in the beginning, but then I learned how to control it.

"And my girlfriend and I . . . we rolled off into the sunset!

"Let's dare to dream together. Let's dare to dream about a future that includes us all. One that prepares the way for children with disabilities, so that they will not feel their disability is a curse. They will feel proud of themselves. That they will feel powerful that they can do something with their life. That they will not feel so ashamed, and they will join us in this struggle for our rights, and for our future.

"The future is ours, we can change our lives for the better and we can change millions of other peoples' lives for the better. If we expect things of people they will succeed, and we will have succeeded."[5]

Weick looked out at the mesmerized audience. They were smiling joyfully. But they also seemed ready to cry. Their heavy minds splashed through memories of the many times they or their children had been demeaned and turned away. His tales of rejection and discrimination resonated with their own, touching their deepest sadness.

But the justice warrior with the mischievous glimmer in his eye also offered them a comforting image and a new sense of hope. Leaning on the side of Ed's iron lung as the Berkeley afternoon sun cast long shadows, they held him in their arms and dreamed of a better future.

Ed became an integral figure in the program. He told Colleen Wieck that Partners should go national. He and his World Institute staff collaborated with the Minnesota Developmental Disabilities council on a federal grant application. Partners soon expanded to twelve additional states.

As Ed traveled the country making speeches, he convinced other states to jump on the Minneapolis bandwagon or start up their own version. He became the regular house band for the Partners program, performing his stories and telling his corny jokes dozens of times across America, embracing small groups of parents and disabled people with unexpected warmth and optimism.

"I'd rather speak to (Partners) than a thousand physicians," Ed told Colleen Wieck. Of all his activities, spending time with the Partners' training participants was his favorite. He rearranged his busy schedule in every way possible to fly to South Dakota, or New Mexico, or Louisiana to teach his best friends.

During the coffee and meal breaks, the Partners' training participants gathered around Ed. They shared their life stories, their hopes and dreams, the atrocities and insults, the frustrations and obstacles. He was their hero, confidant, and shaman. They took turns posing for commemorative photos. They nestled close, sensing that his soft-spoken words and the touch of his blanket would fill them with a renewed outlook.

A mother of a nine-year-old boy with a developmental disability expressed her resentment at a school principal telling her that "handicapped kids need to be with their own kind." A young woman with cerebral palsy, tears sliding down her face, told of difficulties getting reliable transportation to attend her community college classes.

Ed listened and comforted. Together they brainstormed solutions and cracked bitter jokes. There were ways to fight the system. It was all about strategy and persistence, he told them. When you run out of gas, lean on him and your Partners friends. Stick together.

Often, at the end of the conversation, Ed looked the person in the eye and said, "I expect great things from you." They went away feeling a solemn responsibility to Ed and his high expectations.

When they got home, they sent Ed swarms of cards and letters.

An Iowa mother wrote: "I really needed that infusion. Strong as I seem at times, I am sometimes not very strong. Sometimes I get tired of fighting for everything for Sarah."

A mother from Texas felt gratitude. "I want to thank you for the tremendous difference you have made in my life. When I first met you at the Texas Partners last September, I was completely overwhelmed and in awe. . . . Thank you for telling us that we should not have to defend inclusion. Rather we should make others defend exclusion and segregation. That has had a profound effect on me."

A Delaware participant joked, "Are you tired of hearing that you are an inspiration?"

Another Texas mother felt like inclusion was now possible. "I have a great need to share with others across our state that it's time for everyone to be included in everything, every day, every moment! . . . My heart absorbed every word you spoke to us."

A South Dakota mother felt ready to do what couldn't be done. "I learned that history begins with one person willing to take on the 'impossible' and go all the way with it. . . . Thank you, Ed, for all you have done in making our children's lives better."

A mother from Minnesota sent a photo of her five-year-old son Aaron using his new wheelchair. Ed had encouraged her to get an electric wheelchair, claiming that the technology would help Aaron take charge of his life. Ed was right. His hand on the joystick of his own powerchair, the boy became much more outgoing and assertive. At the next Partners meeting in Minneapolis, Ed brought Aaron up on the stage, "He is one of our leaders of the future."[6]

One day, Aaron's glasses fell to the pavement while playing with his friends. A passing car crushed the spectacles. Aaron told his mother, "Let's call Ed. He'll get them." To a little boy in Minnesota, Ed was a superhero who could right all wrongs.[7]

Many parents of children with disabilities came away with a new appreciation for their own children. They had been told by the broader culture and the public schools to focus only on weaknesses and deficits. Ed taught them to see their child's beauty and goodness and talent.

A Minnesota mother said: "You have made me examine my own outlook of people with various disabilities. I appreciate my daughter more as a person and not only as a 'mentally retarded' child. PS, Keep giving 'em hell!"

A Texas father wrote: "One of the biggest benefits of Partners in Policymaking has been an education in the capabilities of people with significant disabilities. Other than my own daughter Katie I've had very limited opportunities to personally know people with disabilities."

He couldn't believe that Ed practiced karate. After watching Ed and his instructor Tony Johnson give a demonstration, he said, " I thought you were bullshitting about karate lessons. I just wasn't buying it. Your demo convinced me that I still have a long way to go to get past the problems of assuming what people cannot do."

The whole idea of the Partners program was to prepare people to be informed and take action in their own lives and communities. Often the participants told Ed the positive steps they took after the training. They wanted him to know that they truly were doing the great things that he expected.

A Delaware mother wrote, "I would like to share with you something I did last week that I don't think I would have done before going to the Partners classes and listening to people like you. I went to the State Joint Finance Committee and talked to them about the need for more early intervention nurses here in lower Delaware rather than caseworkers which is what the Committee wants to do instead. Two other ladies went along with me. One from Partners last year. That evening I got a phone call and found out that when the DMR Council found out that we were going to testify, they found a half time slot for a nurse down state and another half time slot open for something else and decided to combine the slots to a full time nurse slot. We have already made a difference. I can't get over it."

Ed had a special connection with the many mothers of disabled children and teens. In them, he saw his mother, Zona, standing up for her rejected kid. Now he was helping mothers became the Zonas of the next generation.

But there was an additional level of emotion at work for Ed. The loss of his wife, Cathy, and the breakup of his family, left him with lingering sadness. He desperately missed his son, Lee, who lived with Cathy. Ed spent every available moment with his son, often sending his fastest-driving personal attendant racing three hours north to retrieve Lee for the weekend. During summer breaks from school, Lee traveled with Ed to conferences and speaking engagements.

But it was never enough for Ed. The repetitive sadness of waking each morning without Lee at his side never abated.

Nursing his own wounds, Ed reached out to console hundreds of mothers of children with disabilities. Like a brokenhearted therapist, he shared their grief. By helping others, he also comforted himself.

.   .   .

Harriet McBryde Johnson, a disabled woman and lawyer, gained fifteen minutes of fame when she debated Princeton philosopher Peter Singer. The ethics professor argued that parents should have the right to euthanize their newborn child with severe disabilities. Such infants, by Singer's account, didn't necessarily count as persons. Johnson argued cogently that "that the presence or absence of a disability doesn't predict quality of life." She pointed out that Singer's exalted reasoning was fundamentally flawed. He assumed disability was synonymous with misery.[8]

Before she became a noted disability activist, Johnson was at her wit's end. A woman with a progressive neuromuscular disease who used a wheelchair, she was living on her own. She had achieved the independent life that Ed often talked about. It would appear that she was successful.

But she knew better. Her precarious independence relied on too many factors beyond her control. If the winds shifted, the card house would topple. If her health deteriorated or if she didn't have enough money to pay for necessary support services, she'd end up in what she called "the disability gulag," the haunting default of institutional care where disabled people lose control of everything that matters.[9]

As a new college graduate in 1978, Johnson worked providing technical assistance to organizations about how to comply with the new Section 504 regulations. She gave a workshop for the management team at the Coastal Center, a residential institution for people with disabilities in South Carolina. Some of her childhood special education pals lived there.

At lunchtime, Johnson asked if she could eat with her old school friends. It was a strange question. No one wanted to eat with the gulag residents. The staff reluctantly agreed.

Johnson and her six old friends, wheelchair users with cerebral palsy, huddled joyfully together for the impromptu reunion.

A staff member interrupted, "Is this the new girl from Whitten Center?" Whitten was a similar South Carolina institution about 150 miles north.

"She's from outside," Johnson's friends tried to correct the staff member.

The worker was not convinced. "Did you say from the outside?"

Finally, it dawned on Johnson that the staff member thought she was a new institution resident. The staff member saw a woman in a wheelchair, her rail-thin body doubled over in what Johnson described as "deep twisty S-curve," eating lukewarm tater tots and green Jello on a tray. She must be a resident. This is where she belongs.[10]

Sensing the misunderstanding, Johnson talked fast, answering the staff member's many questions. She was a free woman. She showed off her evident signs of living beyond institution walls—her clean, long, carefully braided hair and gold bracelets.

After lunch, Johnson returned to her workshop with the Coastal managers, feeling shaken by the experience. Only the thinnest veil separated her independent life in the community and the segregated existence her friends had on the inside. Her cherished independence could fall apart at any time without warning. Johnson felt deeply discouraged.

Then she attended a Delaware Partners training session where she heard Ed speak. She was immediately transformed.

"All it takes to teach me how wrong I have been is about 45 seconds. . . . With each whoosh" of his ventilator, "he is changing my worldview." Johnson's life was changed by "not what he has done. Not what he is saying. Not who he is. It's his presence."

Although his body was "frail" and "decrepit," Ed was "tough and amazingly funny." Although he appeared only two shallow breaths on the better side of death, he burned with a savage irreverence. He took a "bad-boy delight in truth-telling," kicking authority figures in the teeth, rolling on with a "hellcat gusto for proving the world wrong."

Harriet Johnson came away that day thinking, "A life like his can turn a life like mine upside down."[11]

Johnson went on to be an influential disability rights activist and author. Her debate with the Princeton ethicist became the basis for the play "The Thrill." With her every breath, Johnson's rich and impactful life refuted the philosopher's misguided belief.[12]

Like Johnson, Jamie Wolfe was a disabled woman who felt a jolt of lightning when she heard Ed speak. His encouragement turned her into an empowered activist, standing up for herself and others with disabilities.

Wolfe was born with arthrogryposis, a condition causing muscular weakness and joint contractures. When physicians saw that her body was "twisted like a pretzel," they recommended that her parents place her in an institution. They refused.

"There was no chance that was going to happen," her mother later explained, "We weren't ashamed of her."[13]

As a young woman attending the Delaware Partners meeting, Wolfe met Ed. His words filled her with a new sense of pride and hope. She later wrote him a letter explaining how he impacted her.

"When I was listening to you, it was such a relief listening to someone who had the same philosophy of life as mine and was able to make others not only listen but understand. When I tried to tell people about how people with disabilities should have anything they need to make their lives as fulfilling as possible, they thought I was some radical who was doing it for selfish gain. They thought I wanted to have everything I asked because I thought they owed me something in return for my handicaps. Even members of my family thought I should stop asking people to make changes and just accept what people offered.

"While I was listening to you, I finally realized that I can take my personal experiences and education and not only help people with disabilities take control of their lives but to take control of mine as well. Thank you for giving so many people inspiration, hope, and freedom."[14]

Wolfe earned a master's degree from Delaware State University. For many years, she chaired the Delaware Developmental Disabilities Council. She was one of the founders of the disability studies program at the University of Delaware. Her persistent, skillful advocacy was pivotal in passing state legislation to use federal Medicaid dollars to support the independence of disabled persons.

"She had no fear," observed former Delaware health secretary Dr. Rita Landgraf, when Wolfe passed away.[15]

Through his work in the Partners in Policymaking program, Ed touched the lives of hundreds of disabled persons and parents of disabled children. They came to him beaten down by the worst stereotypes the larger society perpetuated. With warmth and humor, he sent them back into their communities armed with the defiant spirit necessary to spit into the wind and live with enthusiastic abandon.

24 Men of Adventure

In the years following his divorce from Cathy, Ed relied on the good-hearted companionship of male friends. His jolly coterie of best buddies romped and joked like overgrown frat boys. Often they shared adventures seemingly much too risky for a respiratory quad. That was the whole idea.

Two pals expanded and celebrated his life in daring escapades, whale scientist Roger Payne and karate instructor Tony Johnson. Each encouraged Ed to go where no paralyzed person had ever gone.

At the 1984 MacArthur Fellows ceremony in Chicago, Ed met Roger Payne, a marine biologist famous for discovering that humpback whales communicate in surprisingly beautiful musical melodies. He was a leading figure in the international effort to conserve endangered whale species.

After the MacArthur Fellows induction, Payne checked out the Art Institute's medieval armor collection. A strange guy in a giant wheelchair cracked bawdy jokes about the enlarged codpiece. Ed spoofed the sexual implications of the elaborate costumes and weaponry, leaving the ocean scientist rolling in stifled laughter.

To Payne's delight, he quickly fell into Ed's preposterous world. He became a regular participant in Ed's wandering male-bonded squadron of joy. It was all about having excessive fun. But it was also about being a physically disabled man in the world in ways that people did not expect. Large, brash, loving, and silly. Even in friendship, Ed was teaching, changing minds about what having a disability meant.[1]

After listening to Payne present his research on thirty-ton humpback whales to the MacArthur Fellows, Ed shared an audacious wish with his chum. He wanted to swim with the great, gentle beasts.

Payne and his colleague John Atkinson built a custom, ocean-worthy chair out of fiberglass and industrial polyurethane foam. At the edges they affixed rope handles and cinch straps to secure Ed's chest and legs. Ed's respirator rested in a microwave-sized float, delivering air through a five-foot plastic hose ending in a duct-taped snorkel mouthpiece.[2]

Over the 1993 Thanksgiving holiday, Payne, Atkinson, and Ed took the chair for a test run in the Florida Keys. They were accompanied by Ed's attendant Jon Oda and teenage son Lee.

The Dolphin Research Center was the home of the dolphins that starred in the 1963 movie *Flipper*. Surrounded by his son and friends, Ed tried out the new chair in a protected, saltwater lagoon. Oda carefully monitored the floating respirator and the oxygen hose. A trainer tooted a referee's whistle, calling a dolphin over to gently nuzzle its beak to Ed's cheek.[3]

The floating chair was designed to spin like a raffle ticket drum, holding Ed underwater to observe sea life through a diving mask. He wanted to view the sea life below.

"What if he needs help?" Lee asked. The father and son worked out a signaling system. Payne and Atkinson cautiously flipped the chair over, plunging Ed underwater like a do-it-yourself aqualung diver. Lee dove beneath this father and closely watched his eyes for a two-blink distress call.

The respirator alarm screeched. The electric unit sunk accidentally under the water and automatically turned off. Ed was getting no air. The men quickly spun Ed back over and he spit out a mouthful of salt water.

Oda hoisted the device onto a nearby dock. He jumped up, desperately trying to repair the unit. As a young man, Ed could swallow air for hours at a time. By his mid-50s, his frog-breathing limit was a few short minutes. He needed the respirator back on quickly.

The personal attendant yanked the extension cord to shut off the power. An electric shock ran through his hand, up his arm, and knocked him on his butt. Stunned, he shook it off and got back to work. Oda had the waterlogged machine functioning again in minutes.[4]

Despite the mishap, the experiment was a success. The floating ocean chair worked just as designed. Now Ed was ready for the deep sea.

Payne and Ed made a deal with the Discovery Channel network to film a documentary television special about the leader of the American disability rights movement swimming with the humpback whales of Hawaii. An environmental scientist and a paralyzed man share the ocean adventure of a lifetime. It would be must-see TV.

The network sent the ocean explorers on a trial run with a film crew in the Pacific waters off the west coast of the Big Island. Payne, Atkinson, Ed and Lee, and Ed's attendant Otto Roderisch flew to Hawaii in April 1994.

Payne and Atkinson felt understandably anxious about dropping their disabled friend into the deep ocean waters over an hour from emergency medical assistance. This was no secluded Florida lagoon. The waves and the whales would be powerful and unpredictable.

Chartering a commercial fishing boat in Keauhou Bay, the crew encountered their first logistical challenge. The only space on the boat large enough for the bulky wheelchair was atop the cabin roof. And there was no accessible gangplank wide enough for a power wheelchair. They stretched the narrow boarding ramp from the wooden dock up to the top of the high cabin. The wide powerchair barely fit.

Ed would have to perform a circus stunt, driving his wheelchair up a twenty-degree grade some twelve feet above the water. If a single wheel veered off the slender plank, Ed and chair would plummet into the ocean like a giant lead sinker.

Ed crept his chair carefully up the precarious catwalk. He reached the halfway point safely. Payne sighed and bit his lip. So far so good.

Then a motorboat approached the dock at high speed. It roared past, sending a wake that gyrated the skinny ramp like a suspension bridge in an earthquake. Payne noticed that the top lip of the ramp was inching off the wheelhouse roof. Soon the whole ramp would tumble.

"Ed!" he screamed, "Floor it!"

Ed smacked the joystick to full throttle. The oversized tires spun. The overpowered chair rocketed forward like a hopped-up funny car.

At the top of the cabin Ed slid to a precise stop. The chair's weight pinned down the sliding plank as the wake dissipated. He was safe.

Roderisch leaped up to check on Ed. He held a joint to Ed's lips. With a quick puff, he leaned his head back and grinned like a kid who had just ridden the Space Mountain roller coaster.

They piloted the fishing boat miles offshore. Payne searched the Pacific for a pod of humpbacks. It was late in the season. He knew they might strike out.

They finally sighted a school of long-finned pilot whales. It would have to do. Much smaller than humpbacks, the dark gray, bulbous-headed pilots topped out at twenty feet long and three tons weight.

Payne, Atkinson, Roderisch, and Ed boarded the first inflatable motorboat, and two television cameramen followed closely in the second. The delicate process of transferring Ed and his floating chair into a Zodiac lashed to the starboard side of the fishing boat took thirty minutes. Roderisch positioned a rolled-up towel between Ed's thin legs—he was wearing a short wetsuit—to keep his knees from bumping together.

Ed rested for a moment like he was tanning in a pool lounger on the deck. He took one last draw from the respirator tube and began frog-breathing. The crew used ropes to strap the floating chair to the boom. They swung it across the deck until Ed hung above the dinghy, and then gently lowered him down. Placing the respirator box into the Zodiac, Roderisch tucked the hose mouthpiece into Ed's mouth. In seconds, he was relaxing deeply.

Atkinson raced the motorboat into the path of the pilot whales and cut the engine. This was the spot. Small waves lapped the side of the boat.

Donning a snorkel mask, Atkinson slid into the water. Roderisch perched on the boat's edge. Removing the air hose from Ed's mouth, Payne quickly scooped up the end of the green chair. He and Roderisch shuttled the floating chair over the side, and Atkinson pulled it into the water. Payne returned the mouthpiece back into Ed's mouth.

Ed made it. He was floating in the mighty Pacific Ocean.

Payne noticed that Ed was struggling to speak. He removed the mouthpiece.

"Roger," Ed asked his friend, "Can you blow my nose?"

He pinched Ed's nose and wiggled the nostrils until mucus flowed into his hand. He washed his hand in the salt water.

Ed was excited. Soon he would submerge, an undersea diver enveloped in the expansive swishing serenity, greeting colossal creatures with eyes of wonder. Turned over in his fiberglass and foam chair, he would share the ocean with the whales.

Payne directed Atkinson: "Duck under. See if you can see the whales."

Atkinson dove beneath Ed to search for the oncoming school. He burst back to the surface with a horrified expression.

"Rog, there's a shark down there!"

"Just kick him away," Payne replied casually. He had often encountered sharks on his research dives. A little nudge would send the pest away.

"I can't kick him away," Atkinson sputtered. "He's fourteen feet long!"

It was a tiger shark, an aggressive species known for eating humans. They had to get Ed out of the water.

Atkinson threw his shoulder under Ed's chair and lunged upward. Payne clutched the top of the chair desperately. With his whole body, he yanked the chair and Ed up the side of the dinghy. Roderisch and Payne frantically tugged until Ed fell into the boat. Then they jerked Atkinson to safety.

Panting for air, the men fell back in exhaustion. Everyone was safe. The captivating experience of utter fear and adrenaline response pounded through their bodies as they lay sprawled about the little motorboat.

Then Payne started laughing. It was too ridiculous. Months of intensive work and planning shot to hell by a one-in-a-million shark scare.

Ed bit his mouthpiece and launched into a comedy routine. "I can see the headlines now. I can see it, Roger. All the TV channels will pick up the story. Roger Payne, famous environmentalist, discoverer of whale songs, MacArthur Foundation genius, fed disability rights activist Ed Roberts to the sharks!"

The boat of pals exploded in laughter.

Ed continued, "The great Roger Payne unceremoniously dumped a paralyzed man into the ocean where a six-ton man-eating shark turned him into a quick and tasty snack."

Bouncing the Zodiac over waves as the late-day winds kicked up, Payne, Atkinson and Roderisch bawled with laughter. Fresh from the jaws of disaster, exalting in the body-high of relief and joy, they roared at the Pacific Ocean and open skies. Ed never did get to swim with the whales.[5]

. . .

Tony Johnson and Ed were an odd pair. Ed was thin and frail, his muscles diminished over years of disuse. Tony was a Gibraltar of muscle, a monument of wide shoulders and rippling arms rising to a broad neck and smiling face. Placed together, the two seemed as physically misaligned as the old cartoon characters Mutt and Jeff.

Where the two men matched was exuberance. Ed's friend David Goode once described them both as "Bodhisattva warriors, each devoting himself in his own way to relieving the suffering of others, and each having a personal history of suffering that enabled this." They were both unlikely explosions of hopefulness and giving.[6]

Grief corroded Tony Johnson's heart during his Vietnam War service in the Special Forces. He was a member of an elite patrol that prowled the thick jungles, killing with frightening brutality and efficiency. He returned home a seething, aimless man in desperate need of a safe purpose. Teaching karate saved him. Even more, saving others saved him.

He opened a karate school in Los Angeles for society's rejects: Vietnam veterans, gang members, and people with disabilities. His dojo was a diverse family built on respect for self and others. The toughest, bitterest people learned to value themselves and to help one another.

Johnson frequently wandered the poorest neighborhoods. Standing on an urban streetcorner, the only white guy on a predominantly African American or Hispanic block, he sang at highest volume, "Oh what a beautiful morning, Oh what a beautiful day!"

Often an inhospitable crowd of young men gathered around. Then the missionary Hulk rushed forward with his hand outstretched, "Hey, I'm Tony Johnson. I'm glad to meet you."

Caught off guard, the neighborhood guys hesitated. Who was this bulked-up Barry Manilow warbling on their streetcorner?

Within minutes, Johnson had his new friends chatting and laughing. He asked them about their families and their children. He invited them to learn karate at his school. He offered to teach a free class for their kids in a nearby church or community center. An hour later, he left with phone numbers and plans to connect later.

When Ed met Tony Johnson in Los Angeles, the sensei immediately invited him to learn karate. Ed thought Johnson was joking. Of course, he couldn't learn to fight. Johnson pushed until Ed finally agreed to try.

Under Johnson's careful instruction, Ed learned to use his apparent weakness—the fact that he used a wheelchair—as a strength. In well-trained hands, the heavy chair was a formidable weapon that could subdue any attacker.

The karate master and his student worked many hours developing and practicing moves designed for Ed. He tackled the workouts with the intensity of an athlete in training, thrilled at the sheer physicality of combat. He mastered a series of powerful defensive moves that could easily drop any aggressor.

They created a performance called "Claiming Your Power" featuring Ed's surprising self-defense skills. When Johnson first grabbed a knife and told the audience that he would attack the man in the wheelchair, the guy drinking air through a tube, the audience recoiled. It all seemed so far-fetched. Certainly, the behemoth would be play-acting like a father intentionally losing a wrestling match to his toddler son.

The battle was fast and physical. Johnson launched his enormous body, the knife thrusting forward, toward the apparently defenseless man in the wheelchair. The audience gasped. It was real.

With a finger flick, Ed spun the chair to the left, swiping his outstretched legs like a broadsword across the outside of Johnson's knee. The attacker's leg buckled. He stumbled awkwardly to the ground. Ed had successfully fended off his first advance.

Johnson tried again, throwing a forceful assault at Ed's left flank. Skillfully, Ed's fingers pushed the joystick, turning his chair into a deft weapon. He was quick and surprisingly strong. His red face beamed. Sweat dripped off his forehead.

Ed rushed forward like a bull, knocking Johnson to the ground. The instructor tried to regain his feet, but Ed's extended legs overwhelmed him like a snowplow. Trapped under Ed's feet, the sensei scrambled backwards, until Ed had him pinned against the wall. Johnson hand-signaled a white flag, and Ed backed away.

The crowd burst into applause. They still didn't understand what they had just seen. They only knew that it was incredible and unexpected.

After one such demonstration, Ed spotted a skeptical face in the crowd. She was a little person, standing about four feet tall. Ed invited her forward to learn self-defense with Tony Johnson.

"I can't do this," the woman claimed, her eyes falling to the ground.

"You can," Johnson responded. He knelt to speak to her face to face. "What's your name?"

"Millie," she replied shyly.

The big teacher reached out his hand. "I'm Tony. I'm going to teach you."

Doubtful, she held out her fingers and grasped his massive hand. Johnson summoned Ed's teen son Lee to be part of the lesson. Smiling and eager, Lee bounded forward.

"Lee, you come at me with outstretched arms. I won't hurt you. You're the attacker," Johnson instructed. "Millie, watch closely. Your turn is next."

Lee towered over the kneeling instructor. Arms raised, he lunged at Johnson. With a precise sweep of his hand, the master tapped the soft spot behind Lee's right knee. It folded, and the boy fell to the ground.

"I can't do that," Millie shook her head.

Johnson took Millie's hand and balled her fingers tightly into a fist. Then he whispered a few words into her ear. She turned toward Lee with her right fist nervously resting in her left palm. She appeared more ready to run away than fight off an assailant.

"OK, Lee," called Johnson. "Attack!"

Lee threw his hands out and charged forward.

Millie swung her right fist roundhouse style, striking the hollow behind the knee joint. Lee's leg collapsed and he tumbled to the mat. The expression on his face was priceless. He didn't expect this from the seemingly meek woman.

Millie looked at Lee on the ground and then her clenched fist, wondering what she had done. The crowd erupted in cheers. She smiled and hugged Johnson.[7]

Tony Johnson accompanied Ed on many trips in the early 1990s, performing their self-defense exhibition for audiences around the world. The two men were twin brothers who rose up from their own challenges by joyfully giving to others.

25 *Lenin's Tomb Is Inaccessible*

When the plane stopped at the gate, officials instructed Bruce Curtis to wait until the other passengers got off. He watched out the window as a vehicle with flashing red lights crossed the dark tarmac. Two burly men lifted him up and carried him awkwardly down the airstairs to the ambulance. A nurse attended at his side as the ambulance ferried him to a medical unit inside the airport terminal where a white-coated physician took custody. After a prolonged procedure involving numerous forms, the strong men placed him in his manual wheelchair, and he was finally released.

Exhausted from the long flight, Curtis stared out the taxi window on the ride to the hotel. Except for an occasional streetlight and the well-lighted billboard of the Marlboro man in a cowboy hat looking oddly confident, the roads of Moscow were dim. The lights inside office buildings were off. There were no other lighted advertisements. It was November 1992, and Western capitalism hadn't yet filled the Russian capital with electrified hubbub.

Curtis soon discovered that disability access was nonexistent. No curb cuts, no accessible restrooms, typically no elevators. Almost every move he made involved very muscular men hoisting him in his manual wheelchair onto their shoulders.

What struck Curtis most about the state of disability rights in Moscow was the residents' attitudes. The notion that the sidewalks and buildings should be or could be made accessible for disabled people was not even a topic of consideration. There appeared to be no appetite for change.

Curtis was the WID's international specialist, spreading the ideas and lessons of the independent living movement to foreign countries. He was tasked with starting a new program funded by the United States Agency for International Development (USAID), ostensibly bringing the good news of capitalism and democracy to the disabled people of Russia. Truthfully, he launched a disability rights collaboration between WID and a relatively unknown group called the All-Russia Society for the Disabled (ARSD).

Curtis was a paraplegic with shoulder-length hair and a talent for wheelchair dancing, an unheard-of avocation for a disabled person in Russia. He first connected with Ed in 1976 after reading a newspaper article about how the new state rehabilitation director was building independent living centers across California. Curtis asked Pasadena's city manager for start-up funds. With $10,000, an office, and two temporary job training workers, he opened an independent living center in Pasadena. He contacted Ed and became the tenth center to receive state monies.

In his first meeting with the Moscow leaders of the ARSD, Curtis was astonished. His wheelchair was the only one in the room. All the organization's members moved about with crutches and canes.

Curtis asked his hosts about Russians who used wheelchairs. Where were they? He learned they were hidden away in government institutions or private apartments. They didn't go out in public.

It had long been common practice for Russian families to give up their infants with physical impairments to the state. Thousands of children each year were sent to live in orphanages under horrific, impoverished conditions where they received only a minimal education. Typically, at age eighteen, they either moved to large adult institutions or apartments which they rarely left. The Moscow streets were empty of wheelchair users except an occasional bedraggled beggar in a public square.[1]

The Russian government had a prevalent "out of sight, out of mind" policy on disability. When a Western journalist attending the 1980 Moscow Olympics asked a Soviet official if his country would field a team to compete in the Paralympic games, he was told, "There are no invalids in the USSR!"[2]

Curtis traveled the Moscow sidewalks as an invisible man. Passersby turned their heads away, as if his bodily impairment might spread by proximity or eye contact. An occasional charitable soul stuffed a few rubles into his hand.

He learned that the ARSD was not a disability rights organization. It was a national coalition of thousands of small businesses operated by and employing people with physical disabilities. Over years of diligent effort, disabled people had carved out an entire sector of the Russian economy for their own companies, constituting a national system of disabled worker employment.

The ARSD members mostly ran small handicraft guilds and low-tech industrial firms making brooms and cheap tourist souvenirs. Their most lucrative venture was a corporation that exported oil. All told, 1,300 ARSD businesses employed 40,000 workers. Almost half were people with disabilities.[3]

WID set up a Moscow office with a small group of disabled staffers. Curtis brought over WID representatives, including Joan Leon, Pam Mendelsohn, and Mary Lou Breslin, to lead the ARSD training seminars. They taught the Russians how to work with the media, provide direct consumer services, and give legal advocacy for disabled people. Management consultant Dale Flowers ran sessions on basic business practices for success in a competitive market.[4]

In April 1993, Ed joined Bruce Curtis for a series of training meetings in Moscow. Ed was accompanied by his teen son Lee, personal attendant Jon Oda, and karate teacher Tony Johnson.

Twenty-five ARSD leaders watched Ed and Johnson give their usual self-defense demonstration. Many had never seen a power wheelchair. They sat open-mouthed, astounded as Ed burst their every conception of the abject existence of a person with a severe physical disability.

It wasn't just that Ed engaged in activities unimaginable. It was his attitude, his shocking enthusiasm. By the end of the exercise, Ed was sweating and breathing heavily. A man who by all accounts should have been homebound and helpless was a fun-loving athlete.

To the Muscovites, Ed was an outrageous supercrip dreamed up in Hollywood. He was the American can-do ethos on steroids. They had never seen a quadriplegic with a portable respirator living such a full and happy life.

Traveling the sidewalks and public squares of Moscow, Ed was a rolling carnival. Power wheelchairs were extremely rare in Russia. Large crowds gathered to see the breathing "invalid" doing circus tricks. He spun his chair in circles like a victorious NASCAR driver popping the cork.

Bruce Curtis and Ed took their American disability road show to the famous Izmailovski Market, a sprawling outdoor swap meet in a park near the Kremlin. Vendors peddled furniture, crafts, and Eastern European delicacies. The two disability activists sported fuzzy *ushanka* hats and chatted with the curious crowd. When Ed showed interest in a chess set, the seller gave it to him and refused to let him pay.[5]

"I felt like the Pied Piper," Ed later commented. Dozens of women and young children followed him through the market. An older lady pushed excitedly through the crowd and planted a kiss on his cheek. Children repeatedly chanted in Russian for Ed to whirl his chair in circles. He happily obliged, putting on the show until he felt dizzy.[6]

Ed was an instant Moscow celebrity. A popular television program aired across the Soviet bloc nations requested an interview. WID staffer Pam Mendelsohn asked their hotel for a meeting room where the television crew could set up their cameras and lights. Two hotel workers repeatedly denied her requests.

Suddenly one of the denying hotel employees realized something. Her eyes widened. She turned to her coworker and shouted, "Edward Roberts!"

The second worker asked back, "Edward Roberts?" and did an imitation of Ed breathing from his respirator hose. For the American named Edward Roberts, a meeting room was immediately available.

Ed taught the Russian TV audience the basics of physical access: "I can't get into Lenin's tomb. It's inaccessible." An American wanted to honor the great communist forefather. Without curb cuts and architectural modifications, he couldn't get in.[7]

Millions watched the incredible wheelchair hero from America tell stories about his life and the worldwide disability rights movement.

"It doesn't matter if you're in Russia or if you're in Brazil or if you're in the United States. The issue is still the same. We are fighting for our place in the sun. And it's a wonderful struggle. And it gives us strength and in the process we will change ourselves and we will change this world. We will change Russia and we will change attitudes toward Russia because it's the old attitudes that are our worst enemy."[8]

The ARSD organized a bus trip for forty-five disabled people to visit the Goritsky Monastery two hours north of Moscow. The historical campus of picturesque white baroque buildings was a popular tourist site on a high bluff overlooking cold Lake Pleshcheyevo.

Outside the entrance to the Church of the Transfiguration, a curious throng gathered around Ed. Religious devotees concluded that

Ed was there to seek a miracle of divine healing. Women in dark wool coats pressed against him on all sides, laying their hands on his head and praying fervently. One woman grasped his hand from the wheelchair armrest and thrust it up above her head as she beseeched the Lord to cure him.

Ed joked, "I don't mind being healed, but don't make me walk. I might lose my job."

When the woman finally released Ed's arm, his hand landed hard on the joystick controls. The big powerchair lurched forward. Ed wasn't healed, but the sea of praying woman parted as he sped across the plaza.[9]

While Bruce Curtis and Ed waited to board the bus for their ride back to Moscow, a bird flew overhead. It dropped poop on Ed's shoulder. The two friends laughed. It must be a sign from above. God had issued a definitive response to the prayers for cure. Ed wasn't worthy.

The WID program in Russia went on for years, but it often suffered from poor cultural translation. The ideas and practices of Western disability rights activism were as alien to the Russians as Ed's electric wheelchair.

The WID training team felt frustrated that many of the ARSD leaders, the old guard of the organization, had little interest in advocating for their rights. They often argued that they weren't the experts or the authorities on disabilities. The medical establishment and the government had determined that they deserved a very limited kind of life. Disabled people had secondary citizen status, and that was, in the deferential opinion of the ARSD leaders, appropriate given their physical impairments.

Bruce Curtis and Ed decided to bring the ARSD members to Berkeley to witness American disability rights firsthand. They toured the Berkeley CIL where they learned about personal attendants, peer counseling, and the entire repertoire of available services. They studied accessible transit systems, learning how Hale Zukas and others had successfully opened up the Bay Area Rapid Transit system. The Moscow leaders visited Sacramento and met with state legislators to understand the passage of access and nondiscrimination laws.[10]

Despite the WID team's efforts, independent living centers did not catch on in Russia. But one piece of the disability rights education delivered to the ARSD leaders took root.

The Russians were fascinated by the Americans with Disabilities Act, the national antidiscrimination law passed in 1990. They viewed it as the kind of law that had real potential in their homeland. In CIL seminars, they studied the text of the ADA carefully and began working out early drafts of similar legislation for their own country.

By early 1995, the ARSD leaders had a solid piece of legislation prepared. It passed the Duma, the rather weak Russian legislative body. But President Boris Yeltsin rejected it.

Disability Rights and Education Defense Fund (DREDF) leader Mary Lou Breslin went to Sochi, a resort town on the Black Sea, to work with the ARSD leaders on how to organize and advocate for approval of the new legislation. She met with the ARSD bosses to strategize.

The ARSD members were reluctant to take further action. Yeltsin had made his decision. It was done. They didn't believe they had any further role in the matter.

Arguments broke out in the meetings as the frustrated Breslin pushed her Russian colleagues to organize opposition to their president's decision. They were largely submissive: "We let our leaders speak for us."

Breslin prodded them, "How many are you? How big is this country? There's forty of you in this room? And there are two guys in Moscow who are supposed to do it all?"[11]

The ARSD leaders wanted to pack up and go home. The Americans didn't understand how their country worked. Angered by Breslin's brazen assertiveness, they walked out of the meeting.

The attitude of the Berkeley disability rights activists was relentless persistence, knocking on doors, working the phones, rallying the troops again and again. There were no defeats, only temporary setbacks to be countered by further activism and advocacy. The fight was endless.

Breslin brought American-style disruptive energy to the Russian disability leaders, shaking them out of their fatalism. First, they had to become experts on the issues and the legislation. They spent hours studying the issues, examining how lack of access to employment, housing, and transportation impacted disabled people. Their goal was to be able to run logical rings around the thin arguments of dismissive government officials.

The group then studied strategies to influence the press, how to use their in-depth knowledge to explain the issues through television, radio, and newspapers. It was all about preparation, knowing the issues and the legislation, and being ready to present the information clearly so that the media could understand and everyday people could care.[12]

In November 1995, after two Yeltsin vetoes, the Act for the Social Protection of the Disabled was signed into law in Russia. It outlawed discrimination against persons with physical impairments and provided a series of social programs supporting disabled people.[13]

Even if the enforcement and funding were unclear, it was a triumph. ARSD leader Alexander Lomakin celebrated: "Now we have this law that shows a disabled person has all the rights of other citizens, and we need to help him return to a normal, productive life."[14]

After the original USAID grant dried up, the WID Moscow office transitioned into a new organization called Perspektiva. Backed by European governments and the United States, this nongovernmental organization blossomed into a disability advocacy group working on integration, laws, and jobs. Perspektiva built employment programs with international corporations doing business in Russia. It later expanded beyond physical disabilities to support people with intellectual disabilities and autism. Today it continues to provide job training and placements to disabled people in six cities in Russia.

Vladimir Lenin, the revered father of the Russian Revolution, used a wheelchair during his final years of life. His tomb is located at the bottom of a steep set of stairs inside a red and black stone mausoleum. Lacking a ramp or elevator, he tomb is still inaccessible to people using wheelchairs.[15]

26 *Passing the Torch*

The connection between the 1977 Section 504 sit-in victory and the passage of the Americans with Disabilities Act in 1990 was a straight line. Section 504 granted protections to disabled Americans involved in activities and entities receiving Washington dollars. ADA expanded those antidiscrimination protections to the rest of society. The ADA was 504 beautifully spread to Walmart, Wendy's, and Wall Street.

But the path of events from 504 to ADA would only be similarly straight under the right president. Ronald Reagan, no friend to disability rights, defeated Jimmy Carter in 1980 and held the office for two terms. When Vice President George H.W. Bush outpolled Governor Mike Dukakis in 1988, there was a glimmer of hope for disability rights activists. Although conservative, Bush understood that disabled Americans were held back by prejudice.

President Bush filled the White House with Lone Star State conservatives. The activists pushing the ADA over the finish line would wear cowboy hats and speak with a Texas twang.

In 1978, a wealthy Texas businessman traveled to California to learn from Ed and Judy Heumann. Justin Dart, Jr., was a polio survivor who used a wheelchair, but he was new to disability activism.

He was, by many accounts, a nasty guy with a bad reputation.

Dart had a sordid past of extravagant greed and a long list of troubling addictions. Funded by family wealth, raised for merciless selfishness, he had spent decades chasing money, women, alcohol, and drugs.

His aunt Mari Carlin Dart described him as "born to privilege and power—the kind that breeds contempt and a sense of entitlement." His grandfather founded the Walgreens drug store chain. His father ran the big corporation while rising to the highest circles of the Republican Party, serving as a member of President Ronald Reagan's kitchen cabinet of economic policy advisors.[1]

Dart's response to his cold, cutthroat upbringing was all-out rebellion. He was kicked out of seven of the finest prep schools in America. He earned the infamous honor of beating Humphrey Bogart's record for the most disciplinary demerits at prestigious Andover Academy.

His long, serpentine road to redemption began when he contracted polio at age eighteen. "I count the good days in my life from the time I got polio," he told Boston activist Fred Fay and disability historian Fred Pelka.[2]

Los Angeles County Hospital doctors advised his parents he would die in a few days. But "not to worry" because he was "better off dead than crippled." The Dart family heard the same sad line that the family doctor pitched to Zona Roberts. His parents moved him to White Memorial Hospital where the paralyzed teen was overwhelmed by an experience completely unfamiliar. Total, uncompromising love.[3]

The White Memorial nurses were devout Seventh Day Adventists who viewed every life as sacred and worthy of love. Dart soaked up their effusive warmth like a coatless man wandering the Arctic.

"They resurrected my spirit," he later explained. "Love lifted me."[4]

But one dose didn't cure his damaged soul. "I felt the power of love," Dart reflected, "but I didn't have the slightest idea how to use it."[5]

His second round of spiritual rehabilitation began two years later when he read Mahatma Gandhi's *My Experiments with Truth*. The Indian activist's words struck him deeply. Change the world by finding and living the truth. To Dart, these were marching orders, a forthright prescription for personal action in a world filled with cruelty.[6]

Again Dart fell into old habits. In 1963 he accepted a job working for his father, bringing Tupperware products to Japan. He poured his outsized energies into the business with wild success. His company expanded from three employees to 2,500 in only two years.

Dart chased a high-octane lifestyle, "posturing for the media and photo ops with stars, big houses and flashy cars." Neglecting his children, burning through his second marriage, he engulfed himself in "womanizing (and) prescription drugs."[7]

The Vietnam War filled the Tokyo news. Dart sought easy publicity for his company in a charity trip to a Saigon orphanage for disabled children. It was an ideal photo opportunity, a public display of the corporate executive's empathy and kindness.

It didn't go as planned.

Dart later described the horrific scene: "There was a large shed with a tin roof. There were 50 children aged perhaps 3 to 10, wearing white loin cloths. They had bloated bellies, bulging eyes and matchstick arms and legs. They lay covered in flies on the hot concrete floor in a swamp of their own urine and feces. They were starving to death. One little girl reached out and took my hand. She looked into my eyes. I felt a love, a serenity, a passion to live that was thunderous in its silence, profoundly beautiful in its transcendence over horror. She was looking for God. What she found was a counterfeit saint."[8]

Dart quit his job and divorced his second wife. He vowed this time to finally change his life. He married Yoshiko, the devoted companion who would care for him and work tirelessly at his side for the rest of his life.

In 1968, the couple retreated to a remote Japanese farmhouse without plumbing, heat, or a telephone. Dart spent six years wood-shedding his battered soul, studying history and philosophy like an intellectual warrior preparing for combat. He was overwhelmed by fear that he could not live up to his Ghandian commitment to be the love and change the world needed. He battled his internal demons, alcohol and drug addiction and depression.

Finally returning home to Texas, he found his salvation in the dis-ability rights movement. Anyone who met him after 1978 encoun-tered not a greed-riddled addict. He had remade himself into a civil rights mystic pouring forth love and hope.

He traveled to Berkeley to learn from the best. Ed and Judy Heu-mann fully schooled the newcomer on independent living philoso-phy. Dart later recalled, "They took me to kindergarten." He was a thoughtful and dedicated student, gobbling up big mouthfuls of their hard-won wisdom. Little did they know what they were preparing the indefatigable Texan to accomplish.[9]

Using his family's political connections Dart climbed quickly. In 1980, Texas governor Bill Clements appointed him chair of the Gov-ernor's Committee for Persons with Disabilities. A year later, Presi-dent Ronald Reagan picked him to serve as vice chair of the National Council on Disability (NCOD).

Dart remade the underpowered NCOD into a federal govern-ment disability rights squad. He and Yoshiko embarked on the first of their many national tours, driving around the country in a pickup truck, meeting with disability activists in every hamlet, crossroads, and metropolis. He educated himself from the bottom up, asking dis-abled Americans about the everyday obstacles they faced.

In 1986, President Reagan picked him to run the Rehabilitation Services Administration (RSA), the large federal agency overseeing all rehabilitation programs and research. Not surprisingly, he ran smack into the same bureaucratic lethargy and old-fashioned attitudes that bedeviled Ed in California. Following Ed's Sacramento formula, Dart brought disabled people into the agency as expert advisors and evaluators. He steered the enormous bureaucratic machine toward a new mission of vigorous disability advocacy. Entrenched professionals responded with stiff resistance. A decade after Ed's experience in Sacramento, the ugly question remained, How can a guy with a severe disability be in charge of rehabilitation?

Dart fought a very public battle with Madeleine Will, assistant secretary of the Department of Education. The 1986 amendments to the Rehabilitation Act corrected a long-standing policy flaw, finally mandating that disabled people run the federally funded independent living centers. The Department of Education was tasked with administering the crucial new provision.

Responsible for enforcement, Will took a surprising stance. Supported by Education secretary William Bennett, she simply refused.

In June 1987, the Senate Subcommittee on the Handicapped, led by Lowell Weicker and Tom Harkin, took Dart's side. All federally supported independent living centers must "have a board which is comprised of a majority of handicapped individuals."[10]

Will told Senator Harkin that, by her reading, the legislation didn't really require that disabled persons be in charge of the leadership boards. Despite the bill's clear language, the Education Department somehow interpreted the new regulation as optional.[11]

Harkin rallied the grassroots disability activists to apply pressure on the White House. He contacted Marca Bristo, leader of the National Council on Independent Living (NCIL). Bristo was a fierce activist who originally founded a center in Chicago. She immediately fired off heated letters to President Reagan and Secretary Bennett. She issued a nationwide alert to all independent living centers, calling the frontline troops to bury Washington in angry letters.[12]

Dart was a crafty politician. He won the skirmish by sidestepping the obstructive assistant secretary. In late October, he had the RSA head of rehabilitation services Francis Corrigan order all independent living centers to comply with the new rule.[13]

But that move was a political poison pill. Dart knew he was on his way out. His firebrand style of leadership wore out his welcome atop the RSA in only fifteen months.

In November 1987, seeing his days numbered, he testified before a congressional hearing that his own agency was deeply corrupt. The RSA was stifled by "paternalistic central control, non-professional management, and policies of hostility . . . institutionalized for years." The problem, Dart told Congress with brazen honesty, was the upper-level RSA administrators. The system was rotten at the top. Accepting his fate, he tore into the intractable federal leaders who opposed social progress.

"We are confronted by a vast, inflexible federal system which, like the society it represents, still contains a significant proportion of individuals who have not yet overcome obsolete, paternalistic attitudes about disability and indeed about government itself."

The national agency responsible for supporting disabled Americans blocked their attempts "to liberate themselves finally from the subservient dependency produced by millennia of prejudice and authoritarian paternalism, and to participate in the productive mainstream of society as fully independent, fully equal citizens of the first class."[14]

President Reagan asked Dart to resign. Quietly, he stepped down. He gathered up his poker chips and stored them away. This was far from over.[15]

In May 1988, with President George H. W. Bush signaling stronger support for the ADA than his predecessor, New York congressman Major Owens set up the Task Force on the Rights and Empowerment of Americans with Disabilities. He appointed Dart and Elizabeth Boggs as cochairs. A mother of a son with an intellectual disability, Boggs was one of the founders of the Association for Retarded Citizens of the United States, an influential advocacy organization later called the Arc.

Immediately, Dart called Ed for advice. He sought counsel on strategy from the seasoned activist. He also paid respectful tribute to the father of the movement. The torch passed from the Berkeley generation of activists to Dart and his right-hand man Lex Frieden, the Texans who had the trust of the Bush White House.

Dart sent Ed a heartfelt note of personal appreciation, "Continue to appreciate your leadership. You laid the foundation for the ADA! Lead on!" At the bottom of the page, he scribbled, "*Together*"— underlining the word for emphasis—"we shall overcome!"[16]

Undoubtedly, Ed felt disappointed as he watched from the sidelines. But he had a strong affection for Dart, his passionate student who lived with the kind of unbridled audacity Ed loved. He was thrilled that his friend was the star quarterback in the biggest game ever.[17]

Under political cover of the congressional Task Force, Justin Dart was a one-man show. He led with the passion and effusive love of a savior reclaimed from a profligate past. In late 1988, he and Yoshiko again climbed into their pickup truck to crisscross America on a listening tour, holding local forums for disabled people to offer advice on what he called "the civil rights law of the future." He gathered reams of firsthand testimony of disability discrimination, creating a rich archive of grassroots support for the bill.[18]

The final report of the Task Force, typed in all-caps as if to issue a deep-throated scream to both Houses of Congress, included a heartbreaking litany of personal stories of disabled people, their everyday suffering due to discrimination in employment, housing, transportation, and healthcare.[19]

As the Darts rode the circuit, hearing heartfelt stories and spreading the possibility of greater justice, legislative leaders from both sides of the aisle set the table. Congressman Tony Coehlo and

Senators Tom Harkin and Ted Kennedy rallied the Democratic votes. Senators Bob Dole and Orin Hatch, pushing against the opposition of arch-conservative Jesse Helms, gathered the Republican support. Disability advocates from across the nation submitted their opinions in the form of tens of thousands of phone calls and letters.

Beginning with the original draft worked up by legal scholar Robert Burgdorf, Pat Wright and DREDF revised the bill, delicately traveling a harrowing process of negotiations among activists and Capitol Hill staff members. The final text truly was a compromise, trading off punitive damages for an injured party in return for a widened scope of public accommodations. For example, a disabled worker winning a lawsuit against an ADA-violating employer would get their job back, legal fees, and the missing back pay. But they couldn't seek additional payments to punish the plaintiff. For Wright, Judy Heumann, and others, this was an A minus. Still a top grade.[20]

On July 13, 1990, the Senate passed the Americans with Disabilities Act by an overwhelming margin. For the first time ever, a United States senator made a floor speech in American Sign Language. Senator Tom Harkin gave an emotional tribute to his brother Frank, a man with a hearing impairment: "Today we say no to ignorance, no to fear, no to prejudice."

Senator Orrin Hatch, his eyes welling with tears, dedicated the bill to his brother-in-law, who died of polio twenty years earlier. Ted Kennedy, fighting back emotions, saluted his sister Rosemary, who had an intellectual disability, and his son Ted, a leg amputee.[21]

The sweeping bipartisan bill provided protection from discrimination and exclusion for over forty million disabled Americans, broadly spanning employment, education, public accommodations, communications, and public transportation. Workplaces, restaurants, parks, buses, airlines, houses of worship, universities, hospitals, telephones . . . all must be accessible. The law covered persons with all types of mental and physical disabilities as well as those with

AIDS and drug or alcohol addictions. The *Washington Post* triumphantly declared the law "the world's strongest civil rights protection for the disabled."[22]

On July 26, 1990, under the scorching summer sun on the South Lawn of the White House, President Bush signed the Americans with Disabilities Act. He proclaimed to a jubilant crowd of over two thousand, "Let the shameful wall of exclusion finally come tumbling down."[23]

Sitting at the president's side was Justin Dart, Jr., in his trademark cowboy hat. He played the part of the eccentric, demanding, outrageously upbeat civil rights leader. It was the oversized movie star role perhaps originally written for Ed Roberts. Dart played the lead role to perfection, and Ed cheered with heartfelt joy from Berkeley.

27 *To the Smithsonian*

On Tuesday morning, March 15, 1995, personal attendant Jonathan Gold folded towels. In the iron lung, as he did almost every morning, Ed dialed the telephone with a small wooden stick gripped between his lips.

Gold watched the stick fall slowly. Something was wrong. He had never seen Ed drop the stick. He rushed across the room. Ed's eyes were open and blank.

"Ed, I'm counting to five. If you don't move, I don't care if you're joking or not. I'm calling 911."

His eyes remained open and still. Gold phoned 911. Minutes later two EMTs rushed into Ed's apartment. They quickly slid Ed out of the iron lung.

"Be careful with his legs," Gold advised the medics. "He's a quad, but he feels. . . . everything."

An EMT pulled Gold aside and whispered sadly, "Don't worry. He's not feeling anything."

Ed died of congestive heart failure. Over four decades after the polio virus first damaged his heart, it finally gave out.

A thousand mourners gathered in the old Harmon Gym on the Cal campus to pay tribute.

"One by one they drove their wheelchairs up a ramp," observed a *San Francisco Examiner* reporter, "and onto a podium to talk about how their lives had been changed for the better due to Ed Roberts. . . . [It was] an afternoon filled with sadness and celebration." Friends, family, and admirers shared stories of this man who touched their hearts and changed the world.[1]

WID researcher Debby Kaplan captured the emotions in the gym, "I've never had this feeling at a memorial service before. I'm usually overcome by a lot of grief. . . . But he lived really well and he did what he wanted with his life and I don't know anybody—anybody I've ever met—that I can say that for and really feel it." Ed had lived completely, as maybe no one else did, and there were no regrets.[2]

Ed's personal attendants raided his closet, grabbing the assortment of multicolor vests he wore every day. They kept his torso warm and spread a bit of psychedelic Berkeley everywhere he traveled. Zona and the family wore the vests, a symbolic way of bringing Ed to his own goodbye party.[3]

Judy Heumann started the ceremony: "Ed will be remembered by those of us who were privileged to know him for his undying optimism, for believing all things are possible. . . . Although we're here to celebrate his wonderful life—he made many contributions for all of us—the battle is not over."[4]

Zona recounted cherished memories of her son's incredible journey from the polio ward to high school, college, and the world. She spoke of fighting side by side with her son for his rights, breaking open society so that others could follow behind him with heads held high.[5]

Ed's brothers Ron and Mark and his son Lee told their favorite Ed stories. Joan Leon recalled how she first met him and became involved in the early development of the CIL. She spent over twenty years at his side, soaking up his magic.

Tom Bates joked, "Ed is up in heaven right now organizing the disabled and the seniors to take over. No one doubted that Ed would install curb cuts and restroom hand rails across heaven in his first week there."

Judy Heumann read a statement from Justin and Yoshika Dart: "Like all great leaders, his power . . . came from the depths of his vulnerability, of his passion for life and his love for people."

The memorial closed with a thousand voices singing as Ed would want them to.

> Oh, deep in my heart, I do believe,
> We shall overcome someday.

Six weeks later, a hundred of Ed's best friends and family scattered his ashes in the Pacific Ocean just outside the San Francisco Bay. Fittingly, the hearse that delivered Ed to his final rest was the USS *Potomac*, Franklin Delano Roosevelt's presidential yacht.

FDR hid his disability from the public, comforting Depression-era America with the carefully fabricated myth of his physical vigor. Of the thousands of press photos of FDR, only two showed him using his wheelchair. He never tried to convince the public that his physical limitations had nothing to do with his strength, competence, or courage. That argument he couldn't win.

But Ed could.

The roots of Ed's emancipated life began decades earlier with FDR playing in the jovial confines of a little community of physically disabled companions in Warm Springs, Georgia. Hidden from the public, among his closest disabled pals, FDR was free to be an openly disabled man. He laughed and cracked wise as he crawled across the pavement to drop into the swimming pool. There were no secrets among disabled pals.

Warm Springs was a rare 1930s space where disability was normal and acceptable, where FDR and his "crippled" friends enjoyed picnics and card games. At day's end, jolly Roosevelt mixed cocktails for everyone. Following a sumptuous dinner, the disabled comrades sang and danced together until the early morning hours.

Ed's life story picked up where President Roosevelt left off. He fought for a world where the joy, friendship, and freedom that disabled people created privately with one another traveled far beyond a hidden resort in Georgia or the CIL offices in Berkeley. Across the country, and around the world, independent living centers became islands of disability solidarity and support. They offered sweet respite from the harsh stigma and prejudice of the broader society. Disabled people found themselves surprisingly whole and loveable and ready to live their fullest lives.

Independent living centers were the scattered seeds of the revolution. From these unique cloisters of support, the movement leaped outward. The spirit and the depth of acceptance practiced within the center was broadcast and spread into the surrounding society.

That society was undoubtedly filled with danger. Trampling ignorant old attitudes and reinventing disability as a natural way for bodies to exist in the world—just one of many ways of being human, and a damned good one at that—meant following Ed down the riskiest roads. That's where the darkest enemies resided.

But even more, Ed taught that the safest paths were the dullest. Disabled people needed to swim with the whales, dolphins, and sharks. The deepest ocean waters offered the greatest opportunities, the sweetest friends, and the loudest laughter.

For the parents whose disabled children were underappreciated by outdated, uninspired public schools, and the many disabled adults who grew up under a cloud of shame and stigma, Ed gave them permission to be proud. He pushed their downward chins up to the open blue sky. There is a new kind of life for disabled people to live, he told them, and the time is now.

On the ship of the disabled American president, Zona carried her son's ashes to his final resting place. Brothers Ron and Mark brought their families from Oregon and Hawaii. Many members of Verne's side of the family, including his sister Maydelle, attended. Louie Haas, Ed and Ron's boyhood friend from Burlingame, came to say good-bye.

Ed's earliest mentors and supporters honored him. Jean Wirth was Ed's community college mentor. She believed Ed could earn a college degree long before he did. Dr. Henry Bruyn was the Cowell Hospital administrator who first opened the university doors to Ed. John Hessler was his first conspirator who coinvented the audacious idea of disability rights.

Joan Leon was Ed's lifelong best friend. She worked as his talented collaborator for two decades. Judy Heumann was the mighty and wise disability activist that Ed lured to Berkeley from New York. Arguably the most influential of all American disability rights leaders, she was his capable comrade at the CIL and the World Institute on Disability.

His attendants Jonathan Gold, Jon Oda, Otto Roderisch, and Mike Boyd were four men who knew Ed best of all. His cherished daily companions put him to bed at night, held joints to his lips, and shared the greatest belly laughs. The depth of their loving service to Ed was beyond calculation.[6]

Cruising beneath the Golden Gate Bridge, a gentle rain sprinkled on the mourners.

Zona gathered Ed's loved ones at the ship's bow. With a few heartfelt words, she emptied his ashes into the ocean, just beyond the Bay waters where he spent many boyhood days with his father chasing striped bass in their small rowboat.

· • ·

Longtime personal attendant Mike Boyd took Ed's death hard. He sat in his apartment staring at Ed's giant wheelchair.[7]

He had been a longshoreman, a loyal union man working the Long Beach docks. When he suffered a brain injury in a car accident, a host of neurological functioning issues forced him to give up his career. He wandered lost until he took a job as Ed's attendant. With his mentor and best friend, he discovered a purpose for his life.

Alone in his apartment with the empty wheelchair, an enormous Ed monument filling up the living room, Boyd could still hear his mentor's voice.

"When I die, I want my wheelchair in the Smithsonian Museum. Promise me that."

"OK, Ed. The Smithsonian," Boyd agreed, not taking his friend completely seriously.

After staring through tearful eyes for weeks at the strangely motionless chair, Boyd decided it was time. He jumped into action. He launched a grand plan to fulfill his promise.

A colossal electric wheelchair weighing hundreds of pounds is like a small car. Without a driver skillfully steering the machine, it is almost impossible to move.

Boyd built a solid wooden platform with four sturdy rolling casters. He fastened the chair securely with the strap-down hardware repurposed from the back of Ed's van. Attaching a thick length of rope to the front of the improvised vehicle, he was ready.

He called the terminal manager at Oakland Airport. "It's the final journey," Boyd told him. Dozens of times Boyd had assisted the luggage crew loading the chair safely into the underbelly of the aircraft. Boyd pushed Ed's chair into the storage compartment for one last flight to Washington, DC.

Getting around Washington wasn't too difficult. Grasping the rope, Boyd towed Ed's chair onto the Metro. Curious onlookers gawked at the strange man with his own parade float.

A memorial tribute was scheduled at the Dirksen Office Building, named for Illinois Republican senator Everett Dirksen, who broke a filibuster to pass the 1964 Civil Rights Act. The senators and congressional representatives would make speeches. It was high-brow, fancy-lace stuff that didn't appeal to Boyd. As far as he was concerned, the men in snappy suits and tight ties didn't really care about disabled people and didn't really know Ed.[8]

First was a good-bye tour of the city Ed had visited many times. Boyd took Ed's chair to all their favorite haunts, the coffee shops with the kindest waitresses and the restaurants with the tastiest entrees.

Towing the heavy chair down the sidewalk for many blocks, Boyd recalled a time they went shopping in Pentagon City, a commercial district near Arlington. A woman approached them. Her face softened and her voice issued like child's candy. Looking past Ed, the invisible man, she spoke to his assistant, "Oh, is he enjoying his time in Washington?"

"Yes, he is," replied Boyd with a hint of sarcasm. They had seen this kind of strange behavior before, a person talking to the attendant as if Ed were a toddler.

Ed played along, squeaking in a preschooler's high-pitched voice, "I'm going to see the President tomorrow!"

"Oh, my," the overly sweet woman jested back, "Is he going to see the President?"

"Yes, he is," Boyd grunted truthfully. He didn't have Ed's patience for this insulting nonsense. He threw a sideways bitter grin at Ed who smiled back like an innocent youngster.

Ed was in Washington to meet with President Bill Clinton. The president invited a small group of disability rights leaders to commemorate the third anniversary of the Americans with Disabilities Act. The contingent included DREDF lawyer Pat Wright, a leading figure in crafting the ADA, and Gallaudet University's first D/deaf president, I. King Jordan.

A task force headed by First Lady Hillary Clinton was working on an ultimately unsuccessful bill to establish healthcare for all Americans. Ed and the other disability rights leaders used the audience with the president to discuss details of personal attendant care funding in the initiative.[9]

Finally, the condescending woman waved bye-bye and walked away. Mike Boyd couldn't help himself. He bellowed angrily after her, "This man is Ed Roberts, the Martin Luther King of the disability rights movement!"

Ed snickered at his pal's futility. Sometimes there was nothing to do but laugh.

Boyd continued the final Capitol city tour, towing Ed's power wheelchair like a solemn pallbearer. He remembered the address of Ed's old Berkeley CIL friend Don Galloway, a pivotal early leader of blind services and peer counseling programs.[10]

The front door of Galloway's apartment was blocked by a tall row of steps. Boyd tugged the rolling memorial down an alley and pounded on the side door.

"Don!" he shouted. "It's me, Mike Boyd. I brought Ed!"

A surprised Galloway appeared in the doorway.

"It's me, Mike," Boyd identified himself to the blind man.

"Hi Mike. What are you doing?"

"I brought Ed's wheelchair to the Smithsonian. It's our final journey."

Galloway laid his hands on the familiar armrest of Ed's old chair. The two men chatted for a few minutes. Boyd had to leave in time to make the Dirksen memorial.

Stepping off the Metro at Union Station, Boyd hauled Ed's chair two blocks down First Street. Running on his last reserve of adrenaline, he pushed his weary body onward. Curious Capitol hill staffers and tourists gathered, asking what he was doing. He boasted about Ed with pride and sadness.

At Dirksen, Boyd positioned the wheelchair at the front of the big room. Maybe a hundred people, mostly politicians and their office staff, gathered to remember Ed. They nodded and half-bowed in respect to the wheelchair as it passed like a funeral casket.

To Boyd, the many speeches of praise and remembrance were empty wind. The speakers meant well, but they talked about Ed as if he were someone they had read about in the newspaper.

But not Senator Tom Harkin of Iowa. Mike always liked Harkin. He spoke from the heart, talking honestly about the loss of his dear friend. His long, wrinkled face fell downward with genuine feeling as he said, "We are all fortunate to live in this world which Ed so deeply touched, so richly celebrated."[11]

Finally Boyd took the Metro to the Smithsonian Castle, the museum information center on the south side of the Capitol Mall. He lumbered a half block to the front entrance of the red sandstone building with four towers reaching upward like a house of royalty.

He placed Ed's powerchair at the front entrance where it couldn't be missed. He pinned a rumpled paper scrap to the armrest. The note read, "I am delivering to you the motorized wheelchair of Ed Roberts."

Like a heartbroken mother abandoning her newborn on church steps, Boyd stepped away hesitantly. He looked over the chair one last time. On the side, a sticker with purple letters screamed "YES!" It was Ed's simple motto. The world told him "No," and he shouted back "Yes." Boyd loved that sticker. Ed had said "Yes" to him day after wonderful day.

"Hey!" a museum security guard interrupted. "You can't leave that there!"

"This is Ed Roberts' chair," Boyd argued. "He was the Martin Luther King of the disability rights movement."

The security guard had no patience. He didn't know what this guy was talking about. Boyd and the guard jawed angrily back and forth.

"Call Dick Alt," Boyd demanded, "I know Dick. He'll take care of this." Alt was a retired Air Force general who had headed up Smithsonian security two decades earlier. Boyd hoped that summoning his name would do the trick.

The current Smithsonian security boss finally arrived. He listened to the ranting man with tears running down his face make an impassioned speech about historical importance of Ed Roberts and the disability rights movement.

"I'll take care of the wheelchair," the manager said calmly. He took custody of the item. It was duly cataloged and placed in storage with the thousands of other historical artifacts held by the national museum.[12]

Too often the genius and sacrifice that innovated social progress is reduced to half-empty symbols. The African American civil rights movement became a Martin Luther King, Jr., holiday, just another Monday off school. The fight for women's suffrage and equality ended up as a rarely circulating Susan B. Anthony coin. The long, harrowing path of LGBT rights was rendered as an annual Pride Day, a street party often lacking recognition of the real historical struggles.

Perhaps a child enjoying a school-free day wonders who Martin Luther King, Jr., was and why we named a holiday after him. Maybe a man digging into his pocket for change to pay for a cup of coffee takes notice of Susan B. Anthony's image and googles her name. There's a chance that a Pride Day reveler sees a fellow celebrant wearing a Harvey Milk t-shirt and asks, "Who is that?"

The American disability rights movement usually doesn't rise even to that underwhelming level of tokenism. Public school textbooks ignore it. Disability service professionals like rehabilitation counselors and special education teachers know surprisingly little about the people who achieved curb cuts, Section 504, or the ADA. Disabled people and their history of pride and accomplishment are largely invisible.

Three years after Mike Boyd donated Ed's wheelchair to America's most prominent museum, Smithsonian curator Katherine Ott and disability studies scholar Simi Linton collaborated to create a disability rights museum exhibit. Ed's chair came out of mothballs for public display for the first time.

Ott took Linton, herself a wheelchair user, into the vast Smithsonian archives to find Ed's wheelchair. They entered what looked like the giant warehouse in the final scene of the movie *Raiders of the Lost Ark*. The Ark of the Covenant, the sacred chest believed to hold the Ten Commandments stone tablets, was housed in a plain wooden box in the random array amidst thousands of other crates.

Ott and Linton located Ed's chair, coated in a thin dust layer. Unlike Ed, it was motionless and silent. It wasn't driving at outrageous speed, flashing lights, and demanding that America open her doors to embrace and love disabled people. It wasn't charging forward with the laughter and anger of the disability revolution. It just sat there. Her eyes resting on the empty, still wheelchair, Simi Linton couldn't help but cry.[13]

28 *Interdependence*

In July 2017, over one thousand activists from nineteen countries gathered in Washington, DC, for the Global Summit of the World Independent Living Center Network. With participants from Asia, North America, Central America, Europe, and Africa, the conference was living testimony to the continuing vitality of the international disability rights movement. The first Berkeley CIL pebble in the pond had rippled outward for decades to become hundreds of independent living programs and centers, each bearing the cultural character of its location. Ed Roberts's fingerprints were everywhere.[1]

Running through the heart of Ed's contributions to independent living and improved access to society is a powerful idea that continues to resonate. On the surface, advocacy for disability rights obviously focuses on the well-being of disabled people, bringing a misunderstood and maligned population in from the cold to live with surprising measures of pride and strength. Undoubtedly, the movement is all that. But Ed also taught that disability rights benefits everyone, people with and without disabilities. The key to his thinking is the concept of interdependence.

From curb cuts to inclusive public school classrooms to antidiscrimination laws, recalibrating society for the active participation of disabled people wasn't an act of goodwill or deep empathy. It was simply common sense for the common good. Human beings vary greatly in the functioning of our bodies, in what we can and cannot do from situation to situation. Rather than crudely sorting the world into two piles of humanity, those who can and those who can't, Ed believed we are better off understanding all persons as complex, unstable mixtures of capacity and incapacity. As the shadowy visitor to his Cowell Hospital room taught Ed long ago, the human body is both weak and strong, vulnerable and reliable.

Conveyed daily by these contradictory bodies, what we all share is a need for assistance. Every human relies on the help of countless others. If a person receives an array of support without undue notice or devaluing stigma, that person is called nondisabled. If the array of daily assistances that allow a person to make it through the day are viewed as unusual, "special," or stigmatizing, that person is understood to have a disability. Ed taught that the ultimate goal of any society is to supply all manner of help to everyone as human, natural, and necessary.

Beginning with castles in the air conversations in Cowell Hospital, the Berkeley activists strategically used the word "independence" as the centerpiece of the movement. The term signaled a value that individualistic and even hyper-competitive Americans could get behind. With the passage of Section 504 and the ADA, liberal and conservative politicians embraced this goal of independence. Every person should hold the steering wheel of their own life, controlling the main decisions—housing, employment, education, relationships, recreation—that give daily character and content to their existence.

Over the decades, Ed came to chant the movement's independence mantra with a knowing wink. For he truly taught that independence always means interdependence. All people rely on a host of others every day, leaning on them in ways seen and unseen, appreciated and unacknowledged. If Mr. Rogers counseled America to look for the helpers, then Mr. Roberts advised citizens that, in the best society, if we do it right, the helpers are always there. The measure of a society is the presence, through a variety of informal and formal arrangements, of ready and willing human assistance for all persons.

Fully aware that helpfulness too often served the helpers, relegating the recipients to silent, submerged status, Ed's version of human aid had a strong dose of equity. First instituted at the Berkeley CIL, the idea was to invest primary control in the person receiving the assistance, dubbing that person master of their own life and care. It was also imminently practical because individuals tend to know what they truly need.

Ed and his close friend Dr. Bill Bronston put these principles into practice in the development of a summer camp for teens. In 1981, as part of the celebration of the International Year of Disabled Persons, the duo launched Camp Interdependence, a consciousness-raising program for disabled and nondisabled teens in the green hills of La Honda, California.

Bronston was no Marcus Welby. The medical director of the California Department of Developmental Services was a veteran disability rights warrior who fought in the infamous Willowbrook Wars. In the early 70s, he was a staff physician at Willowbrook State School in Staten Island, New York, the largest state residential facility for people with developmental disabilities—then called "severely retarded"—in the country.

The residential facility designed to house three thousand people held over five thousand children and adults. The hospital wards were factories of unimaginable misery. Individual staff members supervised fifty or more residents who sat around with nothing to do. The food was inedible, hygiene insufficient, and medical care inadequate.

When Senator Robert F. Kennedy stopped by for an unannounced tour, he found the residents unclothed on the tile floor in their own feces and urine. Powerful tranquilizers like thorazine and phenobarbital as well as straitjackets subdued the bored and traumatized patients. The senator called the place "a snake pit."[2]

Parents, politicians, professionals, and journalists who toured Willowbrook saw what Senator Kennedy saw: "many—far too many—living in filth and dirt, their clothing in rags, in rooms less comfortable and cheerful than the cages in which we put animals in the zoo—without adequate supervision or a bit of affection—condemned to a life without hope."[3]

In May 1972, Willowbrook superintendent Jack Hammond argued in a *New York Times* opinion piece that visitors like Senator Kennedy weren't actually appalled by the wretched hospital conditions and cruelty. They were simply having a normal emotional response to seeing people with severe mental and physical impairments. The professionals and staff hired to care for the residents bore no responsibility because utter despair was a natural consequence of the disability itself.[4]

With his colleagues Dr. Mike Wilkins and social worker Liz Lee, Bronston fought the institution management. They sponsored open public meetings to share the problems with local citizens and community groups. They emboldened a group of parents of institution residents to demand better care and improved conditions.

Wilkins and Bronston sneaked a relatively unknown television reporter named Geraldo Rivera with a cameraman into a Willowbrook building. Rivera's shocking expose showed scores of moaning, half-clothed residents in unfurnished spaces. What stunned Rivera most, he told New York television audiences, was what his cameras could not capture. It was the overpowering odor, the overwhelming stench of the hundreds of neglected people stewing in their own waste.

In March 1972, Bronston and Wilkins organized lawyers and the parents of residents to file a class action lawsuit. After many rounds of court decisions and appeals, Willowbrook State School, the most notorious of many abusive state institutions for people with developmental disabilities, closed in 1987.

The utopian minds of Ed and Dr. Bronston created Camp Interdependence as the wonderful opposite of Willowbrook. The camp enacted and developed Martin Luther King, Jr.'s, ethical concept of the "inescapable network of mutuality." Everyone was in this together, and loving human assistance was guaranteed.[5]

They recruited students representing the many California racial and ethnic groups while balancing genders. Twenty California high schools each nominated five disabled students and five nondisabled students to attend the annual weeklong adventure and recreation program. The five nondisabled students were intentionally selected because of their social status and leadership in their school. The five disabled students had a wide variety of physical and mental impairments.

Ed gave rousing fireside presentations that framed disability within a diverse American democracy. "Differences shouldn't divide us. They should be [a] source of unity as we help each other. . . . When we talk about integration, it's not just for people who are black or Asian. It's for all of us. It's for all of us to be part of each other."[6]

He appealed to the adolescents' awareness of racial divisions in society, creating a quick way for them to learn a minority-group model of disability rights. He challenged the students to view differences, even those commonly stigmatized and marginalized, as shared across the community. He invited the campers to recast diversity as a source of unity rather than division and acrimony.

The central idea embedded in the camp activities, that all people depend on one another—no one is truly independent—played out repeatedly. The teens participated in cooperative activities such as a ropes adventure course that emphasized team-building and interpersonal trust. The group adventures placed the young people in positions of social and physical vulnerability. The emotional and physical safety of each camper as well as the success of the group relied on intensive bonding and social support.

The days were filled with cheering, hugging, and crying. The popularity façades that protected the high-status youth fell away. So did the stigmatized identities that often resulted in the mistreatment of disabled students. They were just kids—equal humans—having fun together in the California woods.

After the intense outdoor challenges, the students sat in a circle on rocks and logs to share their feelings and thoughts. In a rap session format harkening back to early Berkeley feminist and disability groups, the teens shared their lives with one another.

Disabled youth taught the group about their impairments, how they felt about their bodies and how other people viewed them. One boy said, "I have muscular dystrophy. It eats like my muscle . . . it makes me weak."

Nondisabled campers opened up about their private struggles. One young man admitted that he loved sports but wasn't talented enough to make the high school athletic teams. A young woman with downcast eyes disclosed, "I keep my feelings bottled up inside because I don't really trust people to understand."

Finally, one camper summed up the conversation by proclaiming, "You're disabled. He's disabled. Everyone's disabled. Just some you can see and some are not noticeable."

Camp Interdependence returned the international disability rights hero to his teen years, reimagining the long days spent painfully alone staring up at the bright lights of the hospital polio unit. This time the lonely boy didn't have to daydream himself as a racehorse somehow convincing the competition to let him win. This time he escaped to the sunny California countryside with a fantastic community of high school friends bonded by their differences. No matter the health and functioning of their bodies, at the most basic level of humanity, the personal storehouse of weaknesses, flaws, fears, and vulnerabilities, all were equal. Simply and gloriously, the only point of it all was for each to help one another.

Ultimately, the disability rights movement born of the experiences of disabled college students in Berkeley, that grew through the efforts of activists and political allies across the country, changed both human behavior and attitudes. The laws creating physical and social access to society plus the two federal antidiscrimination statutes—Section 504 and ADA—helped to regulate behavior, forcing open many historically closed doors to participation.

But Ed always knew that the golden ring was the attitudes of the citizens, how they thought and felt about disabled people. That goal was harder and would take more time. That work continues today.

If Ed had his way, one day that woman in the Burlingame five-and-dime who prayed for his miraculous healing would simply appreciate him as a human being. She would spark up a neighborly conversation about the unseasonable weather or the upcoming Stanford Cardinal football season. One day the university administrator who complained "we've tried cripples before" would warmly greet a new disabled student. He would proudly offer a series of accessible housing options and useful educational accommodations. One day Lenin's tomb would feature new sidewalk ramps, accessible restrooms, an elevator, and tour guides proficient in multiple sign languages. Patrons of Moscow's Izmailovski Market would greet people with disabilities as comrades and friends. One day the world would be reasonable, accommodating, and filled with ready helpers. For Ed Roberts, that one day had to be today.

Notes

1. Fight

1. "Students Accuse State Worker," *San Francisco Chronicle*, September 19, 1969, p. 2.

2. Mike Fuss, interview by Sharon Bonney, Disability Rights and Independent Living Movement Oral History Project, Bancroft Library, University of California, Berkeley, 1995, p. 60. Eric Dibner, interview by author, July 18, 2018. Eric Dibner, interview by Kathryn Cowan, June 2000, Disability Rights and Independent Living Movement Oral History Project, Bancroft Library, University of California, Berkeley. Fred Collignon, interview by Mary Lou Breslin, March 1998, Disability Rights and Independent Living Movement Oral History Project, Bancroft Library, University of California, Berkeley. Zona Roberts, interview by author, September 25, 2018. Charles Grimes, interview by David Landes, Disability Rights and Independent Living Movement Oral History Project, Bancroft Library, University of California, Berkeley, 2000.

3. Mary Lou Breslin, interview by Susan O'Hara, Disability Rights and Independent Living Movement Oral History Project, Bancroft Library, University of California, Berkeley, 1998. Mary Lester, interview by Susan O'Hara, Disability Rights and Independent Living Movement Oral History Project, Bancroft Library, University of California, Berkeley, 2000. Scot Danforth, "Becoming the Rolling Quads: Politics at the University of California, Berkeley, in the 1960s," *History of Education Quarterly* 58, no. 4 (2018): 506–536.

4. Mike Fuss, interview by Sharon Bonney, Disability Rights and Independent Living Movement Oral History Project, Bancroft Library, University of California, Berkeley, 1995. Ed Roberts, interview by Susan O'Hara, Disability Rights

and Independent Living Movement Oral History Project, Bancroft Library, University of California, Berkeley, 1995. Edna Brean, interview by Susan O'Hara, Disability Rights and Independent Living Movement Oral History Project, Bancroft Library, University of California, Berkeley, 1995. Linda Perotti, interview by Cathy Cowan, Disability Rights and Independent Living Movement Oral History Project, Bancroft Library, University of California, Berkeley, 1998.

5. Herb Willsmore, interview by Susan O'Hara, Disability Rights and Independent Living Movement Oral History Project, Bancroft Library, University of California, Berkeley, 1999. Letters, Rolling Quads to Rod Carter, September 1969; Larry Biscamp to Rod Carter, September 18, 1969; Catherine Caulfield to Rod Carter, October 9, 1969; James Donald to Rod Carter, October 8, 1969; John Hessler to Rod Carter, September 21, 1969; Herbert R. Willsmore to Rod Carter, September 19, 1969; Larry Langdon to Rod Carter, September 19, 1969; Donald Lorence to Rod Carter, September 17, 1969; Ed Roberts to Rod Carter, September 1969, all in Disabled Students Program Records, carton 1, Bancroft Library, University of California, Berkeley. Gerald Belchick, interview by Sharon Bonney, 1998, Disability Rights and Independent Living Movement Oral History Project, Bancroft Library, University of California, Berkeley, p. 189. Ed Roberts, interview.

6. Robert Cohen, *Freedom's Orator: Mario Savio and the Radical Legacy of the 1960s* (New York: Oxford University Press, 2009); W. J. Rorabaugh, *Berkeley at War: The 1960s* (New York: Oxford University Press, 1990); Hal Draper, *Berkeley: The New Student Revolt* (New York: Grove Press, 1965); Robert Cohen and Reginald E. Zelnik, eds., *The Free Speech Movement: Reflections on Berkeley in the 1960's* (Berkeley: University of California Press, 2002).

7. Ed Roberts, interview.

8. Gerald Belchick, interview, p. 188.

9. Gerald Belchick, interview, p. 190. Eric Dibner, interview. Billy Charles Barner, interview by Kathy Cowan, Disability Rights and Independent Living Movement Oral History Project, Bancroft Library, University of California, Berkeley, March 27, 2000.

10. "Students Accuse State Worker," p. 2, and "UC Cripples Score Cut of Monies," *Berkeley Daily Gazette*, September 20, 1969, p. 1. "They Fought Disabilities and Won," *Daily Ledger* (Antioch, CA), May 2, 1982, p. 10.

11. Jeremiah J. Garretson, *The Path to Gay Rights: How Activism and Coming Out Changed Public Opinion* (New York: NYU Press, 2018).

12. California Department of Rehabilitation, *Vocational Rehabilitation of the Severely Disabled in a University Setting, Progress Report for Fiscal Year 1969-70*, by Lucile F. Withington and Michael T. Savino, Sacramento, November 18, 1969.

Gerald Belchick, interview. Lucile Withington, interview by Sharon Bonney, Disability Rights and Independent Living Monument Oral History Project, Bancroft Library, University of California, Berkeley, 1998.

13. Belchick, interview.

2. The Crippler

1. "A Vaccine for Polio," *Time*, February 9, 1953, 43.

2. Gregory L. Armstrong, Laura A. Conn, and Robert W. Pinner, "Trends in Infectious Disease Mortality in the United States During the 20th Century," *JAMA* 281, no. 1 (1999): 61–66, doi:10.1001/jama.281.1.61. Gareth Williams, *Paralysed with Fear: The Story of Polio* (London: Palgrave Macmillan, 2013).

3. Williams, *Paralysed with Fear*.

4. "March of Dimes, A Little Drama Starring Mickey and Judy" (circa 1938), https://www.youtube.com/watch?=v74xJB0I9M. David M. Oshinsky, *Polio: An American Story* (New York: Oxford University Press, 2005). Jane S. Smith, *Patenting the Sun: Polio and the Salk Vaccine* (New York: William Morrow, 1990).

5. "The Daily Battle," March of Dimes, 1948, https://www.youtube.com /watch?=vRgJjmrkKlm4&t=7s.

6. Hugh Gregory Gallagher, *FDR's Splendid Deception* (New York: Dodd, Mead, 1985), 65. Turnley Walker, *Roosevelt and the Warm Springs Story* (New York: Wyn, 1953).

7. Gallagher, *FDR's Splendid Deception*.

8. Smith, *Patenting the Sun*, p. 37. Marc Shell, *Polio and Its Aftermath: The Paralysis of Culture* (Cambridge, MA: Harvard University Press, 2005).

9. Richard S. Krannich, "Abortion in the United States: Past, Present, and Future Trends," *Family Relations* 29, no. 3 (1980): 365–374. Flora Davis, *Moving the Mountain: The Women's Movement in America Since 1960* (New York: Simon and Schuster, 1991). Paul Saurette and Kelly Gordon, *The Changing Voice of the Anti-Abortion Movement: The Rise of "Pro-Woman" Rhetoric in Canada and the United States* (Toronto: University of Toronto Press, 2015).

10. Zona Roberts, interview, September 25, 2018. Mark Roberts, interview by author, June 7, 2019, June 7, 2019. Zona Roberts, interview by Steve Brown, December 27, 1996. Zona Roberts, interview by Susan O'Hara, Disability Rights and Independent Living Movement Oral History Project, Bancroft Library, University of California, Berkeley, 1995.

11. Zona Roberts, interview, September 25, 2018. Mark Roberts, interview, June 7, 2019. Zona Roberts, interview by Steve Brown, December 27, 1996. Zona Roberts,

interview by Susan O'Hara, Disability Rights and Independent Living Movement Oral History Project, Bancroft Library, University of California, Berkeley, 1995.

12. Paul Michel Taillon, "Americanism, Racism, and 'Progressive' Unionism: The Railroad Brotherhoods, 1898–1916," *Australasian Journal of American Studies* 20 (2001): 55–65. Paul Michel Taillon, "What We Want Is Good, Sober Men: Masculinity, Respectability, and Temperance in the Railroad Brotherhoods, c. 1870–1910," *Journal of Social History* 36, no. 2 (2002): 319–338. Paul Michel Taillon, "Casey Jones, Better Watch Your Speed! Workplace Culture, Manhood, and Protective Labor Legislation on the Railroads, 1880s–1910s," *Australasian Journal of American Studies* 30, no. 1 (2011): 20–38.

13. Joanne Meyerowitz, "Beyond the Feminine Mystique: A Reassessment of Postwar Culture, 1946–1958," *The Journal of American History* 79, no. 4 (1993): 1455–1482. Melody L. Miller, Phyllis Moen, and Donna Dempster-McClain, "Motherhood, Multiple Roles, and Maternal Well-being: Women of the 1950s," *Gender and Society* 5, no. 4 (1991): 565–582. Claudia Goldin, "The Quiet Revolution That Transformed Women's Employment, Education, and Family," *The American Economic Review* 96, no. 2 (2006): 1–21. Debra Michals, "Toward a New History of the Postwar Economy: Prosperity, Preparedness, and Women's Small Business Ownership," *Business and Economic History* 26, no. 1 (1997): 45–56.

14. Betty Friedan, *The Feminine Mystique* (New York: W. W. Norton, 1963), p. 15.

15. "Sex Education: Oregon Film Provides New Approach to Delicate Problem," *LIFE*, May 24, 1948, pp. 55–58, 62. Elizabeth Peterson and Michael Aronson, "NO BIRDS, NO BEES, NO MORALIZING: Lester F. Beck, Progressive Educational Filmmaker," *The Moving Image: The Journal of the Association of Moving Image Archivists* 14, no. 1 (2014): 49–70.

16. The Kitchen Debate—transcript, July 24, 1959, US Embassy, Moscow, Soviet Union, https://www.cia.gov/readingroom/docs/1959-07-24.pdf.

17. Horace Gray, "Trapped Housewife," *Marriage and Family Living* 24, no. 2 (May 1962): 179–182.

18. Zona Roberts, interview, September 25, 2018. Mark Roberts, interview, June 7, 2019. Zona Roberts, interview by Steve Brown, December 27, 1996. Zona Roberts, interview by Susan O'Hara, Disability Rights and Independent Living Movement Oral History Project, Bancroft Library, University of California, Berkeley, 1995.

3. Vegetable

1. David R. Wessner, "Discovery of the Giant Mimivirus," *Nature Education* 3, no. 9 (2010): 61.

2. Gareth Williams, *Paralysed with Fear: The Story of Polio* (London: Palgrave Macmillan, 2013). Scott Young, *Neil and Me* (Toronto: McClelland and Stewart, 2006).

3. Williams, *Paralysed with Fear*.

4. Williams, *Paralysed with Fear*. David M. Oshinsky, *Polio: An American Story* (New York: Oxford University Press, 2005). Jane S. Smith, *Patenting the Sun: Polio and the Salk Vaccine* (New York: William Morrow, 1990).

5. Zona Roberts, interview, September 25, 2018.

6. Zona Roberts, interview, September 25, 2018. Mark Roberts, interview, June 7, 2019. Zona Roberts, interview by Steve Brown, December 27, 1996. Zona Roberts, interview by Susan O'Hara, Disability Rights and Independent Living Movement Oral History Project, Bancroft Library, University of California, Berkeley, 1995.

7. Ed Roberts, "When Others Speak for You, You Lose," Disabled Peoples' International, Melbourne, Australia, January 1983, Ed Roberts Papers, carton 1, folder 28, Bancroft Library, University of California, Berkeley.

8. Daniel J. Wilson, "And They Shall Walk: Ideal versus Reality in Polio Rehabilitation in the United States," *Asclepio. Revista de Historia de la Medicina y de la Ciencia* 41, no. 1 (2009): 175–192. Daniel J. Wilson, *Living with Polio: The Epidemic and Its Survivors* (Chicago: University of Chicago Press, 2007). Donald A. Neumann, "Polio: Its Impact on the People of the United States and the Emerging Profession of Physical Therapy," *Journal of Orthopedic Sports Physical Therapy* 34, no. 8 (2004): 479–492.

9. Zona Roberts, interview, September 25, 2018. Zona Roberts, interview by Steve Brown, December 27, 1996. Ed Roberts, interview by Susan O'Hara, Disability Rights and Independent Living Movement Oral History Project, Bancroft Library, University of California, Berkeley, 1995.

4. Reborn

1. Ed Roberts, "Effective Strategies for Social Change," Ed Roberts Papers, carton 4, folder 16, Bancroft Library, University of California, Berkeley.

2. Zona Roberts, interview, September 25, 2018. Mark Roberts, interview, June 7, 2019. Zona Roberts, interview by Steve Brown, December 27, 1996. Zona Roberts, interview by Susan O'Hara, Disability Rights and Independent Living Movement Oral History Project, Bancroft Library, University of California, Berkeley, 1995.

3. Leonard Kriegal, *The Long Walk Home* (New York: Appleton-Century, 1964).

4. Zona Roberts, interview, September 25, 2018. Mark Roberts, interview, June 7, 2019. Zona Roberts, interview by Steve Brown, December 27, 1996. Zona

Roberts, interview by Susan O'Hara, Disability Rights and Independent Living Movement Oral History Project, Bancroft Library, University of California, Berkeley, 1995. *60 Minutes* transcript, 1988, Ed Roberts Papers, carton 11, folder 18, Bancroft Library, University of California, Berkeley. Ed Roberts, "Effective Strategies for Social Change," Ed Roberts Papers, carton 4, folder 16, Bancroft Library, University of California, Berkeley.

5. Clarence W. Dail, John E. Affeldt, and Clarence R. Collier, "Clinical Aspects of Glossopharyngeal Breathing: Report of Use by One Hundred Postpolio-myelitic Patients," *Journal of the American Medical Association* 158, no. 6 (1955): 445–449.

6. J.C. Geiger, "Poliomyelitis in San Francisco," *American Journal of Public Health* 39 (1949): 1567–1570; Hulda E. Thelander, Maxine Sehring, and Edward B. Shaw, "Poliomyelitis, Six Year Study of Cases at Children's Hospital, San Francisco," *Pediatrics* 6, no. 4 (1950): 581–592; Edward B. Shaw and Hulda E. Thelander, "Clinical Concept of Poliomyelitis," *Pediatrics* 4 (1949): 277.

7. Zona Roberts, interview, September 25, 2018. Mark Roberts, interview, June 7, 2019. Zona Roberts, interview by Steve Brown, December 27, 1996. Zona Roberts, interview by Susan O'Hara, Disability Rights and Independent Living Movement Oral History Project, Bancroft Library, University of California, Berkeley, 1995.

8. Kevin Starr, *Embattled Dreams: California in War and Peace, 1940–1950* (New York: Oxford University Press, 2003).

9. Zona Roberts, interview, September 25, 2018. Zona Roberts, interview by Steve Brown, December 27, 1996.

10. Zona Roberts, interview, September 25, 2018. Zona Roberts, interview by Steve Brown, December 27, 1996.

5. King of the Cripples

1. Kevin Starr, *Embattled Dreams: California in War and Peace* (New York: Oxford University Press, 2003), p. 203. Bennett M. Berger, "Suburbia and the American Dream," *The Public Interest* 2 (1966): 82.

2. William E. Leuchtenburg, *A Troubled Feast: American Society Since 1945* (Boston: Little, Brown, 1973), p. 89.

3. Leuchtenburg, *A Troubled Feast*. William H. Chafe, *The Unfinished Journey: America Since World War II* (New York: Oxford University Press, 2003).

4. Gunnar Myrdal, *An American Dilemma: The Negro Problem and Modern Democracy* (New York: Harper and Brothers, 1944), p. 30. "Ten Most Famous Paint-

ings by Norman Rockwell," *USA Art News*, https://usaartnews.com/art/ten-most-famous-paintings-by-norman-rockwell. Deborah Solomon, *American Mirror: The Life and Art of Norman Rockwell* (New York: Farrar, Straus and Giroux, 2013). Jennifer A. Greenhill, "The View from Outside: Rockwell and Race in 1950," *American Art* 21, no. 2 (2007): 70–95. Bridget R. Cooks, "Norman Rockwell's Negro Problem," *Cultural Critique* 105 (2019): 40–79.

5. Leuchtenburg, *A Troubled Feast*, p. 11. David Chalmers, *And the Crooked Places Made Straight: The Struggle for Social Change in the 1960s* (Baltimore: Johns Hopkins Press, 1991).

6. Fred Davis, *Passage Through Crisis: Polio Victims and Their Families* (Piscataway, NJ: Transaction Publishers, 1991), p. xv.

7. Johnnie Lacy, interview by David Landes, Disability Rights and Independent Living Movement Oral History Project, Bancroft Library, University of California, Berkeley, November 1998.

8. "Neil Marcus: Performance Artist," interview by Esther Ehrlich, Oral History Center, Bancroft Library, University of California, Berkeley, 2006.

9. Zona Roberts, interview, September 25, 2018. Zona Roberts, interview by Steve Brown, December 27, 1996. Zona Roberts, interview by Susan O'Hara, Disability Rights and Independent Living Movement Oral History Project, Bancroft Library, University of California, Berkeley, 1995.

10. Ed Roberts, "Is There?" *Fresh Flame*, Burlingame (CA) High School, January 1959, Ed Roberts Papers, carton 1, folder 1, Bancroft Library, University of California, Berkeley.

11. Mark Roberts, interview, June 7, 2019.

6. Learning to Fight

1. Zona Roberts, interview, September 25, 2018. Mark Roberts, interview, June 7, 2019. Zona Roberts, interview by Steve Brown, December 27, 1996. Zona Roberts, interview by Susan O'Hara, Disability Rights and Independent Living Movement Oral History Project, Bancroft Library, University of California, Berkeley, 1995. Ed Roberts, speech at California Behavior Analysis Conference, March 30, 1977, Ed Roberts Papers, carton 1, folder 20, Bancroft Library, University of California, Berkeley. Ed Roberts, interview by Susan O'Hara, Disability Rights and Independent Living Movement Oral History Project, Bancroft Library, University of California, Berkeley, 1994.

2. Hugh Gregory Gallagher, *Black Bird Fly Away: Disabled in an Able-Bodied World* (St. Petersburg, FL: Vandermere Press, 1998), p. 121.

3. Zona Roberts, interview, September 25, 2018. Mark Roberts, interview, June 7, 2019. Zona Roberts, interview by Steve Brown, December 27, 1996. Zona Roberts, interview by Susan O'Hara, Disability Rights and Independent Living Movement Oral History Project, Bancroft Library, University of California, Berkeley, 1995.

4. Zona Roberts, interview, September 25, 2018. Mark Roberts, interview, June 7, 2019. Zona Roberts, interview by Steve Brown, December 27, 1996. Zona Roberts, interview by Susan O'Hara, Disability Rights and Independent Living Movement Oral History Project, Bancroft Library, University of California, Berkeley, 1995.

7. Dr. Bruyn's Program

1. Kevin Starr, *Golden Dreams: California in the Age of Abundance, 1950–1963* (New York: Oxford University Press, 2009).

2. Taylor Branch, *Parting the Waters: America in the King Years, 1954–63* (New York: Simon and Schuster, 1988). Iwan Morgan and Philip Davies, *From Sit-Ins to SNCC: The Student Civil Rights Movement in the 1960's* (Gainesville: University of Florida Press, 2012).

3. Eric Marcus, *Making Gay History: The Half-Century Fight for Lesbian and Gay Equal Rights* (New York: HarperCollins, 2002), p. 99. Dudley Clendinen and Adam Nagourney, *Out for Good: The Struggle to Build a Gay Rights Movement in America* (New York: Simon and Schuster, 1999). Jeremiah J. Garretson, *The Path to Gay Rights: How Activism and Coming Out Changed Public Opinion* (New York: NYU Press, 2018). Lillian Faderman, *The Gay Revolution: The Story of Struggle* (New York: Simon and Schuster, 2015).

4. Flora Davis, *Moving the Mountain: The Women's Movement in America Since 1960* (New York: Simon and Schuster, 1991). Ruth Rosen, *The World Split Open: How the Modern Women's Movement Changed America* (New York: Penguin, 2000). Barbara Ryan, *Feminism and the Women's Movement: Dynamics of Change in Social Movement Ideology and Activism* (New York: Routledge, 1992).

5. Paul J. Corcoran, interview by Fred Pelka, Disability Rights and Independent Living Movement Oral History Project, Bancroft Library, University of California, Berkeley, 2004, p. 111.

6. Branch, *Parting the Waters.*

7. Henry Bruyn, interview by Susan O'Hara, Disability Rights and Independent Living Movement Oral History Project, Bancroft Library, University of California, Berkeley, 1994. Arleigh Williams, interview by Germaine LaBerge, Uni-

versity History Series, Regional Oral History Office, Bancroft Library, University of California, Berkeley, 1989.

8. Ed Roberts, interview by Susan O'Hara, Disability Rights and Independent Living Movement Oral History Project, Bancroft Library, University of California, Berkeley, 1995, p. 7.

9. Zona Roberts, interview, September 25, 2018. Zona Roberts, interview by Steve Brown, December 27, 1996. Zona Roberts, interview by Susan O'Hara, Disability Rights and Independent Living Movement Oral History Project, Bancroft Library, University of California, Berkeley, 1995. Ed Roberts, interview by Susan O'Hara, Disability Rights and Independent Living Movement Oral History Project, Bancroft Library, University of California, Berkeley, 1995. Henry Bruyn, interview by Susan O'Hara, Disability Rights and Independent Living Movement Oral History Project, Bancroft Library, University of California, Berkeley, 1994.

10. Ed Roberts, interview by Susan O'Hara, Disability Rights and Independent Living Movement Oral History Project, Bancroft Library, University of California, Berkeley, 1995.

11. "Helpless Cripple Attends UC Classes Here in Wheelchair," *Berkeley Gazette,* December 5, 1962, p. 20.

12. Henry Bruyn, interview by Susan O'Hara, Disability Rights and Independent Living Movement Oral History Project, Bancroft Library, University of California, Berkeley, 1994.

13. Ed Roberts, interview by Susan O'Hara, Disability Rights and Independent Living Movement Oral History Project, Bancroft Library, University of California, Berkeley, 1995. Mark Roberts, interview, June 7, 2019.

14. Mike Fuss, interview by Sharon Bonney, Disability Rights and Independent Living Movement Oral History Project, Bancroft Library, University of California, Berkeley, 1995. Mark Roberts, interview, 1998. Arleigh Williams, interview by Germaine LaBerge, University History Series, Regional Oral History Office, Bancroft Library, University of California, Berkeley, 1989.

8. Death and Renewal

1. Zona Roberts, interview, September 25, 2018. Zona Roberts, interview by Steve Brown, December 27, 1996. Zona Roberts, interview by Susan O'Hara, Disability Rights and Independent Living Movement Oral History Project, Bancroft Library, University of California, Berkeley, 1995. Mark Roberts, interview, June 7, 2019. Ed Roberts, interview by Susan O'Hara, Disability Rights and Independent

Living Movement Oral History Project, Bancroft Library, University of California, Berkeley, 1995.

2. Betty Friedan, *The Feminine Mystique* (New York: W.W. Norton, 1963).

3. Ruth Rosen, *The World Split Open: How The Modern Women's Movement Changed America* (New York: Penguin, 2000).

4. Carol Hanisch, "The Personal Is Political," in *Notes from the Second Year: Women's Liberation*, ed. Shulamith Firestone and Anne Koedt, pp. 76–77 (New York: New York Radical Women, 1970). Corbett O'Toole, interview by Denise Jacobsen, Disability Rights and Independent Living Movement Oral History Project, Bancroft Library, University of California, Berkeley, 1998. Corbett O'Toole, interview by author, May 15, 2019.

5. Zona Roberts, interview, September 25, 2018. Zona Roberts, interview by Steve Brown, December 27, 1996. Zona Roberts, interview by Susan O'Hara, Disability Rights and Independent Living Movement Oral History Project, Bancroft Library, University of California, Berkeley, 1995. Ed Roberts, interview by Susan O'Hara, Disability Rights and Independent Living Movement Oral History Project, Bancroft Library, University of California, Berkeley, 1995. Mark Roberts, interview, June 7, 2019. Eric Dibner, interview, July 18, 2018. Eric Dibner, interview by Kathryn Cowan, Disability Rights and Independent Living Movement Oral History Project, Bancroft Library, University of California, Berkeley, 2000.

9. Radical Berkeley

1. Timothy Pfaff, "A Conversation with Ed Roberts: California Q & A," *California Monthly*, February 1985. James Donald, interview by Cathy Cowan, Disability Rights and Independent Living Movement Oral History Project, Bancroft Library, University of California, Berkeley, 1998. Hal Draper, *Berkeley: The New Student Revolt* (New York: Grove Press, 1965). Robert Cohen, *Freedom's Orator: Mario Savio and the Radical Legacy of the 1960s* (New York: Oxford University Press, 2009). W.J. Rorabaugh, *Berkeley at War: The 1960s* (New York: Oxford University Press, 1990).

2. Todd Gitlin, *The Sixties: Years of Hope, Days of Rage* (New York: Bantam, 1987), p. 285.

3. Jim Newton, *Man of Tomorrow: The Relentless Life of Jerry Brown* (New York: Little Brown, 2020). Darle E. Lembke, "Oakland War Protest Quelled," *Los Angeles Times*, October 18, 1967, p. 1. Darle E. Lembke, "Third Day of Oakland Antiwar Protests Results in 91 Arrests," *Los Angeles Times,* October 19, 1967, p. 3. "Newsmen Groups Protest Oakland Police Tactics," *Los Angeles Times*, October 18, 1967, p. 3.

4. Charles Grimes, interview, p. 24.

5. Herb Willsmore, interview. Zona Roberts, interview. Jim Donald, interview by Kathryn Cowan, 1998, Disability Rights and Independent Living Movement Oral History Project, Bancroft Library, University of California, Berkeley. Billy Charles Barner, interview. Cathy Caulfield, interviewed by Susan O'Hara, 1996, Disability Rights and Independent Living Movement Oral History Project, Bancroft Library, University of California, Berkeley. Carol Billings, interview by Kathryn Cowan, Disability Rights and Independent Living Movement Oral History Project, Bancroft Library, University of California, Berkeley, 1999.

6. Rorabaugh, *Berkeley at War*, p. 115. Gitlin, *The Sixties*. Cohen, *Freedom's Orator*. Robert Cohen and Reginald E. Zelnik, eds., *The Free Speech Movement: Reflections on Berkeley in the 1960s* (Berkeley: University of California Press, 2002). William E. Leuchtenburg, *A Troubled Feast: American Society Since 1945* (Boston: Little, Brown, 1973), p. 11. David Chalmers, *And the Crooked Places Made Straight: The Struggle for Social Change in the 1960s* (Baltimore: Johns Hopkins University Press, 1991).

7. Edna Brean, interview by Susan O'Hara, Disability Rights and Independent Living Movement Oral History Project, Bancroft Library, University of California, Berkeley, 1995.

8. Martha Biondi, *Black Revolution on Campus* (Berkeley: University of California Press, 2012). Muhammad Ahmad, "On the Black Student Movement," *The Black Scholar* 9, no. 8/9 (1978): 2–11. Harvey Dong, "Third World Liberation Comes to San Francisco State and UC Berkeley," *Chinese America: History and Perspectives* (2009): 95–106, 157.

9. Felicia Kornbluh, "Disability, Antiprofessionalism, and Civil Rights: The National Federation of the Blind and the 'Right to Organize' in the 1950s," *The Journal of American History* 97, no. 4 (2011): 1026.

10. California Department of Rehabilitation, *Vocational Rehabilitation of the Severely Disabled in a University Setting, Progress Report for Fiscal Year 1968–69*, by Lucile F. Withington and Michael T. Savino, Sacramento, November 18, 1969. Brian Woods and Nick Johnson, "Power to Independence: A Historical Glimpse at the Interactions Between Powered Wheelchairs and the Physically Disabled Students Program at Berkeley," Conference of the Disability Studies Association, Lancaster University, UK, September 2003. Mary Tremblay, "Going Back to Civvy Street: A Historical Account of the Impact of the Everest and Jennings Wheelchair for Canadian WWII Veterans with Spinal Cord Injury," *Disability and Society* 11, no. 2 (1996): 149–170. Julie Anderson, "'Turned into Taxpayers': Paraplegia, Rehabilitation, and Sport at Stoke Mandeville, 1944–1956," *Journal of Contemporary History* 38, no. 3 (2003): 461–475. Geoffrey Reaume, *Lyndhurst: Cana-*

da's First Rehabilitation Center for People with Spinal Cord Injuries, 1945-1998 (Montreal: McGill-Queen's University Press, 2007).

11. Ed Roberts, interview by Susan O'Hara, Disability Rights and Independent Living Movement Oral History Project, Bancroft Library, University of California, Berkeley, 1994, p. 46.

12. Scot Danforth, "Becoming the Rolling Quads: Politics at the University of California, Berkeley, in the 1960s," *History of Education Quarterly* 58, no. 4 (2018): 506-536.

13. Charles Grimes, interview. Woods and Watson, "Power to Independence."

14. Herb Willsmore, interview by Susan O'Hara, Disability Rights and Independent Living Movement Oral History Project, Bancroft Library, University of California, Berkeley, 1999.

15. *60 Minutes* transcript, 1988, Ed Roberts Papers, carton 11, folder 18, Bancroft Library, University of California, Berkeley.

16. Jacobus tenBroek, "Cross of Blindness," National Federation of the Blind Convention, New Orleans, July 6, 1957, https://nfb.org/sites/default/files/images/nfb/publications/bm/bm11/bm1107/bm110712.htm.

17. Bernard Taper, "The Right to Compete," *New Yorker,* January 3, 1958:23. Jacobus tenBroek, "Cross of Blindness,"

18. Kornbluh, "Disability, Antiprofessionalism, and Civil Rights."

19. Audra Jennings, *Out of the Horrors of War: Disability Politics in World War II America* (Philadelphia: University of Pennsylvania Press, 2016).

20. Taylor Branch, *Parting the Waters: America in the King Years, 1954-63* (New York: Simon and Schuster, 1988), p. 475.

21. Often the term "Deaf" is used to describe a linguistic minority, a cultural community who uses American Sign Language (ASL) as their primary language. The word "deaf" is used to indicate the presence of a hearing impairment, a functional loss of hearing. Combining the two words into "D/deaf" is a common way of pointing to both meanings.

22. Jeff Moyer, interview by author, May 1, 2019.

10. A New Movement

1. Dudley Clendinen and Adam Nagourney, *Out for Good: The Struggle to Build a Gay Rights Movement in America* (New York: Simon and Schuster, 1999), p. 28.

2. Letter, Barbara A. Kirk to Don Lorence, August 27, 1969, Disabled Students Program Records, carton 1, Bancroft Library, University of California, Berkeley. Letter, Bod Find, United States Department of Health, Education, and Welfare,

to Colleen Nutt, Membership Director, California Alumni Association, Berkeley, December 8, 1969, Disabled Students Program Records, carton 1, Bancroft Library, University of California, Berkeley. Sociology 198, class meeting notes, Disabled Students Program Records, carton 4, Bancroft Library, University of California, Berkeley. "They Fought Disabilities and Won," *Daily Ledger* (Antioch, CA), May 2, 1982, p. 10.

3. Hale Zukas, interviewed by Sharon Bonney, Disability Rights and Independent Living Movement Oral History Project, Bancroft Library, University of California, Berkeley, 1998. Eric Dibner, interview by Cathy Cowan, Disability Rights and Independent Living Movement Oral History Project, Bancroft Library, University of California, Berkeley, 2001.

4. "Hear Ye, Hear Ye," *Berkeley Barb*, April 18–24, 1969, p. 2.

5. "Herrick Injury Reports," *Berkeley Barb*, May 23–29, 1969, p. 4. "Medic Amidst Madness," *Berkeley Barb*, May 23–29, 1969, p. 6. Robert Sommer and Robert L. Thayer, "The Radicalization of Common Ground People's Park, Berkeley: An Unnatural History," *Landscape Architecture Magazine* 67, no. 6 (November 1977): 510–514. Jon David Cash, "People's Park: Birth and Survival," *California History* 88, no. 1 (2010): 8–29, 53–55.

6. Herb Leibowitz, interview by Susan O'Hara, Disability Rights and Independent Living Movement Oral History Project, Bancroft Library, University of California, Berkeley, 2000, p. 10. "Students Accuse State Worker," *San Francisco Chronicle*, September 19, 1969, p. 2. Gerard J. De Groot, "Ronald Reagan and Student Unrest in California, 1966–1970," *Pacific Historical Review* 65, no. 1 (1996): 107–129.

7. Lonnie Hancock interview, May 16, 2019.

8. Steven E. Brown, "The Curb Ramps of Kalamazoo: Discovering Our Unrecorded History," *Disability Studies Quarterly* 13, no. 3 (1999): 203–205.

9. "Curb cuts outside Altgeld Hall," photo, RS 16/6/13, Series 1, carton 1, folder 3, University of Illinois Archives. "Man on ramp outside rehabilitation center," photo, RS 16/6/13, Series 1, carton 1, folder 3, University of Illinois Archives.

10. Kitty Cone, interview by David Landes, Disability Rights and Independent Living Movement Oral History Project, Bancroft Library, University of California, Berkeley, 1998.

11. "Ridgewood Taking Down Obstacles to Wheel Chairs," *New York Times*, March 26, 1975, p. 88. Mildred Jailer, "Handicapped to Get Aid at Bergen Polls," *New York Times*, October 28, 1973, p. 100.

12. Paul Weingarten, "Simpson to Seek Parking, Ramps for the Handicapped," *Chicago Tribune*, July 28, 1976, p. 4. Richard J. McCauley, "Ramps for Handicapped," *Chicago Tribune*, December 6, 1976, p. C2.

13. Hearings Before the Subcommittee on Select Education and Committee on Education and Labor, House of Representatives, Ninety-Fifth Congress, Second Session (Washington, DC: US Government Printing Office, 1978), p. 699. "Aids for Wheelchair Users; Curb Ramp Project Nears Completion," *Los Angeles Times,* October 30, 1977, p. CS7. John T. McQuiston, "Easing the Way for the Handicapped: Building Hope for the Handicapped," *New York Times,* January 15, 1978, p. LI1.

14. Bess Williamson, *Accessible America: A History of Disability and Design* (New York: NYU Press, 2019).

11. Humblest Beginnings

1. Fred Collignon, interview by Mary Lou Breslin, Disability Rights and Independent Living Movement Oral History Project, Bancroft Library, University of California, Berkeley, March 1998. Fred Collignon, interview by author, January 21, 2019.

2. Mike Fuss, interview, p. 65.

3. Charles Grimes, interview by David Landes, Disability Rights and Independent Living Movement Oral History, Bancroft Library, University of California, Berkeley, 1998.

4. Jeff Moyer, interview.

5. Robert L. Metts, *Stories for My Friends* (Kindle Edition, 2021), chap. 18.

6. Corbett O'Toole, interview by Denise Jacobson, July 18, 2000, Disability Rights and Independent Living Movement Oral History Project, Bancroft Library, University of California, Berkeley, p. 30.

7. Susan Marie Schweik, *The Ugly Laws: Disability in Public* (New York: NYU Press, 2009).

8. Corbett O'Toole, interview by Denise Jacobson, July 18, 2000, Disability Rights and Independent Living Movement Oral History Project, Bancroft Library, University of California, Berkeley, p. 29. Corbett O'Toole, interview, May 15, 2019.

9. Crosby, Stills, Nash, and Young, "Chicago," *Four Way Street*, Atlantic Records, 1971.

10. Jo Freeman, "The Tyranny of Structurelessness," *Berkeley Journal of Sociology* 17 (1972): 151–164.

11. Herb Leibowitz, interview by Susan O'Hara, Disability Rights and Independent Living Movement Oral History Project, Bancroft Library, University of California, Berkeley, 2000, p. 15.

12. Fred Collignon, interview, January 21, 2019.

13. E. B. Whitten, "Rehabilitation for Independent Living," editorial, *Journal of Rehabilitation* 23, no. 4 (1957): 2.

14. A.D. Puth, "Passing and Implementing Effective Legislation," editorial, *Journal of Rehabilitation* 27, no. 6 (1961): 2. I.J. Brightman, "The Proposed Federal Legislation for Independent Living Rehabilitation," *American Journal of Public Health and the Nation's Health* 51, no. 5 (1961): 753–759. Louis B. Newman, Robert S. Wilson, and Joseph S. Stratigos, "Dignified Living for the Severely Disabled: The Role of Physical Medicine and Rehabilitation," *Quarterly Bulletin of Northwestern University Medical School* 35, no. 1 (1961): 61–69.

15. H.D. Young, *Independent Living: A Study of Rehabilitation of Physically Handicapped Adults Living in Foster Homes; Social Work Intervention in the Adaptation to Family Environment*, Final Report, Rehabilitation Services Administration, 1966, p. 199. E. Katz, *An Independent Living Rehabilitation Program for Seriously Handicapped Mentally Retarded Adults*, Final Report, Rehabilitation Services Administration, 1965.

16. Fred Collignon, interview, January 21, 2019.

17. Carole Fewell Billings, interview by Kathy Cowan, July 24, 1998, Disability Rights and Independent Living Movement Oral History Project, Bancroft Library, University of California, Berkeley, p. 9.

18. Letter, Ramona A. Watras to Ed Roberts, November 21, 1993, Ed Roberts Papers, carton 4, folder 20, Bancroft Library, University of California, Berkeley.

19. Charles Cole, "Social Technology, Social Policy, and the Severely Disabled: Issues Posed by the Blind, Deaf, and Those Unable to Walk" (PhD, dissertation, University of California, Berkeley, 1979), p. 401. Carole Fewell Billings, interview by Kathy Cowan, July 24, 1998, Disability Rights and Independent Living Movement Oral History Project, Bancroft Library, University of California, Berkeley.

20. Fred Collignon, interview, January 21, 2019.

21. Manning Peterson, "Highlighting Disabled Activism's Incubator," *The Advocate: The Student Voice of Contra Costa College*, October 29, 2015, https://cccadvocate.com/3037/opinion/highlighting-disabled-activisms-incubator/.

22. Timothy J. Conlan, "The Politics of Federal Block Grants: From Nixon to Reagan," *Political Science Quarterly* 99, no. 2 (1984): 247–270.

23. Tom Bates and Lonnie Hancock, interview, May 16, 2019.

24. Tom Bates and Lonnie Hancock, interview, May 16, 2019.

12. Joan

1. Joan Leon interview, Paul K. Longmore Institute on Disability Collection, San Francisco State University, https://diva.sfsu.edu/collections/longmoreinstitute/bundles/230605.

2. Barbara McIntosh, "Man in the Iron Lung," *San Jose Mercury News*, November 4, 1984, pp. 1L–2L.

3. Joan Leon, interview, November 18–19, 2018. Joan Leon, interview by Susan O'Hara, Disability Rights and Independent Living Movement Oral History Project, Bancroft Library, University of California, Berkeley, 2000.

4. Ed Roberts, "When Others Speak for You, You Lose," Disabled Peoples' International, First National Assembly, Melbourne, January 1983, Ed Roberts Papers, carton 1, folder 28, Bancroft Library, University of California, Berkeley.

5. Joan Leon, interview, November 18–19, 2018. Joan Leon, interview by Susan O'Hara, Disability Rights and Independent Living Movement Oral History Project, Bancroft Library, University of California, Berkeley, 2000.

6. Herb Leibowitz, interview by Susan O'Hara, Disability Rights and Independent Living Movement Oral History Project, Bancroft Library, University of California, Berkeley, 2000.

7. Joan Leon, interview, November 18–19, 2018. Joan Leon, interview by Susan O'Hara, Disability Rights and Independent Living Movement Oral History Project, Bancroft Library, University of California, Berkeley, 2000.

13. Judy

1. Judith Heumann and Kristen Joiner, *Being Heumann: An Unrepentant Memoir of a Disability Rights Activist* (Boston: Beacon Press, 2020). Judy Heumann, interview by Jonathan Young, Susan Brown, and David Landes, Disability Rights and Independent Living Movement Oral History Project, Bancroft Library, University of California, Berkeley, 2001. Judy Heumann, interview, September 4, 2020.

2. Andrew H. Malcolm, "Polio Victim, 22, Is Denied License to Teach in City's Schools," *New York Times*, April 1, 1970, p. 35.

3. "License Miss Heumann," *New York Times*, April 2, 1970, p. 38.

4. Heumann and Joiner, *Being Heumann*. Judy Heumann, interview by Jonathan Young, Susan Brown, and David Landes.

5. Charles M. Shapp, "Hiring Handicapped," *New York Times,* April 11, 1970, p. 29.

6. Heumann and Joiner, *Being Heumann*, p. 59.

7. Lillian Faderman, *The Gay Revolution: The Story of Struggle* (New York: Simon and Schuster, 2015).

8. Andrew H. Malcolm, "Woman in Wheel Chair Sues to Become Teacher," *New York Times,* May 27, 1970, p. 33.

9. "New Medical Exam Set for Teacher Applicant," *New York Times,* June 2, 1970, p. 49. Judy Heumann, interview by Jonathan Young, January 2, 1998, Disability Rights and Independent Living Movement Oral History Project, Bancroft Library, University of California, Berkeley, p. 150. "Polio Victim Wins Teacher's License," *New York Times,* June 20, 1970, p. 17.

10. Richard K. Scotch, "Politics and Policy in the History of the Disability Rights Movement," *The Milbank Quarterly* 67 (1989): 380–400.

11. "Disabled Tie Up Traffic Here to Protest Nixon Aid-Bill Vote," *New York Times,* November 3, 1972, p. 43.

12. "Handicapped Stage a Times Square Protest on Health Measures," *New York Times,* November 7, 1972, p. 38.

13. E. W. Kenworthy, "200,000 March for Civil Rights in Orderly Washington Rally; President Sees Gain for Negro," *New York Times,* August 29, 1963, p. 1.

14. Taylor Branch, *Parting the Waters: America in the King Years, 1954–63* (New York: Simon and Schuster, 1988). Taylor Branch, *Pillar of Fire: American in the King Years, 1963–65* (New York: Simon and Schuster, 1998). "Seminarians Quietly Maintain 24-Hour Rights Vigil: Fresh Force Nightly," *Washington Post,* May 11, 1964, p. A6.

15. Heumann and Joiner, *Being Heumann.* Judy Heumann, interview by Jonathan Young, Susan Brown, and David Landes. Judy Heumann interview, September 4, 2020.

14. I'm Here, We're Here

1. Jenny Perry, "His Ambition Is to 'Free' the Handicapped," *Santa Barbara News-Press,* May 6, 1979, p. A-3.

2. Megan Kirschbaum, interview by Kathy Cowan, Disability Rights and Independent Living Movement Oral History Project, Bancroft Library, University of California, Berkeley, 2001. Hal Kirschbaum, interview by Kathy Cowan, Disability Rights and Independent Living Movement Oral History Project, Bancroft Library, University of California, Berkeley, 2000.

3. Hal Kirschbaum, interview by Kathy Cowan, Disability Rights and Independent Living Movement Oral History Project, Bancroft Library, University of California, Berkeley, 2000, p. 175.

4. Ed Roberts, speech at California Behavior Analysis Conference, March 30, 1977, Ed Roberts Papers, carton 1, folder 20, Bancroft Library, University of California, Berkeley.

5. Ed Roberts, speech at California Behavior Analysis Conference, March 30, 1977, Ed Roberts Papers, carton 1, folder 20, Bancroft Library, University of California, Berkeley.

6. Nancy Skelton, "The 'Helpless Cripple' Steers a Fresh Course," *Sacramento Bee,* January 18, 1976, p. A3. "'Helpless' Cripple Helps California's Handicapped," *Fremont Argus,* December 10, 1975, p. 1.

7. Ed Roberts, Workshop on Hiring the Handicapped, March 24, 1977, Ed Roberts Papers, carton 1, folder 18, Bancroft Library, University of California, Berkeley.

8. Carol Billings, interview by Kathy Cowan, Disability Rights and Independent Living Movement Oral History Project, Bancroft Library, University of California, Berkeley, 1998.

9. Ed Roberts, speech at California Behavior Analysis Conference, March 30, 1977, Ed Roberts Papers, carton 1, folder 20, Bancroft Library, University of California, Berkeley.

10. Ed Roberts, speech at California Behavior Analysis Conference, March 30, 1977, Ed Roberts Papers, carton 1, folder 20, Bancroft Library, University of California, Berkeley.

11. Megan Kirschbaum, interview by Kathy Cowan, Disability Rights and Independent Living Movement Oral History Project, Bancroft Library, University of California, Berkeley, 2001, p. 46.

12. Megan Kirschbaum, interview by Kathy Cowan, Disability Rights and Independent Living Movement Oral History Project, Bancroft Library, University of California, Berkeley, 2001, p. 46.

13. Megan Kirschbaum, interview by Kathy Cowan, Disability Rights and Independent Living Movement Oral History Project, Bancroft Library, University of California, Berkeley, 2001, p. 46.

14. Mary Lou Breslin, interview by Susan O'Hara, Disability Rights and Independent Living Movement Oral History Project, Bancroft Library, University of California, Berkeley, 1998. Arlene Mayerson, interview by Mary Lou Breslin, Disability Rights and Independent Living Movement Oral History Project, Bancroft Library, University of California, Berkeley, 2004, p. 30. Fred Pelka, *What We Have Done: An Oral History of the Disability Rights Movement* (Amherst: University of Massachusetts Press, 2012).

15. Mary Lou Breslin, interview by Susan O'Hara, Disability Rights and Independent Living Movement Oral History Project, Bancroft Library, University of California, Berkeley, 1998, p. 116.

16. Pelka, *What We Have Done.*

17. Arlene Mayerson, interview by Mary Lou Breslin, Disability Rights and Independent Living Movement Oral History Project, Bancroft Library, University of California, Berkeley, 2004. Pelka, *What We Have Done*.

18. Mary Lou Breslin, interview by Susan O'Hara, Disability Rights and Independent Living Movement Oral History Project, Bancroft Library, University of California, Berkeley, 1998. Arlene Mayerson, interview by Mary Lou Breslin, Disability Rights and Independent Living Movement Oral History Project, Bancroft Library, University of California, Berkeley, 2004.

19. Twentieth Anniversary of ADA [Americans with Disabilities Act], C-Span, https://www.c-span.org/video/?294746-1/americans-disabilities-act-anniversary-historical-perspective. Arlene Mayerson, interview by Mary Lou Breslin, Disability Rights and Independent Living Movement Oral History Project, Bancroft Library, University of California, Berkeley, 2004.

20. Taylor Branch, *Pillar of Fire: America in the King Years, 1963–65* (New York: Simon and Schuster, 1998), p. 521.

21. Mary Lou Breslin, interview by Susan O'Hara, Disability Rights and Independent Living Movement Oral History Project, Bancroft Library, University of California, Berkeley, 1998. Arlene Mayerson, interview by Mary Lou Breslin, Disability Rights and Independent Living Movement Oral History Project, Bancroft Library, University of California, Berkeley, 2004.

22. Don Galloway, interview by Fred Pelka, Disability Rights and Independent Living Movement Oral History Project, Bancroft Library, University of California, Berkeley, December 9, 2001.

23. W. J. Rorabaugh, *Berkeley at War: The 1960's* (New York: Oxford University Press, 1989). Charles M. Wollenberg, *Berkeley: A City in History* (Berkeley: University of California Press, 2008).

24. Billy Charles Barner, interview by Kathy Cowan, Disability Rights and Independent Living Movement Oral History Project, Bancroft Library, University of California, Berkeley, March 27, 2000.

25. Johnnie Lacy, interview by David Landes, Disability Rights and Independent Living Movement Oral History Project, Bancroft Library, University of California, Berkeley, July 2, 1998, p. 44.

26. Ron Washington interview, Paul K. Longmore Institute on Disability Collection, San Francisco State University, https://diva.sfsu.edu/collections/longmoreinstitute/bundles/230595. Johnnie Lacy, interview by David Landes, Disability Rights and Independent Living Movement Oral History Project, Bancroft Library, University of California, Berkeley, July 2, 1998, p. 106.

27. Don Galloway, interview by Fred Pelka, Disability Rights and Independent Living Movement Oral History Project, Bancroft Library, University of California, Berkeley, December 9, 2001, p. 69.

28. Don Galloway, interview by Fred Pelka, Disability Rights and Independent Living Movement Oral History Project, Bancroft Library, University of California, Berkeley, December 9, 2001.

29. Elaine Brown, *A Taste of Power: A Black Woman's Story* (New York: Anchor, 1993), p. 441.

30. Ron Washington interview, Paul K. Longmore Institute on Disability Collection, San Francisco State University, https://diva.sfsu.edu/collections/longmoreinstitute/bundles/230595.

31. Johnnie Lacy, interview by David Landes, Disability Rights and Independent Living Movement Oral History Project, Bancroft Library, University of California, Berkeley, July 2, 1998, p. 104.

32. Elaine Brown interview, Paul K. Longmore Institute on Disability Collection, San Francisco State University, https://diva.sfsu.edu/collections/longmoreinstitute/bundles/230640. Don Galloway, interview by Fred Pelka, Disability Rights and Independent Living Movement Oral History Project, Bancroft Library, University of California, Berkeley, December 9, 2001. Mary Lester, interview by Susan O'Hara, Disability Rights and Independent Living Movement Project, Bancroft Library, University of California, Berkeley, 2000. Susan Schweik, "Lomax's Matrix: Disability, Solidarity, and the Black Power of 504," *Disability Studies Quarterly* 31, no. 1 (2011): n.p.

33. Taylor Branch, *Parting the Waters: America in the King Years, 1954-63* (New York: Simon and Schuster, 1988). Branch, *Pillar of Fire.* Iwan Morgan and Philip Davies, *From Sit-Ins to SNCC: The Student Civil Rights Movement in the 1960's* (Gainesville: University of Florida Press, 2012). John R. Rachal, "The Long, Hot Summer: The Mississippi Response to Freedom Summer, 1964," *The Journal of Negro History* 84, no. 4 (1999): 315-339.

34. Ruth Rosen, *The World Split Open: How the Modern Women's Movement Changed America* (New York: Penguin, 2000), p. 108. "SNCC Position Paper, November, 1964," https://www.crmvet.org/docs/snccfem.htm.

35. Rosen, *World Split Open.*

36. Mary Lester, interview by Susan O'Hara, Disability Rights and Independent Living Movement Oral History Project, Bancroft Library, University of California, Berkeley, 2000. Judy Heumann, interview by Jonathan Young, January 2, 1998, Disability Rights and Independent Living Movement Oral History Project, Bancroft Library, University of California, Berkeley, p. 285. Corbett O'Toole, in-

terview by Denise Jacobson, July 18, 2000, Disability Rights and Independent Living Movement Oral History, Bancroft Library, University of California, Berkeley, p. 32.

15. Across America

1. Joan Leon interview, Paul K. Longmore Institute on Disability Collection, San Francisco State University, https://diva.sfsu.edu/collections/longmoreinstitute/bundles/230605.

2. Arlene Mayerson, interview by Mary Lou Breslin, Disability Rights and Independent Living Movement Oral History Project, Bancroft Library, University of California, Berkeley, 2004.

3. Fred Fay, interview by Fred Pelka, Disability Rights and Independent Living Movement Oral History Project, Bancroft Library, University of California, Berkeley, 2001. Lex Frieden, interview by author, May 19, 2022.

4. "Max Starkloff and Colleen Kelly Starkloff," Starkloff Disability Institute, https://starkloff.org/max-starkloff/. Ed Roberts Memorial, March 19, 1995, Ed Roberts Papers, carton 11, folder 22, Bancroft Library, University of California, Berkeley.

5. Lex Frieden, interview, May 19, 2022.

6. Lex Frieden, "Independent Living: The Movement and Its Programs," *American Rehabilitation* 3, no. 6 (1978): 6–9.

7. Lex Frieden, "Independent Living: The Houston Experience," *American Rehabilitation* 4, no. 6 (1979): 26.

8. Lex Frieden, "Independent Living Program Models," *Rehabilitation Literature* 41, no. 7-8 (July-August 1980): 169. Lex Frieden and Joyce Frieden, "Organized Consumerism at the Local Level," *American Rehabilitation* (September-October 1979): 3–6.

9. Frieden, "Independent Living: The Movement and Its Programs." Frieden, "Independent Living: The Houston Experience." Lex Frieden and L. Richards, "Independent Living: Choosing from a Variety of Programs," *Disabled USA* 2, no. 9 (1979): 11–14. Frieden and Frieden, "Organized Consumerism at the Local Level." Frieden, "Independent Living Program Models."

10. Lex Frieden, interview, May 19, 2022.

11. Joan Leon, interview, November 18-19, 2018.

12. Lex Frieden, "Independent Living Arrangements for Severely Disabled Persons," National Independent Living Conference, Berkeley, October 21-23, 1975.

13. Ed Roberts, "Placements," August 1975, Ed Roberts Papers, carton 1, folder 36, Bancroft Library, University of California, Berkeley.

14. Dudley Clendinen and Adam Nagourney, *Out for Good: The Struggle to Build a Gay Rights Movement in America* (New York: Simon and Schuster, 1999), pp. 53–54. Eric Marcus, *Making Gay History: The Half-Century Fight for Lesbian and Gay Equal Rights* (New York: HarperCollins, 2002).

15. Ruth Rosen, *The World Split Open: How The Modern Women's Movement Changed America* (New York: Penguin, 2000), p. 87.

16. Jeff Moyer, interview, May 1, 2019. Mary Lester, interview by Susan O'Hara, Disability Rights and Independent Living Movement Oral History Project, Bancroft Library, University of California, Berkeley, 2000.

16. Revolution in Sacramento

1. Roger Payne, interview by author, November 12, 2019.

2. Janet McEwen Brown, interview by Sharon Bonney, Disability Rights and Independent Living Movement Oral History Project, Bancroft Library, University of California, Berkeley, 1998.

3. Mary Lester, interview by Susan O'Hara, Disability Rights and Independent Living Movement Oral History Project, Bancroft Library, University of California, Berkeley, 2000.

4. Joan Leon, interview, November 18–19, 2018. Joan Leon, interview by Susan O'Hara, Disability Rights and Independent Living Movement Oral History Project, Bancroft Library, University of California, Berkeley, 2000. Steven E. Brown, "Zona and Ed Roberts: Twentieth Century Pioneers," *Disability Studies Quarterly* 20, no. 1 (2000): 26–42, http://www.independentliving.org/docs3/brown00a.pdf.

5. Jeff Moyer, interview. Ed Roberts, Department of Rehabilitation press release, November 17, 1975, Ed Roberts Papers, carton 8, Bancroft Library, University of California, Berkeley. Richard Ramellsa, "Rehabilitation Chief Speaks from Iron Lung," *Berkeley Gazette*, October 28, 1975, p. 6. Nancy Skelton, "The 'Helpless Cripple' Steers a Fresh Course," *Sacramento Bee*, January 18, 1976, p. A3.

6. Barbara McIntosh, "Man in the iron Lung," *San Jose Mercury News*, November 4, 1984, pp. 1L–2L.

7. Robert Gnaizda, interview by author, March 8, 2019.

8. Skelton, "The 'Helpless Cripple' Steers a Fresh Course." Robert Gnaizda, interview, March 8, 2019.

9. Brown, "Zona and Ed Roberts: Twentieth Century Pioneers," p. 38. Barbara McIntosh, "Man in the Iron Lung," *San Jose Mercury News*, November 4, 1984, pp. 1L–2L.

10. UPI, "'Helpless' Cripple Helps California's Handicapped," *Fremont Argus*, December 10, 1975.

11. Ramellsa, "Rehabilitation Chief Speaks from Iron Lung." Ed Roberts, "Placements," August 1975, Ed Roberts Papers, carton 1, folder 36, Bancroft Library, University of California, Berkeley.

12. Ramellsa, "Rehabilitation Chief Speaks from Iron Lung."

13. Nancy Skelton, "The 'Helpless Cripple' Steers a Fresh Course," *Sacramento Bee,* January 18, 1976, p. A3. Ramon Jiminez, interview by author, January 23, 2019. Joan Leon, interview, November 18–19, 2018. Joan Leon, interview by Susan O'Hara, Disability Rights and Independent Living Movement Oral History Project, Bancroft Library, University of California, Berkeley, 2000.

14. Skelton, "The 'Helpless Cripple' Steers a Fresh Course."

15. Skelton, "The 'Helpless Cripple' Steers a Fresh Course."

16. Chapter 1196, Statutes of California, Statutes of 1976, vol. 2, pp. 3977–3979.

17. Stephen O'Connell, interview by author, April 20, 2022. Joan Leon, interview, November 18–19, 2018. Joan Leon, interview by Susan O'Hara, Disability Rights and Independent Living Movement Oral History Project, Bancroft Library, University of California, Berkeley, 2000.

18. Skelton, "The 'Helpless Cripple' Steers a Fresh Course."

19. Joan Leon interview, Paul K. Longmore Institute on Disability Collection, San Francisco State University, https://diva.sfsu.edu/collections/longmoreinstitute/bundles/230605.

20. Charles Carr, interview by Fred Pelka, Disability Rights and Independent Living Movement Oral History Project, Bancroft Library, University of California, Berkeley, 2001.

21. Stephen O'Connell, interview, April 20, 2022. Joan Leon, interview, November 18–19, 2018. Joan Leon, interview by Susan O'Hara, Disability Rights and Independent Living Movement Oral History Project, Bancroft Library, University of California, Berkeley, 2000.

17. Winning

1. Lillian Faderman, *The Gay Revolution: The Story of Struggle* (New York: Simon and Schuster, 2015). Ray Uzeta and Connie (Soucy) Uzeta interview, Paul K.

Longmore Institute on Disability Collection, San Francisco State University, https://diva.sfsu.edu/collections/longmoreinstitute/bundles/231041.

2. George Miller, interview by author, May 18, 2022. Robert Gnaizda, interview, March 8, 2019.

3. Robert Fairbanks, "Prop. 13—More Battles Lie Ahead: Prop. 13—Voters Send a Message but . . . ," *Los Angeles Times,* June 7, 1978, p. A10. Richard Bergholz, "Voters Deliver Tax Message in Prop 13 Landslide," *Los Angeles Times,* June 7, 1978, p. A3. Jim Newton, *Man of Tomorrow: The Relentless Life of Jerry Brown* (New York: Little Brown, 2020).

4. Maggie (Shandera) Linden, interview by author, June 7, 2021. Tom Bates and Lonnie Hancock, interview, May 16, 2019.

5. Ed Roberts, "Hiring the Handicapped" speech, March 24, 1977, carton 1, folder 18, Ed Roberts Papers, Bancroft Library, University of California, Berkeley.

6. Letter, Charles H. Cruttenden to Assemblyman Alfred Siegler, April 9, 1975, California State Archives, Sacramento.

7. Letter, Stanley J. Fontez to Assemblyman Jack Fenton, April 14, 1975, California State Archives, Sacramento. Letter, Charles H. Cruttenden to Assemblyman Alfred Siegler, April 9, 1975, California State Archives, Sacramento. Letter, J. E. Markey to Assemblyman Alfred Siegler, April 16, 1975, California State Archives, Sacramento. Letter, Peggy Brownlow to Assemblyman Alfred Siegler, April 17, 1975, California State Archives, Sacramento.

8. Legislative Analyst, Analysis of Fiscal Impact of AB 1194, May 2, 1975, California State Archives, Sacramento. Hearing Notes, State Assembly Committee on Labor Relations, April 21, 1975, California State Archives, Sacramento.

9. Jerry Buck, "The Real Doctor in 'Medical Center,'" *San Jose Mercury,* October 10, 1974, California State Archives, Sacramento. Press release, MGM Television News, October 8, 1974, California State Archives, Sacramento.

10. Press release, Alan S. Gutterman, Office of Assemblyman Alfred C. Siegler, March 18, 1975, California State Archives, Sacramento.

11. Chapter 431, Statutes of California, 1975-76, vol. 1, pp. 923-927. Press release, Medical Center, March 18, 1975 (CBS-TV).

12. Chapter 869, Statutes of California, 1975-76, Statutes of 1976, pp. 1978-1979. Chapter 700, Statutes of California, 1975-76, Statutes of 1976, pp. 1714-1715.

13. Chapters 1096 and 1097, Statutes of California, 1975-76, Statutes of 1976, pp. 4959-4966. Chapter 700, Statutes of California, 1975-76, Statutes of 1976, pp. 1714-1715.

14. Michael J. Kluk, "Prohibiting Employment Discrimination on the Basis of Disability: The Need to Expand California Law," *U. C. Davis Law Review* 14, no. 3 (Spring 1981): 731–766.

15. Chapter 1150, Statutes of California, 1975–76, vol. 2, pp. 2835–2836. Letter, Barbara Ortega to Eugene Chappie, August 19, 1975, California State Archives, Sacramento.

16. Chapter 1145, Statutes of California, 1975–76, vol. 2, pp. 2830–2831.

17. Arlene Kanter and Rebecca Russo, "The Right of People with Disabilities to Exercise Their Right to Vote Under the Help America Vote Act," *Mental and Physical Disability Law Reporter* 30, no. 6 (November-December 2006): 852–857.

18. Phyllis W. Cheng, "The Unruh Civil Rights Act: Sixtieth Anniversary," *The California Employment Labor Review* 33, no. 6 (2019): 2.

19. Chapters 971 and 972, Statutes of California, 1975–76, Statutes of 1976, pp. 2269–2274. Chapter 293, Statutes of California, Statutes of 1977, pp. 1194–1195.

18. Pride in 25 Days

1. Ron Shaffer, "Carter Asks Md. Support," *Washington Post*, December 1, 1975, p. C1. Jules Wilcover, "Carter: Man Who Didn't Plan to Lose," *Washington Post,* July 15, 1976, p. A1.

2. David S. Broder, "Carter Pledges Restoration of 'Strength, Hope,'" *Washington Post*, September 7, 1976, p. A1. Jimmy Carter, "Remarks on Starting Formal General Election Campaign Activities in Warm Springs, Georgia," September 6, 1976, The American Presidency Project, https://www.presidency.ucsb.edu /documents/remarks-starting-formal-general-election-campaign-activities -warm-springs-georgia.

3. Flora Davis, *Moving the Mountain: The Women's Movement in America Since 1960* (New York: Simon and Schuster, 1991). Joyce Gelb and Marian Lief Palley, "Women and Interest Group Politics: A Comparative Analysis of Federal Decision-Making," *The Journal of Politics* 41, no. 2 (1979): 362–392.

4. James L. Cherry, "Cherry vs. Mathews: Fifty Years and Counting," *Ragged Edge* 4 (2001), http://www.raggededgemagazine.com/0701. Kitty Cone, interview by David Landes, Disability Rights and Independent Living Movement Oral History Project, Bancroft Library, University of California, Berkeley, 1998. Jon Margolis, "Protest for Guaranteed Rights Isn't Handicapped by Disabilities," *Chicago Tribune,* April 10, 1977, p. 10.

5. Kitty Cone, interview by David Landes, Disability Rights and Independent Living Movement Oral History Project, Bancroft Library, University of

California, Berkeley, 1998. Kitty Cone interview, Paul K. Longmore Institute on Disability Collection, San Francisco State University, https://diva.sfsu.edu /collections/longmoreinstitute/bundles/230592.

6. Evan White interview, Paul K. Longmore Institute on Disability Collection, San Francisco State University, https://diva.sfsu.edu/collections/longmoreinstitute /bundles/230598.

7. Judith Heumann, *Being Heumann: An Unrepentant Memoir of a Disability Rights Activist* (Boston: Beacon, 2020). Kitty Cone interview, Paul K. Longmore Institute on Disability Collection, San Francisco State University, https://diva .sfsu.edu/collections/longmoreinstitute/bundles/230592. Kitty Cone, interview by David Landes, Disability Rights and Independent Living Movement Oral History Project, Bancroft Library, University of California, Berkeley, 1998. Corbett O'Toole, interview by Denise Jacobson, July 18, 2000, Disability Rights and Independent Living Movement Oral History Project, Bancroft Library, University of California, Berkeley. Ron Washington interview, Paul K. Longmore Institute on Disability Collection, San Francisco State University, https://diva.sfsu.edu /collections/longmoreinstitute/bundles/230595.https://diva.sfsu.edu/collections /longmoreinstitute/bundles/230592.

8. Evan White interview, Paul K. Longmore Institute on Disability Collection, San Francisco State University, https://diva.sfsu.edu/collections/longmoreinstitute /bundles/230598.

9. Ed Roberts, 504 rally speech, Ed Roberts Papers, carton 1, folder 21, Disability Rights and Independent Living Movement Oral History Project, Bancroft Library, University of California, Berkeley.

10. Jeff Moyer, interview, May 1, 2019.

11. Kitty Cone, interview by David Landes, Disability Rights and Independent Living Movement Oral History Project, Bancroft Library, University of California, Berkeley, 1998, p. 128.

12. Heumann, *Being Heumann*. Kitty Cone, interview by David Landes, Disability Rights and Independent Living Movement Oral History Project, Bancroft Library, University of California, Berkeley, 1998. Ray Uzeta and Connie (Soucy) Uzeta interview, Paul K. Longmore Institute on Disability Collection, San Francisco State University, https://diva.sfsu.edu/collections/longmoreinstitute/bundles/231041. HolLynn D'Lil, *Becoming Real in 24 Days: One Participant's Story of the 1977 Section 504 Demonstration for Disability Rights* (Graton, CA: Hallevaland Productions, 2015), https://diva.sfsu.edu/collections/longmoreinstitute/bundles/231041.

13. Ron Washington interview, Paul K. Longmore Institute on Disability Collection, San Francisco State University, https://diva.sfsu.edu/collections

/longmoreinstitute/bundles/230595. Lillian Faderman, *The Gay Revolution: The Story of Struggle* (New York: Simon and Schuster, 2015).

14. D'Lil, *Becoming Real in 24 Days*.

15. D'Lil, *Becoming Real in 24 Days*, p. 66.

16. Myra MacPherson, "Newly Militant Disabled Waging War on Discrimination," *Washington Post*, May 9, 1977, p. A2. George Miller interview, Paul K. Longmore Institute on Disability Collection, San Francisco State University, https://diva.sfsu.edu/collections/longmoreinstitute/bundles/230647. Kitty Cone interview, Paul K. Longmore Institute on Disability Collection, San Francisco State University, https://diva.sfsu.edu/collections/longmoreinstitute/bundles/230592. Bruce Oka interview, Paul K. Longmore Institute on Disability Collection, San Francisco State University, https://diva.sfsu.edu/collections/longmoreinstitute/bundles/230601. Ray Uzeta and Connie (Soucy) Uzeta interview, Paul K. Longmore Institute on Disability Collection, San Francisco State University.

17. Martha Biondi, *Black Revolution on Campus* (Berkeley: University of California Press, 2012). Eric Marcus, *Making Gay History: The Half-Century Fight for Lesbian and Gay Equal Rights* (New York: HarperCollins, 2002).

18. Bruce Oka interview, Paul K. Longmore Institute on Disability Collection, San Francisco State University, https://diva.sfsu.edu/collections/longmoreinstitute/bundles/230601. Kitty Cone, interview by David Landes, Disability Rights and Independent Living Movement Oral History Project, Bancroft Library, University of California, Berkeley, 1998. Ray Uzeta and Connie (Soucy) Uzeta interview, Paul K. Longmore Institute on Disability Collection, San Francisco State University, https://diva.sfsu.edu/collections/longmoreinstitute/bundles/231041. Evan White interview, Paul K. Longmore Institute on Disability Collection, San Francisco State University, https://diva.sfsu.edu/collections/longmoreinstitute/bundles/230598.

19. Nancy Hicks, "Handicapped Use Protests to Push H.E.W. to Implement '73 Bias Law," *New York Times*, April 11, 1977, p. 12. Nancy Hicks, "Equity for Disabled Likely to Be Costly," *New York Times*, May 1, 1977, p. L29.

20. Editorial Board, "Dispatches from the Domestic Front," *Washington Post*, April 7, 1977, p. A18. Editorial Board, "Fairness for Homosexuals," *Washington Post*, February 2, 1971, p. A14.

21. Evan White interview, Paul K. Longmore Institute on Disability Collection, San Francisco State University, https://diva.sfsu.edu/collections/longmoreinstitute/bundles/230598.

22. Heumann, *Being Heumann*. D'Lil, *Becoming Real in 24 Days*.

23. Heumann, *Being Heumann*.

24. Ray Uzeta and Connie (Soucy) Uzeta interview, Paul K. Longmore Institute on Disability Collection, San Francisco State University, https://diva.sfsu.edu/collections/longmoreinstitute/bundles/231041. Kitty Cone, interview by David Landes, Disability Rights and Independent Living Movement Oral History Project, Bancroft Library, University of California, Berkeley, 1998.

25. Joan Leon interview, Paul K. Longmore Institute on Disability Collection, San Francisco State University, https://diva.sfsu.edu/collections/longmoreinstitute/bundles/230605.

26. Joan Leon interview, Paul K. Longmore Institute on Disability Collection, San Francisco State University, https://diva.sfsu.edu/collections/longmoreinstitute/bundles/230605.

27. George Miller interview, Paul K. Longmore Institute on Disability Collection, https://diva.sfsu.edu/collections/longmoreinstitute/bundles/230647.

28. Disability Rights Education and Defense Fund, *The Power of 504*, https://www.youtube.com/watch?=v52XqupjXHIM.

29. D'Lil, *Becoming Real in 24 Days*, p. 110.

30. Heumann, *Being Heumann*. D'Lil, *Becoming Real in 24 Days*.

31. Heumann, *Being Heumann*, p. 124.

32. Heumann, *Being Heumann*, pp. 124–125.

33. Kitty Cone, interview by David Landes, Disability Rights and Independent Living Movement Oral History Project, Bancroft Library, University of California, Berkeley, 1998. Heumann, *Being Heumann*.

34. Heumann, *Being Heumann*. Kitty Cone, interview by David Landes, Disability Rights and Independent Living Movement Oral History Project, Bancroft Library, University of California, Berkeley, 1998. D'Lil, *Becoming Real in 24 Days*.

35. Heumann, *Being Heumann*. Evan White interview, Paul K. Longmore Institute on Disability Collection, San Francisco State University, https://diva.sfsu.edu/collections/longmoreinstitute/bundles/230598.

36. HolLynn D'Lil interview, Paul K. Longmore Institute on Disability, San Francisco State University, https://diva.sfsu.edu/collections/longmoreinstitute/bundles/230597.

37. Evan White interview, Paul K. Longmore Institute on Disability Collection, San Francisco State University, https://diva.sfsu.edu/collections/longmoreinstitute/bundles/230598. Heumann, *Being Heumann*.

38. Evan White interview, Paul K. Longmore Institute on Disability Collection, San Francisco State University, https://diva.sfsu.edu/collections/longmoreinstitute/bundles/230598.

39. George Miller interview, Paul K. Longmore Institute on Disability Collection, https://diva.sfsu.edu/collections/longmoreinstitute/bundles/230647.

40. Kitty Cone interview, Paul K. Longmore Institute on Disability Collection, San Francisco State University, https://diva.sfsu.edu/collections/longmoreinstitute/bundles/230592.

41. Heumann, *Being Heumann*. Letter, Harrison A. Williams, Jr., to Joseph Califano, April 22, 1977, in D'Lil, *Becoming Real in 24 Days*, pp. 156–157. Richard K. Scotch, "Politics and Policy in the History of the Disability Rights Movement," *The Milbank Quarterly* 67 (1989): 380–400.

42. Judy Heumann, interview by Jonathan Young, January 2, 1998, Disability Rights and Independent Living Movement Oral History Project, Bancroft Library, University of California, Berkeley. Statement of Edward V. Roberts, Committee on Veteran's Affairs, Congress, March 5, 1980, Ed Roberts Papers, carton 1, folder 38, Bancroft Library, University of California, Berkeley. Lowell Weicker, Jr., "Historical Background of the Americans with Disabilities Act," *Temple Law Review* 64 (1991): 387–392.

43. D'Lil, *Becoming Real in 24 Day*. Heumann, *Being Heumann*.

44. HolLynn D'Lil interview, Paul K. Longmore Institute on Disability, San Francisco State University, https://diva.sfsu.edu/collections/longmoreinstitute/bundles/23059. Letter, Alan Cranston to Joseph Califano, April 22, 1977, in D'Lil, *Becoming Real in 24 Days*, pp. 154–155.

45. Letter, George Miller and others to President Carter, April 20, 1977, in D'Lil, *Becoming Real in 24 Days*, pp. 158–159.

46. Dudley Clendinen and Adam Nagourney, *Out for Good: The Struggle to Build a Gay Rights Movement in America* (New York: Simon and Schuster, 1999).

47. Kitty Cone interview, Paul K. Longmore Institute on Disability Collection, San Francisco State University, https://diva.sfsu.edu/collections/longmoreinstitute/bundles/230592. Kitty Cone, interview by David Landes, Disability Rights and Independent Living Movement Oral History Project, Bancroft Library, University of California, Berkeley, 1998. Heumann, *Being Heumann*. Ron Washington interview, Paul K. Longmore Institute on Disability Collection, San Francisco State University, https://diva.sfsu.edu/collections/longmoreinstitute/bundles/230595.

48. Kitty Cone, interview by David Landes, Disability Rights and Independent Living Movement Oral History Project, Bancroft Library, University of California, Berkeley, 1998.

49. Kitty Cone, https://blogs.dickinson.edu/modern-us-history/1977-patient-no-more-kitty-cones-victory-speech/.

50. Ed Roberts, 504 victory speech, Tuesday, April 5, 1977, Ed Roberts Papers, carton 1, folder 21, Bancroft Library, University of California, Berkeley.

51. Kitty Cone, https://blogs.dickinson.edu/modern-us-history/1977-patient-no-more-kitty-cones-victory-speech/. Ron Washington interview, Paul K. Longmore Institute on Disability Collection, San Francisco State University, https://diva.sfsu.edu/collections/longmoreinstitute/bundles/230595. Myra MacPherson, "Newly Militant Disabled Waging War on Discrimination," *Washington Post,* May 9, 1977, p. A2.

19. Nationwide Independence

1. George Miller, interview, May 18, 2022.

2. Hearings Before the Subcommittee on Select Education and Committee on Education and Labor, House of Representatives, Ninety-Fifth Congress, Second Session (Washington, DC: US Government Printing Office, 1978), p. 80.

3. Hearings Before the Subcommittee on Select Education and Committee on Education and Labor, House of Representatives, Ninety-Fifth Congress, Second Session (Washington, DC: US Government Printing Office, 1978), p. 60.

4. Hearings Before the Subcommittee on Select Education and Committee on Education and Labor, House of Representatives, Ninety-Fifth Congress, Second Session (Washington, DC: US Government Printing Office, 1978), p. 60. George Miller, interview, May 18, 2022.

5. Hearings Before the Subcommittee on Select Education and Committee on Education and Labor, House of Representatives, Ninety-Fifth Congress, Second Session (Washington, DC: US Government Printing Office, 1978), p. 77.

6. Joyce Gelb and Marian Lief Palley, "Women and Interest Group Politics: A Comparative Analysis of Federal Decision-Making," *The Journal of Politics* 41, no. 2 (1979): 362–392.

7. Hearings Before the Subcommittee on Select Education and Committee on Education and Labor, House of Representatives, Ninety-Fifth Congress, Second Session (Washington, DC: US Government Printing Office, 1978), p. 281.

8. Hearings Before the Subcommittee on Select Education and Committee on Education and Labor, House of Representatives, Ninety-Fifth Congress, Second Session (Washington, DC: US Government Printing Office, 1978), p. 283.

9. Hearings Before the Subcommittee on Select Education and Committee on Education and Labor, House of Representatives, Ninety-Fifth Congress, Second Session (Washington, DC: US Government Printing Office, 1978), p. 520.

10. Hearings Before the Subcommittee on Select Education and Committee on Education and Labor, House of Representatives, Ninety-Fifth Congress, Second Session (Washington, DC: US Government Printing Office, 1978), p. 316.

11. Hearings Before the Subcommittee on Select Education and Committee on Education and Labor, House of Representatives, Ninety-Fifth Congress, Second Session (Washington, DC: US Government Printing Office, 1978), pp. 317-318.

12. Susan Stoddard, "Independent Living Concepts and Programs," *American Rehabilitation* 3, no. 6 (July-August 1978): 2-5.

13. Hearings Before the Subcommittee on Select Education and Committee on Education and Labor, House of Representatives, Ninety-Fifth Congress, Second Session (Washington, DC: US Government Printing Office, 1978), p. 401.

14. Hearings Before the Subcommittee on Select Education and Committee on Education and Labor, House of Representatives, Ninety-Fifth Congress, Second Session (Washington, DC: US Government Printing Office, 1978), p. 414.

15. Hearings Before the Subcommittee on Select Education and Committee on Education and Labor, House of Representatives, Ninety-Fifth Congress, Second Session (Washington, DC: US Government Printing Office, 1978), p. 444.

16. Flora Davis, *Moving the Mountain: The Women's Movement in America Since 1960* (New York: Simon and Schuster, 1991). Elizabeth M. Schneider, *Battered Women and Feminist Lawmaking* (New Haven: Yale University Press, 2000). Kathleen J. Tierney, "The Battered Women Movement and the Creation of the Wife Beating Problem," *Social Problems* 29, no. 3 (1982): 207-220.

17. Carl M. Brauer, "Kennedy, Johnson, and the War on Poverty," *The Journal of American History* 69, no. 1 (1982): 98-119. J. Travis Bland, "Authentic Participatory Engagement," *Public Administration Quarterly* 42, no. 2 (2018): 213-251. Susan Abrams Beck, "The Limits of Presidential Activism: Lyndon Johnson and the Implementation of the Community Action Program," *Presidential Studies Quarterly* 17, no. 3 (1987): 541-557. Richard M. Flanagan, "Lyndon Johnson, Community Action, and Management of the Administrative State," *Presidential Studies Quarterly* 31, no. 4 (2001): 585-608. Alice O'Connor, *Poverty Knowledge: Social Science, Social Policy, and the Poor in Twentieth-Century U.S. History* (Princeton: Princeton University Press, 2001).

18. Hearings Before the Subcommittee on Select Education and Committee on Education and Labor, House of Representatives, Ninety-Fifth Congress, Second Session (Washington, DC: US Government Printing Office, 1978), pp. 454, 812.

19. Hearings Before the Subcommittee on Select Education and Committee on Education and Labor, House of Representatives, Ninety-Fifth Congress,

Second Session (Washington, DC: US Government Printing Office, 1978), p. 647. Lex Frieden, interview, May 19, 2022.

20. Richard K. Scotch, "Politics and Policy in the History of the Disability Rights Movement," *The Milbank Quarterly* 67 (1989): 380–400. Fred Pelka, *What We Have Done: An Oral History of the Disability Rights Movement* (Amherst: University of Massachusetts Press, 2012). Teodor Mladenov, Ines Bulic Cojocariu, Lilia Angelova-Mladenova, Natasa Kokic, and Kamil Goungor, "Special Issue Editorial: Independent Living in Europe and Beyond: Past, Present, and Future," *The International Journal of Disability and Social Justice* 3, no. 1 (April 2023): 4–23.

20. Vegetables Unite!

1. Fred Fay, interview by Fred Pelka, Disability Rights and Independent Living Movement Oral History Project, Bancroft Library, University of California, Berkeley, 2001. Gerben DeJong, "Independent Living: From Social Movement to Analytic Paradigm," *Archives of Physical Medicine and Rehabilitation* 60 (1979): 435–446. Gerben DeJong, interview by author, October 5, 2022.

2. Diane Driedger, interview, September 18, 2022, Visions and Victories, Canadian Abilities Foundation, https://www.abilities.ca/uncategorized/vision-and-victories/.

3. R.J. Stickley, "A Report of the Independent Living Centre of the Waterloo Region," *Canadian Journal of Mental Health* 9, no. 2 (1990): 19–23.

4. Alfred H. Neufeldt and Henry Enns, *In Pursuit of Equal Participation: Canada and Disability at Home and Abroad* (Concord, Ontario: Captus Press, 2003).

5. Diane Driedger, *The Last Civil Rights Movement: Disabled Peoples' International* (New York: St. Martin's Press, 1989). Diane Driedger, interview, September 18, 2022.

6. Brian Cole, "Rave Review for Bestseller: New Telephone Directory Will Keep Trivia Buffs Busy," *Winnipeg Free Press*, June 4, 1980, p. 2. Lea Blauvelt, "Canada Salutes Gardening," *Wilson (NC) Daily Times*, June 11, 1980, p. 20. "Won't Have to Knock," photo, *Winnipeg Free Press*, June 5, 1980, p. 19. Manfred Jager, "World Congress in City: Delegates from 77 Countries Tackle Problems of the Disabled," *Winnipeg Free Press*, June 23, 1980, p. 7.

7. Neufeldt and Enns, *In Pursuit of Equal Participation*.

8. Neufeldt and Enns, *In Pursuit of Equal Participation*.

9. Henry Fairlie, "Are Handicapped Spoiled?" *Winnipeg Free Press*, June 20, 1980, p. 12.

10. Manfred Jager, "Wages Called Substandard," *Winnipeg Free Press*, June 24, 1980, p. 5. Manfred Jager, "Disabled Could Fight," *Winnipeg Free Press*, June 24, 1980, p. 5.

11. Manfred Jager, "Begin Predicts Push for Rights for the Handicapped," *Winnipeg Free Press*, June 24, 1980, p. 41.

12. Laurie Streich, "International Coalition Created by the Handicapped," *Winnipeg Free Press*, June 26, 1980, p. 16. Driedger, *Last Civil Rights Movement*. Diane Driedger, interview, September 18, 2022.

13. Neufeldt and Enns, *In Pursuit of Equal Participation*, p. 84.

14. Driedger, *Last Civil Rights Movement*. Diane Driedger, interview, September 18, 2022. Neufeldt and Enns, *In Pursuit of Equal Participation*.

15. Neufeldt and Enns, *In Pursuit of Equal Participation*.

16. Driedger, *Last Civil Rights Movement*.

17. Driedger, *Last Civil Rights Movement*, p. 48.

18. Ed Roberts, speech to Disabled Peoples' International Conference, Singapore, December 1981, Ed Roberts Papers, carton 1, folder 27, Bancroft Library, University of California, Berkeley.

21. A Magical Place

1. Tim Palmer, *Stanislaus: The Struggle for a River* (Berkeley: University of California Press, 1982).

2. Dakota Goodman, "The Personification of Natural Waterscapes: A Brief History of Friends of the River (1970–1992)," Stanislaus River Archive, https://www.stanislausriver.org/collection/dakotagoodmans-collection/.

3. Mark Dubois, interview, April 20, 2022. Ward Sinclair and John Berthelsen, "Engineers Halt Flooding to Search for Chained-Up Protester," *Washington Post*, May 23, 1979.

4. Palmer, *Stanislaus*, p. 270.

5. Robert L. Metts, *Stories for My Friends* (self-published, 2021).

6. Micheal Pachovas, interview by Mary Lou Breslin, Disability Rights and Independent Living Movement Oral History Project, Bancroft Library, University of California, Berkeley, 1999.

7. Mark Dubois, interview, April 20, 2022. Palmer, *Stanislaus*.

8. Micheal Pachovas, interview by Mary Lou Breslin, Disability Rights and Independent Living Movement Oral History Project, Bancroft Library, University of California, Berkeley, 1999. Palmer, *Stanislaus*.

9. Palmer, *Stanislaus*, p. 197.

10. Patricia Shifferle, interview by author, May 2, 2022.

11. Wayne King, "Officials Take to Rafts to Save a White-Water River," *New York Times*, August 18, 1980, p. A12.

12. Patricia Shifferle, interview, May 2, 2022.

13. Patricia Shifferle, interview, May 2, 2022. Mark Dubois, interview, April 20, 2022.

14. King, "Officials Take to Rafts to Save a White-Water River."

15. Mark Dubois, interview, April 20, 2022.

16. Ed Roberts, Fair Housing Amendments Testimony, May 1987, Ed Roberts Papers, carton 1, folder 44, Bancroft Library, University of California, Berkeley,

17. Untitled Ed Roberts speech, May 19, 1980, Ed Roberts Papers, carton 1, folder 24, Bancroft Library, University of California, Berkeley.

18. Patricia Shifferle, interview, May 2, 2022. Palmer, *Stanislaus*.

19. Jonathan Gold, interview, November 21, 2018.

22. Grief and Genius

1. Steven Brown, "Zona and Ed Roberts: Twentieth Century Pioneers," *Disability Studies Quarterly* 20, no. 1 (2000). Zona Roberts, interview, September 25, 2018. Mark Roberts, interview, June 7, 2019. Zona Roberts, interview by Steve Brown, December 27, 1996. Zona Roberts, interview by Susan O'Hara, Disability Rights and Independent Living Movement Oral History Project, Bancroft Library, University of California, Berkeley, 1995.

2. Kurt Vonnegut, *Hocus Pocus* (New York: Putnam, 1990), p. 238.

3. "Notes and Briefs: Social Welfare Expenditures, Fiscal Year 1980," *Social Security Bulletin* 46, no. 8 (August 1983). "Notes and Briefs: Social Welfare Expenditures, Fiscal Year 1985," *Social Security Bulletin* 51, no. 4 (August 1988). David K. Henry and Richard P. Oliver, *The Defense Buildup, 1977–1985: Effects on Production and Employment* (Washington, DC: Bureau of Labor Statistics, 1988). David Stoesz and Howard Jacob Karger, "Deconstructing Welfare: The Reagan Legacy and the Welfare State," *Social Work* 38, no. 5 (1993): 619–628.

4. Dan Walters, "Brown Redux, Part 2: Could He Have Been President?" *CalMatters*, December 28, 2018, https://calmatters.org/commentary/2018/12/could-jerry-brown-have-been-president/. Stephen O'Connell, interview, April 20, 2022. Burr Snider, "Up and Fighting for Rights of the Disabled," *San Francisco Examiner*, February 13, 1983, pp. 1, 3 (Sunday Scene/Arts section). Richard Scheinin, "Breaking the Barriers," *San Jose Mercury News*, June 8, 1980, pp. 1c, 4c.

5. Fahizah Alim, "Disabled Hold Rallies to Protest Funds Cut," *Sacramento Bee*, January 13, 1981.

6. Ed Roberts, Testimony on the Impact of Federal Human Services Cutbacks on the Disabled for the House of Representatives Ways and Means Committee Hearing, January 18, 1982, Sacramento, Ed Roberts Papers, carton 1, folder 39, Bancroft Library, University of California, Berkeley.

7. Ed Roberts, Testimony on the Impact of Federal Human Services Cutbacks on the Disabled for the House of Representatives Ways and Means Committee Hearing, January 18, 1982, Sacramento, Ed Roberts Papers, carton 1, folder 39, Bancroft Library, University of California, Berkeley.

8. Dudley Clendinen and Adam Nagourney, *Out for Good: The Struggle to Build a Gay Rights Movement in America* (New York: Simon and Schuster, 1999).

9. Stephen O'Connell, interview, April 20, 2022.

10. Joan Leon, interview, November 18-19, 2018. Jonathan Gold, interview, November 21, 2018. Stephen O'Connell, interview, April 20, 2022.

11. Independent Living Programs National Directory, Independent Living Center Utilization Project, Houston TX, Summer 1981, Ed Roberts Papers, carton 8, folder 3, Bancroft Library, University of California, Berkeley.

12. Proposal Summary, January 1983, World Institute on Disability Papers, carton 1, folder 12, Bancroft Library, University of California, Berkeley.

13. Letter, Joan Leon to Herb Gunther, March 5, 1983, World Institute on Disability Papers, carton 3, folder 1, Bancroft Library, University of California, Berkeley. Letter, Joan Leon to Davlin Paint Company, February 7, 1984, World Institute on Disability Papers, carton 3, folder 3, Bancroft Library, University of California, Berkeley. Letter, Joan Leon to Garland Chambers, February 15, 1984, World Institute on Disability Papers, carton 3, folder 3, Bancroft Library, University of California, Berkeley. Letter, Joan Leon to Don Davis, Berkeley Unified School District, January 23, 1984, World Institute on Disability Papers, carton 3, folder 3, Bancroft Library, University of California, Berkeley. WID revenue graph, World Institute on Disability Papers, carton 1, folder 17, Bancroft Library, University of California, Berkeley. Joan Leon interview, Paul K. Longmore Institute on Disability Collection, San Francisco State University, https://diva.sfsu.edu/collections/longmoreinstitute/bundles/230605.

14. Martin Morse Wooster, "The MacArthur Mistake," *Commentary*, December 2010, https://www.commentary.org/articles/wooster-martin-morse/the-macarthur-mistake/. Martin Morse Wooster, "Those Unassailable 'Genius Grants,'" *Philanthropy Daily*, October 30, 2014, https://www.philanthropydaily.com/those-unassailable-genius-grants/. Samuel Goldman, "The Recurring

Problem with the MacArthur 'Genius' Grants," *The Week,* October 1, 2021, https://theweek.com/culture/1005474/whats-a-genius.

15. Barbara McIntosh, "Man in the Iron Lung," *San Jose Mercury News,* November 4, 1984, pp. 1L–2L.

16. Robert Gnaizda, interview, March 8, 2019. Sam Roberts, "Robert Gnaizda, 83, Who Saw Injustice and Did Something About It, Is Dead," *New York Times,* August 9, 2020, p. A26.

17. Letter, Robert Gnaizda to Kenneth Hope, February 1, 1984, carton 11, folder 11, Ed Roberts Papers, Bancroft Library, University of California, Berkeley.

18. Barbara McIntosh, "Man in the Iron Lung," *San Jose Mercury News,* November 4, 1984, p. 2L. Letter, John E. Corbally and J. Roderick Macarthur to Ed Roberts, October 11, 1984, oversize box, folder 6, Ed Roberts Papers, Bancroft Library, University of California, Berkeley. World Institute on Disability Proposal and Plan, January 1983, World Institute on Disability Papers, carton 1, folder 12, Bancroft Library, University of California, Berkeley.

19. Gareth Williams, "Irving Kenneth Zola (1935–1994): An Appreciation," *Sociology of Health & Illness* 18, no. 1 (1996): 107–125.

20. Joan Leon interview, Paul K. Longmore Institute on Disability Collection, San Francisco State University, https://diva.sfsu.edu/collections/longmoreinstitute/bundles/230605.

21. Letter, Joan Leon to Herb Gunther, March 5, 1983, World Institute on Disability Papers, carton 3, folder 1, Bancroft Library, University of California, Berkeley. Letter, Bob Griss to Joan Leon and Judy Heumann, February 26, 1988, World Institute on Disability Papers, carton 4, folder 11, Bancroft Library, University of California, Berkeley. Andrew Batavia, "Representation and Role Separation in the Disability Movement: Should Researchers Be Advocates?" *Archives of Physical Medicine and Rehabilitation* 70, no. 4 (1989): 345–348.

22. By-laws, 1983, World Institute on Disability Papers, carton 1, folder 14, Bancroft Library, University of California, Berkeley.

23. Revenue graph, World Institute on Disability Papers, carton 1, folder 17, Bancroft Library, University of California, Berkeley. Board meeting minutes, November 13, 1993, World Institute on Disability Papers, carton 1, folder 19, Bancroft Library, University of California, Berkeley.

24. Dudley Clendinen and Adam Nagourney, *Out for Good: The Struggle to Build a Gay Rights Movement in America* (New York: Simon and Schuster, 1999).

25. Colman McCarthy, "Gay Rights and Gay Acceptance," *Washington Post,* October 9, 1982, p. A19.

26. Alan I. Abramowitz, "Campaign Spending in U.S. Senate Elections," *Legislative Studies Quarterly* 14, no. 4 (1989): 487–507. Anthony Corrado, "Money and Politics: History of Federal Campaign Finance Law," in *The New Campaign Finance Sourcebook,* pp. 7–47 (Washington, DC: Brookings Institution Press, 2005).

27. Frank Bowe, *Disabled Adults in America: A Statistical Report Drawn from Census Bureau Data* (Washington, DC: President's Committee on Employment of the Handicapped, 1983). Edward H. Yelin, "The Recent History and Immediate Future of Employment Among Persons with Disabilities," *The Milbank Quarterly* 69 (1991): 129–149.

28. Judith Heumann, *Being Heumann: An Unrepentant Memoir of a Disability Rights Activist* (Boston: Beacon, 2020). Joan Leon and Judy Heumann, interview, September 4, 2020.

29. Board meeting minutes, March 23, 1988, World Institute on Disability Papers, carton 1, folder 16, Bancroft Library, University of California, Berkeley.

30. *60 Minutes* transcript, 1988, Ed Roberts Papers, carton 11, folder 18, Bancroft Library, University of California, Berkeley, "Mr. Roberts," https://www.youtube.com/watch?v = ZxidR5SZXxA.

31. Board meeting minutes, January 25, 1984, World Institute on Disability Papers, carton 1, folder 16, Bancroft Library, University of California, Berkeley.

32. Simi Litvak, Hale Zukas, and Judith Heumann, *Attending to America: Personal Assistance for Independent Living: A Survey of Attendant Service Programs in the United States for People of All Ages with Disabilities* (Berkeley, CA: World Institute on Disability, 1987).

33. Simi Litvak, interview, June 30, 2023.

34. Simi Litvak, interview, June 30, 2023.

35. Jae Kennedy and Simi Litvak, *Case Studies of Six Personal Assistance Programs Funded by the Medicaid Personal Care Option* (Washington, DC: US Department of Health and Human Services, 1991). Lance C. Egley, "The Cost of a National System of Personal Assistance Services," in *End Results and Starting Points: Expanding the Field of Disability Studies*, ed. Elaine Makas and Lynn Schlesinger, pp. 127–132 (Portland, ME: Edmund Muskie Institute of Public Affairs, 1996).

36. Raymond E. Glazier, "The 'Re-Invention' of Personal Assistance Services," *Disability Studies Quarterly* 21, no. 2 (2001), https://dsq-sds.org/article/view/285.

37. Margaret A. Nosek, "Personal Assistance Services: A Review of the Literature and Analysis of Policy implications," *Journal of Disability Policy Studies* 2, no. 2 (1991): 8.

38. Theda Skocpol, Margaret Weir, and James J. Mongan, "The Rise and Resounding Demise of the Clinton Health Security Plan," in *The Problem that Won't Go Away: Reforming U.S. Health Care Financing*, ed. Henry J. Aaron (Washington, DC: Brookings Institute Press, 1996), p. 34.

39. Theda Skocpol, Margaret Weir, and James J. Mongan, "The Rise and Resounding Demise of the Clinton Health Security Plan," in *The Problem That Won't Go Away: Reforming U.S. Health Care Financing*, ed. Henry J. Aaron, pp. 34–69 (Washington, DC: Brookings Institute Press, 1996). Lawrence R. Jacobs, "What Health Reform Teaches Us About American Politics," *PS: Political Science and Politics* 43, no. 4 (2010): 619–623.

40. Joshua M. Wiener, Carroll L. Estes, Susan M. Goldenson, and Sheryl C. Goldberg, "What Happened to Long-Term Care in the Health Reform Debate of 1993–1994? Lessons for the Future," *The Milbank Quarterly* 79, no. 2 (2001): 207–252.

41. Stephen O'Connell, interview, April 20, 2022.

42. Stephen O'Connell, interview, April 20, 2022.

43. David Ashley, "Symptoms Back to Haunt Some Ex-Victims as Adults," *San Jose Mercury News*, April 9, 1985, pp. E1–2.

44. Larry Schneider, "Those Passing Years," *Rehabilitation Gazette* 22 (1979): 64. Polio Survivors Association, *Rehabilitation Gazette* 22 (1979): 64.

45. Gini Laurie, Frederick M. Maynard, D. Armin Fischer, and Judith Raymond, eds., *Handbook on the Late Effects of Poliomyelitis for Physicians and Survivors* (St. Louis: GINI, 1984). Lauro S. Halstead, "A Brief History of Postpolio Syndrome in the United States," *Archives of Physical Medicine and Rehabilitation* 92 (2011): 1344–1349.

23. Partners

1. Michael Lesy, *Rescues: The Lives of Heroes* (New York: Farrar, Straus, and Giroux, 1991), pp. 121–122.

2. Thomas J. Zirpoli, David Hancox, Colleen Wieck, and Edward R. Skarnulis, "Partners in Policymaking: Empowering People," *The Journal of the Association for People with Severe Handicaps* 14, no. 2 (1989): 163–167. Colleen Wieck, interview by author, March 12, 2019.

3. Colleen Wieck, interview, March 12, 2019.

4. Saul Alinksy was a community organizer who authored *Rules for Radicals*, a 1971 book teaching low-power, marginalized groups how to disrupt and defeat corporations and the government.

5. Ed Roberts, "The Real Meaning of Independence and Independent Living as Civil Rights," United Cerebral Palsy Association Conference, Hyatt Regency Hotel, Minneapolis, April 30, 1987, Ed Roberts Papers, carton 4, folder 16, Bancroft Library, University of California, Berkeley.

6. Letter, Krista J. Westendorp to Zona Roberts, April 15, 1995, Ed Roberts Papers, carton 11, folder 25, Bancroft Library, University of California, Berkeley.

7. Letter, Krista J. Westendorp to Zona Roberts, April 15, 1995, Ed Roberts Papers, carton 11, folder 25, Bancroft Library, University of California, Berkeley.

8. Harriet McBryde Johnson, "Unspeakable Conversations," *New York Times Magazine*, February 16, 2003, https://www.nytimes.com/2003/02/16/magazine/unspeakable-conversations.html.

9. Harriet McBryde Johnson, "The Disability Gulag," *New York Times Magazine*, November 23, 2003, p. 59.

10. Johnson, "Unspeakable Conversations."

11. Johnson, "Disability Gulag."

12. Johnson, "Unspeakable Conversations."

13. Beth Miller, "Advocate Defies Doctors, Fights for the Disabled," *Delaware News Journal*, April 15, 2006.

14. Letter, Jamie Wolf to Ed Roberts, February 2, 1993, Ed Roberts Papers, carton 4, folder 20, Bancroft Library, University of California, Berkeley.

15. Meredith Newman, "Fierce Disability Rights Advocate Jamie Wolfe Dies at Age 52," *Delaware News Journal*, August 22, 2018.

24. Men of Adventure

1. Jon Oda, "Traveling in the Ed Zone," *Mouth,* January/February 1996, 33–35.

2. John Atkinson, interview by author, January 16, 2020. Roger Payne, interview, November 12, 2019.

3. Our History, Dolphin Research Center, https://dolphins.org/our_history. Dolphin Swim Marathon Key video, *Discovery Channel*, November 1993. Building Ed's Floating Chair video, *Discovery Channel*, November 1993. *Discovery Channel* videotapes courtesy of John Atkinson.

4. Oda, "Traveling in the Ed Zone."

5. John Atkinson interview, January 16, 2020. Roger Payne interview, November 12, 2019. Scot Danforth, "Two Geniuses, One Wheelchair and an Audacious Plan to Swim with the Whales," *Narratively,* July 2020, https://narratively.com/two-geniuses-one-wheelchair-and-anaudacious-plan-to-swim-with-the-whales/.

6. David Goode, A Tribute to Ed Roberts' Karate Instructor, Minnesota Developmental Disabilities Council, https://mn.gov/mnddc/ed-roberts/tony-johnson.html.

7. Ibid. Jon Oda, "Ed Roberts on Sex, Karate, and Life with a Disability," *Mouth,* July-August 2003, 20–25.

25. Lenin's Tomb Is Inaccessible

1. Bruce Curtis, interview by author, October 22, 2019.

2. Sarah D. Phillips, "'There Are No Invalids in the USSR!' A Missing Soviet Chapter in the New Disability History," *Disability Studies Quarterly* 29, no. 3 (2009), https://dsq-sds.org/article/view/936/1111.

3. Bruce Curtis, interview. October 22, 2019. Harry Jupiter, "Wheeling into the Limelight," *San Jose Mercury News,* June 6, 1993, pp. B1, B3.

4. Mary Lou Breslin, interview by Susan O'Hara, Disability Rights and Independent Living Movement Oral History Project, Bancroft Library, University of California, Berkeley, 1998.

5. Jupiter, "Wheeling into the Limelight."

6. Jupiter, "Wheeling into the Limelight."

7. Soviet TV interview of Ed Roberts, April 1993, Ed Roberts Papers, carton 1, folder 34, Bancroft Library, University of California, Berkeley,

8. Soviet TV interview, April 1993. Bruce Curtis, interview. October 22, 2019.

9. "Ed Stories," by Pam Mendelsohn, Ed Roberts Papers, carton 11, folder 28, Bancroft Library, University of California, Berkeley.

10. Mary Lou Breslin, interview by Susan O'Hara, Disability Rights and Independent Living Movement Oral History Project, Bancroft Library, University of California, Berkeley, 1998.

11. Mary Lou Breslin, interview by Susan O'Hara, Disability Rights and Independent Living Movement Oral History Project, Bancroft Library, University of California, Berkeley, 1998, p. 301.

12. Mary Lou Breslin, interview by Susan O'Hara, Disability Rights and Independent Living Movement Oral History Project, Bancroft Library, University of California, Berkeley, 1998.

13. "About Social Protection of Disabled People," Federal Law of the Russian Federation, https://cis-legislation.com/document.fwx?rgn=1751.

14. Stephanie Simon, "Willing and Able in Russia; Society Has Long Seen the Disabled as Helpless Wards of the State, Unfit to Work or Study. Armed with a

New Law, Activists Are Fighting to End the Smothering Coddling," *Los Angeles Times*, January 13, 1996, p. 1.

15. "Lenin Mausoleum," Encyclopedia Britanica, www.britannica.com /place/Lenin-Mausoleum. "Moscow, Russia, Wheelchair Accessible Travel Guide," Wheelchair Travel, www.wheelchairtravel.org/moscow/. "Vladimir Lenin's Last Photo," Rare Historical Photos, www.rarehistoricalphotos.com /vladimir-lenin-last-photo-1923/.

26. Passing the Torch

1. Mari Carlin Dart, "The Resurrection of Justin Dart, Jr.: A Quest for Truth and Love," *Ability*, 2002, 32.

2. Fred Fay and Fred Pelka, "Justin Dart, An Obituary," *Ability*, 2002, 36.

3. Dart, "The Resurrection of Justin Dart, Jr."

4. Dart, "The Resurrection of Justin Dart, Jr.," p. 33. Fay and Pelka, "Justin Dart, An Obituary," p. 36.

5. Dart, "Resurrection of Justin Dart, Jr.," p. 33.

6. Fred Pelka, "Empowerment: The Testament of Justin Dart, Jr.," *Mainstream* magazine (March 1998): 17–18.

7. Pelka, "Empowerment," p. 20.

8. Pelka, "Empowerment," pp. 20–21.

9. Jean Dobbs, "And Justin for All," *Mobility*, March 1998, 36.

10. Letter, Subcommittee on the Handicapped, Committee on Labor and Human Resources, United States Senate, to Justin Dart, Jr., June 2, 1987, Ed Roberts Papers, carton 8, folder 3, Bancroft Library, University of California, Berkeley.

11. Letter, Madeleine Will, Assistant Secretary, United States Department of Education to Sen. Tom Harkin, August 12, 1987, Ed Roberts Papers, carton 8, folder 3, Bancroft Library, University of California, Berkeley.

12. Letter, Tom Harkin to Marca Bristo, August 18, 1987, Ed Roberts Papers, carton 8, folder 3, Bancroft Library, University of California, Berkeley. Letter, Marca Bristo to President Ronald Reagan, August 27, 1987, Ed Roberts Papers, carton 8, folder 3, Bancroft Library, University of California, Berkeley. Letter, Marca Bristo to William Bennett, August 26, 1987, Ed Roberts Papers, carton 8, folder 3, Bancroft Library, University of California, Berkeley. Memo, Marca Bristo to National Council on Independent Living, "Alert—Need for Letters to Go to Washington," August 26, 1987, Ed Roberts Papers, carton 8, folder 3, Bancroft Library, University of California, Berkeley.

13. Memorandum, Acting Commissioner of Rehabilitation Services Francis Corregan to State Commissioners of Rehabilitation, October 21, 1987, Ed Roberts Papers, carton 8, folder 3, Bancroft Library, University of California, Berkeley.

14. Justin W. Dart, Jr., Testimony, Subcommittee on Select Education, United States House of Representatives, November 18, 1987, Ed Roberts Papers, carton 8, folder 3, Bancroft Library, University of California, Berkeley.

15. "White House Fires Outspoken Official," *Chicago Tribune*, December 2, 1987.

16. Minutes of meeting of Task Force on the Rights and Empowerment of Americans with Disabilities, May 20, 1989, Ed Roberts Papers, carton 4, folder 3, Bancroft Library, University of California, Berkeley.

17. Handwritten note, Justin Dart to Ed Roberts on the meeting minutes of the Task Force on the Rights and Empowerment of Americans with Disabilities, May 20, 1989, Ed Roberts Papers, carton 4, folder 3, Bancroft Library, University of California, Berkeley. Joan Leon, interview, November 18–19, 2018.

18. Fay and Pelka, "Justin Dart, An Obituary," p. 37. Lennard J. Davis, *Enabling Acts: The Hidden Story of How the Americans with Disabilities Act Gave the Largest US Minority Its Rights* (Boston: Beacon Press, 2016).

19. Report of the Task Force on the Rights and Empowerment of Americans with Disabilities, Ed Roberts Papers, carton 4, folder 3, Bancroft Library, University of California, Berkeley.

20. Davis, *Enabling Acts*. Judith Heumann and Kristen Joiner, *Being Heumann: An Unrepentant Memoir of a Disability Rights Activist* (Boston: Beacon Press, 2020).

21. "Senate Sends Disabled Rights Bill to Bush Legislation: It Is Hailed as an 'Emancipation Proclamation' by One Lawmaker," *Los Angeles Times*, July 14, 1990, p. 23. Stephen A. Holmes, "Rights for Disabled Is Sent to Bush," *New York Times*, July 14, 1990, p. 6. Davis, *Enabling Acts*. Helen Dewar, "Senate Approves Disabled Rights Bill," *Washington Post*, July 14, 1990, p. A1.

22. Ann Devroy, "In Emotion-Filled Ceremony, Bush Signs Rights Law for America's Disabled," *Washington Post*, July 27, 1990, p. A18.

23. Devroy, "In Emotion-Filled Ceremony, Bush Signs Rights Law," p. A18.

27. To the Smithsonian

1. Steven A. Chin, "Champ of the Disabled Honored; 750 Pay Homage to Ed Roberts; He Dedicated His Life to Independent Living," *San Francisco Examiner*, March 20, 1995, p. A2.

2. Deborah Kaplan speech, Ed Roberts Memorial, March 19, 1995, Ed Roberts Papers, carton 11, folder 22, Bancroft Library, University of California, Berkeley.

3. Zona Roberts speech, Ed Roberts Memorial, March 19, 1995, Ed Roberts Papers, carton 11, folder 22, Bancroft Library, University of California, Berkeley.

4. Judy Heumann speech, Ed Roberts Memorial, March 19, 1995, Ed Roberts Papers, carton 11, folder 22, Bancroft Library, University of California, Berkeley.

5. Zona Roberts speech, Ed Roberts Memorial, March 19, 1995.

6. Memorial Services, Ed Roberts Papers, carton 11, folder 23, Bancroft Library, University of California, Berkeley.

7. Mike Boyd, interview, February 6, 2019. Joan Leon, interview, November 18–19, 2018.

8. David Chalmers, *And the Crooked Places Made Straight: The Struggle for Social Change in the 1960's* (Baltimore: Johns Hopkins Press, 1991).

9. Agenda, Disability Community Meeting, White House, July 27, 1993, Ed Roberts Papers, carton 6, folder 41, Bancroft Library, University of California, Berkeley.

10. Don Galloway, interview by Fred Pelka, Disability Rights and Independent Living Movement Oral History Series, Bancroft Library, University of California, Berkeley, December 9, 2001.

11. Tom Harkin, May 16, 1995, Ed Roberts Congressional Memorial, Ed Roberts Papers, oversized box, folder 1, Bancroft Library, University of California, Berkeley.

12. Mike Boyd, interview, February 6, 2019.

13. Victoria Dawson, "Ed Roberts' Wheelchair Records a Story of Obstacles Overcome," *Smithsonian Magazine*, March 13, 2015, https://www.smithsonianmag .com/smithsonian-institution/ed-roberts-wheelchair-records-story-obstacles -overcome-180954531/.

28. Interdependence

1. "Wrap Up: NCIL Annual Conference on Independent Living," *The Advocacy Monitor*, https://advocacymonitor.com/wrap-up-ncil-2017-annual-conference-on-independent-living/. "Activists All over the World Gathered for the Global IL Summit in DC!" https://winwebsite2017.wixsite.com /winontheweb.

2. "Excerpts from Statement by Kennedy," *New York Times,* September 10, 1965, p. 21.

3. "Excerpts from Statement by Kennedy."

4. Jack Hammond, "Another View of Willowbrook," *New York Times,* May 6, 1972, p. 35. McCandlish Phillips, "Hospital's Wards: A Study in Misery, Willowbrook Director Denies Charges, Concedes Crowding," *New York Times*, September 10, 1965, p. 21.

5. Martin Luther King, Jr., "Letter from a Birmingham Jail," April 16, 1963, https://www.africa.upenn.edu/Articles_Gen/Letter_Birmingham.html.

6. William Bronston, *Discover Independence* (Sacramento: World Interdependence Fund, 1992).

Selected Bibliography

Brown, Steven E. "The Curb Ramps of Kalamazoo: Discovering Our Unrecorded History." *Disability Studies Quarterly* 13, no. 3 (1999): 203-205.

Danforth, Scot. "Becoming the Rolling Quads: Politics at the University of California, Berkeley, in the 1960s." *History of Education Quarterly* 58, no. 4 (2018): 506-536.

Davis, Fred. *Passage Through Crisis: Polio Victims and Their Families.* Piscataway, NJ: Transaction Publishers, 1991.

Davis, Lennard J. *Enabling Acts: The Hidden Story of How the Americans with Disabilities Act Gave the Largest US Minority Its Rights.* Boston: Beacon Press, 2016.

DeJong, Gerben. "Independent Living: From Social Movement to Analytic Paradigm." *Archives of Physical Medicine and Rehabilitation* 60 (1979): 435-446.

D'Lil, HolLynn. *Becoming Real in 24 days: One Participant's Story of the 1977 Section 504 Demonstration for Disability Rights.* Graton, CA: Hallevaland Productions, 2015.

Dobbs, Jean. "And Justin for All." *Mobility*, March 1998. https://newmobility.com/justin-dart/.

Driedger, Diane. *The Last Civil Rights Movement: Disabled Peoples' International.* New York: St. Martin's Press, 1989.

Frieden, Lex. "Independent Living Program Models." *Rehabilitation Literature* 41, no. 7-8 (1980): 169.

———. "Independent Living: The Houston Experience." *American Rehabilitation* 4, no. 6 (1979): 23-26, 27.

———. "Independent Living: The Movement and Its Programs." *American Rehabilitation* 3, no. 6 (1978): 6–9.

Gallagher, Hugh Gregory. *Black Bird Fly Away: Disabled in an Able-Bodied World.* St. Petersburg, FL: Vandermere Press, 1998.

———. *FDR's Splendid Deception.* New York: Dodd, Mead, 1985.

Heumann, Judith, and Kristen Joiner. *Being Heumann: An Unrepentant Memoir of A Disability Rights Activist.* Boston: Beacon Press, 2020.

Jennings, Audra. *Out of the Horrors of War: Disability Politics in World War II America.* Philadelphia: University of Pennsylvania Press, 2016.

Kriegal, Leonard. *The Long Walk Home.* New York: Appleton-Century, 1964.

Oda, Jon. "Ed Roberts on Sex, Karate, and Life with a Disability." *Mouth,* July-August 2003, 20–25.

———. "Traveling in the Ed Zone." *Mouth,* January/February 1996, 33–35.

Oshinsky, David M. *Polio: An American Story.* New York: Oxford University Press, 2005.

Pelka, Fred. *What We Have Done: An Oral History of the Disability Rights Movement.* Amherst: University of Massachusetts Press, 2012.

———. "Empowerment: The Testament of Justin Dart, Jr." *Mainstream* magazine (March 1998): 17–18.

Phillips, Sarah D. "'There Are No Invalids in the USSR!' A Missing Soviet Chapter in the New Disability History." *Disability Studies Quarterly* 29, no. 3 (2009): n.p.

Schweik, Susan. "Lomax's Matrix: Disability, Solidarity, and the Black Power of 504." *Disability Studies Quarterly* 31, no. 1 (2011): n.p.

Schweik, Susan Marie. *The Ugly Laws: Disability in Public.* New York: NYU Press, 2009.

Scotch, Richard K. "Politics and Policy in the History of the Disability Rights Movement." *The Milbank Quarterly* 67 (1989): 380–400.

Shell, Marc. *Polio and Its Aftermath: The Paralysis of Culture.* Cambridge, MA: Harvard University Press, 2005.

Smith, Jane S. *Patenting the Sun: Polio and the Salk Vaccine.* New York: William Morrow, 1990.

Walker, Turnley. *Roosevelt and the Warm Springs Story.* New York: Wyn, 1953.

Williams, Gareth. *Paralysed with Fear: The Story of Polio.* London: Palgrave Macmillan, 2013.

Williamson, Bess. *Accessible America: A History of Disability and Design.* New York: NYU Press, 2019.

Wilson, Daniel J. *Living with Polio: The Epidemic and Its Survivors.* Chicago: University of Chicago Press, 2007.

Zirpoli, Thomas J., David Hancox, Colleen Wieck, and Edward R. Skarnulis. "Partners in Policymaking: Empowering People." *The Journal of the Association for People with Severe Handicaps* 14, no. 2 (1989): 163–167.

Index

Founded in 1893,
UNIVERSITY OF CALIFORNIA PRESS
publishes bold, progressive books and journals
on topics in the arts, humanities, social sciences,
and natural sciences—with a focus on social
justice issues—that inspire thought and action
among readers worldwide.

The UC PRESS FOUNDATION
raises funds to uphold the press's vital role
as an independent, nonprofit publisher, and
receives philanthropic support from a wide
range of individuals and institutions—and from
committed readers like you. To learn more, visit
ucpress.edu/supportus.